USAA

A TRADITION OF SERVICE

1922-1997

USAA

A TRADITION OF SERVICE

1922-1997

BY

PAUL T. RINGENBACH

USAA
A Tradition Of Service
1922–1997

BY

PAUL T. RINGENBACH

Copyright ©1997, USAA

All rights reserved. No part of this book may be reproduced in any form or by any means, electronic or mechanical, including photocopying, recording or by any information storage and retrieval system, without the permission in writing from the copyright owner. For information write to: USAA, Corporate Communications, 9800 Fredericksburg Road, San Antonio, Texas, 78288.

USAA is not an agency, instrumentality, or affiliate of the U.S. Government.

THE DONNING COMPANY
PUBLISHERS

Printed In USA
02 01 00 99 98 97   10 9 8 7 6 5 4 3 2 1
ISBN 0-89865-993-0
Design and typography by Neal Kimmel & Associates, Dallas

Library of Congress Cataloging-in-Publication Data

Ringenbach, Paul T.
    USAA : a tradition of service, 1922-1997 / by Paul T. Ringenbach.
       p. cm.
    Includes bibliographical references and index.
    ISBN 0-89865-993-0
    1. USAA. 2. Insurance, Automobile — United States. 3. Insurance companies — United States — History. 4. United States — Armed Forces — Officers — Finance, Personal   I. Title.
HG9970.37.U8R56   1997
368'006'573 — dc21

97-11162
CIP

Dedication

This book honors the thousands of USAA employees, past and present. Their dedication to outstanding service built USAA into the success it is today.

and

It is also dedicated to my children — Kathy and John, Paul and Kathy, Dan and Paula, and Ted and Rhonda; my grandchildren; and my extended family. And especially to my wife, Sally, whose patience, support, and understanding made this book possible.

SERVICE is the motto of this Association, it is the reason for our existence — it is the secret of our success.

– from a 1923 USAA advertisement
in the *Army and Navy Register*

Contents

FOREWORD
xi

CHAPTER ONE
THE ROAD LESS TRAVELLED
1

CHAPTER TWO
DEPRESSION AND REVOLUTION
37

CHAPTER THREE
THE WAR YEARS
69

CHAPTER FOUR
THE COLD WAR BEGINS – SERVICING AN EXPLODING MEMBERSHIP
99

CHAPTER FIVE
MODERNIZING THE ASSOCIATION – A BEGINNING
133

CHAPTER SIX
THE SIXTIES – MATURITY AND PROGRESS
177

CHAPTER SEVEN
HIGH ENERGY
217

CHAPTER EIGHT
TURBULENT TIMES
277

Contents

CHAPTER NINE
EXPANDING, SAFETY, AND SUCCESSION
333

CHAPTER TEN
A NEW ERA FOR USAA – FINANCIAL SERVICES
391

CHAPTER ELEVEN
THE NINETIES – A DECADE OF WORLDWIDE CHANGE
449

CHAPTER TWELVE
THE TRANSITION TO NEW LEADERSHIP: GENERAL ROBERT T. HERRES
467

CHAPTER THIRTEEN
MEETING THE CHALLENGES OF CHANGE
483

EPILOGUE
529

APPENDIX
535

ENDNOTES
539

INDEX
561

Foreword

This is not only the first-rate history of a great corporation, but it is also the well-told tale of a grand adventure—the story of imaginative human enterprise that was eventually rewarded, of a daring dream that was ultimately realized, of a simple idea that grew and grew until today it reaches into the lives of millions of Americans.

The idea was that if you fill a need—fill it reliably, efficiently, economically—you will do well while doing good. This was the concept on which Major William H. Garrison Jr., and two dozen other Army officers founded the United Services Automobile Association in San Antonio seventy-five years ago. Their dream was that they could serve the needs of military officers who had trouble buying car insurance in those Model T and Elcar sedan days because they moved around so much, from post to post.

The founders scarcely imagined that, three-quarters of a century later, USAA would have developed into not merely America's fourth largest homeowner insurer and the fifth largest auto insurer but a broad-based, $7 billion dollar-a-year giant that sells a wide range of financial products and investment advisory services and operates out of the largest private office building in the world.

As *Fortune* magazine recently reported, "USAA has, over the years, transformed itself into a life and health insurance company, a discount brokerage firm, a mutual fund manager, a travel agency, a buying club and a bank. This financial services supermarket, which conducts all its business by telephone or post, is now the biggest direct-mail outfit in the country. Consumers rank USAA's life insurance company, its homeowners insurance company and its investment management service Number 1 in consumer satisfaction, according to a survey by Dalbar, a Boston research firm." Add to that the fact that *Money* magazine named the USAA Federal Savings Bank "the best bank in America," praising it for, among other things, offering the nation's best credit-card deals and absolutely free checking.

Chief executive Robert Herres, a retired Air Force general who learned technology in the cockpit of a Sabrejet and served as vice chairman of the Joint Chiefs of Staff under Presidents Reagan and Bush, sums up the strategy for this success in three spare sentences: "First, you decide who you want your customers to be. Then you figure out which of their needs you can meet. And then you do it better than anyone else."

In this book, historian Paul T. Ringenbach, a retired Air Force colonel who earned a Ph.D. at the University of Connecticut and is an Assistant Vice President of Corporate Communications at USAA, gives the rich details of the decisions behind those three simple sentences. The decisions are today the grist of classic case studies at Harvard and other business schools, and are pondered for strategic lessons by leaders of companies in disparate industries the world over.

Take, for example, the question of who you want your customers to be. For most of its life, USAA limited them to U.S. military officers and their dependents; today the company does business with fully 95 percent of active-duty military officers. Talk about market share! Or talk about enviable demographics: the average age of members is fifty-one; 46 percent hold a master's degree or higher, median income is nearly $64,000.

But over the years, USAA has prudently spread out, to keep up with—and ahead of—changing times and needs. With post-Cold War cutbacks in the armed forces, its core membership of active, former and retired officers is shrinking. So the company, which is owned by its policyholders, has expanded to accommodate the children and grandchildren of original members. And early in 1996, it began phasing in service to enlisted men and women; first in Germany and later in six states in the Continental United States. The company plans to expand steadily, aiming to recruit over 500,000 enlisted personnel as members by the year 2000.

Then there is the question of which needs you can meet. Many of them you can meet through cross-selling. The company's insurance customers have an average of five USAA products each; two-thirds of them use a USAA credit card. Others may have a home loan, a car loan, an annuity, a discount brokerage account and much more. And here's a formula for making synergy work: When you buy a product or service from any USAA subsidiary, it gathers and sends no fewer than eighteen pieces of data about you to all other subsidiaries. At the same time, there are some customer needs that USAA chooses not to meet.

Yet the real key to growth is Herres's third point: You do it better than anyone else. And the root of that, as Herres or just about any other USAA employee will tell you, is service.

The company makes almost a religion of service, beginning with its CEO. He regularly meets with a small team to review recent letters from any customers who have a complaint. At each session, Herres says, he hears at least one thing that moves him to start a project that will repair a problem or improve a process.

Ernest Auerbach, senior vice president of UICI, found out how closely the top brass listen to customers. As he wrote in the *Wall Street Journal,* "When I had a service problem with my USAA policy, I wrote to Mr. Herres, and a company officer soon called. He apologized, worked with me to fix the problem and called later to ensure everything was all right. Mr. Herres followed up with a letter, with which he enclosed vouchers to use against my next phone bill. How many insurance companies are this solicitous?"

Clearly, service depends on the employees. They treat customers pretty much the way their own bosses treat them. And year after year, USAA is chosen as one of the 100 best employers in the country. Turnover is low: only 6 percent to 7 percent a year versus an industry average of nearly twice that — and a walloping 44 percent when former Air Force Brigadier General Robert McDermott became CEO in 1968.

"McD," who served for twenty-five years until 1993, brought the company into the modern age and made it a much more enticing place to work. As Dr. Ringenbach recounts on these pages, "McDermott's vision for USAA was a full-service insurance and financial services company. He believed in making available to USAA members all the products and services that they needed for their financial security and well-being."

He diversified boldly. He broadened employees' jobs so that each person would perform more tasks and have more chances to advance. To improve efficiency and customer service, he both emphasized employee training and invested heavily in computers and telecommunications. He aimed to combine "high tech" (make work more rewarding for the employee) with "high touch" (make service more rewarding for the customer).

A *Fortune* article from the McDermott era, in the issue of February 21, 1991, makes some points that are still valid: "In an industry that too often provides dilatory and inattentive service, the company gets high marks from its members, the term USAA uses to describe its property and casualty policyholders. In 1971, USAA became one of the first companies to adopt a four-day, thirty-eight-hour workweek, a move that significantly reduced absenteeism. USAA devotes 2.7 percent of its annual budget to training, nearly double the industry average, and it dispenses some $1.4 million a year in college and graduate school tuition reimbursements. The company is such a desirable place to work that it received 24,000 applications to fill 1,000 vacancies last year."

By now, the figures have grown—a lot. USAA today spends $2.7 million a year in tuition reimbursements alone, for college courses taught at company headquarters and elsewhere. Management figures that better-educated employees make better employees.

As Herres says, "We now expect that in a twenty- to twenty-five-year career, a typical employee will hold six different jobs. We want to keep our employees when we shift to new processes. They come with assets like loyalty, commitment to customers, and understanding our culture and our mission. We've therefore struck a bargain: We'll provide them with the training they need if they're willing to do their part and invest in self-development and education." In sum, employees have a remarkable opportunity to learn new skills and move ahead.

Not so long ago, the *Harvard Business Review* proclaimed that "USAA is everything an operationally excellent company would want to be." USAA managers might think this praise is a bit extravagant—after all, they are perpetually dissatisfied, always trying to improve. It's reasonable to expect that they will do just that. As Herres puts it, looking to the next seventy-five years, "The only real limitation to growth is how well we do our jobs."

—Marshall Loeb
Former Managing Editor,
Fortune and *Money* magazines

Preface

For seventy-five years, USAA employees have been serving the members of the Association so well that the relationship has always been "us and our" rather than "we and they." A series of outstanding leaders and Boards of Directors provided the vision and the support the employees needed to do their jobs well. And both were blessed by members who trusted USAA and who were trusted in turn.

It is not easy to capture this spirit of community in print, but it exists as surely as the sun rises in the morning. As you read about these people and their efforts, you will come to understand why it has been rewarding to write about them. While all their names do not appear in the book, it is not a reflection of lack of respect, but only of space. As you read about the programs, innovations, technical developments, and other things about USAA, remember that they were the product of outstanding leadership and these superior employees.

In writing this book, I have a great number of people to thank. In the history of USAA, no single individual has been so harassed by friends and colleagues about his job as this author has. It made the whole project fun, however, and I greatly enjoyed the good-natured jibes. A large number of individuals willingly consented to interviews for the book. I have listed them in the appendix and thank them for their time. Many, many other USAA people have helped me along the way. These include George McCall, Paul Menchen, Troy Little, Bill Reese, Del Chisolm, George Valdemar, Sylvia Armendariz, Fran Laue, Minnie Fuentes, Jack Mondin, George Ensley, Margaret Anderson, Chris Head, John Henry, Alice Gannon, Eddie Ryan, Mark Ellis, George Weynand, Pam Gardner, Bill Hicklin, Mary Foreman, Katherine Ybarra, Barbara Humlicek, Tracy (White) Boynton, David Santos, Pat Rogers, Doris Dent, Lynn Vale, David Snowden, Mike Hawker, CeCe Abel, Jill Weinheimer, Reggie Williams, Hal Curry, Irene S. Rios, Cynthia Lyle, John Clark, Ed Braswell, Mike Lynch, Art Settles, Ron Anderson, George Tye, Bill James, Brenda Harrier, Bernie Tallerico, Tom Bolander, Staser Holcomb, Bill Cooney, JoAnn Reyes, Denise Harris, Patsy Brecheen, Nancy Hurt, Leticia Casiano, Melba Leal, Shiang

Chen, Norma Jean Salinas, Dave Huffman, Rob Henderson, Kay Parker, Beverley McClure, Steve Marlin, Inzia Miller, Susan Lewis, and the employees who helped prepare historical inputs from their units the past few years. Others from outside USAA include Bill Hoglund and Tom Paterson from The University of Connecticut; Louise Arnold – Friend of the U.S. Army Military History Institute at Carlisle, Pennsylvania; Ron Cole of the Joint Chiefs of Staff's History Office; John Manguso of the Fort Sam Houston Museum; Captain Mike Rein and Jimmy Biggs of the Air Force Personnel Center at Randolph Air Force Base; Colonel Tom Russell of the USMA Association of Graduates; Rod A. Siler of The Camberley Gunter Hotel; and Susan Chandoha, Virginia Nicholas, Kathy Ringenbach, and Tom and Carolyn Duffy.

Over the years, many individuals in my office helped me collect materials and photos to use "some day" for this book. They include Mel Walts, Mel Garza, Claudia Lawson, Kami (King) Fiedler, Martha Mitchell, Greg Webb, and Leslie Todd. Also, Leslie did yeoman work in helping collect the illustrations for this book. Roger Smith did an especially great job enhancing print pieces. Jim Donovan, John Cook, Mike Wagner, Tim Timmerman, and Sue Whinnery read the entire manuscript. They saved me from numerous errors, but those that remain are mine alone. In addition, Jim Wieghart, former editor of the *New York Daily News* and currently Associate Professor of Journalism at Central Michigan University, provided thoughtful editorial suggestions on USAA in the 1990s and made major contributions to the epilogue. Neal Kimmel's book design efforts were exceptional.

I especially appreciated the support, ideas, and encouragement of John Cook, and I thank General Bob Herres for his confidence and the time in allowing me to write this book. Finally, I want to thank Jo Wynn who helped get illustrations, aided in research, and typed the entire manuscript (many times) with great skill and even more patience. She translated my scribbles on yellow legal pads into the book that follows. Without her, there would have been no book at all.

P.T.R.
May 7, 1997
San Antonio, Texas

Gunter Hotel, circa 1920. *(Courtesy Institute Of Texan Cultures)*

CHAPTER ONE

THE ROAD LESS TRAVELLED

June 20, 1922. While the rare days of poet James Russell Lowell's June gently warm the northern United States, those same days in San Antonio are often oppressive. It was just such a day on the 20th, with the temperature in the mid-90s, when twenty-five Army officers began arriving at the Gunter Hotel. Dressed in khaki with Sam Browne belts, they came to talk about automobile insurance, but they had an appointment with history. When the day was over, they would be the charter members and founders of the present-day USAA.

The officers attending were a cross-section of much of the U.S. Army in the 1920s. Medical Corps Lieutenant Colonel R.F. Metcalfe was the Chief of Surgery at the Post Hospital at Fort Sam Houston. Lieutenant Colonel J.H. Barnard was from the Quartermaster Corps. Major H.B. Lewis was the Adjutant General of the 2nd Infantry Division and Lieutenant Colonel W.W. Morris was from the same Division. Lieutenant Colonel George W. Biegler was a Cavalry representative and Medal of Honor winner. Captain Harry McCorry Henderson of the 9th Infantry Regiment came over from Camp Travis, now part of Fort Sam Houston, in his Buick touring car.

Years later, Henderson recalled that his commander had taken a litter of skunks to the Post Veterinarian for surgery to make them sexless and odorless. When visitors came from the Division headquarters and met with the commander, Henderson's assignment was to toss in one of the black and white furry grenades and holler "skunk!" The idea was to see how the visitors would react to this "combat" situation. One of Henderson's favorite memories shared with Biegler and others at the Officer's Club was George Biegler, the Medal of Honor winner, taking refuge from the skunk by standing on his chair.

Also present was infantry officer Major Marion O. French, who walked with a slight limp — a souvenir of fighting the insurrection in the Philippines years before. During the insurrection there, then Lieutenant French, with saber in one hand and pistol in the other, had led his men on a charge over a mud wall, sustaining many wounds. Also stationed with him at Fort Sam Houston was Lieutenant Robert G. Caldwell, a battalion commander.

From the newly constituted Air Service, a part of the Signal Corps, was Major Frank D. Lackland, who would become a general officer and have Lackland Air Force Base in San Antonio named in his honor. He, Air Service officer Major J.A. Pagelow, and several junior flying officers were particularly interested in talking about automobile insurance. They had just lost their premiums and insurance when the Red Dog Automobile Insurance Company of Chicago went belly-up.

Responsible for calling the meeting was Major William Henry Garrison. "Gary," as he was known, was born in Brooklyn, New York, on January 29, 1885. He went to grammar school there, attended a boys' school in Switzerland for two years, and returned to Brooklyn to graduate from high school in 1903. He entered West Point as a member of the Class of 1907, but had academic difficulties and was eliminated. Within two weeks, however, he had secured a new Congressional appointment for himself to the Class of 1908. He graduated in the middle of his class, was commissioned in the Cavalry, and served at a number of posts in the United States and in the Philippines. He also served on the West Point faculty teaching French, which he had learned as a boy in school in Switzerland.

In September 1917, he was assigned as the Commanding Officer of the Air Depot at Middleton, Pennsylvania. Caught up with flying, he cajoled his friends who flew to give him informal lessons. In 1918, he received the official rating of junior military aviator. He may have been the only man to become an Army pilot without the benefit of attending any flying school, military or civilian. Even more amazing, he was then assigned as Commanding Officer of Kelly Field #1 (Duncan Field), a flying base and now part of Kelly Air Force Base in San Antonio.

Major William Henry Garrison Jr.

Garrison's West Point classmates found him cheerful and even-tempered and an agile performer in the baked potato "wars" at dinner, hurling them with great skill at his classmates. His skill at polo was such that the 1908 *Howitzer,* the Academy yearbook, predicted he could become a centaur if he wanted, although Gary opted for the Cavalry. A friend later recalled that his outstanding trait was persistence, because Garrison believed he could accomplish any objective if he really wanted to do it. His record in getting admitted to West Point twice, becoming a flying officer without flying school, and starting an insurance company with no money and little background in business testify to his tenacity.

Regardless of their military specialties, these men shared the common bond held by all military officers. They were professionals, serving their nation with "Duty, Honor, Country." One other aspect set them aside from other civilian professionals such as doctors and lawyers. Sir John Hackett, famed military historian, later put the idea simply: they were all subject to the unlimited liability clause

A Tradition Of Service

Major William Henry Garrison Jr., after the crash of his biplane in June 1922

— their willingness to sacrifice their lives for their country. This understanding was integral to their respect for each other.

For those who had participated in the heady celebrations of Armistice Day on November 11, 1918, the 1920s were filled with uncertainty and change. Demobilization of the armed forces proceeded rapidly and was a concern for those officers wanting to stay in the military for a career. Military publications were filled with news of deactivations and reductions, and even the *San Antonio Express* on June 20, 1922, reported that Congress was considering a further reduction of 19,000 in the U.S. Navy active force. The unsettling news was everywhere.

In addition to the impact of demobilization on the military, enormous political, economic, and social changes were sweeping the United States. In the decade following the war, the Republicans won the White House, industrial production almost doubled, and the gross national product rose almost 40 percent. The automobile was a major factor in this economic boom and was the most visible vehicle for social change in the nation.

As early as 1877, George B. Sheldon had designed a gasoline-propelled vehicle. By the turn of the century, Charles E. Duryea, Henry Ford, and others had begun production of automobiles for general sale. Although relatively expensive at first, the automobile became enormously popular. In 1906, *Harper's Weekly* reported that John Jacob Astor owned thirty-two cars, and that 200 New Yorkers owned five or more. In fact, New Yorkers owned nearly half the cars driven in the United States at that time.[1]

Model "T" Ford

Continuing design improvements by Ford resulted in the Model T in 1908. Word-of-mouth advertising praised the reliability of this automobile and the prices made it affordable for most Americans. A fixed design, improved manufacturing techniques, and mass sales reduced the cost from $850 in 1908 to $600 in 1914 to $260 in 1921. Ford resisted any changes to his vehicle that might cause prices to rise. This even included the color. Buyers could have any color they wanted, Ford insisted — as long as it was black! The eight-hour, five-dollar-a-day jobs of Ford's employees also generated publicity for the Model T and were factors in increased sales.

The car had won the hearts, minds, and pocketbooks of Americans

A Tradition Of Service

Ford advertisement in *San Antonio Light*, June 18, 1922

everywhere. The automobile was a central theme in popular magazines, newspapers, and in the arts. In 1922, Sinclair Lewis's *Babbitt* reached the reading public. George Babbitt, the central character, was a small businessman in the Midwest. Lewis wrote that Babbitt's car was "poetry and tragedy, love and heroism. The office was his pirate ship, but the car his perilous excursion ashore." Frank King's "Gasoline Alley" comic strip portrayed small-town car owners and was tremendously popular in 1921. Robert and Helen Lynd's social study of the twenties, *Middletown*, found that by 1923 there was already one car for about every sixty-two persons in Muncie, Indiana.

Besides the automobile and the related suppliers it fostered, development of the nation's road system grew rapidly as well. Prior to World War I, the system was poor. Substantial areas west of the Mississippi River had no highways at all. Automobile owners and companies like Goodyear with a vested interest pressured government to do something about the situation. In 1921, Congress passed the Federal Highway Act, which enabled national planning and development of an interstate road system. Local authorities were quick to apply for such funds for road development in their jurisdictions.

The officers at the Gunter that day in 1922 were well aware of the impact of the automobile. Parked in the street outside the hotel were their personal vehicles, including Model T Fords, Overland 90s, Studebakers, Hudsons, Chevrolets, and one Elcar, manufactured in Elkhart, Indiana.[2] The local papers that day were filled as usual with articles about the automobile. The Texas Highway Commission announced that it would allot three million dollars of federal funds to begin a network of roads for Texas. Two of the eight goals for the city of San Antonio related to cars. The County Commissioners announced that Babcock and Fredericksburg Roads would be paved. A column on Road Reports noted that the Old Spanish Trail from Houston to San Antonio was "fair to good" with some rough stretches, and a bad mudhole lying waiting on the way to Del Rio from San Antonio. "Joe's Car," a 4-panel cartoon syndicated by *The New York Evening World,* showed the problems of car ownership to *San Antonio Light* readers daily.

"Joe's Car" in *San Antonio Light.* © 1922, *N.Y. Evening World* by Press Publishing Company.

The officers were also all too aware of the dangers of the automobile — to their personal safety and to their financial security. As they sat in the Pink Room waiting for the meeting to begin, they could have read in that day's *San Antonio Express* about the car that collided with a street car on Houston Street, or the traffic officer who was hit while attending a traffic signal. One subscriber wrote to the editor to express his concern for pedestrians and the carelessness of local drivers. He wrote, "It is quite common in San Antonio for motor car drivers to bear down upon pedestrians, sound a shrill horn and making no attempt to reduce speed . . . (sending the pedestrians) scurrying in other directions seeking safety. They drive their cars as though the thoroughfare had been constructed especially for them — others were trespassers, mere worms to be run off . . ." The officers knew they needed insurance, but it was not a simple matter.

The prestige military officers held in society during the war was not an important factor for automobile insurance companies. The war was over now, and even Congress deferred discussion of a military bonus in favor of discussing international trade. The insurance companies did not appreciate the transient lifestyles of career officers and many locally based insurance companies were reluctant to insure them at all. Many other companies were not funded adequately and failed when claims overwhelmed their limited cash reserves. It was Major Garrison's bold idea to organize an association of officers who would insure automobiles for each other.

The idea of consumers getting together in organizations for mutual financial advantage was not a new one. Consumer cooperatives that distributed food date back to mid-eighteenth century Scotland. And in 1844, the weavers of Rochdale, England, formulated a set of principles such as "each member — one vote" which was followed by cooperatives in this country. Farmers' cooperatives were common in the United States and ran such economic ventures as stores, grain elevators, and meat packing plants. Land O' Lakes butter and Sunkist citrus fruit are familiar store brands of farmers' cooperatives.

In addition to the more traditional businesses directly affiliated with agriculture, the farmers also formed many successful township and county fire insurance companies. In 1920 over 1,800 such farmers' mutuals existed. Almost all of these followed generally along the lines of the Philadelphia Contributorship for the Insurance of Houses from Loss by Fire, founded in 1752 and chaired by Benjamin Franklin. In these early mutuals that offered insurance, "mutual" meant that each policyholder was a member and a direct guarantor of fellow members. They prorated losses among members and assessed levies to cover the losses.

George Mecherle had the same idea for farmers at the same time Garrison was formulating his plans for insuring automobiles for military officers. The U.S. Census of 1920 was the first in which the U.S. urban population exceeded rural population. In the decades following the Civil War, farmers increasingly felt betrayed by urban companies and banks. They sought insurance protection with local cooperatives, but it was often not sufficient. Mecherle's dream was to pull all farmers together to help each other. His goal was to establish a liability company based on mutual principles that would sell affordable insurance to the farmers in the state of Illinois. He realized his goal on June 8, 1922, with the establishment of State Farm Mutual Automobile Insurance Company, just twelve days before USAA began.

When it appeared that the officers whom Garrison had invited were ready to begin, he called the meeting to order. To brief the officers on his proposal, Garrison had asked Harold Dunton to attend the session. Dunton was a civilian businessman with some insurance experience, and a reserve officer in the Air Service. Garrison's hope was that if the attendees decided to go ahead with the association, perhaps Dunton could run it for them.

The tall, slender, and dark-haired Dunton began with the litany of problems facing the officers in procuring reliable and inexpen-

A Tradition Of Service

Harold F. Dunton

sive automobile insurance. He had a suggestion. He pointed out that the Army Cooperative Fire Association of Fort Leavenworth, Kansas, had been insuring officers' clothing, household goods, and equipment since 1887. Until recently, this Association had also insured automobiles for fire risks. It demonstrated that a mutual type of organization for officers could be very successful. Another example was the Army Mutual Aid Association, which had existed for over forty years.

Dunton went on to point out that the automobile presented many risks besides fire. Theft, public liability, collision, and property damage all had to be considered, as did insurance protection for cars when officers shipped them by rail or by sea to a new duty station. Local companies and agents were rarely interested when an officer went out of their territory. Dunton concluded by saying that the only way to get the service you need and at a price you can

USAA Board of Directors, circa 1923

afford to pay is to organize your own association. Garrison seconded Dunton's remarks to the assembled officers, who unanimously agreed that they wanted to start their own association to insure each other. And so the United States Army Automobile Insurance Association was born.[3]

With the decision made, the officers elected Garrison as the first president of their Association and elected fourteen others to join him on the first Board of Directors. Garrison agreed to serve as Acting Secretary-Treasurer until the Board made a permanent selection. He also agreed to find a temporary office at Kelly Field #1 where he was the commanding officer. USAA soon opened the doors to its first office in a World War I wooden barracks at Kelly. With a

USAA's first office at Kelly Field

salary of $150 per month, Harold Dunton was selected as the first general manager, and the United States Army Automobile Insurance Association (USAA) was open for business.

The early months of the Association were extremely busy for Garrison, Dunton, and the Board. The Board adopted the first bylaws at its first meeting on June 22. The bylaws stated that the main purpose of the Association was to provide automobile insurance to Army officers from its office in San Antonio. Membership was open to U.S. Army officers and warrant officers, who had the power to

11

elect a board of directors and to change the bylaws at the annual meeting. To protect the members, the Board specified that the Association could not assess members more than one additional premium in the event of severe losses. For military officers accustomed to a chain of command, the Board's failure to specify who was the "commander" of USAA created significant problems. It would take a long time until the membership knew whether the Board Chairman, the Attorney-in-Fact, or the General Manager was the individual in charge.

In addition to these decisions, the Board also appointed an Executive Council of three board members. This council had the authority to act for the Board between meetings. All board members were to receive five dollars per month, and Garrison, who worked on his off-duty hours for the Association, was to receive $100 monthly. The monies due an individual were to be paid in a lump sum when he left the Association.

Just one week after the organizational meeting at the Gunter, Garrison and Dunton had a draft of an insurance application and a power of attorney ready for board approval. Their familiarity with the methods of the reciprocal organization of the Army Cooperative Fire Association was very helpful in developing the documents to run USAA's business. They also adapted forms used by a company known as the Automobile Underwriters of America (AUA), an insurance exchange located in San Antonio. The application was in reality a private contract in which the subscriber (new policyholder) agreed to obtain indemnity by the exchange of these contracts. The subscribers or members also appointed the secretary-treasurer of the Association as their "Attorney-in-Fact" to act for the members if they became liable for matters of common risk.

In the matter of money, the document assured the members that their money would be deposited in banks or invested in "proven gilt-edged" securities. The Attorney-in-Fact could draw money from these funds to pay the members' share of the Association's expenses and adjusted claims. But what if expenses and claims exceeded the funds deposited by members? The form noted the bylaws' restriction that the Board of Directors could assess each member "for not more than one additional premium deposit on any one contract."[4] This limited power of assessment eased the worries of many potential members who had heard horror stories of reciprocals sucking their members dry.

A 1925 Elcar Landau Touring Sedan – similar to the first car insured by USAA

Once the Board approved the "Application, Agreement, and Power of Attorney Form," and laid the foundation for organizing USAA, it recognized that acquiring new members was the highest priority. The Board had already shown its concern by inserting an incentive clause in Dunton's contract. Dunton's salary was $150 per month or $1.50 per new member, whichever was larger. The Board assumed that this incentive would encourage Dunton to find as many members as possible. Incidentally, the first USAA policyholder, and technically its first member, was Major Walter Moore who insured his 1922 Elcar for an annual premium of $114.47. Moore attended the first meeting at the Gunter and was a member of the first Board of Directors. Two months later, the Board agreed to pay Majors Moore and H.B. Lewis 10 percent of the first payment on all insurance policies that they wrote personally. Garrison even wrote to President Warren G. Harding to let him know he was eligible to join by virtue of being "Commander in Chief of the United States Army."[5] Harding was "most appreciative of the courtesy extended to him," but declined.[6]

Dunton was energetic and enthusiastic about the Association. His first marketing venture was a flyer to be distributed to the various military installations in San Antonio. The flyer emphasized why USAA was good for the military officer. The insurance was cheaper than other policies and covered the officer wherever he was stationed. One line of the flyer underlined the fraternal nature of the Association and suggested great service at the same time. "All losses are adjusted by a committee of three of your *fellow* officers, thereby *avoiding delay* in settlement." The member would not be dealing with one of "them," but one of "us." To reassure potential members, the flyer listed the Directors and their military ranks and affiliations. It also noted that Dunton was a thoroughly experienced automobile insurance man. Dunton also visited the area military posts, and other Board members talked with their friends about joining the Association. This word-of-mouth advertising by members was to continue to be enormously successful throughout USAA's history. Faith in USAA, the honesty of the membership, and the willingness to share the USAA "good deal" with professional friends and colleagues would be key ingredients of growth over the years.

The transient lifestyle of the officers soon affected their own Association. Garrison received orders to report to Washington, D.C., via the Command and General Staff School at Fort Leavenworth in September 1922 and carried the presidency of USAA with him. The Board elected Major Lackland to assume the position of Acting Secretary-Treasurer. At its November 20 meeting, the Board decided to act on its officer situation. Although Garrison would remain President until the next annual meeting, the Board directed the Acting Secretary-Treasurer to write Garrison to advise him that his salary was discontinued effective November 30 and to thank him "for his labors in the forming of the Association."

The selection of a permanent Secretary-Treasurer could not wait until the next annual meeting, however. The Board elected Lieutenant Colonel R.G. Caldwell to become the permanent Secretary-Treasurer effective upon his retirement from the Army. It decided to give Caldwell a contract that matched Dunton's. Caldwell retired on December 15 and began his five-year contract with USAA. The Board also gave Caldwell an expense account of $100 monthly, and amended Dunton's contract accordingly to give him an expense account as well.

Lieutenant Colonel Robert G. Caldwell

Born in 1873, Caldwell had dark, curly hair slightly graying at the temples. He was easygoing, likable, and had a wry sense of humor that helped him keep his balance at USAA. After a stint in Argentina as a dispatch rider, he enlisted in the U.S. Army after the Spanish American War and was commissioned with less than three years' service. His last assignment prior to his retirement was as a battalion commander at Camp Travis, Texas.

A Tradition Of Service

As a last piece of business, the Board directed that Dunton move the offices of the Association into the city of San Antonio as soon as practical. Dunton leased an office at 615-617 Calcassieu Building on Broadway at Travis and moved in with his staff of one bookkeeper and three clerks less than two weeks after the Board's request. When Caldwell reported to work, Dunton retained control over the Board minutes and most administrative functions, keeping Caldwell in the dark. When Caldwell complained to board member George Biegler, he was told to do whatever Dunton asked. With Garrison already departed, the Board had decided to keep Dunton as USAA's primary operating manager.

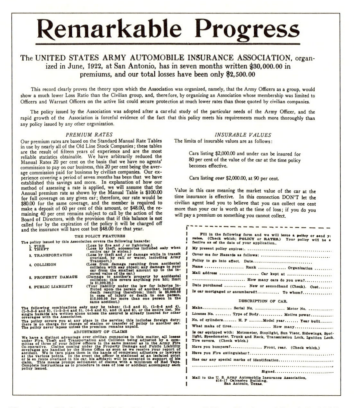

"Bragging Rights," published in the *Army and Navy Register*, March 3, 1923

In January 1923, the Board was pleased with how well things seemed to be going and ran a bulletin advertisement, shown on the previous page, in the *Army and Navy Register.*

It also ran a series of eye-catching advertisements in 1923 to attract more members to the Association. The advertisement with an officer holding an umbrella was a good example — officers did not carry umbrellas while in uniform.

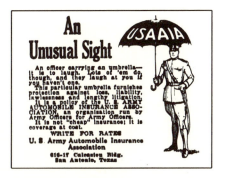

In June 1923, it was time for the Board to review USAA's first year. Of the fifteen original Board members, only six were "present," and two of these, including Garrison, by proxy. Although not a Board member, Dunton chaired the meeting and briefed the Board. He reported a deficit of about $3,300, and the Board voted to in-

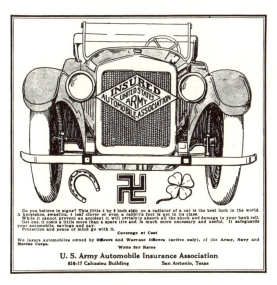

Army and Navy Register, June 30, 1923. (Although many people identify the Swastika with Nazi Germany, it is a symbol of prosperity and good fortune dating back to the ancient world. It is prominent in Navajo, Mayan, Hindu, and Byzantine art)

A TRADITION OF SERVICE

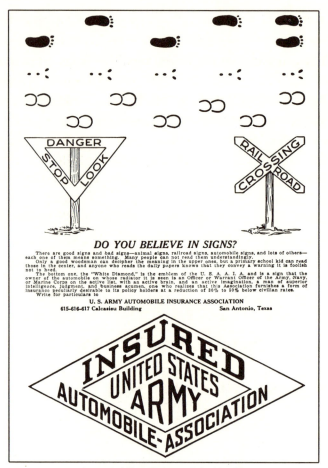

Army and Navy Register, July 28, 1923

crease the premium rate to liquidate the deficit and to create a conservative surplus. In a show of continuing faith, in spite of the loss, the Board raised Dunton's monthly salary to $250.

The first Annual Members' Meeting was held one year to the day from USAA's founding in the same Pink Room of the Gunter Hotel. Of the approximately 800 members, only eighteen actually attended, and they held 183 proxy ballots. Medal of Honor winner Lieutenant Colonel George Biegler was elected president, replacing founder

Garrison. To remedy the problem highlighted by Garrison's move, the membership voted to amend the bylaws to provide for the immediate removal of any member of the Board who was transferred out of San Antonio and for his replacement by the remaining Board. Most significant of all was a change in the bylaws to extend membership eligibility in USAA to include officers and warrant officers of the Navy and Marine Corps on "the *active* list only." With this change, the membership set the precedent of broadening eligibility to include new groups of individuals. The Board suggested that this change be released to the *Army and Navy Journal* and the *Army and Navy Register*.

In an advertisement published in the *Army and Navy Register*, on August 4, 1923, USAA displayed the graphic of a new diamond emblem. The ad compared the USAA diamond to the blue-white diamond

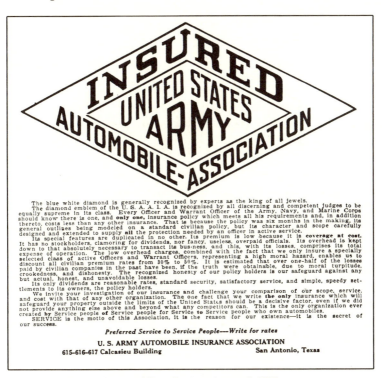

Army and Navy Register, August 4, 1923

A Tradition Of Service

recognized by experts as the king of jewels. The text included reasons why officers should join USAA. It had low premiums because it was "coverage at cost," and it had "no stockholders clamoring for dividends, nor fancy, useless, overpaid officials." It had a low overhead. This,

> combined with the fact that we only insure a specially selected class of active Officers and Warrant Officers, representing a high moral hazard enables us to discount all civilian premium rates from 30 to 50%. It is estimated that over one-half of the losses paid by civilian companies have been . . . due to moral turpitude, crookedness and dishonesty. The recognized honesty of our policy holders is our safeguard against any but actual, honest, and unavoidable losses. Its only dividends are reasonable rates, standard security, satisfactory service, and simple, speedy settlements to its owners, the policy holders.

The ad further pointed out that USAA's insurance was "the *only* insurance" which would safeguard property outside the limits of the United States. If this were the only difference between USAA and other carriers, it should be the decisive factor for military officers. It continued that USAA was the only organization "created by Service people of Service people for Service to Service people who own automobiles." It concluded with the following:

> SERVICE is the motto of this Association, it is the reason for our existence — it is the secret of our success.

This advertisement pretty well described the rationale for the foundation of USAA.

Another advertisement ran in the *Army and Navy Register* on November 24 of the same year, that suggested members should place the USAA emblem on their vehicles. The December 29 issue of the *Register* stated that "The white diamond is the emblem of USAAIA and is a sign that the owner of the automobile on whose radiator it is seen is an officer 'on the active list, with an active brain, and with an active imagination, a man of superior intelligence, judgment, and business acumen' who realizes the great benefits of USAA." While these advertisements might not work today, they did then, and the Association received considerable numbers of inquiries to the pleasure of the Board.

The normal claims procedure in effect in 1923 said a great deal about the respect the Association had for officers. The instructions on the automobile policy advised the following in the event of an accident.

1. Call a Board of three officers, preferably, but not necessarily members of USAA as soon as possible after loss or damage.
2. Fill out the accident report which accompanies the policy and have the board that you selected investigate your claim and fix your award, approving by their signatures on the loss report.
3. Mail the approved report to the Secretary-Treasurer of USAA.

There was not a glimmer of suspicion that a member might get three of his officer friends to certify something not true. The USAA leadership assumed that any officer, member or not, would make an impartial judgment. As such, the Secretary-Treasurer would just pay the claim as certified by the three officers.

After his election as President, Biegler looked more carefully into the office operation and the ongoing dispute between Dunton and Caldwell. He found the books questionable and Dunton guilty of drawing more than his authorized expense allowance. Biegler called a Board meeting and told the Board of his misgivings. These included that the Association's deficit was larger than reported to the membership, that Dunton had deposited USAA funds in banks other than those approved by the Board, and the terrible shape of the minutes and business papers of the Association. Aware that Dunton was speculating in the oil fields and fearing for the Association, Biegler directed that Dunton turn over all the books to Caldwell and confine himself to insurance matters pending a Board investigation.

A Tradition Of Service

Lieutenant Colonel George W. Biegler

After discussing Biegler's report, the Board hired the Perry L. King Auditing Company to perform an audit on USAA immediately. King sent in one of its top men, Leo Goodwin, to perform the audit. With the Board's consent, Biegler also appointed three of the directors to examine the whole problem and to make a report to the Board on August 20. Armed with the King audit report and the results of its own investigation of the Association's records, Major Lackland reported for the committee of three. He stated that Dunton had overdrawn his spending account by $845 and that the checks were signed by the Association's Secretary-Treasurer, Caldwell. The Board voted to cancel Dunton's and Caldwell's contracts and asked for a refund of the overdraft. Because the votes were not unanimous, the Board selected Brigadier General Benjamin A. Poore to serve as arbitrator. The final decision was to offer Dunton a settlement and send him on his way. Caldwell was retained with the support of Biegler because Biegler believed that Caldwell was a "victim of circumstances."

While looking into this case, Lackland reported another surprising development. An organization called the Service Finance Corporation (SFC) was using the Association's offices and clerks without Board authority or payment. This corporation loaned money to officers to buy new cars. One USAA clerk reported that they were behind twenty-four renewals and twenty-five new applications, but still had to do the SFC work first! It turned out Dunton was president and Caldwell was secretary-treasurer of this firm. The Board appointed a separate committee of three to look into SFC.

In his report to the Board in September, Major Fred Cruse explained that the purpose of SFC was to provide automobile financing to Army officers, and its relationship to USAA was a symbiotic one. Most standard commercial finance companies insisted that the officers carry insurance with civilian companies, which hurt USAA. On the other hand, SFC with its favorable consideration of officers for insurance, helped. Cruse pointed out that in just the past three months, USAA had received almost $2,000 in premiums from SFC referrals. His committee found that USAA's actual financial assistance to SFC was trivial and was no longer an issue anyway because SFC had moved into its own offices. The USAA deposits in banks not authorized by the Board turned out to be "courtesy deposits" in banks where SFC discounted its paper. USAA's deposits earned the expected interest and that money was not at risk. The Board found that Dunton's and Caldwell's efforts were positive, if not authorized, and voted to ratify all previous arrangements with SFC. It did direct that no more than three directors or officers of SFC serve on the USAA Board at the same time.

It appears that USAA had already discovered that service meant more than paying fair claims on time. Sometimes USAA could do more. If officers could not buy cars in the first place, there would be no need for insurance. Most of the officers had brought their own cars to the USAA organizational meeting, but virtually all were senior officers. And, on the original Board, there was only one lieutenant. In 1922 there were over 15,500 Army officers on active duty with an average base pay of about $2,100. Needless to say, junior officers made considerably less. The Model T was relatively inexpensive, but Chevrolet Roadsters and Touring cars were over $500 and Pontiac sports touring cars ran over $1,200. Then, as now, "time payments" were a necessity for most potential car buyers. The USAA Board was not prepared to put car loans under the USAA emblem, but it made provisions to help guarantee the success of the Service

Finance Corporation which, in turn, provided a service to the member to the benefit of USAA.

With Dunton on his way out, the Board hired retired Army Major William B. Loughborough as the new general manager. Thirty-eight years old, Loughborough had been in the insurance business since his retirement, and had been considered earlier by the Board to head a possible office in Washington, D.C. Interestingly, when Dunton and Caldwell were being "investigated" by the Board committee, both individuals had contacted Loughborough separately to see if he were interested in replacing each one's antagonist.

Major William B. Loughborough, USA (Ret.)

Loughborough was an Army "brat" born in the Dakota Territory in 1885. He started his college education in Kansas while his father was stationed at Fort Leavenworth, and received his degree in English from Stanford in 1908. He was commissioned as a second lieutenant (infantry), and the Army assigned him to the Philippines in 1909. While on special assignment in Northern Luzon with the Corps of Engineers, he received a leg injury which became infected. To the end of his days, his leg had an open sore and was very painful. When World War I began, he was still a second lieutenant. As a recognized Army expert in new weaponry, he spent the war in training posts, rapidly reaching the rank of lieutenant colonel. After the war, his rank reverted to major and he received a medical-disability retirement.

At the end of 1923, things seemed to be settling down as the Board met on the day after Christmas. Loughborough had developed the premium rate tables that Dunton never got around to doing, and proposed something new to attract new members. Loughborough recommended that USAA make a proposition to hire Garrison to solicit new policies. USAA would pay a 15 percent commission to him on all new policies he could solicit in the Washington, D.C., area. The Board enthusiastically agreed. As later reports showed, USAA had 2,110 members as of December 31 and Caldwell received a bonus of $165 for signing up more members than expected. The Board also authorized the Executive Committee to select securities for the investment of funds in excess of $10,000 belonging to the Association.

In 1924, having been burned by a lack of supervision of USAA's operations, the Executive Committee of the Board became considerably more active. It met more regularly, and most of the changes in bylaws and other things came about as a result of its initiatives. At its March 26 meeting, the full Board made a decision on premium rates that would become a ground rule for the Association for decades. USAA would use the rates published in the *Combination Automobile Insurance Manual,* the standard rates guide for the insurance industry, less 20 percent. Later, USAA would use other services, but the principle of "reduced by 20 percent" remained the same.[7] This decision to use standard manuals at this time was a good one for USAA because of the Board's lack of specific expertise in insurance.

The Executive Committee of the Board also recommended that USAA move out of its downtown location and onto the friendly confines of Fort Sam Houston. By July, the Association completed its second move in two years. USAA's new home was a two-story wooden building, built in 1901, which had serviced the YMCA during World War I.

Fort Sam Houston Clock Tower on the Quadrangle, circa 1922. *(Courtesy of Fort Sam Houston Museum)*

By 1924, USAA's idealistic view of the claims process seemed to have dissipated. Rather than the Secretary-Treasurer automatically paying all claims, the Executive Committee proceedings often included decisions made on claims. One example was the denial of a claim submitted by an officer whose underage dependent was driving. As the Association grew and unusual cases developed, it became obvious that rules regarding claims needed to be spelled out more carefully. On the matter of payment to Board members, the Executive Committee recommended that Board members be paid five dollars in cash at the time of the meeting. Captain Harry Henderson recalled that he and the other members received a five-dollar gold piece on the spot for attendance. The full Board concurred with all the recommendations of its Executive Committee.

An example of the effort to clarify rules concerned insuring autos during military transfers. USAA insured its members' vehicles overseas and also the movement of these vehicles between military assignments. The Association queried the War Department on the transportation of these cars and its shipping rules on U.S. government vessels. The Department advised that all accessories and "all removable parts such as lamps, carburetors, starting motors not an integral part of the motor, magnetos, etc. . . . had to be removed from all such vehicles and securely boxed and sealed."[8] In addition, all gasoline, oil, and water had to be removed as well. The Board made these rules a condition of insurance. Disassembling and reassembling autos were now part of the officers' moving aggravations.

The Annual Members' Meeting in June 1924 was again significant in the precedents that the members approved. The members approved a new set of bylaws, which had some key changes. The formal name of the Association, the "United States Army Automobile Insurance Association" was changed to the "United Services Automobile Association" to better reflect the membership changes approved in 1923. Further, the new bylaws extended membership to retired as well as active officers.[9] The first bylaws had emphasized the "active" status, so this was a significant change in direction. The decision made sense — officers remained officers with the same values after retirement, good members could be retained, and the membership could continue to grow. If USAA insured those on the active list only, the total number of eligibles would be limited to the vagaries of the War Department and Congressional appropriations.

During the first week of August, the USAA leadership was reminded again how little it knew about insurance. The news arrived in the form of a letter from the Texas Department of Insurance in Austin. The letter and its meaning were very clear:

27

> We hear you're writing insurance down there in San Antonio. It's a violation of the insurance laws of Texas to do that without first securing a Certificate of Authority from the Department of Insurance. Our records don't show that we have issued such a Certificate to your Company. Let us know by return mail if you are actually writing insurance, and if so, under what authority you are doing so.[10]

This was a surprising development to those running the Association and pointed out once again the lack of experience in insurance on the Board. USAA had passed the 2,500-member mark on July 31 and seemingly had no such worries. But, after the Civil War the U.S. Supreme Court had ruled that insurance was not covered under the interstate commerce provision of the Constitution. As such, the states were responsible for regulation of insurance, if there were to be any. As federal officers, the Association's leaders never gave state regulation of their activities a thought. Texas had established a code, a State Board of Insurance Commissioners, and a Department of Insurance, but the state authorities had not noticed USAA for more than two years.

Loughborough wrote to B. Werkenthin, Deputy Commissioner of the Texas Department of Insurance, immediately and played the innocent. He noted that all USAA members were military officers and had no permanent residence. Further, USAA's office was in a building owned by the War Department. Werkenthin was polite, but undeterred. He sent along a copy of the insurance code and pointed out USAA was functioning like a "reciprocal or interinsurance exchange" and was subject to the Texas Insurance Code.[11] In November, backed by an opinion issued by the Texas Attorney General that the Insurance Code did indeed apply to USAA, Judge Scott, Commissioner of Insurance, asked USAA to comply. After a series of meetings and actions by USAA to meet minimum requirements, USAA submitted a formal request for a license along with the prescribed one-dollar fee. USAA received its first license on March 23, 1925.[12]

In one way, the Texas Department of Insurance's licensing requirements were a blessing. Prior to receiving the letter, USAA had not established a reserve for unexpected losses. The Perry L. King auditors recommended that a percentage of monthly profits be set aside for this purpose to meet the licensing requirement and to put USAA on a more stable financial footing. The Executive Committee agreed.[13] The year 1924 ended on a positive note. Membership had risen to over 3,300 and USAA held assets of more than $85,000. Even after establishing the reserve, the Board was still able to declare an 8 percent dividend. And to the delight of the USAA employees, the Board decided to give them a Christmas bonus of 40 percent of one month's pay.

Over the next three years, a number of things gave the Board of Directors, membership, and employees of USAA very positive feel-

A 1926 Auburn 4-door sedan with a USAA emblem.

ings about their Association. Most visible was USAA's continued rapid growth — membership more than doubled during this period. This was a product of a number of things, including USAA's growing reputation for service and economical insurance, spread mainly by word of mouth. USAA members also helped spread the word by purchasing USAA car radiator emblems for their vehicles. USAA spent money for paid advertising as well in publications read by officers such as the *Army and Navy Register*, and USAA also made a direct mail appeal annually to all officers who were not USAA members.

New U.S. Army regulations in the 1920s authorizing officers to be reimbursed for use of their own cars on official duty and opening gasoline filling stations on Army posts reflected the growing interest in autos by the military.

Most important in the long run was the Board's willingness to expand the eligibility base by including members other than strictly military officers. In 1925, it was Field Clerks (similar to Warrant Officers) and in 1926 the U.S. Coast and Geodetic Survey, the Secretary of War himself, officers on active duty from reserve status for more than one year, and officers of the Public Health Service. The number of new eligibles was small — 203 in the Public Health Service — for example, but the new precedents were huge.

USAA's growth in size and reputation had many repercussions. The Board asked Caldwell to seek a building permit for a new structure on Fort Sam Houston and directed him to begin placing $500 in reserve each month towards the cost of a new building. USAA's reputation was enhanced when it agreed to a request by the Texas State Insurance Commissioner to help host the National Convention of State Insurance Commissioners. This was a positive show of confidence for a company only recently licensed by the Commissioner.

The reputation for service grew along with USAA's continued efforts in settling claims quickly and fairly and in other ways. When a December garage fire destroyed three members' vehicles at Fort Snelling, Minnesota, the officers received their checks by Christmas. Unusual claims such as damage to members' vehicles by a stray bullet and a burst of steam were paid quickly. Dividends which at first were only issued as a credit towards policy renewals, were now to be paid by check.

The investment program seemed to be going well. Most surplus funds went into U.S. government bonds, but others went to foreign bonds and even some into real estate mortgages. Another investment of $2,000 went towards stock in the Federal Services Finance Corporation. This company, founded by Major Garrison after his Army retirement, financed vehicles for military personnel in the Washington, D.C., area.

USAA also invested in its employees. Modern equipment such as multigraph and bookkeeping machines improved productivity, and the Christmas bonus seemingly had become a tradition. In 1926 employees found increases in their pay envelopes and learned they would now be eligible for 30 days of consecutive sick leave. Things were going well at USAA — or were they?

In some ways, all these successes and achievements were diverting attention from serious problems in the operations of USAA. The Board's failure to designate either the Secretary-Treasurer and Attorney-in-Fact (Caldwell) or the General Manager (Loughborough) as the "Commander" led to serious problems. Loughborough was aggressive, knew insurance, and had support from many Board members, and he soon gained the upper hand.

The problem surfaced in a public way at the June 1925 Annual Members' Meeting. Colonel James V. Heidt, a member of the Board, moved that a very favorable five-year contract for Loughborough be executed. After some discussion, the motion passed. When a similar motion was proposed on Caldwell's contract, the members voted to defer the action until later. Caldwell's contract still had over two years to run so he did not lose his job. It was obvious, however, that Loughborough had the votes he needed on the Board and with the membership to run the Association as he saw fit. It was easier for him to do so than might appear because the Executive Committee held the power, was small, and he met with it often. While the full Board met only three times in 1925 and two times in 1926, the Executive Committee met forty-one times in the same two-year period.

Following the 1925 Members' Meeting, the full Board met and elected Colonel Heidt as USAA's new President and Chairman of the Executive Committee. Born in 1873, this Georgia native entered West Point in 1892, but left after two years under honorable conditions. He enlisted in the Army in 1898 to fight in the Spanish American War and received a commission in 1899. In World War I he won two silver stars for gallantry and was promoted to colonel. When the Board elected him President, he was a senior staff officer to Major General Ernest Hinds, Commanding Officer of the VIII Corps at Fort Sam Houston, who would later head USAA.

Heidt was concerned about the rift between Caldwell and Loughborough and the growing division on the Board. When he visited the office, he was convinced that the job responsibilities were not clear and that the office wasn't being run in accordance with the bylaws. He asked both men to give him a list of the duties they should be performing in their respective jobs. The results showed clearly that there was no agreement between the two men. But Heidt had a 3-2 split against him and for Loughborough in the Executive Committee; he decided not to try to resolve the issue before the full Board immediately. He feared automatic support for Loughborough, and he consulted with USAA's attorney.

In the meantime, in the fall of 1926, Lieutenant Colonel Raymond F. Metcalfe, 1st Vice President of USAA and Executive Board Member, called a meeting of Loughborough and selected other directors at the quarters of Board member Lieutenant Colonel G. L. Hicks at Fort Sam Houston. In further meetings in the spring of 1927, this "rump" Board formulated plans to change the bylaws. They wrote to members outside of San Antonio to secure their proxies. Their letter did not spell out why, but only asked for their vote if they knew or had confidence in one of the nine signees.

Heidt became aware of this just before the regular proxies were mailed for the 1927 Annual Members' Meeting. Furious, he called a number of the signers of the letter and they professed ignorance of the real purpose of the rump Board. Heidt added a statement to the regular proxy cards advising them of Metcalf and Loughborough's attempt to control the Association. He recommended they return the regular proxy card and write in "Vote no changes in bylaws."[14]

Next Heidt called a special meeting of the Board on May 28. The rump representatives and their opponents on the Board engaged in furious charges and counter-charges. Heidt finally persuaded the Board to have a special committee of three, headed by Colonel Ephraim G. Peyton, look at the office operations and the Caldwell-Loughborough problem one more time. When this committee tried to give its report to the full Board, the Board wanted it delayed until after the June 15 Annual Members' Meeting. It was delayed but, as things evolved, only until the meeting itself.

Present at the Board Meeting were twenty-three members, including all twelve directors and eleven other members. The meeting quickly erupted into a series of violent arguments. The majority of the Board members did not want Peyton's report given to the members. One member, retired Army Major Josiah C. Minus, demanded the members be able to hear the report. The result was that the members heard two reports — one by the two "majority" members of the Peyton Committee and one from Peyton which he called a "minority" report.

Both reports agreed that Loughborough did exceed his authority. For example, although the Board authorized Loughborough to sign as "Acting Secretary-Treasurer" when Caldwell was absent, he did so when Caldwell was not really "absent" but only temporarily out of the office, often on business for Loughborough. On one occasion, Caldwell refused to pay Loughborough for an unauthorized trip to Houston. When Caldwell was "out," Loughborough signed a check for himself and cashed it. There were many other criticisms as well. The focus of the majority report was that in spite of these things, Loughborough had taken a company and had made it successful. Although the Board had been aware of many of the problems, it had made no attempt to correct them.

Peyton's minority report was to prove the telling one. He reiterated the character of USAA and its commissioned officer members. He criticized Caldwell for being too weak and for allowing Loughborough to usurp his rightful powers. He criticized Loughborough for his ethical errors in the handling of USAA's business. He bitterly denounced Metcalfe, Hicks, and Loughborough for the role they played in calling secret meetings to plan actions detrimental to the Association. He went on to say:

> Unthinkable as it may seem, it is legally possible for a directorate, vested with such powers, and by the secret process described, to completely change the organization of the Association to one wherein the ownership of stock would enrich individuals who were able to buy, at the expense of the poorer subscribers and at the same time deny the latter a court of last resort — the members — to protect their interests.[15]

After he finished, the members wrangled over the situation, the meeting lasting over six hours. Before it was over, the members removed Loughborough for cause and canceled his membership, and renewed Caldwell's contract for an additional five years at a straight salary of $10,000 per year.

While all the trauma over office administration was going on, the office itself became a problem. USAA had entertained the idea of building a new building on the federal reservation of Fort Sam Houston since its present quarters there were overcrowded. That required permission of the Secretary of War. In the meantime, Caldwell told the Board that the officer in charge of facilities at Fort Sam Houston had told Caldwell that the Army needed the current USAA building back. He told Caldwell that the possibility of getting another desirable government building was remote.

Caldwell's suggestion was to purchase a building in the civilian community right off the Post. In fact, he had looked at a house that had promise on Grayson Street, across the street from the Quadrangle at Fort Sam Houston. As it was summer and the Executive Committee thought it had time, it took no action on its study of the issues. The Army was on a different calendar, however. It wanted USAA to vacate as soon as possible. Heidt explained to the Board that the Executive Committee authorized the Association to purchase the building at 1400 Grayson Street without full Board authorization. Caldwell asked the Board to approve the action which it did.[16] The office was temporary because of its size and the Association now incurred taxes on the property, but USAA was in operation again in its fourth location in five years. The plan was to modify the structure to expand the work and storage areas and to make provisions for a vault.

The fierce fight at the Annual Members' Meeting left a bitter residue at USAA. Board supporters of Loughborough continued their arguments for him and against Caldwell at the next two Board meetings. Loughborough instituted a suit against USAA, Heidt, and Caldwell. Members in attendance at the Annual Members' Meeting spread the word on the situation at USAA, and confidence in the Association dropped in spite of continued growth in members and in assets. The General Manager's position was now vacant and the

Board did not have confidence in Caldwell's abilities to run USAA's operations alone. What USAA needed was a leader who could command the respect of the Board, employees, and membership.

CHAPTER TWO

DEPRESSION AND REVOLUTION

On the eve of the Depression, the nation still surged with confidence. Charles Lindbergh had completed his solo flight to Paris in 1927 and Henry Ford produced his 50 millionth car. The *New York Times* index of twenty-five industrial stocks marked 100 in 1924 and by the end of 1927 reached 245.[1] In spite of its problems in 1927, USAA's optimism was high nonetheless when 1928 began. It now had over 7,500 members and assets totaling over $300,000. Most important of all, USAA began the year with a new leader, retired Army Major General Ernest Hinds, whom all respected and admired.

Hinds was born in 1864 in Marshall County, Alabama. At the age of eighteen, he took a competitive exam for West Point and secured an appointment from Congressman Joseph Wheeler, a former Confederate general. Wheeler's own son came in second to Hinds in the examination and lost the appointment. (In the following year, Wheeler's son lost a Naval Academy appointment to Hinds' brother, Walton, who was destined to rise to the rank of Admiral.[2]

Ernest Hinds as a West Point Cadet

Hinds graduated eighth in the Class of 1887, was appointed a second lieutenant of Artillery, and married his tutorial student, Minnie Miller, who would share his life for more than fifty years. He aggressively sought combat duty and demanding assignments throughout his career and performed exceptionally well. Typical of his zeal was his experience in the Spanish-American War. Hinds received an assignment to Cuba to Light Battery "F," Second Artillery. When he arrived at Tampa, the troop ship had already departed. Unwilling to wait for another, he jumped aboard a freighter full of mules. When he arrived at Cuba, he learned his unit was already in action. He picked up his blanket roll and walked all night to reach Santiago.

When Hinds arrived on the morning of July 2, the battery commander, Academy graduate Captain Charles Parkhurst, had just been wounded. Hinds took command and Parkhurst reported of a later engagement that the "good work" of "F" battery "was due to his [Hinds'] energy" in moving the battery "right of the line and within a range of 800 yards of the advanced Spanish entrenchments."[3] Because of his outstanding performance at Santiago, the Army promoted Hinds to Brevet (temporary) Major. Following his duty in Cuba, he was assigned as a battalion commander to help put down the insurrection in the Philippines, where he captured one of the most notorious rebels along with his cache of arms.

During the remainder of his active career, his success as an artillery expert dominated his military records. He helped develop the basis of modern field artillery techniques and when Artillery became a separate branch in 1907, he transferred to it. He stood towards the top of his class in all the service schools he attended including Mounted Service School and the forerunner of Command and Staff School. In General William P. Duvall's nomination of Hinds for the Army War College, he said that Hinds "is conspicuously the type of officer that should preferably be sent to the War College: studious, broad, well-read, ambitious — in short, a sterling officer in every respect."[4] The U.S. entrance into World War I was to preclude his attendance at the Army War College, however.

The Great War found him in France, where he served as Commandant of the Saumaur Artillery School until January 1918. He rapidly rose through command assignments until General John J. Pershing named him as Chief of Artillery for the American Expeditionary Forces. He was responsible for training about 15,000 officers and 340,000 enlisted men. Official German records discovered after the war praised the American artillery for its "machine-like accuracy and deadliness," which they suggested was a major factor in defeating the German forces. Pershing said, "Hinds was an exceptionally able officer, and withal extremely modest. I value his friendship highly."[5]

All of Hinds' commanders held him in highest regard. Following the war, his commander at Fort Sill, Alabama, called him one of the most remarkable officers in the service. He called him thorough in his work with a judicial temperament and pleasant and agreeable manners. He said that he always had the respect, admiration, and loyal support of those serving under him. He concluded by stating that "his principles, both personal and official are the highest. Of the thirty-three brigadier generals whom I know personally, I place General Hinds No. 1."[6]

It was at Fort Sam Houston where General Hinds would complete his career as Commanding Officer of the VIII Corps Area. He was one of a very small number of major generals selected to remain on active duty after demobilization. A classmate later pointed out that his brilliant record of achievements paled next to his personal characteristics. He had "no concept of vanity and it was as natural for him to do the honorable thing and to be considerate of others as it is for the sun to shine." His actions "inspired confidence and assured success." His concern for the welfare of others "won the loyalty and affection of those associated with him."[7]

It is no wonder that Heidt's proposal to the Board to offer the positions of Secretary-Treasurer, Attorney-in-Fact, and General Manager to Hinds was received so enthusiastically. Heidt had talked

Major General Hinds and his Aide entertain visitors on the breezeway of the Fort Sam Houston Quadrangle – 1927. *(Courtesy of Fort Sam Houston Museum)*

to Hinds informally to see if he would be interested. Hinds was interested, but was not willing to campaign for the position. He knew more about USAA than the average member because of discussions with his son-in-law, Major Fred Cruse, who had been a member of the USAA Board. On the personal side, he and his wife were planning on retiring in San Antonio anyway. In fact, while horseback riding, they had picked out a piece of land on a hilltop in Terrell Hills, close to Fort Sam Houston.

Heidt suggested to Hinds and then to the Board that any proposal from USAA could be made effective upon the general's retirement. This would solve the problem that had troubled USAA for years — who was in charge of running USAA? Hinds would hold all three positions: Secretary-Treasurer, Attorney-in-Fact, and General Manager.[8] Hinds wrote to Heidt three days later and accepted the offer, but asked that it be held confidential until he formally submitted his retirement. Such big news does not stay secret in a small military community, however. The word was already out at Fort Sam Houston as one Board member noted who heard the story while attending a dance at the post.

The problem with making this proposal work was that Caldwell already held the positions as Secretary-Treasurer and Attorney-in-Fact under his contract with USAA. Heidt had gone to Caldwell and discussed with him his proposal about Hinds. In order for it to work, Caldwell would have to resign. Heidt and Caldwell worked it out so that after Caldwell resigned, Hinds would get a contract, and then the Board would appoint Caldwell as Assistant Secretary-Treasurer, working for Hinds at a reduced salary. Showing unusual loyalty, Caldwell agreed to do this for the good of the Association. That settled, USAA looked forward to the General reporting to work.

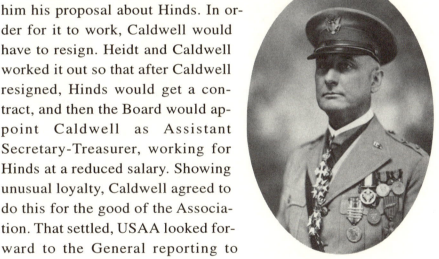

Major General Ernest Hinds

Hinds began his duties on the first day after New Year's Day in 1928. USAA had about two dozen employees at that time, mostly women. This was certainly a major change for Hinds who commanded men almost exclusively during his service career. Contractually Caldwell was to be his second in charge, but his health was weakened due to stress and occasional bouts with alcohol. As a result, after Loughborough, the General Manager, left USAA,

A TRADITION OF SERVICE

Caldwell depended a great deal upon Leo Goodwin and other USAA staff members. Goodwin, who originally came to the Association as an auditor with Perry L. King to help straighten out USAA's books, had been hired by Caldwell in 1925. His first USAA position was as Chief Accountant. Goodwin was born in Missouri in 1886 and prior to his hiring at USAA worked as an accountant or auditor for the railroad and in the oil industry in West Texas. His wife, however, favored San Antonio and he began working for Perry L. King as an auditor there.[9]

Leo Goodwin Sr. was hired in 1925, and became a key staff member to Caldwell.

Goodwin had no insurance background, but his intelligence and accounting experience made him a key staff man for USAA. Prior to Hinds' arrival he had helped negotiate a reinsurance contract for USAA, had provided advice on USAA investments, and pushed for modernization of the USAA office equipment. He also helped realign USAA investments, and he fixed the accounting system to comply with the Texas Insurance Commissioner's negative findings on USAA operations in these areas. Hinds admired Goodwin a great deal and was pleased with the many other excellent employees at USAA. He and Caldwell hired several other outstanding individuals during their tenure.

To run the crucial claims area, Caldwell had hired young San Antonio attorney Max Wier. Wier was born in 1888 and was raised on a farm close to San Antonio. He went to local country schools and received a teaching certificate by examination at Pearsall, Texas. After a short stint at teaching, he worked for the State Hospital and then as a conductor and cashier for the electric trolley in San Antonio. Eventually, the company moved him to its claims department. In 1916, the local Aetna office hired him to head its claims department. While there, he began spending his free time studying law. In 1920, he felt he was ready and traveled to Austin to take the state

Max Wier Sr., a San Antonio attorney, was hired by Caldwell to manage the claims department at USAA.

bar exam. Upon his arrival, he fell and broke his arm. Three hours later, he went to the law examination and for the next three days, took the series of exams — splint, pain, and all. In spite of the handicap, he passed. Prior to coming to USAA, he continued to work with Aetna, opened his own law office, and was an officer at a San Antonio bank.

Assisting Wier with claims was Eva Long. Eva was the daughter of a Methodist minister who headed the Alamo Heights Methodist Church. She started out at USAA as Loughborough's secretary, but showed a penchant for claims work. After Hinds' arrival, Long began night classes at the San

Eva Long

Antonio School of Law (later absorbed by St. Mary's University). She passed the bar in 1932 and remained with USAA for more than thirty years.

Another outstanding woman professional who stayed with USAA for more than thirty years was Consuelo Kerford. Tall and slender with bright eyes, Kerford was born in Mexico City of American parents. When she joined USAA she was only twenty-three, but quickly made her mark because of her intelligence, reliability, and conscientious behavior. She became an underwriter and served as a secretary to General Hinds. Hinds subsequently gave her the additional duty of Secretary to the USAA Board of Directors. Kerford was destined to become USAA's first woman officer and served USAA until 1976.

Stuart Gwyn rejoined USAA in 1928 as Goodwin's Chief Assistant in underwriting. Born in Waco, she showed early talent in art, but she was later to show a talent in business that was to prove of long-term benefit to USAA. Before joining USAA, Gwyn had held responsible positions in fire and casualty insurance, and as an attorney-in-fact for the general agency of a large stock company. At USAA, she also held the position of principal assistant to the Office Manager. It was while dealing with her on personnel problems that Hinds often called her "Portia" from the character in Shakespeare's *Merchant of Venice* who was always pleading for someone. In everyone's view, she was a highly respected professional who gave much to USAA.

After Caldwell's death, due to a heart ailment, on April 23, 1929, the Board selected Colonel Herbert A. White as his replacement as Assistant Secretary-Treasurer. White knew USAA well, having served on the USAA Board of Directors and as President since August 1928. He was to prove to be an outstanding manager who would serve USAA for over twenty years. Other members of the professional management team who started in this period and made tremendous contributions to USAA included Meta (Nemkey) Willis, who first came to USAA as a bookkeeper and stayed with USAA for nearly forty years. Another was Bertie Covo, who due to her previous business and secretarial expertise, was assigned the dual responsibility of Policy Writer in the Underwriting Department and Secretary to General Hinds.

Meta Nemkey Willis

This group of professionals provided technical expertise, hard work, and stability to USAA. Many of their careers with the Association spanned decades and created history as they went. Under the leadership of USAA's primary officers and managers, these outstanding individuals laid the foundation of the modern property and casualty company the USAA membership enjoys today.

The mood at the 1928 Annual Members' Meeting was in marked contrast to the tumultuous one the year before. Hinds had developed a remarkably smooth relationship with the USAA Board. He was a voting member of the full Board, but a nonvoting recorder for the Executive Committee meetings. In spite of the fact that he did not have a vote on the Executive Committee, he exercised considerable influence on the selection of Board members because of his outstanding leadership qualities and his ability to get along.

Hinds' reputation throughout his service career had been one of "taking care of his troops," and his troops accorded him tremendous respect and support in return. During his first years, Hinds hired new personnel when workload demanded and gave pay raises when deserved. He sought and won a group life insurance policy for all employees, with the Association paying 25 percent of the premium. Male department heads received $3,500 policies and female department heads $2,500 policies, apparently without complaint. He also developed a comprehensive salary plan in which the pay of the employee depended not only on the work performed itself, but also on such factors as loyalty, devotion to duty, and the ability to work in harmony with others. It was natural to Hinds to include the same characteristics in evaluating employees that brought him personal success in his Army career. He sold his plan to the Board by demonstrating that when business expansion was considered, USAA's percentage of earned premiums funneled into salaries would actually decline from 1927 levels. That year, the employees again enjoyed a Christmas bonus.

Whenever Hinds spoke of USAA's employees, he was always positive about their contributions to the Association and its members. They were friendly, yet professional with the members. In turn, the members always felt they were communicating with more than insurance company representatives — rather, with friendly partners in their Association. One member, now retired Colonel Margaret P. Graham, recalled recently that her grandfather and father were both USAA members. When her father was stationed in San Antonio at this time, she recalls that the USAA employees were always friendly. One employee had her beautiful long reddish golden hair cut for a flapper hairdo. She gave her hair to Margaret's mother to use on a China doll for Margaret which she treasured. It is memories and stories like this that furnish the special warmth that has always made the Association more than an insurance company.[10]

The USAA office memos from the late 1920s give a snapshot of work life in a growing company. There were insurance operations memos on rates, dividends, and service, as well as on general office decorum. In sending insurance cancellations to overseas locations, to provide better service, employees were to send them thirty-five days early to Europe and Asia instead of five days as specified in the contract. Telephone calls were to be answered promptly and courteously and the phone was to be answered "United Services."

USAA employees during the Depression era

Personal and business activities were kept very separate, and rules on this subject were quite strict. Conversation between employees, other than on strictly business matters, was prohibited. Desks were not to be cleared until 4:00 p.m. at the close of the business day — no earlier. Employees leaving or closing earlier received disciplinary action. Normally, notices of personal telephone calls would not be given to the employees until 12 noon or until the workday was finished, when they could return the calls. At the same time, USAA management did show it had a heart. When USAA employee Lottie Cherrier was to get married, a memo advised that everyone desiring to attend the 8 a.m. wedding at St. Mary's Catholic Church was "privileged to be late to work on the morning of September 14, 1929."[11]

As 1929 began, USAA's confidence reflected the national mood of optimism. In his inaugural address, Hoover talked of the future in glowing terms. Speculation in the stock market continued pushing prices of stocks far beyond their values. By Labor Day, the *New York Times* average of selected industrial stocks reached 452, an increase of over 200 points since the beginning of 1928. Conservative bankers and financiers appealed for caution and President Hoover and the Federal Reserve Board's warnings to banks and the New York Stock Exchange for temperance went unheeded.

On October 23, the prices of securities collapsed as speculators hastened to unload their holdings. Black Thursday was to see a record of almost thirteen million shares sold. Five days later, the record for sales fell again along with the value of the total stock market. By the second week of November, the market had lost 47 percent of its value. After a short-lived rebound in early 1930, the market shuddered and continued its decline to its nadir in 1932. Over the same period, over 100,000 businesses failed, as did over 4,000 banks. National unemployment climbed from four million in 1930 to almost eleven million by the fall of 1932. Those working earned less and less as hours and salaries fell.

Although the impact of the Depression hit San Antonio later than other areas of the nation, it did arrive. The Depression would have an interesting impact on USAA. It would have been easy to speculate that an insurance company in place less than ten years would fail, but USAA did surprisingly well over the Depression years. It is useful to look at USAA's investments for one reason why.

When Hinds arrived at USAA, the Board-required investment policy of the Association was very simple. With singular exceptions all of USAA's surplus went into real estate-guaranteed bonds. USAA purchased all these securities from the Investment Securities Company of Dallas and the National Title and Trust Company of San Antonio. Further, the National Surety Company of New York was the guarantor on all the bonds offered by these two companies. Hinds was concerned that USAA had no diversification of its investments. As he put it, "all of our eggs were in one basket."[12]

Working closely with Hinds, Assistant Secretary-Treasurer White suggested to a September 1928 Executive Committee meeting that the existing policy was dangerous. He proposed a break with precedent by investing $15,000 in high-grade bonds. The committee agreed, and as a matter of practice, USAA purchased no more real estate bonds after this meeting. A year later, the Board established an Investment Committee, made up of the Executive Committee, the Secretary-Treasurer, and one of USAA's other Attorneys-in-Fact.

After the stock market crash, USAA still held $210,000 of the real estate bonds guaranteed by the National Surety Company. During the short and temporary rebound of the bond market in the spring of 1930, the Executive Committee agreed to Hinds and White's recommendation to exchange $155,000 worth of these for other types of bonds. This resulted in a small loss, but all of the $55,000 not exchanged went into default. If USAA had held onto all $210,000 worth, the results would have been disastrous. Of those exchanged, $20,000 in Republic of Cuba bonds were repudiated by the successors to the Machado government there. These bonds were sold at a loss and the proceeds put into common stock in General Electric, the Chesapeake and Ohio Railroad, the Pennsylvania Railroad, U.S. Steel, and AT&T. The hope was that when permanent prosperity returned, the increase in value would offset the losses in the Cuban offering. USAA's overall change in investment policy was a success. The January 11, 1932, issue of *Barrons* noted that the depreciation of all securities reached 32.5 percent. USAA's holdings depreciated only 15.9 percent.

With each passing year in the 1930s, USAA gained financial strength through its investment policies. Hinds made studies of the efficacy of investing in government bonds rather than other investments. He recommended that USAA could earn more interest in investments other than U.S. Government Bonds. The Board agreed and, with the exception of 1933 when USAA investments were funneled into U.S. Government Securities for safety purposes, diversification of investments remained the rule. If there were a preference, it was towards high-grade state and municipal bonds in 1937.[13]

A major, but temporary impact on USAA's investment policy was a proposed 1935 federal Internal Revenue Service ruling that USAA was liable for tax retroactive to 1922. USAA quickly hired the firm of Carneiro, Chumney and Cagney to represent USAA before the IRS. Concerned about a possible six-figure tax bill, USAA placed funds in reserve to cover any tax liability. In 1936, USAA received great news. The Commissioner of Internal Revenue ruled that under the Revenue Act of 1936 and prior acts, USAA was exempt from federal income tax. This turned out to be not only good news for the Association, but also for the individual members. The Board voted to transfer the income tax reserve to the reserve for dividends and to pass it on to the members.[14]

Following this ruling, the Board again emphasized its diversification philosophy and provided some general guidance to the Investments (Finance) Committee. Among the recommendations was to purchase municipal bonds only issued by communities with over 5,000 people and to invest in high-grade utilities. While the Board did not believe that the railroads would disappear in the near future, it preferred other industrials. The Board did state that aviation should not be considered at that time. It had no doubt about the future of the industry, but felt that aviation bonds were speculative. The industry was developing so quickly and so many were engaged that "almost overnight a plane might be developed by one company that would put all other companies practically out of business."[15]

Although USAA was apparently doing well without much professional expertise, Hinds decided to look for outside advice on USAA's investment portfolio. He traveled to Chicago, New York, and Boston and received advice from some of the top financial houses in the country. These included Moody's Investor Services, J.S. Bache & Company, Chase National Bank, and First Boston, where he met with a retired Army officer whom he had known throughout his service career. The collective view of the various experts was that USAA had a good portfolio — better than most banks and insurance companies. Since USAA was not subject to income taxes, the experts pointed out that the tax-exempt features of U.S., state, and municipal bonds were of no consequence and USAA should reevaluate its holdings in this area.

There was not general agreement on USAA's holding of a large percentage of Texas bonds. The state of Texas levied a tax of 3¼ percent on all net business written for members stationed in Texas unless 25 percent of the assets were in Texas securities. In this case, the state reduced the tax to 1¼ percent. Some experts felt that USAA should just pay the 3¼ percent for the greater freedom of investing, others said the opposite. Hinds' recommendation was to keep the Texas bonds. All in all, however, USAA had a right to be pleased with its investment performance, because USAA remained sound in a financial world filled with turmoil. Under the broad Board guidelines, the Finance Committee would pursue the policy of "as high a yield as possible as is consistent with adequate security."[16] Nothing was left to chance. One Attorney-in-Fact and one Board member routinely inspected and verified the security certificates that were supposed to be on hand.

An unexpected impact of the Depression was an attack on the Association and its policies led by a former Board member, Major Josiah C. "Josh" Minus. Lieutenant Colonel W. F. Jones had nominated Minus to the USAA Board in 1927. Jones believed that retired officers should have more representation on the Board, and argued that Minus was an outstanding candidate. Minus was elected easily.

Minus was an 1899 graduate of West Point and was commissioned as a Second Lieutenant of Infantry. He served in the Spanish Ameri-

Major Josiah C. Minus
USA (Ret.)

can War and retired in 1908 as a result of a service-connected disability. During World War I, he reentered the Army and was honorably discharged in 1919. After the war, Minus became a businessman in San Antonio, joining the Service Finance Corporation (SFC), then headed by Dunton. Minus succeeded him as President in 1923.

The SFC made loans to officers and some others who sought to buy automobiles, and USAA offered SFC varying support over the years. As the Depression deepened, SFC found it more difficult to make a profit. Military officers were facing pay cuts and auto sales were down. It became more difficult for SFC to obtain money to loan, and when it did have money, the interest rates it charged met with resistance from buyers. When Minus sought investment money from USAA, the Finance Committee turned down his request. Reasons included conflict with USAA investment policy and the obvious conflict of interest between Minus the USAA Board Member and Minus the President of SFC. Perhaps more important, the certain hostile reaction by members when they learned that USAA was loaning money at 5 or 6 percent that was being loaned to them at 13 to 15 percent was a deciding factor. Minus was furious.

So began a second attempt by a minority group of members to take over USAA's management. Still on the Board of Directors, Minus proposed that USAA eliminate its surplus except for the minimum required by Texas and return the rest as dividends to the membership. He suggested that USAA raise the discount from 20 to 40 percent on insurance premiums and then allow members to pay only 60 percent of their premiums in cash and tender a note for the rest. He also wanted reductions in the number of employees and salaries for those remaining. Undoubtedly, he felt that extra money channeled to members would assist in his own business.

In league with Minus was retired Army Colonel E. O. Sarratt, a resident of San Antonio, who proposed a major structural change in the bylaws. In essence, Sarratt wished to establish a special auditing and proxy committee made up of three members appointed by local commanders. This committee would perform independent audits, collect proxies, and report directly to the members at their Annual Meeting. Sarratt argued before the Board that the whole proxy system was a sham, as it enabled the managers in place to control the Association. Further, he opposed the pending Board proposal to increase the number of members who could call a members' meeting from twenty-five to 1 percent of the membership. Another retired colonel, W. A. McDaniel of San Antonio, complained bitterly to the Board that the salaries of Hinds and White were exorbitant. His suggestion was to halve their salaries and those of the remaining employees as well.

During the next three months, feverish activity ensued in preparation for the Annual Members' Meeting. The Board formally rejected the various proposals by Minus, Sarratt, and McDaniel. Hinds and White offered to voluntarily reduce their own salaries, but the Board refused. Defeated by the Board, Minus wrote and petitioned the membership, as did Hinds and White. The meeting was to be a stormy one, but the outcome was never in doubt. Of the more than 12,000 proxies, Minus and his band controlled only a little over 600. The melodrama began with Minus submitting his resignation from the Board, which the members accepted with alacrity. Sarratt appealed directly to the assembled members for his proposals and those of Minus as well. He presumed that he was "not the only one fighting arterio-sclerosis" and that the members should be able to discuss the Association's funds "without going away peeved at each other like children."[17] The membership turned down the proposals by a 23 to 1 margin. The victors had had enough. White moved that

Minus be stripped of his membership and his insurance canceled. Minus threatened to go to the War Department because he was being thrown out for no reason. The vote was 7,553 to 1,295. White next proposed the same for Sarratt. One Board member protested that the whole thing was going too far. To "throw them out on their necks" for expressing what they thought was best for the Association was not right. The vote was called and Sarratt was out, 6,962 to 2,395. The meeting was then adjourned with the second "revolution" in eleven years at an end. This insurrection, like the previous one, lost because those trying to take over had violated the code of ethics and honor of the professional officer by trying to have the Association serve their own business interests. The guardians of "Duty, Honor, Country" at USAA had prevailed.

The other direct impact of the Depression on USAA was the reduction in federal salaries imposed by Congress. Just after the Depression began, the services were forced to accept a payless furlough for 8 1/3 percent of their active duty forces. The plight of the military was spotlighted by the thousands of World War I veterans who marched into Washington, D.C., to demand payment of their bonuses early. The so-called Bonus Marchers camped on Anacostia Flats until regular Army units, under the personal command of General Douglas MacArthur along with junior officers Dwight Eisenhower and George Patton, drove them out. While the marchers received sympathy from many, they received no money. The Depression was still alive and well and Congress wanted more cuts. In the spring of 1933, Congress changed the limited payless furlough to a straight 15 percent cut in pay that applied to all grades. The privates now drawing $17.85 per month were operating the Civilian Conservation Corps Camps for unemployed men who were receiving $30 per month.[18]

General Hinds' response to the 15 percent pay cut of USAA members was unequivocal. He renewed his offer to the Board to take a salary reduction of 15 percent. He made this offer, he said, "because of the fact that our clientele are suffering a 15 percent reduction in their pay." He emphasized that the reason was not that he didn't earn his pay, but for "psychological conditions only." The Board accepted his generous offer.[19] Colonel White offered to cut his salary 15 percent as well, but Hinds vigorously opposed the cut and the Board did not accept White's offer. Hinds had also previously fought pay cuts and layoffs for the forty-nine regular USAA employees. He told the Board that the Association was doing well and there was no reason to run it like a failing organization. He said that the employees of USAA were a fine body of conscientious, efficient women, earnest and loyal. He didn't believe that the Association should pay them less than they were worth for the sake of

USAA Policy and Rating Departments, 1937

56 cents per member per year. There was no reason to grind down the employees. Hinds related that the members wouldn't even care — they were more than satisfied with the net cost of their insurance as it is.[20]

> We of the Board of Directors are here to represent the 18,600 present membership. We should be just to them and just to our employees. These women have to accept at this time whatever salaries we offer — there is no other course open to them. Shall we take advantage of their helplessness, or shall we regard the trust reposed in us by the members and by our employees in the light of the GOLDEN RULE: Do unto others as you would have them do unto you?[21]

The Board of Directors readily agreed to Hinds' emotional appeal. Hinds fought for the employees in other ways as well. In 1935, he had the work areas air-conditioned, which was a blessing in San Antonio's hot summers. And he ensured USAA employees had the opportunity for a bonus each year based on the efficiency of USAA.

If not for some of the events related above, it would be difficult to tell within the USAA operation that the country was in a Depression. The only suggestion of problems for the membership was the Board decision to allow members in some hard-hit urban areas to make their insurance payments in six months rather than in the usual four.[22] The restoration of the 15 percent military pay cut in 1935 was a major help. Incidentally, the Board followed by restoring the 15 percent to Hinds' salary.

Hinds was right in his appeal for the employees to the Board. USAA was not "a failing organization," but rather a successful one. USAA continued to grow steadily in spite of the problems suffered by the nation's economy. Although actual growth slowed somewhat, USAA saw gains every year in members. Also, the number of policies in force indicated many members were now insuring more than one car. Just as positive, the expense ratio to net premiums written slowly fell.

Positive Trends in the Depression Years

	1929	**1930**	**1931**	**1932**	**1933**
*Members	11.8	13.6	15.5	15.9	17.0
*Policies in Force	11.8	13.6	15.9	18.2	19.6
Expense Ratio	19.6	20.3	18.4	18.4	17.9

*In Thousands

By the end of 1939, USAA membership had more than doubled since Black Thursday, and now numbered over 27,000.

One loss USAA did suffer as the Depression began to stall out was Leo Goodwin. By 1934, widower Goodwin had gone as high as he could in USAA. The full-time President and Attorney-in-Fact positions had always been filled with retired military officers. Goodwin was not. He sought capital to start his own company and Cleaves Phea, a self-made Dallas businessman and banker, agreed to back him. Goodwin resigned from USAA effective March 15, 1935, and founded what is today Government Employees Insurance Company. Less than a year later, he returned to San Antonio to marry Lillian Wilson, Cashier of USAA. The couple then moved to Washington, D.C., to establish the headquarters of their new company there.

Lillian Wilson

USAA's growth and continuing success in the 1930s can be attributed to many things. The bottom line seemed to be, however, that the members trusted USAA as their Association and appreciated the service and economical insurance it afforded to them. One reason for the trust was the confidence the members placed in General Hinds and Colonel White. The Board was so pleased with their service to the Association that it offered both of them new ten-year contracts in 1938. The Board reasoned that the members would appreciate the stability. Especially in light of Hinds' age, the Association would be protected by a disability clause in both contracts. The members also trusted their fellow officers serving as Board members, even though its members changed frequently.

Because of the requirement in the bylaws for a Board member to live in San Antonio, turnovers on the Board and even in the Presidency itself were frequent. (Hinds served USAA under nine different presidents in his thirteen-plus years.) The philosophy of Board selection was explained by Colonel Brooke, President of USAA, to the Members' Meeting in 1933. Brooke noted that:

> We try as far as possible to represent as many arms or departments of the Army as possible. That is one of the reasons for having thirteen directors, and we try to get as much diversification in the different arms of the Army as possible.

One member cautioned that the Association should not put too much reliance on retired officers, but that the active Army officers should be as strongly represented as possible. He also noted that the Navy was not represented, but with naval officers not being assigned to San Antonio, this was not a possibility. The selection process eventually got to the point where Board members' slots were sometimes held open until their military replacements arrived in San Antonio. In spite of this apparent lack of stability, the Board seemed to function well.[23] And last but not least, the members appreciated the USAA employees.

Colonel Roger Brooke

DEPRESSION AND REVOLUTION

The USAA Board and leadership never regarded USAA as a closed corporation, but often considered new groups of individuals for memberships and occasionally reviewed current policies for eligibility. In 1929, the cadets of the Air Corps were included. That year, the Board also closed a loophole that had enabled non-dependent relatives to receive USAA insurance. A policy of issuing "and/or" policies based on the application of a member or an individual eligible to be a member was discontinued.[24]

In 1931, the Board drew a distinction between two classes of retired enlisted men. The first category was former Warrant Officers and World War I officers who resigned their commissions and got appointments as non-commissioned officers to get credit for a thirty-year retirement. The Board granted eligibility to these retired non-coms because they had served as officers or Warrant Officers on active duty. The second category was retired enlisted personnel who had served as Emergency Officers in World War I, but who were never Warrant Officers in the regular service. The Board denied membership to these individuals and, in the following year, also declared all Emergency Officers under the Act of 1924 ineligible. The Board was concerned that these disabled individuals would be unable to drive safely and would pose an unacceptable risk for automobile insurance.[25]

The Board discussions on the retired enlisted status of Warrant Officers and Emergency Officers had touched on the consideration of enlisted eligibility for membership. In those two cases, active service as an officer was the determining factor. In 1933, a Navy Commander stationed in Boston wrote USAA President Colonel Roger Brooke and discussed the question of membership for the three highest grades of non-commissioned officers in the Navy. He noted that Master Sergeant and Chief Petty Officers (CPOs) each received $126 per month base pay. He pointed out that the CPOs rarely had less than ten years' service and often performed duties on small ships that were assigned to officers on large ones. In his view, the Petty Officers 1st and 2nd Class, equivalent to Technical Sergeants and Staff Sergeants in the Army, were sometimes "unreliable and financially irresponsible." While the CPOs would probably do well, he argued that as a class, the next two grades could only afford old secondhand cars which "get out of control and into accidents."[26]

The Board then explored the proposal and whether it should pose the matter to the membership at this time. After considerable discussion, one Board member suggested that Brooke get the sense of the Board informally. Brooke asked, "All in favor of taking in Chief Petty Officers of the Navy and Master Sergeants of the Army, please so indicate by raising your hand." Not a single Board member raised his hand and so the Board moved on to other business.[27]

As USAA's members aged, many had concerns for their wives; they wanted USAA to insure their wives if the member predeceased his spouse. Colonel Clyde E. Hawkins, a USAA member, wrote to General Hinds and asked that steps be taken to modify the bylaws to make widows eligible. Hawkins' letter hit a responsive chord among the Board members. The Board voted to place the change to the bylaws on widows' eligibility before the membership at the next Members' Meeting in June. At the meeting, the members voted to make widows of members and those eligible for membership "eligible for membership in the Association until change of status is affected by marriage."[28] The Board also decided to offer membership to officers of the Foreign Service of the Department of State stationed in the U.S. and its possessions, Mexico, and Canada.[29] In 1937, the territorial restrictions were removed. Thus, the members had increased eligibility to cover the most immediate members of the military family, their wives, and another group of individuals considered on a par with active duty officers. The changes in eligibility were logical — and consistent.

In addition to adding more members to the eligibility lists, USAA also marketed its insurance in a number of ways. Besides word-of-mouth and print advertising and sales commissions to individuals who sold USAA policies, USAA also paid for auto insurance referrals that were passed on by the Army Cooperative Fire Insurance Company. It also paid the Service Finance Corporation for referrals SFC was able to procure during periodic trips to West Point to loan new graduates money for the purchase of cars. By the end of the 1930s, however, most of these special commission programs had been terminated.

Typical 1930s USAA advertisement. *Army and Navy Register*, July 15, 1939

USAA also sought to counter the possible negative impact of other firms using "United Services" in their names. By 1939, the Board was so concerned that it directed USAA management to place a one-half page advertisement to state the Association's position.

A key element of service was to provide the products and services the membership needed. Changing circumstances dictated a

A Tradition Of Service

IT IS DEEMED ADVISABLE TO REMIND OUR MEMBERS THAT THIS ASSOCIATION IS **NOT** AFFILIATED WITH ANY OTHER CONCERN. THIS ASSOCIATION WRITES THE FOLLOWING FORMS OF INSURANCE **ONLY:**

AUTOMOBILE

AUTOMOBILE ACCIDENT

HOUSEHOLD GOODS AND PERSONNEL EFFECTS

United Services Automobile Association
Fort Sam Houston, Texas

ERNEST HINDS   H. A. WHITE   W. F. JONES

Army and Navy Register, November 25, 1939

necessity for new types of insurance to protect the members' financial security and to provide peace of mind. The original USAA automobile insurance coverage focused on the vehicles themselves.

DEPRESSION AND REVOLUTION

As most of the original members were active-duty officers with access to military hospitals, coverage for personal injury was apparently of little concern. As the Association grew and with retired officers eligible, the diverse membership no longer routinely had easy access to military hospitals. Many retired members settled in their hometown areas or moved to warmer climates where military installations were a distance away. The problem for the members was a significant one and becoming more so. The Board and USAA management studied the matter carefully. In the announcement of the 1931 Annual Members' Meeting, General Hinds told the members that this personal injury insurance could be offered "to the convenience and profit of the members of the Association without endangering the strong and safe position of the organization."[30]

The final proposal included insurance for members and their immediate families against injuries sustained while in an auto, being hit by an auto, or even in traveling in any conveyance except an airplane. It would even cover injuries sustained by cranking an automobile or changing a tire, but the Board drew the line and offered no insurance for injuries involving tanks, armored cars, and motorcycles. This protection covered only those from eighteen to seventy years of age (eighteen to sixty-five for females), but those over seventy could get coverage at an increased price.

In addition to this "accident" insurance, the Board also proposed to offer fire insurance for household goods and personal effects. In deference to the Army Cooperative Fire Association at Fort Leavenworth that had been offering such coverage for more than thirty years, USAA would not offer fire insurance to Army officers, but only to other members. The only change to this would be if through a majority vote of its members, the Army Cooperative Fire Association decided to merge with USAA. The Board also proposed "to insure household goods and personal effects against the risks of fire, lightning, navigation and transportation, theft, pilferage, and larceny." This coverage had previously been available through Fidelity & Guaranty Fire Corporation of Baltimore and was known as the Government Service Policy. The USAA Board reasoned that the profits of this insurance should go to the members, rather than some other commercial company.[31] All three proposals passed easily.

Automobile safety became an important issue for USAA in the 1930s as accident rates climbed. General Hinds instituted a safety campaign in 1932 which he hoped would increase dividends. He pointed out that if an accident was caused by a non-member's car, the Association would pay for the member's car only. If the member caused the accident, however, the Association would have to pay for both cars and the injuries as well. "If those who drive cars would exercise more than average care in driving, the net cost of our insurance would be less than 50 percent of the annual premiums." USAA letterhead paper carried the following line, printed in red ink:

SAFETY FIRST! CUT DOWN YOUR OWN LOSSES AND INCREASE YOUR DIVIDENDS BY CAREFUL DRIVING.[32]

All over the United States, the number of accidents continued to rise. In its January 11, 1935, issue, *Best's Insurance News* reported that a Travelers Insurance Company study found that at least 36,000 deaths in automobile accidents had occurred, a rise of 16 percent over the previous year. USAA's experience was even worse. Member auto-accident deaths jumped from twelve in 1933 to twenty-five in 1934. USAA's claims climbed from 3,496 to 3,980 in 1934, an increase of 14 percent, while the number of policies rose only 8 percent. The USAA *Annual Report* for 1934 pointed the finger at "excessive speed and carelessness." The Report admonished that "careful driving increases dividends" and "it also saves lives." Another issue for the Executive Committee was that it reviewed claims exceeding $500 — so its workload grew significantly. As one result, the Board members' compensation rose to ten dollars per meeting.

The year 1935 saw the number of auto accident deaths nationally climb to over 36,000. Deaths attributed to excessive speed amounted to 31 percent. USAA's death toll was almost steady at twenty-four, but bodily injuries climbed 26 percent. USAA supported a Lumberman's Mutual Casualty Company program called the "Not Over 50" Club. Requirements for membership were only to paste a small red arrow bearing the words "not over 50" directly on the speedometer. USAA also ran advertisements calling for careful driving.

Army and Navy Register, September 15, 1937

In 1936, deaths nationally rose to over 38,000 while those at USAA dropped to twenty-one. In 1937, the member deaths again climbed — to thirty. Not only the totals, but the rates were worse.[33]

1936 = 1 death for each 1,053 policies in force

1937 = 1 death for each 800 policies in force

Since pleading with members seemed to have little effect, the Board decided to try money. Effective February 1, 1938, USAA instituted a Safe Driver Award Plan. The plan would reward any member with no claims for Bodily Injury or Property Damage for one year with a credit of 15 percent of the premium. For the first eleven months of 1939, 81.3 percent of members whose policies expired received two dividends. The percentage who did not get the award, however, suffered twenty-one deaths and a total of 6,207 claims registered, the highest in the Association's history.

In addition to bodily injury, USAA was also concerned about the rise in damage claims. The *Annual Report* of 1939 reported that because of contemporary automobile construction, a car could be damaged in front to the extent of $100 "without injury to the motor itself!" Lights in fenders and the beginnings of uni-body construction were also cited. The *Report* commented that the manufacturers would have no reason to revamp their cars — so the drivers would have to do better.

Driving under the influence was another major cause of accidents. One New York City study stated that in 1937, 47 percent of accident deaths in the city were alcohol-related. The Association's advice was:

DON'T DRINK AND DRIVE:
and DON'T DRIVE AND DRINK.

Drivers could be arrested and convicted with only the smell of liquor on their breath. In the state of California, if the police surgeon smelled even the faintest odor, the driver was guilty without appeal.[34] The warning went, "Don't drink at the Club and get behind the wheel." One Board member feared increased losses to the Association if Prohibition ended. The USAA efforts in safety were part of its service to the members. Through its campaigns, it hoped to reduce costs and to ensure its members' lives were not adversely affected by the automobile.

Depression And Revolution

Another change was to use "actual value" of cars instead of "stated value" effective January 1, 1939. The change benefited members in two ways. In 1939, the actual value of a vehicle varied greatly depending on the location of the car. A member who bought a car in the East, in the proximity of a manufacturer, would find his car much more valuable when he arrived at his overseas location. If the car were destroyed there, the member would now receive the value of the car in the Philippines and not the "stated" value of the car when purchased. A second benefit was the greatly decreased cost of USAA employees calculating values after each move. Since total losses from fire were one in 4,450 and theft were one in 4,660, there was no sense in doing them all. The workload was less and members benefited from reduced overhead costs at San Antonio.

While USAA's efforts in these matters were major elements of service, it added many other service features for its members in the 1930s. If members' cars were under repair for sixty days or more, USAA gave a refund for that period of time on their insurance premiums. Members received a 2 percent discount if they paid their bills within ten days. For members being transferred to foreign soil where USAA did not offer policies, USAA made arrangements with the American International Underwriters Corporation to handle them. And finally, Colonel White wrote a series of leaflets on insurance matters to help educate members. The leaflet titles included "The Necessity for Auto Insurance" and "Different Forms of Coverage: How Rates are Determined." These leaflets were sent free to members upon their request.

Overall, USAA's efforts in the 1930s were much appreciated by the members. Their view was confirmed by examiners from the Texas State Insurance Department in 1933. Mr. H. Economidy, Examiner-in-Charge, noted that:

> A considerable number of tests were made of closed claims and no evidence was furnished of any but fair treatment of all

claimants against the Association. Correspondence files disclose fair and courteous treatment of the claims of all members.

This organization presents, in the estimate of your examiners, a model organization. The records are complete, concise, accurate and clear. The inter-departmental coordination practiced in this office results in better records and more expeditious service. The history of every member in the Association is uninterrupted with a complete experience under every policy carried or ever carried by each member.

As USAA matured, everyone associated with it had the right to be proud of its accomplishments. The Association had survived a Depression, two internal revolutions, and four moves. Many important precedents had been set for the years ahead. World War II would pose new challenges for the youthful company.

CHAPTER THREE

THE WAR YEARS

On September 18, 1931, Japanese units attacked the Chinese Army's 7th Brigade barracks at Peitaying, near Mukden in Southern Manchuria. The Japanese claimed the attack was in response to an incident in which someone blew up tracks of the Southern Manchurian Railway. So began the long and slippery descent into total war.

The world seemed much larger then, and Manchuria was too far removed from Americans to cause more than a slight ripple in the national thought. The intensity of the "Living Room War" in the days of Vietnam was a product of technical improvements, television, and aggressive news gatherers across the globe. In the 1930s the intensity was diminished by the geographical distance and the isolationism of the American people.

For a nation of immigrants whose past was deeply rooted in Western Europe, early events there had surprisingly little practical impact on Americans. The rise of Hitler and Mussolini even brought early praise from American intellectuals and others, and brought little or no action from Congressional leaders. Even legislation to increase the American defensive posture often remained without appropriations. The size of the Army officer corps remained the same, about 12,000, in the face of Japanese aggression and Hitler's move into the Rheinland in 1936. Hitler had feared confrontation there, but no opposition materialized. U.S. military officers were left to practice their leadership skills performing public services such as running radio stations in Alaska, serving areas savaged by natural catastrophes, and operating the Civilian Conservation Corps camps.

A *Tradition Of Service*

Meanwhile, in Europe, Hitler continued his aggressive policies towards his neighbors. In May 1935, Congress had provided for the commissioned strength of the Army to go to 16,719, but over a ten-year period. It was obvious that Congress was still complacent about the impending crisis. President Franklin D. Roosevelt pledged neutrality in response to the pacifist sentiment in the nation. As late as August 1936 he told an audience at Chatauqua, New York, that "we shun political commitments which might entangle us in foreign wars; we avoid connection with the political activities of the League of Nations." When the Spanish Civil War erupted, the U.S. observed, but again took no military action. Surely it would not affect us! Ernest Hemingway in *For Whom the Bell Tolls* was more prophetic when he wrote that "The bell in Spain tolled not just for that unhappy country, it tolls for thee!"[1]

In 1938, the eyes of the world shifted to Central Europe once again. Calling Austrian Chancellor Kurt Von Schuschnigg to Berchtesgaden, Hitler demanded the surrender of Austria. Von Schuschnigg had no choice. Germany took over Austria and Von Schuschnigg and his wife spent the war years in a cabin in a sanitized and wooded part of Buchenwald. Next, Hitler placed demands on the government of Czechoslovakia on behalf of the German minority there. In September, British Prime Minister Neville Chamberlain met with Hitler, Premier Edouard Daladier of France, and Mussolini. Without a Czech representative present, the group agreed to let Hitler annex the Sudetenland, populated mainly by ethnic Germans. Except for the Czechs, the world felt a great relief as Chamberlain announced "peace in our time."

The worldwide relief and hope for peace echoed at USAA. During Hinds' trip to the East Coast to discuss the USAA investment portfolio, the economic leaders discussed the world situation with him. In November of 1938, Hinds' report to the Finance Committee, upon his return, reflected their optimism. Hinds reported that

THE WAR YEARS

"the passage of the European War crisis — for the present at least — affords a basis for the hope of improvement in economic conditions there."

Hinds' message of hope for the improvement of economic conditions in Europe and for peace was not to be realized. But he was not to know. On December 27, 1940, the General entered the military hospital at Fort Sam Houston for treatment of leukemia. By April, he seemed to be improving and wrote to the Board of his hope to return part-time to USAA in the near future. On June 16, surrounded by his wife, daughter Marjorie, and son John, Hinds must have known he was near the end. Instead of saying "goodnight," as usual, he said goodbyes to his children using his childhood nicknames for them. "Goodbye, Little Girl. Goodbye John-up," he murmured.[2] Hinds died quietly the next day.

On June 18, the Board met and elected Colonel Herbert Arthur "Artie" White as USAA's new Secretary-Treasurer and Attorney-in-Fact. Retired Army Colonel William F. Jones was elected Attorney-in-Fact and Assistant Secretary-Treasurer. Later, retired Brigadier General Joseph A. Atkins was elected Second Assistant Secretary-Treasurer and Attorney-in-Fact. White was a superior choice as USAA's new number-one man. He had previously served USAA as a Director, President, and, in the twelve years since his retirement from the Army, as Assistant Secretary-Treasurer of USAA and Hinds' right-hand man. After Hinds became seriously ill in

Herbert A. White as a West Point cadet

December, White actually succeeded him. He was a little over seventy when he officially took over, but he was in good health and retained his keen mind. The Board had no hesitation in selecting him.

White was born in Worth County, Iowa, on July 31, 1870. He followed his two brothers to West Point and enrolled as a member of the Class of 1895. At West Point, he was an excellent student, graduating eighth. He was well-liked and a recognized leader among his classmates. Upon graduation, he received his preferred assignment as a Cavalry officer in the 6th Cavalry at Fort Myer, Virginia. He studied law off duty at Columbian University (later renamed George Washington University) and received his Bachelor of Laws degree in June 1898.

Following this assignment, he fought with the Cavalry in the Spanish American War, against the Philippine insurrection, and in the Boxer Rebellion in China. In China, his unit fought alongside those from both Asiatic and European nations to relieve the many foreign legations trapped in Peking. When the Rebellion ended, White was transferred to the Infantry and Cavalry School at Fort Leavenworth, Kansas. In addition to his duties in teaching cavalry and law, he also edited the *U.S. Cavalry Journal.* He was very popular and gained the respect of the students, many who later became top military leaders, including the controversial Billy Mitchell.

After attending War College, and seeing no war for the U.S. in the near future, he transferred to the Army's Judge Advocate General Department. Now married to his childhood sweetheart, Ida Lillian Beckett, he was transferred to the Panama Canal Zone. When the U.S. entered World War I, the Army ordered him to the War Department in Washington, D.C., and he served there until the Armistice. Next he went to Europe as Judge Advocate for the American occupation forces and, after a short follow-on tour in Washington, became Professor of Law at West Point in 1922. In 1923, the Army transferred him to Fort Sam

Houston, Texas, as Staff Judge Advocate of the VIII Corps Area Headquarters under General Hinds.

In 1925, an event occurred which profoundly affected the military career of White — the court-martial of General Billy Mitchell.[3] Mitchell had been the U.S. senior Air Service officer in the Allied Expeditionary Force in World War I. Following the war, he publicly advocated airpower in ways the senior Army leadership opposed, and he was charged with insubordination. When President Calvin Coolidge ordered Mitchell's court-martial under those charges, Mitchell asked the Army to have White be assigned to help defend him. Mitchell had known White at Fort Leavenworth in 1904 and had followed his career with admiration. During the court-martial, White took his duties seriously, and he aggressively defended his client before a board of senior Army generals. Believing that two of the generals were prejudiced, White challenged them and had them both removed, one peremptorily and the other for cause. In spite of his heroic efforts, Mitchell was convicted, and many viewed him as a martyr. White's West Point classmate, Brigadier General Perry L. Miles, suggested later that White may have become a martyr as well. He believed that White's failure to become the Army's top lawyer may well have been affected by his vigorous defense of Mitchell before the Army establishment.

In any case, White had been delighted to join USAA in 1928 and had done an outstanding

Colonel Herbert A. White

A Tradition Of Service

job for the membership since his arrival. He was a trusted confidant of Hinds and worked closely with him. In support of Hinds' goal of taking care of the employees, for example, he helped engineer the first employee group medical insurance. He had an outgoing, gregarious personality and a good sense of humor. At the same time, he had a low boiling point; was explosive and even occasionally used profane language. He was to be popular and well-respected by USAA employees. He trusted the employees and delegated much more authority to them. They returned his faith with outstanding performance.

Meanwhile, as the war gathered momentum in Europe and in Asia, the President and Congress took action to increase preparedness, but without the intensity that the situation deserved. In spite of Hitler's success in Poland and with the Blitzkrieg in the Low Countries, Congress still moved slowly until the fall of France. Then Congress appropriated billions, but the Selective Service Act still took almost three months to pass. The continuing advance by the Axis Powers and the bombing of Great Britain finally drove the President to declare an "unlimited emergency" as the United States struggled to undo nearly forty years of neglect in its armed forces. The officer and enlisted strength of the nation's military forces climbed rapidly. This increase in officer strength was reflected in USAA's growth as the war approached. While USAA gained about 2,000 members each in the years 1937, 1938, and 1939, growth in 1940 was over 3,000, and over 6,000 in 1941. That amounted to an almost 20 percent growth in members in 1941 alone. Being so closely connected to the active force and sensitive to the deteriorating world situation, the Association's leaders began making preparations for the war that looked more certain each day. For example, Stuart Gwyn began stockpiling office supplies which would carry USAA through the war years.

At 7:53 a.m., December 7, 1941, the fateful moment arrived. Japa-

THE WAR YEARS

nese Commander Mitsuo Fuchida called out "Tora! Tora! Tora!" on his radio. The Japanese air armada had achieved complete surprise. In his plane over Pearl Harbor, Fuchida would see much of the U.S. Pacific Fleet erupt in explosions, smoke, and flames. Lieutenant Commander Frank Welden was one of the USAA members on duty during the attack. Nearly sixty hours later he was relieved and was driving home during a blackout when he had an accident. This basis of his claim would be one of the dozens of cases the USAA Board would have to decide that were peculiar to wartime conditions.

On December 8, the USAA Board met to make some decisions on the Association's operations in light of the Japanese attack on Pearl Harbor. "To render service for our members" White renewed for sixty days all policies expiring on or after one minute after midnight on December 8 if the member's address were outside the continental United States.[4] USAA would make a pro rata charge for the sixty days on these policies. If a member sold his car or did not wish to carry insurance any longer, USAA would refund the money as soon as it received the member's decision in writing. White decided not to mail any savings checks to such addresses, but to credit the savings to the individuals' savings accounts. The USAA management team also decided to encourage members to place their insurance affairs with some family member or other responsible party in the United States. This would enable USAA to handle the insurance business with the member's designee until the member returned. The 1941 *USAA Annual Report* assured members that it would continue to meet unusual conditions rising out of the war "in the spirit of service."

Service also meant maintaining the financial stability of USAA. All insurance companies protect themselves in the event of war, insurrection, riot, and civil disorder. They do this by including a clause in the policies that specifically states that the policy does not cover damages due to any of these occurrences. Ten days following the Japanese attack on Hawaii, the Board of Directors met. White told them that the existing exclusion clause in USAA's policies covered either declared or undeclared war. He explained further that USAA management had considered War Risk coverage, but would deny any such requests from members for the time being because of the fiscal danger to USAA.

USAA was following the lead of the world's insurance community. Three days after Pearl Harbor, most fire insurance companies announced they would no longer offer war risk and bombardment insurance to property owners. At the same time, Lloyd's of London canceled all reinsurance contracts covering these risks. To try to assist its members, USAA sought companies willing to reinsure war risks. The Association had only one modest success. USAA received a reinsurance rate quote of $10.37 per $100 valuation, but it would cover only shipment of autos from Hawaii to the U.S. Fortunately, USAA's adjusters found carriers in Honolulu that would carry this war risk coverage for a cost of $3.05 per $100 valuation. From this point on, USAA referred its members in Hawaii to these local companies.

USAA's management team continued to study the war risk question and made comparisons with policies of major insurance carriers such as North American and Provident. It found that these companies carried a specific "War Exclusion" clause and recommended to the Board that USAA do the same. The Board agreed and a specific "War Exclusion" clause was added to USAA's policies. The exclusion read as follows:

Section C. War Exclusion

This policy does not apply:

(1) To any injury or loss if it results from an accident involving a Government owned or privately owned passenger car, motor vehicle, truck, motorcycle, or any other motor or power driven vehicle, if the accident occurs while such automobile, vehicle, etc.,

THE WAR YEARS

is being operated in connection with any military exercises, maneuvers, and/or if the insured is at the time engaged officially in such activity:

(2) Or to any injury or loss if it results from an accident due to proximate connection with a hostile act of war.

(3) During black-outs under above conditions and during any blackout where insured neglects or fails to act in accordance with or fails to obey and abide by orders or regulations governing at the time, place and occasion.

Although USAA was already covered legally, White felt this would make things clearer to members during the war and would reduce inquiries to the home office. The creation of a new Reconstruction Finance Corporation subsidiary to provide "reasonable protection" against losses resulting from enemy attacks on private property also reduced pressure on USAA to offer such coverage.[5]

The blackout question was a new one for American insurance companies. Aircraft added a new dimension to war and to the rules for insurance as well. No court decisions existed to establish an insurance company's responsibility to guide USAA's actions. The aerial attack on Hawaii and members' claims resulting from blackouts forced the issue before the USAA Board. In a letter dated February 20, 1942, Commander Welden, whose original claim stemming from the accident during the blackout after the attack on Pearl Harbor was denied, appealed a USAA decision not to cover his claim. His original denial resulted from a USAA interpretation that damage sustained during a blackout is derived directly or indirectly from war or invasion. As such, USAA would not honor the claim. Later, however, USAA reversed itself and paid the claim.

White's concern was that USAA members' property was subject to much greater danger than that of the ordinary populace. Some insurance companies could pay and were paying for claims rising out of blackouts without endangering their reserves. If USAA were to cover all such claims indiscriminately, however, it might be taking an unacceptable risk. If a member had a vehicle in a "Theater of Operations," the hazard would normally be too great to cover with non-war rates. Because of the airplane, USAA could not clearly define such a Theater as it could have done in past years. Due to the nature of the war with Japan, White felt it was reasonable to consider the Philippines and the Hawaiian Islands as within a Theater of Operations. As such, USAA would deny claims, including blackouts in these areas. While a hardship on members stationed there, White said it was "one of the misfortunes of war which we cannot right." Paying claims there could endanger USAA reserves.

Areas like the U.S. East and West Coasts would be considered Theaters of Operations when an enemy was attacking or threatening to attack. In such cases, USAA would not honor claims there either. White argued that if the blackouts were purely precautionary or for safety, USAA could pay the damages as long as the policyholder adhered to all blackout regulations in effect at that time and place. Because of the complexity of the issue, the Board finally left determination on individual cases up to management, subject to review by the Executive Committee and the Board.[6]

The decision regarding Commander Welden's claim and others reflected the ambivalence that the Board and USAA management had in operating USAA during the war. They interpreted service broadly, with the focus on the entire membership when the financial stability and reserves were at stake. The USAA leadership's initial impulse was to isolate the Association from such risks completely. Blackout coverage, a small risk for some companies, could become untenable for the Association. On the other hand, most of the Board members had "been there" and were sympathetic to the plight of individual officers in defense of their country. This was intensified as the Board learned that other companies were doing

THE WAR YEARS

more to serve individuals in risky situations than USAA was doing. If officer-members went with other insurance companies, they could get better coverage than USAA was willing to provide. This was not acceptable. In the final analysis, the Board established parameters to protect the fiscal integrity of the Association when it was critical to do so. At the same time, however, it granted management the authority to make exceptions in individual cases where it seemed warranted.

Another example of this was the issue of USAA policyholders using their personal cars in support of the war effort. USAA's initial reaction was not to cover these vehicles. On May 9, 1942, USAA's reinsurer, the Employers Reinsurance Company, on its own initiative, wrote to USAA and proposed an amendment to its reinsurance contract with USAA. It stated its willingness to approve a liberal construction of its policy provisions "to extend coverage to the policyholders in connection with use of their own or other automobiles in furtherance of war or defense activities." The USAA Board tabled the proposal and directed White to thank the reinsurer, but to say "no." USAA's letter to the reinsurer pointed out the hazards to the Association if it should move into such coverage.[7]

Over eighteen months later, on November 13, 1943, the Employers Reinsurance Company wrote to USAA and raised the matter again. This time the Board had received information that all the leading old line insurance companies were now including this protection in their contracts. In view of this development, the Board was concerned that USAA could be held liable in the event of a trial of a case involving an accident under such usage. Also, the reinsurer offered to provide the additional protection at no additional cost. These arguments, and the opportunity to provide better service to the member, carried the day, and the Board voted to extend this coverage to the membership.[8] It was unwilling to offer coverage on government-owned cars in carpools, however.[9]

A Tradition Of Service

In areas where the Board of Directors felt that the impact of the war did not threaten USAA's overall survival, the Association continued to seek ways to assist the members. In August 1942, Colonel White received a letter from a USAA member that included an advertisement for the Government Employees Insurance Company. The GEICO ad offered reduced automobile insurance rates because of gasoline rationing and the thirty-five mile per hour speed limit. Colonel White immediately had his staff study the issue.

At the next Board meeting, White briefed the results of his staff's study. In the seventeen states where gasoline rationing was in effect under the initial government order, many insurance carriers were offering discounts. Soon all states would be subject to rationing, and other insurers were using the following guidelines. Those holding "A" cards received a 20 percent discount on the Manual Rates on bodily injury coverage, while those holding "B" and "C" ration cards received a 10 percent discount. ("A" card holders received the highest ration of gasoline because of their occupations, and so on.) White argued that to try to find out and then to keep track of which members held which ration cards would be too expensive. He proposed a straight 30 percent discount on manual rates across the Board. This would give USAA members better rates than they could get anywhere else, and the program would be simple and inexpensive for the Association to administer. The Board agreed and left it to management to put the

Herbert A. White

discount into effect.[10] USAA advertisements during the rest of the war reflected the wartime discount.

INSURANCE AT COST

AUTOMOBILES

PERSONAL PROPERTY

AUTOMOBILE ACCIDENTS

★ ★ ★

Rates on Automobile Insurance are Made
To Meet War Restrictions on Driving

★ ★ ★

All Savings are Returned to Members
Upon Expiration of Policy

★ ★ ★

MEMBERSHIP RESTRICTED
To Officers in Federal Services

★ ★ ★

UNITED SERVICES AUTOMOBILE ASSOCIATION

Box 275, Grayson Street Station
SAN ANTONIO, TEXAS

Army and Navy Register, October 23, 1943

USAA made many other wartime decisions in an effort to serve the membership. The Board authorized the continuation of policies for members who had been transferred overseas and had left their cars with a close relative. Because of the multiple moves by officers during the war, USAA decided not to adjust rates until a car had been at the new location for a minimum of six months. Some decisions hurt individual members, but the Board felt it had to make them to protect the membership. For example, as the Japanese advanced in the Pacific in the early part of the war, USAA acted. It canceled automobile policies in the Philippines, Wake Island, and Guam with the hopeful provision that it would reinstate the insurance if the cars were later found to be "intact."[11]

These decisions by management set ground rules for the membership as a whole while USAA employees continued to provide excellent service to each member as best they could. Sometimes the service was very unusual. On more than one occasion, USAA members received assistance from USAA employees in finding housing in San Antonio for their families. Another example occurred when a young officer departed San Antonio, leaving his sweetheart behind. Months later, a USAA employee received a special request. The next day the employee delivered a birthday cake to the Lieutenant's surprised sweetheart. The members asked, and the employees gave the assistance with no thought of whether this was an insurance-related activity. The Association was taking care of its own. Through it all, the members maintained their sense of humor. Lieutenant Harry Rice, under his household policy, put in a claim for "what he termed *theft* of two automobile tires by the Defense Services Corporation in Cleveland." The reason? The negligible amount which was paid on his turned-in tires. The result? Denial with a smile!

Sensitivity towards members in the war years continued after the war as well. In 1950, the question of canceling a war widow's insurance came before the Executive Committee with a claim. Normally, it would have been done. In this case, the widow's husband had been beheaded while a prisoner of war. After being informed of his death, she became an alcoholic, and her teenaged daughter was declared delinquent by the authorities. Because of the circumstances that began the tragic chain of events, the Committee decided to give the widow another chance to pull herself together.

In its 1942 *Annual Report*, USAA management reassured members that the Association was going to support them in spite of the war. They were reminded that all of the officers of USAA, members of the Board, and Attorneys-in-Fact were all commissioned officers. The report emphasized that:

> Naturally their mental approach to all Association problems is an enlightened one and leads them to a liberal and not technical solution of problems presented. Our members may rest assured that the attitude of those responsible for the direction and control of our activities is one of service.[12]

As the war continued, getting mail to members became a significant problem. Mail delivery was irregular and the Association took that into consideration in doing routine business. Members "missing in action" and "prisoners of war" presented a unique problem. This was also true of members who had no such "official" status, but who had made no contact with USAA either. Management maintained open files for these individuals "due to non-receipt" and established a reserve fund of $80,000 to cover monies owed to these members for various reasons. In addition, USAA held the Annual Reports for these individuals at the home office until it established their final status. Another complicating factor was the censorship rules that applied to all USAA outgoing mail. The Association followed the rules closely, but they made communications with members more difficult.

USAA also did whatever it could to support the overall war effort. The Association changed its investment policy and bought only U.S. government bonds. The one exception was to hold enough Texas securities to maintain USAA's favorable state tax status in Texas. The chart below illustrates the steady growth in USAA's holdings of U.S. government securities.

Percentage of USAA Investments in U.S. Government Bonds

1941	1942	1943	1944	1945
30.9	48.1	51.0	55.8	57.1

It would take about ten years after the U.S. entrance into the war before USAA investments in U.S. government securities would return to prewar levels.

There were other areas where USAA cooperated as well. When the War Production Board asked USAA for the number of typewriters it had on hand and how many it could spare, USAA gave up five. USAA also supported a ride-sharing plan initiated by the Office of Price Administration. Under this plan, USAA agreed to extend automobile insurance coverage to members participating in ride sharing. In addition, USAA stopped sending calendars to members in 1942. The calendars had bases made of metal which would better serve the members when used in the production of American airplanes and other war weapons.

In the personnel area, the Association was able to grant 5 percent salary increases each year on a regular schedule. Any changes in job classifications or special increases beyond the already approved regular schedule had to go before the War Labor Board. In most cases, the local office of the Board was able to grant special increases. When it could not, however, it forwarded the requests to Washington. USAA did its best to keep to the spirit as well as the letter of the requests and supervision of the War Labor Board. This Board was part of the government's overall program to control inflation in the wartime economy, and USAA was in complete accord with this effort.

During the war years, the turmoil and frequent changes in military assignments created some instability in the USAA Board of

THE WAR YEARS

Directors. Under the bylaws, Board members were required to live in Bexar County, the location of the USAA home office. Because of this, reassignments away from San Antonio terminated Board membership. For example, an Army reorganization moving a headquarters to Dallas resulted in the loss of five Board members in October 1942. Of the thirteen Board members in place when the war began, only seven were left three and one half years later at the end of the war.

Besides White and Jones, retired Army Brigadier General Alexander T. Ovenshine helped provide continuity in the leadership. Ovenshine had been President for a short time in 1933. After a limited absence from San Antonio, he returned to the city and the Board in 1934. In 1939, the membership elected him as its new President, and as such, he headed the Executive Committee. He would hold this position until 1955. The continuity provided by Ovenshine was especially important because he chaired the Executive Committee, which met weekly throughout the war. Its principal function was to decide on claims cases. His presence at these meetings helped ensure the claims decisions were equitable from year to year. There were a wide variety of claims cases to handle, ranging from auto accidents with multiple deaths to a lieutenant colonel who sought reimbursement from USAA for "a one-tooth bridge (part gold at least)" allegedly stolen from his hotel room.[13] The Executive Committee and Board also approved the annual report before it was sent to the members. An important

Brigadier General Alexander T. Ovenshine

historical footnote was the election of the first U.S. Navy representative to the USAA Board of Directors in 1943. The war had brought the Navy to inland San Antonio, and the membership welcomed Lieutenant Commander James E. Brett to the Board.

Regardless of service affiliation, members respected their fellow officers serving on the USAA Board of Directors on their behalf. In 1944, the wife of Major Wilmer C. Landry executed the USAA Power of Attorney for her husband because he was not available to sign it. She did not designate a specific officer on the Board. Her reason was that "any of the officers of the U.S.A. Association is agreeable to either Major Landry or myself as all officers of said Association are always excellent fine gentlemen."

During the war years, new groups occasionally petitioned the Board of Directors for USAA membership. Commissioned officers of a new Specialist Corps were approved by the Directors for USAA membership. These were civilian technical experts who were incorporated into the Reserves with officer status for the duration of the war. Requests from British officers on assignment to the United States and Treasury Department representatives in Cuba, however, were rejected. A request from a newly retired reserve officer elicited some sympathy. Nonetheless, the Board turned down his request because the bylaws specified current active duty service for reservists. Retirement terminated active duty and USAA membership. White argued that the Association should wait until after the war to see the future size of the Army and Navy and status of the Reserve officers. He acknowledged his conservative outlook, but said that it was a good characteristic to have in the casualty insurance business.[14] The Board agreed with White and placed no major bylaw changes before the membership until after the war.

In addition to the unique insurance questions and problems surfacing during this period, USAA faced others that had little or no relationship to the war. One challenge to USAA's way of doing busi-

THE WAR YEARS

ness and claims philosophy occurred as the result of a tragic accident. On the night of October 13, 1940, an Air Corps Reserve lieutenant stationed at Randolph Field drove into and killed two people on the Austin Highway in San Antonio. USAA investigated the case and found the lieutenant to be responsible beyond all reasonable doubt. The investigator suggested that a charge of voluntary manslaughter would be difficult to reduce to involuntary manslaughter in light of the lieutenant's actions. Because the victims were man and wife with no children and no direct dependents, USAA paid the relatively small sum of $4,000 to settle the case.

A few months later, White received a scathing letter from Lieutenant Colonel Charles H. Dowman, appointed by the Randolph commander to investigate the case. Dowman argued that USAA had been remiss in its moral responsibility. By settling at such a low figure, USAA may have incited the animosity of the aggrieved and "thereby provoked criminal proceedings." (The lieutenant had been charged with manslaughter.) USAA's action, he felt, caused "a permanent and irreparable injury" to the Association. All officers at Randolph, he stated, "felt there has been a miscarriage of justice in this case."[15]

Dowman's letter angered White, and he wrote a strongly worded reply which he cleared with the Board of Directors before mailing. Dowman's suggestion that the Association's settlement had incited the aggrieved to seek retribution was without evidence. Further, Dowman's inference that a larger settlement would have prevented "subsequent criminal proceedings" raised ethical questions. In other words, if the Association had put up enough money, the implication was that the State might not have acted in starting criminal proceedings. White called the suggestion a strange one, "and unexpectedly strange in a Federal official." He continued that the only answer to Dowman's letter was that USAA would not "engage in the practice of paying money to secure immunity from criminal acts, and thus become a party to compounding crime." USAA had no legal and certainly no moral obligation to follow Dowman's reasoning, argued White. The Association did everything that it could do to help its members and leaned over backwards doing so. It would not, however, go to the extent of protecting criminal acts.[16] White's statement of USAA's position was clear. USAA would act to assist its members only within the bounds of integrity and honor revered by all professional officers.

In spite of the increased difficulty the war brought to USAA management, the Board continued to listen to members' requests for new insurance products. In 1941, USAA added medical insurance with two limits — either $250 or $350 per person, per accident. It required the insured to have bodily injury liability, and the new policy covered persons riding in, entering, or getting out of an auto. It paid for reasonable and necessary medical, surgical, ambulance, hospital, and even funeral expenses in the event of death up to the policy limits.[17]

Regular Army members had often requested fire insurance and were confused by USAA's refusal to sell them any. While Regular Army officers could not get their fire insurance from USAA, their Reserve Army officer friends could. This policy dated back to 1931, when USAA began offering policies on household goods and a personal effects floater policy. At that time, USAA made a gentleman's agreement with the Army Cooperative Fire Association (ACFA) at Fort Leavenworth, Kansas, not to offer fire insurance in competition with ACFA. Thus, USAA would not write fire insurance for regular Army officers unless an officer already carried the $4,800 maximum offered by ACFA and wanted additional coverage. Only then would USAA write the additional amount desired.

In 1944, the USAA Board of Directors decided it was time to extend fire coverage to all eligible officers including Regular Army officers. USAA wrote to ACFA, explained the situation, and sug-

The War Years

gested a merger. On July 20, ACFA wrote to USAA and stated its Executive Committee had decided against the proposed merger. ACFA continued:

> If the United Services is considering entering the field of fire protection of personal effects, household goods, and, in addition, writing policies against storm, earthquake, and transportation hazards, we will welcome you as a 'friendly competitor'.[18]

At the 1945 Annual Meeting, the membership decided by an 11 to 1 margin to begin writing fire coverage for all members. In the 1945 *Annual Report* issued in February 1946, Colonel White demonstrated once again the concern for the membership that made USAA special. He advised USAA members who had fire insurance coverage through ACFA, and who had reasonable reserves in that Association, not to transfer their insurance to USAA. You "would not be warranted," he wrote, "in forfeiting such reserves by transferring coverage to our Association."[19] Honesty with the members and ethical behavior were more important than writing new business.

USAA management was heartened by the Association's continuing, if slowed, growth during the war years. In 1943, the *Annual Report* noted that the loss of members going overseas was being offset by new members drawn from the huge numbers of officers entering active service. USAA management expected that "our field of potential members will not appreciably diminish" in the future, and that the number of policies would continue around 50,000 "for some years." In February 1945, the *Annual Report* for 1944 was distributed, and its tone was optimistic about the future of USAA. It looked to a larger standing force of military after the war than before the war, one that would enlarge USAA's field of eligibility. Even in 1946, when membership dropped 5,000 from over 41,000 in 1945, the mood was optimistic. Management explained that the

89

decrease was simply caused by members returning to civilian life and the inability to procure new cars because of slow production. Major auto manufacturers like Ford (jeeps), Pontiac (torpedoes), Oldsmobile (aircraft cannons), Chevrolet (propeller blades), Chrysler (tanks), and Studebaker (tanks) had to reconvert factories to civilian use. It was just a matter of time before USAA would begin to grow again. Just one year later, membership had again climbed to over 41,000 and policies in force jumped over 7,000.

USAA Growth

	1941	1943	1947
Members	36,900	40,500	41,400
Policies in Force	47,500	49,800	53,000

As satisfied as USAA management was with growth of the Association, it was troubled by the rise in accidents and claims. After a disastrous year in 1941, the numbers of accidents and claims after the U.S. entered the war tumbled. Gas rationing, fewer cars available, and large numbers of members overseas all played a role. In 1944, the total number of claims began climbing again and when gas rationing ended, accelerated quickly past prewar levels. The number of claims per policies in force began dropping, however. The Board discussed a 1946 *New York Times* article in which the newspaper was highly critical of the rising accident statistics. It pointed out that the death toll was higher so far in 1946 than in a corresponding period in 1941, even though there were five million fewer cars on the road. In the long term, the *New York Times* placed its hope in education, and in the short term, on more strict enforcement. The article concluded, "It is both absurd and disgraceful to talk peace with our world neighbors while we wage, through gross carelessness, lethal war upon our own fellow-citizens at home."[20]

USAA Automobile Claims Record

Year	Number of Claims Paid	Claims per 100 Policies in Force
1941	8,896	4.14
1942	6,207	6.27
1943	4,148	9.33
1944	5,344	7.51
1945	6,728	6.00
1946	9,896	3.77
1947	9,713	3.87

The cost of the claims was also rising very quickly. Reasons included increased costs for damages because of inability to secure parts, and less experienced workmen. The average monthly claims losses during gasoline rationing were just about $34,000. In 1946, with rationing gone, the average monthly losses were over $81,000.

The Board of Directors pointed to carelessness and speeding as primary causes. It also noted that if members put more emphasis on the condition of their cars, things would improve. In short, the Board warned that "if any of our members drive prewar cars on prewar tires at a high rate of speed, then we must be prepared to continue coverage for widows and executors."[21]

The tremendous and growing carnage on the nation's highways caught the attention of more than insurance companies such as USAA. Individual states, responsible for safety within their borders, became concerned over who or what was to pay for the destruction. Most states' initial response was to enact Financial Responsibility Laws. One state, Massachusetts, had enacted a compulsory automobile insurance law in the 1920s. By the late 1940s, most states and eight Canadian provinces had enacted Financial Responsibility Laws to assure that innocent victims were compensated.

While the laws varied from state to state, they were similar in principle and in how they worked. The assumption of these laws was that each driver was a good driver until proved otherwise. The proof that any driver was not a good one would include a violation of traffic laws, failure to satisfy a court judgment, driving while intoxicated, or leaving the scene of an accident. When this occurred, the laws required the driver to deposit $11,000 with the appropriate state authority, or to post a bond in that same amount. A third way to satisfy this requirement was to show an insurance contract for that amount with a carrier recognized in that state. This was by far the most common and cheapest way to satisfy the requirement. This was a problem for USAA — it was licensed only in the state of Texas. Failure to have a state license did not affect the actual insurance coverage for a member, but it did make it against the law for that driver to operate on the roads of another state.

USAA management's initial assumption that these laws would affect only a small number of USAA members proved to be true. In 1940, only 26 of over 40,000 members had sought insurance certificates. In these cases, USAA made arrangements with carriers such as Employers Reinsurance Company, which was licensed in all states, to issue certificates to state authorities on behalf of USAA members.

In 1942, the strict Financial Responsibility Law of New York State went into effect. White told the Board of Directors that USAA must now look into such laws seriously. If other states were to strengthen theirs as well, the Association must be prepared to lose members who wanted bodily injury and property damage in those states. For the long term, USAA must consider getting licensed in states besides Texas. In the meantime, White sent Max Wier Sr. to New York, where he was able to make satisfactory arrangements with the State

THE WAR YEARS

Insurance Department. Facilitated by an amendment to the New York Financial Responsibility Law, the Association received permission to file Financial Responsibility Certificates to cover USAA members who were not legal residents of New York.

In 1945, the problem arose again, this time in the state of Virginia. Again, White sent Wier to make arrangements for USAA members in Virginia. This time the results were different. The State Insurance Department informed Wier that the Association would have to get a Virginia license if it intended to continue operating in that state. After discussing this issue, the Board decided to go ahead with an application in Virginia. USAA soon became licensed there. The Board also heard that the Commanding General of the U.S. Marine Corps at Cherry Point, North Carolina, had directed members of his command to get their automobile insurance only from a carrier licensed in North Carolina. Although USAA worked things out with the General, and was able to sell insurance at his installation, it was clear that getting licensed in most states would be a future requirement.

While the states were getting more involved in automobile insurance, it appeared for awhile that the federal government was going to get involved as well. In 1943, a bill was introduced into the House by Representative Sam Hobbs that would have severely restricted "mail order" insurance carriers such as USAA. White lobbied against the bill through Congressman Paul J. Kilday. Leo Goodwin of GEICO also worked against the bill from his Washington, D.C., office. In mid-April, Goodwin sent a telegram to White and told him that the bill was dead. Next, in early June of 1944, the U.S. Supreme Court overruled a lower court precedent and ruled that insurance was now subject to interstate commerce laws. The federal government took no action, however, and the ruling had no practical effect. After intensive lobbying, the 79th Congress enacted the McCarran Act in early 1945, declaring "that the continued regulation and taxation by the several states of the business of insurance is in the public interest."²² The states were again in the driver's seat. USAA would have to continue to work with the individual states, but at least the federal government was out of the business for the time being.

One of the welcome dividends of the war's end was the return of those members who had been prisoners of war or missing in action. Stuart Gwyn, then Chief Underwriter, began a policy of sending a "welcome home" telegram to them. Besides the heartfelt greeting, her telegrams notified the returnees that their policy information would follow by letter. These individuals always remembered Gwyn's kindness with warm feelings toward USAA.

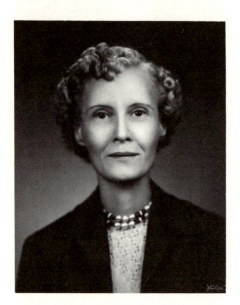
Stuart Gwyn

Many of these members stopped by the USAA home office after the war to thank Gwyn and the Association for their support. Consuelo Kerford, USAA's Chief Underwriter, related the story of one former POW who had been captured at Bataan and held in a Japanese prison camp for three years. Prior to his capture he had put his 1941 USAA Household Goods Policy and a USAA dividend check in the sole of one of his shoes. With nothing to read and little to do (obviously), the officer and his fellow POWs spent hours memorizing the insurance policy and discussing its contents. Kerford happily helped him cash his bedraggled and faded check. When the veteran began reciting the provisions of the policy, however, Kerford had to tell him gently that the policy had been completely revised. "Well," he said, "I'm not going back to Bataan just to memorize this new policy."[23]

A major decision at war's end concerned what to do about the members overseas who became part of the occupying force and were joined by their dependents. White wrote to the membership that USAA desired to cover its members wherever they were, if the hazards were

Consuelo Kerford

not too great. He pointed out that USAA had never written automobile insurance in Europe and would not now. If USAA members stayed in the occupied areas, then provost courts could handle claims settlements. The problem was that the European continent was small, and countries outside the occupied zones such as France, with its fine wines and foods, were within an easy drive. The assumed difficulty in settling claims in former Allied and neutral states led USAA to assist members in getting their insurance through the American International Underwriters Corporation.

In the Far East, the differences were significant. In occupied Japan, American tribunals were available to settle claims. USAA could insure its members easily there, and did. To start with, the Association used the San Francisco schedule of rates for those autos insured in Japan.[24] On the smaller islands, the relatively small number of cars posed no significant hazards or problems for the Association. In the Philippines, USAA bet on the influence of almost a half century of American rule to provide the proper judicial climate. On the other hand, USAA decided not to extend coverage to China, Korea, or elsewhere on the Asian continent. White hoped that the USAA members in Europe would not think that USAA had "casually overlooked them, but have been guided in our action by what we deemed best for the Association."[25]

Meanwhile, the end of the war meant many changes for the USAA employees in San Antonio. The War Labor Board had closely controlled the personnel classification of employees and salary adjustments. With that body dissolved, the USAA Board directed the Attorneys-in-Fact "to rearrange our classifications of the clerical personnel and to adjust salaries effective January 1, 1946."[26] To make the workplace more efficient and more comfortable, the Board hired an architect to determine what alterations and additions to the Grayson Street office were required.

Management also decided to upgrade to more sophisticated automated equipment. These included alphabetic duplicating key punch machines, a transfer posting machine, two alphabetic accounting machines, and a collator, for a monthly rental cost of over eight hundred dollars. Meta Willis, USAA Auditor and Statistician, and co-worker Oleta Payne worked long hours to convert all accounts to the new system. The new equipment replaced what some considered USAA's first computer — the 1936 automatic multiplying punch machine, which computed members' dividends. The machines would lessen clerk workloads and would improve the system in place in the bookkeeping department. The increased cost of the machines was to be met by the loss of six clerks. (Because it would be months before the machines would arrive, White hoped to find places for the six through normal attrition and other changes.) These efforts made USAA the pioneer in the use of this automated equipment in the southwestern part of the United States.[27]

Perhaps of most significance to the employees was the Board's

THE WAR YEARS

adoption of the first Old Age Pension Plan for the employees of the Association. The Board had discussed a pension plan earlier, but dropped consideration when Social Security was put into place in 1935. The Board decided that it was now time to implement one for the Association's employees. The plan called for individual annuity contracts placed with the Southwestern Life Insurance Company at a total cost to USAA of from $20,000 to $22,000 per year. White told the members that USAA had a valuable staff of older employees. The adoption of this plan would help guarantee the Association of their continued service for years. He pointed out that the plan would have little effect upon savings to members because of USAA's reserves.[28]

Emerging from the shadows of war, USAA was in remarkable shape. *Best's Insurance Report*, the leading authority on insurance companies in the United States in the 1940s, gave USAA its highest rating, A+ (excellent), for each year of the war. *Best's* noted that "the underwriting record of the exchange has been remarkable with loss and expense ratios of 40.1 percent and 15.9 percent respectively, for the last five years."[29] In a Report of Examination of USAA dated December 31, 1944, the Examiners of the Insurance Department of the State of Texas were very positive about the Association. They said that USAA "has been very efficiently managed and economically operated." It praised the USAA management for its conservative approach in the establishment of reserves for unexpected losses and for voluntary additions to the unpaid claim reserves.[30]

Colonel White was justifiably proud when he told the membership that USAA stood "as a model of economic organization" and that it was "meeting with fairness and justice, the requirements of this disturbed age, while maintaining a high degree of solvency."[31] He predicted that USAA would be good for the membership indefi-

A Tradition Of Service

nitely. What White and most others didn't know was that the shooting war just ended would give way to a new type of war, one with profound implications for USAA.

CHAPTER FOUR

THE COLD WAR BEGINS—SERVICING AN EXPLODING MEMBERSHIP

As Colonel Paul Tibbetts and his *Enola Gay* crew watched the mushroom cloud rise far above the earth, they knew that war would never be the same again. For the United States, peace would never be the same again either. Outside of its war casualties, the nation had emerged from the war virtually untouched, and as a real global power for the first time in its existence. It was not only the premier postwar military force, but the world's top economic power as well.

Representatives of the Allied powers and the Japanese government assembled aboard the U.S.S. *Missouri* for ceremonies attending the surrender of Japan. General of the Army Douglas MacArthur, as Supreme Commander, affixes his signature to the document. September 2, 1945. *(Courtesy of Fort Sam Houston Museum)*

A TRADITION OF SERVICE

Also emerging from the war was a growing Soviet-American rivalry over the power vacuums left by the defeated Axis powers and the Allied Colonial powers that won the war, but lost their empires.[1] This rivalry, of course, grew into the Cold War, which was to last almost forty years. As early as 1946, Winston Churchill coined the term "iron curtain" to describe the separation of the Eastern and Western powers. Crises erupted from Iran to Berlin, but at first the U.S. military strength remained at levels close to the World War II demobilization figures. USAA's principal interest, the active-duty officer strength, fell from 422,000 in 1946 to 169,000 in 1948. As late as 1950, the number of officers on active duty was still only 182,000.

Although the number of active-duty officers was down considerably from wartime levels, USAA's growth surged after the momentary drop in membership in 1946. By the end of 1947, the membership totals equaled the 1945 numbers, policies in force were up dramatically, and assets totaled almost five million dollars. On the crest of USAA's success, one of its architects, USAA chief Colonel "Artie" White, died on December 7, 1947, at the age of seventy-seven at Fort Sam Houston Hospital. Ten days later the USAA Board met. Its resolution saluted USAA's leader and his many contributions to the growth and management of USAA. Perhaps most important was the Board's determination to "carry on" in the best military tradition:

> We can best express our feeling and admiration of his character and ability by firmly resolving to carry on the work he so successfully conducted, adhering to his practices and not departing from his principles.[2]

To succeed White, the Board elected retired Army Colonel William Fitzhugh "Jack" Jones as Secretary-Treasurer and Attorney-in-Fact. At the time of his election, Jones was almost seventy years of age. As his First Assistant Secretary-Treasurer, the Board advanced

Servicing An Exploding Membership

Colonel Mert Proctor. Proctor was eight years Jones' junior and a possible successor. For the Second Assistant Secretary-Treasurer, Jones had provided the Board with five nominees. He suggested that this position be filled with a man at least eight years younger than Proctor for succession purposes. Active duty Army Colonel Charles E. Cheever, Staff Judge Advocate, and USAA Board member, was the only nominee who fit that criteria. Even more important, he had strong support among the Board members, and he was elected by an eleven-to-one margin. To fill White's place on the Board, the Board elected Navy Captain Eugene M. Waldron. Later, at the June 1950 Annual Members' Meeting, the membership voted to give Jones the additional title of "General Manager" as more descriptive of his role for the Association.

Jones had served the USAA membership for more than twenty years and was highly regarded and well liked. He had been a USAA Director as early as 1927 and had been White's Assistant Secretary since 1938. Born on May 26, 1878, in Alabama, his father had been a Colonel in the Confederate Army who lost a leg in the Battle of Vicksburg in 1863. Jones' grandfather, Richard Wilmer, was an Episcopal Bishop and the young "Jack" traveled the state with him, assisting him in readings and conducting services.

Colonel William F. Jones as Commanding Officer of the 12th Field Artillery, 1935 to 1937.

When the Spanish American War began, Jones volunteered for military service in the 2nd Alabama Infantry, but his unit never left the Continental United States. While Jones liked the idea of military service, he had no ready avenue to pursue a military career until President William McKinley got something in his eye on a trip to Alabama. McKinley went to a doctor's office; by chance, the doctor was Jones' uncle and the son of Bishop Wilmer. There, McKinley learned of young Jones' interest in the military and offered him the opportunity to take an exam for a Regular commission. Jones passed with ease and was commissioned a Second Lieutenant of Artillery in 1901.

Jones married his childhood sweetheart, Sally Brassfield, the daughter of a former surgeon in the Confederate Navy. They were to spend more than fifty years together. Their Army life began at a small seacoast artillery fort located on an island off the North Carolina coast. In 1907, when the Artillery split into two separate branches, Coast and Field, Jones volunteered for Field Artillery and was assigned to the 2nd Field Artillery. It was here that he picked up the additional nickname "Deacon" because of his early ties with his bishop grandfather.

Following this assignment, Jones completed several different tours of duty: three in the Philippines, one in Washington state where he first had met Lieutenant Mert Proctor, and one in New Orleans. In 1916, he went with General Pershing on the American expedition into Mexico as commander of a truck company. While there, Jones designed a mobile field kitchen that the Army used widely for many years.

During World War I, Jones saw combat duty that included participation in the Meuse-Argonne offensive as a regimental commander of the 111th Field Artillery of the Virginia National Guard. Following the war, he graduated from the School of the Line, Command and General Staff School, and Army War College. In 1922, after War College, he assumed the command of the 18th Field Artillery at Fort Sill, Oklahoma, under the overall command of General Hinds. In 1924, he was stationed in San Antonio for the first

Lieutenant William F. Jones in the Philippines, circa 1910. *(Courtesy of Jeanne Rowlett)*

time — as a staff officer again serving under General Hinds. After three more assignments, Jones returned to Fort Sam Houston in 1935 as Commander of the 12th Field Artillery and later as Executive Director for the Civilian Conservation Corps for the VIII Corps Area. He retired in 1939 in the grade of Colonel after thirty-seven years of service.

As a civilian, his physical appearance belied his intelligence and leadership ability. He was thin and about six feet tall, and his civilian clothes never fit his frame as well as his uniform had. He was always a gentleman and well respected by USAA employees who sometimes affectionately called him "Uncle Willy" when out of earshot. He spoke slowly with a Southern drawl that followed him from Alabama. Possibly as a result of his upbringing and his age, he tended to think everything over carefully and was conservative about change. The irony in this was that dramatic changes in membership eligibility under his administration fueled the explosive growth of USAA in the 1950s.

As World War II drew to a close, the movement for establishing an independent Air Force had gathered momentum. In spite of strong support from President Harry S. Truman, General Dwight David "Ike" Eisenhower, and the senior Air Force leadership, the birth

William F. Jones, General Manager of USAA, 1948 to 1952

was an extremely difficult one. The Navy opposition was particularly intense, because it feared the loss of its own aerial mission to the new Air Force. Finally in July 1947, Congress passed the National Security Act, creating a Department of Defense and a separate Department of the Air Force. This Department accomplished most of what the airmen had sought — independence, authority for operating the strategic air mission, unity of control under a single Secretary of Cabinet rank, and equal status with its sister services, the Army and the Navy. The downside, at least to the Air Force leadership at the time, was that all the services retained a flying mission. Typical was Air Force General Ira Eaker, who said the act "legitimized four military air forces."[3] From USAA's business per-

B-17 "Flying Fortress," a bomber used extensively during World War II. *(Courtesy of the National Archives)*

spective, what service the flyers belonged to was not important, but the bylaws had to be changed so that the officers of the new service could become members of USAA.

Technically, the National Security Act removed thousands of officers from the USAA membership eligibility list, and USAA took quick action to incorporate the newly designated Air Force officers. In June 1948, at the first Annual Members' Meeting following the creation of the Air Force, the membership amended the bylaws to include the Air Force officers. This change to the bylaws was not a dramatic one, but more of a technical correction to include the thousands of airmen who were former Army officers and who were already members or eligible to be so. As a footnote, Colonel Michael F. Davis became the first member of the newly constituted U.S. Air Force to serve on the USAA Board of Directors.

The second change in the bylaws set a new precedent although the number of individuals it made eligible for membership was relatively small. The Association's employees had made USAA the outstanding company it had become by 1948 and had especially impressed the Board and the membership with their professionalism over the war years. Employees like Mary Ethel Vaughan, Rita Hopkins, Marynel Neilson, and the many others whose names have been lost to history provided dedicated service to the membership. A few employees were retired military, some were dependent wives whose husbands were stationed in San Antonio or who had gone overseas, and others were military "brats." One of these "brats" was Marynel Neilson, who had been born in the Philippines to U.S. Army Cavalry Lieutenant Frederick Neilson and his wife Mary, daughter of a West Point graduate. Most employees, however, had no personal connections with the military and knew little about it. Frances Moore recalled one young mail clerk who came to her one day because the clerk's search for General Ledger was in vain. "I just can't find him," she told Frances.[4] Together, however, these employees were

Servicing An Exploding Membership

USAA employees of the Automobile Policy Department working in the Grayson Street building

an outstanding team who were dedicated to the membership.

USAA management believed that it was time to recognize these employees in a very special way: to make them members — *voting* members — of USAA. In June 1948, the bylaws change that the Board submitted to the membership to make this so met with very little opposition. The proposal received only 121 more negative votes than were cast against admitting Air Force officers into membership. The approved change was profound in its implications and in its precedent. Individuals who were never members before, with no personal connection to commissioned officers or even to the military, had been admitted to membership. It was a dramatic and important step for USAA. The employees were now serving fellow members — and not "them."

Another change that expanded the roster of USAA membership eligibles related to retired officers. After the 80th Congress passed

Public Law 380 concerning retired officers, Jones and his staff studied it carefully. This law spelled out five different categories of retired officers. Two categories, officers of the Regular Service and retired enlisted personnel of the Regular Establishment who were advanced on the retired list to their highest commissioned rank held, were already eligible. Officers retired for physical disability, National Guard and Reserve Corps Officers retired after twenty years of accumulated service, and officers on the Honorary Retired List were not. In January 1949, the Board decided to add the category of officers retired for physical disability incurred in the line of duty to the membership eligibles.[5] It disapproved adding the remaining two categories. The issue was not settled, however.

About a year later, retired Navy Captain Howard G. Copeland wrote to the Board. Copeland had retired for a physical disability and became a member as a result of the 1949 Board decision. He questioned the Board's decision to deny eligibility for brother officers who retired for years of service rather than for physical disability. It didn't seem fair and it made no sense to him. After Jones looked at the issue again, it made no sense to him either. He found forty-five different laws affecting Army officer retirements. Depending on which of these laws governed an officer's retirement, he might or might not be eligible for USAA membership. Jones recommended to the Board that all retired officers and warrant officers, including those on the honorary list, be eligible for USAA membership. The Board concurred. Now all officers on active duty and all retired officers were eligible for membership.[6] Commissioned Reserve officers who were neither active duty nor retired, however, were in a membership limbo.

During the demobilization of the 1940s and continuing into the early 1950s, USAA was forced under its own bylaws to cancel the membership of thousands of Reserve and National Guard officers when they returned to civilian life. Many of the officers had been members for as long as ten years, and held excellent records with the Association. Needless to say, officers caught in this mass exodus were not happy with their state of affairs and contacted the Board. Major Samuel Campanella wrote that after nineteen years of active duty under a Reserve Commission, he was being relieved from active duty because of an enforced reduction. He re-enlisted as a Master Sergeant to save his retirement, but now he had lost his USAA membership! Another officer who wrote to the Board was Major William C. Bloch, a Reserve officer separating from the Signal Corps. He asked the Board to reconsider continuing membership privileges for Reserve officers on inactive status, if they were members while on active duty.

The Reserve and Guard officers who left the service and lost their membership hurt USAA in another way. By 1950, the Association's management became aware that many Reserve and Guard officers ordered to active duty were not joining USAA. The reservists had heard the stories of those who had preceded them. These new officers were reluctant to place their insurance with USAA because they knew they could not retain it if they went off active duty. Rather, they preferred to build up their reputations as good risks with companies such as Government Employees Insurance Company that would continue to insure them after the officers returned to inactive duty and civilian life.

This issue of separated Reserve and Guard officers was not a minor one for USAA. In 1950, these officers made up over 22 percent of the membership. Just one year later, they constituted over 28 percent of the Association's members. Although these percentages may have included an unknown number of retired officers, the problem was still very significant. At its December 1950 meeting, the Board of Directors appointed a three-man committee to study the issue and to report back to the Board.[7]

About a month later, Colonel William Harris presented his committee's report on eligibility. He noted that USAA management wanted to retain Reserve component officers as long as they served more than ninety days of active duty and retained officer status in any civilian component of the Armed Forces. The reasons were simple — any sound business must continue to expand, and USAA was eliminating members who had demonstrated they were good risks. Further, eliminating these officers discouraged other Reservists from joining in the first place, thus reducing USAA's potential growth. Finally, new companies were rising to furnish insurance to members of the Armed Forces. USAA's restrictive policies were only assisting this new competition.

The Harris committee didn't understand the rationale for dropping the separating Reserve and Guard officers in the first place. USAA insured them on active duty, when they were the poorest risks because of "separation from family ties, lack of restraint from home influence, and that they were just young and less stable." After these same officers completed their service commitment, they usually settled down and accepted greater responsibility, thus becoming "better insurance risks."[8] But at this point, USAA dropped them!

The Cold War threw a shadow over the committee's otherwise solid reasoning, reflecting the fear so prevalent in the U.S. at the time. Russian aerial attacks were thought possible any day — even tomorrow! The popular American press listed Russia's targeted priorities in the United States, all military facilities had medical kits for treating radiation burns, subways became nuclear shelters, and a thriving cottage industry built bomb shelters for private residences. The committee decided that in the event of a nuclear attack on military centers like San Diego, San Francisco, Washington, or San Antonio, the Association might expect severe losses — if USAA had no war risk clause. Insuring separating Reserve officers who would live in thousands of locales across the nation would lessen any potential negative impact on USAA resulting from officer-members concentrated in principal Russian-target areas.

SERVICING AN EXPLODING MEMBERSHIP

The committee did not find arms-open support among some members in favor of incorporating the separating Reserve and Guard officers into USAA. Many senior Regular Army and Air Force officers objected to the proposed change. Some Regular officers feared that expansion might "ultimately result in control of the Association by non-regular officers." Other members thought that USAA expansion, beyond its niche of active-duty and retired officers, would cause other large insurance companies to move into aggressive competition with the Association. The proposed change would also make eligibility determinations much more difficult. How could the Association tell if an officer retained a commission or not? Still others raised the problem of USAA growing into a "really big business"—and with it the difficulty of maintaining the same service levels and financial strength. The committee's final recommendation was to let the USAA Board of Directors make the final decision. It would do this by changing the bylaws provision on eligibility to include the phrase "as may be enumerated from time to time in the policy contract." Under this provision, the Board could expand eligibility to include the separated officers.[9]

After a month to consider the proposal, the Board met on February 21. Unlike some issues that had come before the Board in the past which had generated little disagreement, this one generated a spirited discussion among the Board members. Several of them had sought opinions from friends and members and there seemed to be no middle ground here. Those asked either strongly supported the proposal to include the separated officers or they strongly opposed their inclusion. It was clear that this potentially divisive proposal on separated officers had to be placed before the membership. The decision was to make the proposed eligibility change one that would not require the Association to spend a great deal of time determining each individual officer's eligibility. Colonel Harris, who had chaired the Committee on Eligibility, made the proposal the Board agreed to place on the ballot. It set no specific time requirement of active duty service to qualify for USAA:

> Officers and Warrant Officers of the National Guard and the Reserve Corps of the United States Services when called into Federal Service for extended active duty, and to continue their membership so long as they retain their commissions or warrants in the National Guard or Reserve Corps.[10]

At the 1951 Annual Members' Meeting, the membership voted 18,451 to 890 to include these Reserve and National Guard officers. The membership also supported the change to the bylaws proposed by the Harris Committee on eligibility that clarified and emphasized the authority of the Board of Directors to define categories eligible for membership.[11]

What made these membership decisions extremely significant was the Korean War. Before dawn on Sunday, June 25, 1950, about 75,000 North Korean troops raced through the rain across the 38th parallel. This was the boundary between North and South Korea that the U.S. and the Soviet Union had drawn following World War II. Led by tanks and supported by heavy artillery, the North Koreans attacked along a 150-mile front. The South Korean forces quickly collapsed, and the communist forces rumbled southward. President Harry Truman asked General Douglas MacArthur in Japan to send arms and equipment to the South Koreans and to use United States aircraft to attack the onrushing North Korean spearhead. On Monday evening, the communists neared Seoul. With this development, Truman ordered U.S. aircraft and warships to fully support South Korea below the 38th parallel. In spite of this action, by June 30th the surging North Korean forces had pushed the South Korean forces into a small area in the southeast corner of Korea — the Pusan Perimeter. MacArthur asked for American combat soldiers to enter the Korean conflict, and Truman gave the order.

More than three years later, the adversaries signed an armistice. The "police action" of 1950, dubbed the "forgotten war" in the 1990s, was

USAA member Major Russell Dougherty in Korea. He later became a four-star general and Commander of the Strategic Air Command.

one of the costliest in the twentieth century. Close to five million Asians died. The United States lost over 54,000 dead and more than 100,000 wounded. The National Security Council Paper Number 68 (NSC-68) had been "validated." Formulated in January 1950, NSC-68 treated communism as an evil monolith and supported America's responsibility to be the world's policeman with conventional arms and atomic weaponry. As Cold War scholars Tom Paterson and Garry Clifford put it, "the Korean War's most lasting legacy was its acceleration of the militarization of the Cold War."[12] The numbers of military personnel on active duty reflect their analysis and the underlying principles of NSC-68. In 1950, officers on active duty totaled 182,000. At the end of 1951, the number was 323,000. Over the next fifteen years, officer strength ranged from a low of 315,000 to a high of 378,000, until the Vietnam War when the strength climbed again to over 400,000. For

A Tradition Of Service

USAA, the expanded eligibility requirements meant a nearly doubled pool of active-duty officers and the membership exploded, almost tripling between 1950 and 1955.

In the face of the favorable numbers of eligibles and the increase in new members, USAA continued to advertise aggressively. The Association routinely ran advertisements in many publications with wide military readership. For example, the *Army and Navy Register*, the *Air Force Times*, and the *Army and Navy Journal* contained USAA advertisements that included return coupons. In 1951, USAA received almost 5,000 of these coupons from interested officers. Typical of the early fifties' ads is the one pictured below.

USAA also reintroduced the USAA desk calendars which it had discontinued during the war years because of metal shortages. The calendars were sent annually to all members.

More Than 100,000 Officers Shared $2,995,269 Dividend in 1951

More than 100,000 members in this exclusive, non-profit automobile insurance exchange split that melon during 1951. The average amount of dividends per policy written by this Association during 1951 was $25.04.

Did you get your share? If not, fill in the coupon below. Find out for yourself the benefits enjoyed by policy holders in United Services.

Membership restricted to commissioned and warrant officers.

UNITED SERVICES *Automobile Association*

UNITED SERVICES Automobile Association
Dept. R, 1400 E. Grayson Street - San Antonio 8, Texas
Without obligation, send information on automobile insurance:

Car Year____ Make____ Model____ Body Type____ Pass. Capacity____
Serial No.____ Motor No.____ No. Cyls.____ Cost____ Date Purch.____ New or Used____
Factory Price____ Current Year & State Registration____
Age of Youngest Driver in your Household____
Is Car Used for Business Purposes Other Than to and from Work?____ Yes____ No____
Name & Rank____
Military Address____
If car not at above address, give location of car.____

Get the facts today

Army, Navy, Air Force Register, May 31, 1952

Servicing An Exploding Membership

A creative marketing strategy was USAA's distribution of a reprint of an insurance text used at West Point called *Principles of Insurance*. USAA's General Counsel Cheever traveled to West Point to secure permission and to make the initial arrangements with the author and the Academy to reprint it. The author turned out to be West Point instructor Major Robert McDermott, who was to become USAA's chief executive some eighteen years later. The first mailing of nineteen thousand of the reprints went to Army, Navy, and Air Force ROTC cadets who were graduating in 1951 and being ordered to active duty. Along with the educational *Principles of Insurance,* USAA sent marketing information.[13]

Important to the growth and reputation of USAA were the Association's continuing efforts to take care of its members. In 1950, Jones reported to the Board that in order to give prompt service it had been increasingly necessary to resort to telegrams. USAA had to install a second telegraph machine to help with the 150 telegrams received daily. To keep things moving in the home office when the attorneys were not available, the Board authorized Stuart Gwyn and Nancy Brooks to authenticate policies and endorsements in the event of an emergency. Reducing expenses helped reduce insurance costs to members. Productivity was important and USAA made progress in this area. As one example, Jones reported "that 658 girl hours were required to mail the [*Annual*] reports in 1951 as against 746 girl hours in 1950 when some seventeen thousand less reports were mailed."[14] To assist the Board members in being more productive, the Board changed its policy on maintaining USAA's securities. Until 1949, the USAA securities were kept in a safety deposit box. Board members routinely inventoried the securities and clipped coupons. Contracting this responsibility to Frost National Bank of San Antonio gave the Board members more time to work on other Association matters.

In response to member requests, USAA raised the limit on Fire Insurance to $10,000 and Automobile Medical Payments coverage to $1,000. The Association also broadened the interpretation of the Household Goods policy to include covering potential losses of property while in the hands of shippers. Incredibly, USAA included all of these increased coverages within the existing premium costs. The honesty of the members helped make it possible to make these changes. For example, in the year 1950 only $439 or .000055 percent of the business was charged to bad debts. [15]

Another example of USAA's assistance to members was its efforts to reduce the automobile insurance rates on Governor's Island in New York City. USAA had a large number of members stationed and living at the island's First Army Headquarters installation who were paying New York City's premium insurance rates. This was clearly unfair to those on the island because of the low traffic density and minimum number of accidents. In 1950, Cheever appealed to the New York Insurance Department on behalf of the Governor's Island residents. The following year, the Insurance Department directed the National Bureau of Casualty Underwriters and the National Automobile Underwriters Association to reduce the rates. After looking into the situation, the two rate-making bureaus classified this island the same as Staten Island. The results were savings to USAA members of up to $150 per year — and great gratitude to USAA for Cheever's efforts.

A decision that provided service and facilitated USAA growth was to insure members stationed in Germany. The original USAA decision not to insure members in Germany and Europe had made sense at the time. In Germany, USAA could count on the military judicial system for help. Elsewhere in Europe, USAA had no infrastructure for claims and other things fundamental to the business. The Association had made an arrangement so that USAA members would be handled by the American International Underwriters Corporation, and it seemed satisfactory. In addition, the Army Exchange Service in Germany was also writing automobile insurance. With the increasing intensity of the Cold War, more and more American troops were being stationed in Europe. In fact, Jones told the Board that four or five divisions with many officer-members were going to Europe and a solution to their insurance problems had to be worked out.[16] USAA was missing out on a good piece of business, and Jones began looking into the Association selling its own insurance in Germany. He briefed the Board in June 1951 that he had received letters and application information from Headquarters, European Command (EUCOM). He said his study would continue, but "if it were finally determined that a license to write insurance in Germany would not be granted unless the Association insured enlisted personnel and civilians, the whole idea would be abandoned."[17]

When USAA received the license provisions, the Board discussed it and directed Jones to write to EUCOM to get a clarification of some troubling issues. In the early fall of 1951, Jones wrote a letter to the Commanding General. He pointed out that the military license would authorize USAA to sell insurance to anyone who received U.S. Military Payment Certificates. This would include enlisted personnel and would conflict with USAA's bylaws, if USAA were *obligated* to write insurance for everyone. In this case, USAA "would be unable to qualify to transact business in Germany."[18] Jones pointed out that USAA's principal purpose in seeking a license to write insurance in the U.S. zone was "to be able to follow our members who are ordered there."[19]

The response to USAA from Colonel C.R. Hutchinson of EUCOM was very positive. Hutchinson stated that although USAA would be authorized to write insurance for all Americans in Germany, it would not be required to do so. The only possibility of this in the future was that EUCOM might have to assign risks to USAA, but the chance that this would occur was remote. In addition, USAA's contracted attorney from Munich, Morton K. Lange, appeared to have worked out satisfactory solutions to the other USAA issues.[20] While the reply to the issues Jones raised looked good, three other obstacles arose.

For a member to register a car in Germany, the insureds had to have a Bodily Injury and Property Damage Liability policy in their possession. For USAA, this presented a difficult problem because of the mail lag times. Although officials at EUCOM had told Cheever that an officer could personally certify he had insurance with USAA, EUCOM had not confirmed this offer in writing. Also, the High Commissioner for Germany had promulgated, in Law 22, the abrogation of all exclusions including "war risk" clauses. This did not sit well with USAA. Finally, on October 18, 1951, Congress adopted a resolution declaring a cessation of war between the United States and Germany. USAA management feared that control of insurance might pass from EUCOM to the German government. All of these problems had to be resolved. If they were not, American International Underwriters Corporation had expressed a willingness to handle USAA claims, as long as USAA had no office in Europe. The whole issue required more study.[21]

Based on the existing confusion, USAA notified EUCOM that it would not begin selling insurance in Germany January 1, 1952, as it had previously suggested. On January 5, EUCOM sent a cable to USAA to try to settle the issues. While Jones had mentioned newspaper reports raising the possibility of U.S. forces moving to France, the cable said there were no such plans under discussion. Law 22 and the Congressional resolution were having no apparent effect on the five companies already doing business in Germany since none had raised any problems to the American authorities there. The cable noted that it hoped USAA would enter the insurance market in Europe, estimating that at least 15,000 vehicles would meet USAA eligibility requirements. EUCOM officials "highly recommended that the Association send soonest a competent representative to Heidelberg to look into the situation so that it may be assured . . .

Servicing An Exploding Membership

that its early entry into the U.S. zone will be in the best interests of the Association."[22]

Jones appeared to be very cautious in the face of this positive cable. He sent another letter to EUCOM asking for more specifics about any EUCOM assigned risk plan and the likelihood that USAA would have to raise rates as the other companies had on February 1. Jones also wrote that he believed USAA could not provide efficient service in Europe. When the issue came up in the next Board meeting, Jones told fellow Board members that it was "not feasible at this time" to send a USAA representative to Europe as EUCOM had requested. Colonel Harris disagreed and moved to have an ad hoc committee appointed consisting of one Board representative from each of the major Armed Services and management. The proposal included the provision that this committee make a recommendation on Germany to the Board at its next meeting. After a lengthy discussion, the motion passed seven to five with one abstention.

The committee's recommendation was strongly in favor of selling insurance in Germany. It emphasized that more than one-third of American Army personnel would be serving (and insuring) in Europe as well as additional Air Force, Navy, and Marine officers. This percentage of potential membership that would eventually serve in Germany would actually be much greater due to rotations. If USAA refused to insure them, the officers would feel "let down" by USAA and would go elsewhere — maybe permanently. The report further stated that "U.S. and its Armed Forces are now and will be for an indefinite period, International Forces. Therefore USAA *must go overseas...* to accommodate its members." The committee confirmed that the potential business in Germany would be 15,000 cars annually or about $2 million. In addition, the USAA Board of Directors should recognize that EUCOM had "done its utmost to pave the way for USAA to enter Germany with a minimum of trouble." The preferred solution was to send someone to Europe

Charles Cheever

and to open an office in Germany as soon as possible.[23]

After the Board discussed the report, Jones made a motion to send a USAA representative to Europe as soon as possible. To save time, the representative was to communicate with the Board by cable. The Board of Directors agreed, and Charlie Cheever was named as the Association's representative. Cheever left for Europe at once. His cable of April 22 clarified all the issues. He recommended hiring Welby Logan, head of the Army Exchange Service's insurance operation, as USAA's manager in Europe. Cheever found adjusters and adequate repair facilities available everywhere, with stateside Blue Book values prevailing. As to the issue of insuring the enlisted forces there, Cheever pointed out that according to Provost Marshal statistics, "officers' accident rates were one-third those of the first three grades and one-fifth the rate of those for enlisted personnel below the first three grades."[24] In 1951, officers in Europe registered about 35 percent of all American vehicles and had less than 14 percent of the accidents. The "top 3" enlisted grades registered 31 percent of the vehicles, but had almost 40 percent of the accidents![25] "Officers keenly resent," Cheever said, "paying for the bad accident ratio of others."[26] While this was just one year's statistics and may have been an anomaly, the figures left a residual negative impact on USAA management regarding insuring enlisted personnel.

Cheever's recommendation was to begin operating July 1, 1952, and he requested authority to proceed.[27] Jones moved that the Board

USAA's first overseas office – 229 Fuerstenbergerstrasse, Frankfurt, Germany

approve Cheever's recommendation and execute a two-year contract with Logan. The Board gave Cheever the go-ahead.[28] Cheever moved swiftly. By May 15, he had contracted with Logan to be USAA's European Manager. Warren V. Green was to be claims supervisor, and two other employees, Beate Dau and Charlotte Hildebrandt, were hired. Cheever rented office space in Frankfurt to house the USAA operation in Europe. USAA opened its doors on July 1, 1952.

The continuing growth had an obvious and visible impact on USAA. The number of employees grew, and the Grayson Street building got increasingly crowded. USAA looked to purchasing neighboring land and began building additional space, including a second story. Although the original Board approval for the addition had been for $200,000, Jones had sought an extra $125,000 as the work had neared completion in the spring of 1949. The additional costs included acoustical tile, additional lighting, and reinforcing the original structure to support a second floor. The Board approved the new costs unanimously.[29]

Grayson Street Building

By 1950, the building was again bursting because of the onslaught of new business. Jones requested Board approval to add a two-story addition to the building totaling approximately 22,000 square feet at a cost of about $30 per square foot. The Board approved management's request to begin immediately.[30] In October, Jones told the Board that the cost looked like it would be about $425,000 plus another $105,000 for air conditioning and heating. USAA's efforts to modernize the work environment for its employees did not go unnoticed. In February 1951, *American Business* picked USAA as one of the "Best 100 Offices" in America. The magazine praised the modern equipment which improved productivity, the high-level lighting that reduced fatigue, and the Directors' Room, a reproduction of a room in the famed Raleigh Tavern at Williamsburg, Virginia. And, the

Servicing An Exploding Membership

322 USAA employees enjoyed their breaks at an outdoor patio equipped with picnic tables or in an attractively furnished room.[31]

One year later, before the work was even completed, Jones asked for approval to add a third floor to the new two-story addition. USAA was having trouble keeping up with member growth. By November 1952, the Board was trying to purchase additional land close to the National Bank of Fort Sam Houston. It was also considering getting a city ordinance passed to permit an overhead passage from the Grayson Street building to a newly planned structure across the street. USAA would continue to study the various options for expansion and buy suitable land for it.

Satisfied employees translated into better service to the membership, and the enhanced work environment was an important factor. Especially appreciated was the air conditioning that made the office more comfortable than most employees' homes. The World War II experience at USAA also brought about a major and more satisfying change in the employees' salary structure. During the war, USAA had great difficulty in raising or adjusting salaries because USAA had no fixed structure. Jones recommended to the Board that USAA establish brackets and wage scales approximating those established by the Civil Service Commission. The existing ratio of salary to written premium was less than 8 percent, and the new one would be closer to nine. The Board concurred. The Board further approved salary increases not to exceed 10 percent of the total payroll in years 1951 and again in 1952. The employees now had increased pay and a structured salary system in place.

In addition to the pay increases, the Board approved half a month's salary each year as a Christmas bonus. In 1949, Jones had recommended that the year-end bonus be an out-and-out Christmas gift instead of having it tied to the company's expense ratio. The old way had gotten too complicated to administer because of new laws and the standard forty-hour work week. Also, a retirement plan was approved for employees with a maximum monthly retirement income set at $150 and a minimum of $20.

In spite of the improved benefits, it was becoming increasingly difficult for USAA to obtain and retain enough qualified and trained employees. In mid-1952, Jones reported that for the first time in the history of the Association, USAA had a personnel problem. Many USAA employees were leaving, and finding replacements was difficult. Factors in the losses included the improved economy, better pay available to USAA employees elsewhere in the community, and women who followed their husbands when they were transferred.

Although it involved problems and building expenses, USAA growth rates were reassuring to the USAA Board of Directors. The rising tide of automobile accidents and fatalities was not. The USAA *Annual Report* for 1950 spelled out the bad news. As of November 1950, automobiles, in their short history, had killed more Americans (442,970) than had died in every war the U.S. had been involved in starting with the Revolution and including casualties-to-date in Korea (439,151). At USAA, the growth in claims was outpacing the growth of membership, and the average cost per claim was beginning to rise precipitously.

USAA tried to educate its members about the dangers of driving. The annual reports to the members pointed out the main causes of accidents — speeding, running traffic lights and stop signs, carelessness in backing, following too closely and drinking. They focused on excessive speed as the prime cause for fatal accidents and illustrated this with a chart in the 1950 *Annual Report*. It concluded with a plea for all members to drive carefully and avoid accidents. The headquarters of the U.S. Coast Guard requested and received permission to reprint the chart on the opposit page in a publication going to all Coast Guard units.

The movement for State Financial Responsibility Laws gathered momentum in the face of the acceleration of accidents and the costs of these accidents. The first such laws had been enacted in New England in 1927, and other states followed suit. There were two ways for USAA to serve members in these states. One was to gain

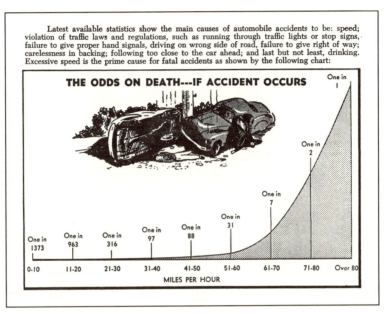

"The Odds on Death"

official status as a non-admitted carrier. In this way, USAA was not licensed, but appointed a state official to act on its behalf "as its true and lawful attorney." In the state of Alabama, for example, this was the Director of Public Safety. The Director then acted as the Agent of USAA "to receive and accept service of notice process in all motor vehicle accident cases and presented in the state of Alabama." Then the state would accept USAA's insurance policy as meeting the Financial Responsibility Law officially. The advantage for USAA as a "non-admitted carrier" was that it avoided taxes and most other regulatory procedures in states where USAA used this option. The principal disadvantage was that USAA could not serve its members directly in the state, but had to act through a third party.[32]

The second way for USAA to function in a state with a Financial Responsibility Law was to secure a license to operate in that state. By 1948, the Board's policy was to get "licensed" in such states when it was possible and desirable to do so.[33] Each state presented its own set of problems, and the USAA staff worked hard to solve them, often meeting with state officials. In the Territory of Hawaii, for example, the new Financial Responsibility Law would preclude USAA's policies from being recognized effective January 1, 1950. The Board decided to keep the goodwill of the membership there by applying for a license. Jones recommended that the Board send Cheever to make the arrangements.[34] Cheever left immediately and on December 21, the Insurance Commissioner of the Territory of Hawaii cabled USAA that its application was approved effective January 1, when the new law went into effect. The cable said that Cheever was "very helpful, constructive (about) your Association's qualification." Its cost to USAA would be a payment of a 2 ½ percent tax retroactive to all business ever written by USAA in Hawaii, plus a 6 percent delinquency fee from the date of delinquency. USAA decided that if it had to pay the tax, it would do so under protest. In any case, it secured a Hawaiian license. In almost every case, as states enacted new Financial Responsibility Laws, USAA senior managers Cheever, Eugene Waldron, and Max Wier Sr. went to each state to negotiate.

The state of New York was to be considerably more difficult. When USAA looked into the situation there, licensing seemed impossible. As a reciprocal, USAA would be required to file with the state a financial statement for each and every policyholder that guaranteed that the member was personally worth $10,000. Even if USAA could do this, it would only be permitted to write automobile insurance and would have to open an office in New York. Max Wier Jr. worked out a solution in late 1947. New York would accept certificates on behalf of members, if USAA would pay the costs to maintain them.

SERVICING AN EXPLODING MEMBERSHIP

Even though USAA agreed, the solution would not cover citizens of New York State.

Just a few months later, in 1948, the state of New York decided to renege on its agreement with Wier and enforce the letter of its law. Since USAA was not licensed in New York, the state would no longer accept Financial Responsibility Certificates from USAA. If New York members tried to provide one from USAA (an unlicensed company) the members would lose their operator's licenses.

Eugene Waldron

The only exception was USAA members' cars that bore Virginia or Texas license plates. This was because USAA was licensed to do business in those states and New York recognized their licensing. (A change to the Soldiers and Sailors Relief Act in 1948 permitted armed services personnel to retain the license plates issued by their home states.) The Board decided to cancel the liability insurance for members (other than those from Texas and Virginia) who were located in New York and to send them to a company that was licensed to do business in that state. USAA then notified the commanders at Mitchel Air Force Base and the Brooklyn Navy Yard.[35] The results were very unsatisfactory to the members who wanted to continue their membership.

The Board sent Cheever to New York to see what could be done. Cheever took along a letter of introduction from the Texas Insurance Commissioner which was very positive about USAA. Because of the New York Commissioner's unfamiliarity with reciprocals, the title "Attorney-in-Fact" had no meaning to him. Cheever solved this on the spot by introducing himself also as USAA's "General Counsel." Upon his return to San Antonio, the Board officially conferred this title on Cheever to assist him in New York and in other states.[36] When Cheever returned to New York, however, he made little progress; New York State law still did not recognize reciprocals. Next, Cheever found an attorney, Paul Taylor, who was willing to take USAA's case. Taylor developed a plan to try to amend the New York insurance law. The Board decided to give it a try and authorized a fee not to exceed $4,500.

In January 1949, Taylor was successful in getting the USAA amendment introduced in the legislature. In May, Jones reported to the USAA Board that both the Multiple Lines Bill and the Anderson Bill, which permitted the licensing of the Association in New York, had passed the New York State legislature and been signed by Governor Thomas E. Dewey. The next step was to apply for a license. It was during this process that Jones learned that USAA had to meet another requirement — a much larger reserve. USAA's existing reserve for unexpected claims was already $500,000, but it was not enough. USAA had a year to raise it to $950,000 with a minimum surplus of $1.675 million. The Board approved the arrangement, but decided to set the reserve at $1 million. At its August Board Meeting, the Directors changed the minimum surplus to $1.75 million. That was not to be the end, however. In 1951, New York revised its law again, forcing USAA to raise its Bodily Injury Liability Coverage from $5,000/$10,000 to $10,000/$20,000. USAA management notified the Board that it had raised the limits and would do so wherever else it was required. The Association was finally fully licensed to operate in the nation's most populous state.

Another facet of getting licensed to sell auto insurance in a particular state was the requirement for an insurance company to take assigned risks from that state. These were individuals who wanted insurance, but who in good faith had not been able to secure insurance elsewhere. (Under normal circumstances, they would not be eligible for membership and USAA would not insure them.) The first Assigned Risk Plan appeared in New Hampshire in 1938, and other states quickly followed the Granite State. In 1946, USAA received its first assigned risk from the state of Virginia, but it raised little concern. A more serious consideration for USAA was in California. In 1948, over 20 percent of USAA's members resided in California, and the Board decided that a California license was a must. It sent Mert Proctor and Stuart Gwyn to California to secure a license to do business there. One of the requirements for the California license turned out to be a financial Trojan horse — the Assigned Risk Plan. Proctor and Gwyn were told that USAA would only have to accept one risk assignment the first year. In subsequent years, the state would assign the number of risks in proportion to the number of policies USAA carried in the state. The USAA representatives tried to limit these risks to those eligible for USAA membership, but they were not successful. Although unenthusiastic about the California requirements, the Board decided to meet them and to change the bylaws to provide non-voting Associate Membership to assigned risks. The change was approved by the membership.

In 1950, the Association was forced to consider another change to the bylaws. The Association had made individuals assigned to USAA under Assigned Risk Plans Associate Members, but with no vote. Some states had declared this action illegal and USAA sought advice from the Texas Insurance Department. Its legal staff suggested that USAA rescind this bylaw at the next Members' Meeting. As of the 1950 Members' Meeting, all states (except Texas) where USAA had been licensed required USAA to join their Assigned Risk Plans. These states made up 40 percent of all USAA policies in force. In spite of over 90,000 policies issued, only about fifty assigned risks belonged to USAA, and none of these had yet submitted a claim. At the time, the assigned risk problem didn't look significant and the membership approved the change. The short-term result was that USAA had a small number of voting members who did not meet eligibility requirements. (By 1970, however, three percent of all USAA's insureds were assigned risks.) The following year, in 1951, the question arose whether Assigned Risks should receive dividends. The Board decided that they should, but less the extra expenses the Association spent in handling the risks.[37]

States continually changed rules and requirements across the nation, forcing USAA to react. For example, a new requirement for a California license was that a fidelity bond for attorneys-in-fact be $50,000 which could be filed with the Texas Insurance Commissioner. The Texas requirement was only $25,000, but the Texas Commissioner consented to accepting the increased bond for each of the attorneys-in-fact to help USAA satisfy the California requirement. A special requirement for a license in Maryland was for USAA to deposit $100,000 in cash or approved securities with the state of Texas. USAA complied by placing $100,000 in U.S. Treasury Bonds in escrow with the State Treasurer of Texas. This, along with the standard Power of Attorney requirement, resulted in Maryland granting a license to USAA to operate in Maryland.

The dynamics of state licensing occasionally led to changes in USAA products. The USAA Personal Accident policy was one example. USAA had first offered the policy in 1931 with the rationale that members who did not have easy access to military hospitals would use it. This turned out not to be the case. Most members apparently had access to the military medical system and did not purchase the policies. At the time USAA was applying for its California license, only 1,356 such policies were in force, and about one-third of those in California and Virginia. The Board learned that it would have to revise the Personal Accident policy drastically and put it under strict state control in order to comply with California and Virginia law. The small member demand for the policy made compliance with the state laws easy. The Board authorized management to discontinue writing these policies.

As 1952 was drawing to a close, the preliminary statistics indicated that USAA would have another great year. As it turned out, USAA that year wrote more business than any other in the Association's history. USAA showed a net gain of over 31,000 members and nearly a $3 million gain in net premiums written. That was about a 30 percent increase in both categories over 1951. Although net underwriting expenses to net premiums written rose, it still was a very respectable 12.6 percent.

So it was with satisfaction that at seventy-five years of age Jones announced at the Board of Directors meeting on November 19 his intention to retire at the end of the year. He told the Board that the contracts of all three attorneys-in-fact would expire on December 31, and he did not intend to renew. That left Mert Proctor and Charles Cheever remaining. Jones formally moved that the older Proctor be appointed as his replacement and that Cheever be moved up to the number-two position. For the third attorney, he nominated Navy Captain E. M. Waldron. All contracts were to be for five years.

Mert Proctor

After considerable discussion, the Board decided to hold a special meeting of the Board of Directors on December 3 for the specific purpose of electing the new USAA management team. On the appointed day, the Board met. First, it established the salaries of the three attorneys-in-fact at

$15,000, $12,0000, and $10,000 per year. It also increased the amount paid to Board members to $25 per meeting attended. Next, Colonel "Jack" Keyes nominated Proctor, Cheever, and Waldron for the three positions under consideration — in the same order as in Jones's original nomination. The procedure was for each Board member to vote for the officer he wished to fill each of the three positions. The vote was announced as follows:

Election Results for the Position of Secretary-Treasurer

	Proctor	Cheever	Waldron
Secretary-Treasurer	3	10	–
1st Assistant Secretary-Treasurer	10	3	–
2nd Assistant Secretary-Treasurer	–	–	13

Cheever was USAA's new Secretary-Treasurer, General Manager, and Attorney-in-Fact. Proctor was his principal assistant and Waldron the new 2nd Assistant Secretary-Treasurer. The Board had rejected Jones's recommendation and had selected Cheever, at fifty-five years of age, as USAA's new Chief Executive Officer. Jones accepted the will of the Board gracefully and then submitted his previously announced resignation from the Board. USAA would continue with experienced leadership following the years under "Deacon" Jones.

CHAPTER FIVE

MODERNIZING THE ASSOCIATION — A BEGINNING

In late 1951, a young Naval officer had a series of auto accidents resulting in cancellation of his insurance and, therefore, his USAA membership. About sixteen months later, the officer wrote to USAA to request his reinstatement. He acknowledged his responsibility for the accidents and stated they were "principally due to his way of life as a bachelor officer." He wrote that he was now married and "settled down." His case was discussed at the weekly Executive Committee meeting. The Committee met each Wednesday afternoon in the Home Office on Grayson Street to discuss problems of individual members. Some cases were debated for up to fifteen minutes; most deliberations resulted in insurance cancellations for sound reasons. The Committee did not just consider cases by the numbers, but attempted to do what was best for both the member and the Association. In this case, the Committee believed the Lieutenant had learned his lesson and would make a good officer and a good member.[1]

This level of service, when combined with other factors, led to continuing growth. As 1953 opened, the surging growth threatened to overwhelm USAA and its service ethic. This was to be one of the central challenges for USAA's new General Manager, Charles Cheever. Cheever had participated in the deliberations on this young officer and hundreds of others as well in his years, so far, at USAA. Under his mentorship, he was determined to have USAA continue to serve individuals and the membership as a whole as USAA moved towards its new status as a major U.S. company.

Charles Emmett Cheever was born on January 5, 1898, in Boston, Massachusetts. He lived in Beacon Hill near Boston Common

A Tradition Of Service

and went through the Boston public school system. At Mechanic Arts High School, he was a good student and played baseball, football, and hockey. After graduation, he studied law for a year at Suffolk University Law School in Boston, but did not complete the program.

Cheever's first paying job was as a part-timer at the Old West Church branch of the Boston Public Library. On Sundays he worked at the main public library on Copley Square. The pay was only twenty cents an hour, but he received an unexpected dividend from his employment. It was through a librarian he knew at the Boston Public Library that he first met Elizabeth "Betty" Daley. Although Cheever had serious intentions almost from the start, Betty was in no rush to get married.

Charles Cheever as a young man

His first acquaintance with the military way of life was as a civilian in the Army Quartermaster Corps. While a teenager and still in high school, he took a competitive examination for a clerk position with the Army. He did well, scoring 37th out of 900 candidates. In 1916, when Pancho Villa attacked Columbus, New Mexico, a major Mexican border crisis erupted. The Army called Cheever into service as a civilian employee and assigned him to the Army Quartermaster Depot in Boston. The crisis quickly passed, however, and the Army released him. Because of his clerking experience in the Army, the Holtzer-Cabot Electric Company hired him to work in its stockroom. The work was not too demanding, but Cheever had the opportunity to observe a modern manufacturing plant operate under enlightened management.

During Cheever's time at Holtzer-Cabot, the newspapers were filled with accounts of the rising tensions between the United States and Germany. Unrestricted submarine warfare was driving the two nations to the brink of war. When German U-boats sank five U.S. vessels on the heels of the release of the Zimmerman Telegram, Wilson urged Congress to declare war.[2] On April 2, 1917, America was officially at war, and the war changed Cheever's life. In May, the Army recalled Cheever as a civilian employee and assigned him to its Northeastern Department Headquarters. He observed the Army's line and staff organization with interest. Its emphasis on delegation of authority particularly intrigued him and would shape his own ideas of management years later.

Within months, Cheever's energy and hard work won him a promotion to Army Field Clerk (similar to a Warrant Officer). In spite of his youth, the Army put him in charge of the mail and records section of the Adjutant General's Office. Cheever led the twenty-man section with distinction. Impressed by his ability to supervise these more mature individuals, others encouraged him to apply for a commission and overseas duty. Unfortunately for Cheever's aspirations, the Chief Clerk of the Headquarters regarded Cheever as too valuable and blocked his attempts to leave.

In 1921, Cheever tried again for a commission and succeeded, gaining an appointment as a Second Lieutenant in the Quartermaster Corps. After completing Quartermaster School in Philadelphia, he was first assigned to Fort Williams, Maine, and then to Fort Hamilton in Brooklyn, New York. While stationed in Brooklyn, he pursued a law degree at New York University in his off-duty time. He earned his LL.B. degree in 1925 and his LL.M. degree in 1926. Although he continued his quartermaster duties, his law degrees gave him the opportunity to occasionally serve as defense counsel and trial judge advocate (prosecutor) as additional military duties. He did so well in his legal work that, when he left Fort Hamilton,

A Tradition Of Service

the Staff Judge Advocate for the 1st Infantry Division there commended Cheever for his outstanding efforts.

In 1927, Cheever attempted to transfer to the Infantry Branch, but the Army turned him down because of a shortage of qualified Quartermaster officers. Cheever's next orders to the Philippines provided the impetus to get married. After about ten years of dating, when Betty realized he was leaving the country, she finally agreed to get married. The ceremony was on May 17, 1927, in Boston, and the young couple was then transferred to Fort McKinley in the Philippines and then to Fort Washington, Maryland. They would spend close to sixty years together as man and wife.[3] When he arrived in the Philippines, he learned that he was to run the cooks and bakers school for the Far East. As he could barely boil water, he found an outstanding NCO to help. Cheever always seemed to have the knack to surround himself with good people. In 1932, he was detailed to the Office of the Judge Advocate General of the Army in Washington. In every assignment, Cheever received high praise from his superiors. When he completed the Army Industrial College as an honor graduate in 1935, General Douglas MacArthur, then Chief of Staff of the Army, took note of Cheever's exceptional performance. He wrote that in spite of his outstanding record, his rank as only a lieutenant would preclude his selection for Army War College at that time. MacArthur continued:

USAA member General Douglas MacArthur on a visit to San Antonio. *(Courtesy of Institute of Texan Cultures)*

I hope . . . that later on I may have the pleasure of seeing you in the class at the Army War College. It is such outstanding work as yours at the Army Industrial College that will mean so much to the Service if we are ever engaged in another major emergency.[4]

In August of 1935, Cheever requested and received a permanent transfer to the Department of the Judge Advocate General. In 1936, he served his first tour of duty as a Staff Judge Advocate at Fort Sam Houston in San Antonio, where he met both General Hinds and Colonel White of USAA. The Cheevers often walked in the evening, and they soon decided that the area could use a bank. Knowing little about banking, the Cheevers went to the library and read everything they could about the subject. With Betty's solid encouragement, Cheever went to work. He had everything in order to establish the Broadway Bank before leaving for his next tour of duty, on the West Point faculty teaching law. The bank actually opened for business in 1941 with a total capitalization of $65,000. Part of the money was from stock sold to Cheever's fellow officers, although he would buy the stock back during the war years when they became concerned about their investment. Academy Cadet Robert McDermott had Cheever as an instructor for a short course on the Uniform Code of Military Justice. McDermott remembered the soft-spoken Cheever as an excellent instructor.

Major Charles Cheever as an instructor at the United States Military Academy.

In 1942, Cheever returned to legal duties at Sherman, Texas, while assigned to the X Corps, commanded by General Courtney H. Hodges. After his promotion to colonel, Cheever was assigned to

A Tradition Of Service

the Third Army at Fort Sam Houston. In early 1944, he accompanied the Third Army to England. There he served as Staff Judge Advocate to General George Patton and was responsible for legal assistance to the Third's 300,000 troops. Prior to the D-Day Invasion, Cheever wrote a ten-page booklet called the *Soldier's Handbook on the Rules of Land Warfare* which included an explanation of the Geneva Convention. This pamphlet was distributed throughout the Army.

Nothing in the Geneva Convention or the handbook prepared Cheever and the troops for what they were to find at Dachau and other German concentration camps, however. During the Third Army's five campaigns in Europe, beginning at Normandy, Cheever performed yeoman duty for Patton. Cheever routinely conferred with Patton on serious court-martial decisions. Over the course of the war, Cheever's staff expanded from nine to seventy-two officers

Colonel Charles Cheever at the Eagle's Nest — Adolf Hitler's home in the Bavarian Alps

and men.⁵ For his distinguished wartime service, Cheever earned the Legion of Merit with one Oak Leaf Cluster, the Bronze Star, and three Croix de Guerre with Palme from France, Belgium, and Luxembourg.

After the war, Cheever received his most demanding assignment as a human being. He was responsible for all preparations and arrangements for the war crimes trials to be held at Dachau. Cheever already was a man who was sensitive to others; this experience would stay with him the rest of his life. He would never discuss this chapter of his life with anyone. The only outward signs of its affect were his strong support of the National Council of Christians and Jews and an increased sensitivity to others.⁶

In 1946, the Army reassigned Cheever to be the Staff Judge Advocate of the Fourth U.S. Army at Fort Sam Houston. There he re-

Concentration camp survivors. *(Courtesy of the National Archives)*

newed his friendship with Artie White, then USAA's Secretary-Treasurer, who nominated Cheever to the USAA Board of Directors. After White's death, the Board selected Cheever as the number-three man at USAA effective upon his retirement in April 1948. In the meantime, Cheever was serving on the Board of the Broadway Bank, and on April 1, 1945, he had been elected Chairman of the Bank's Board.

Cheever brought to USAA experience in business, banking, and law. He had been an accomplished leader and manager throughout his adult life. He was very energetic and willing, if not eager, to try new things. Perhaps more important, Cheever was gregarious and had a warm and friendly personality. His sensitivity to the feelings of others was obvious and he never missed an opportunity to greet an employee with genuine warmth and respect. He knew their first names and their families and cheerfully joined any employee at lunch. Employees responded to him with affection and worked harder than ever for the Association.

He also had the reputation for being very careful with money, probably because of his struggle during the Great Depression. Cheever's trip to Europe to begin USAA's insurance program there provided examples of his thrift. Because of the urgency of the situation, the Board told Cheever to use cable for communication — which he did. He followed up one cable with a letter to Colonel Jones in which he explained why he did not address the cable to Jones personally. After all, he explained, "they charge for every word in the address" and it would have added two words to the cost of the telegram. He also rented a major's personal car at a cut-rate price — $1.50 per day and 2¢ a mile. "Pretty good deal!" wrote Cheever.[7] Fortunately for USAA employees, he did not insist on his thrifty ways when dealing with them concerning pay and benefits.

During Cheever's years at USAA, he was to guide its development into a modern company. One of Cheever's first actions as president was to provide USAA with a facility designed to handle future growth. In April 1953, he pointed out to the Board that the Association was servicing 170,000 policies as of the end of 1952 — an increase of 30 percent over the previous year. The projection for 1953 was another 58,000. Based on the potential eligible members, USAA could gain 50,000 policies per year for the next five years! To handle this workload, Cheever estimated the Association would need an increase of 18,000 square feet per year. By 1957, USAA would need 150,000 square feet and another 56,000 by 1960.

USAA had already planned on three new and separate additions to USAA's existing facility on Grayson Street and had bought neighboring property to make it possible. The overall construction costs for the additions would run about $20 per square foot for the three planned projects. Cheever pointed out that such additions normally meant remodeling of the existing structure to accommodate them. Besides the actual construction costs, hidden costs included lowered operating efficiency due to noise, dust, and moving desks. In addition, during previous USAA modifications, wasted space proliferated, absenteeism rose, and frayed nerves lowered cooperation among employees. Cheever estimated a 10 percent loss in productivity or a cost of about $250,000 over the eighteen months of construction. If the Board decided to modify rather than build new, USAA would also have had to add more space — possibly building an annex in a separate building near the existing Grayson Street site within three years.

Cheever's preferred initial solution was to build a new 150,000 square-foot building in a new location. The consulting architect estimated that the cost would run about $14 per square foot, or a little over $2 million. Land for the building site and parking would run another half million dollars. Proper design would result in an additional 15,000 feet of usable space through reduction of wasted passageways and aisles. It would also permit the most cost-efficient operation of air conditioning, heating, and other utilities. By proper planning, easy and efficient future expansion could be made possible by including in the original design adequate foundations and columns for support of additional floors. Cheever estimated that the cost of bringing the existing building to 150,000 square feet would be a little over $2 million. When he included savings for additional usable space gained in the proposed building and the sale of the existing building, he estimated the cost of the new building would save the Association more than $100,000. He concluded by noting that USAA had sufficient reserves to finance the new building. Along with his briefing, Cheever shared comments on his plan from the firm of Carniero, Chumney, & Company, Certified Public Accountants. The firm concurred with Cheever's recommendations.

Carniero also offered some comments on financing the construction. The firm advised USAA to reduce member savings by 2 percent immediately and by 3 percent the following year to make the project financially feasible. It noted that USAA carried the Grayson Street Home Office on its books for $1.25 million. The projected resale price was $500,000. Unless USAA reserved the additional money for the projected loss from the reduced dividends, the surplus would have to be seriously reduced. Hopefully, increased efficiencies in the future could result in returning these dividends to the members.[8]

The Board agreed with Cheever's recommendations and appointed a committee chaired by USAA President Brigadier General Alexander Ovenshine to look for a suitable site. Ovenshine's committee recommended the site be a minimum of ten acres to accommodate future requirements. It noted that about an equal number of employees used private autos and bus service, and that convenient access to both was essential. The committee suggested that the site should be in the part of the city convenient to the employees that USAA hired — and 60 percent of them lived in the northern half of the city. Generally speaking, low-cost properties around the city were not acceptable because they did not meet the committee's criteria.

The Ovenshine committee looked at various sites in San Antonio. One location in the southeastern part of the city that had favorable topographical features was just north of Brooks Air Force Base. The downside was no public utilities, the nearest bus twelve blocks away, and no restaurants available. In the northeast quadrant of the city, the committee found a ten-acre site for $150,000 at the intersection of San Pedro and Jackson-Keller Road. Although on the "extreme north edge of a good population center," it had no nearby restaurants and the nearest bus service was four blocks away. The committee's final recommendation was a ten-acre property at the intersection of Broadway and Hildebrand Avenue that had belonged to San Antonio surgeon and Mexican expatriate Doctor Aurelio Urrutia. Although the asking price was $500,000, the property was well-located, with nearby restaurants, city utilities, and excellent improvements on adjacent properties. The selling price was high, but the committee felt it was not excessive considering the long-range potential growth of USAA.[9]

The Board discussed the Ovenshine Committee report at length at its May 20 meeting. After discussion of all the sites, the Board decided that the San Pedro site was too risky because the surrounding property had not been developed. The Board was unsure whether there would be future building in the area, and finally settled on the Dr. Urrutia property on Broadway. Management was authorized to acquire not less than ten acres of the property for not more than $500,000. The Board also decided to follow the Carniero firm's advice, and it reduced member savings by 2 percent to protect the Association's surplus.

At the next Board meeting, Cheever had good news. It looked like USAA would be able to purchase the Urrutia property for about $362,000. Further, engineers had favorable results from test borings on the property to determine if the foundations were suitable for the new proposed buildings. At the following Board meeting, Cheever announced that the National Bank of Fort Sam Houston had purchased part of the property USAA had been holding for expansion near Grayson Street. The Board then authorized management to sell the current Home Office Building on Grayson with the understanding it would not be vacated until USAA moved its operations to Broadway. The sale took much longer than hoped, however. Not until 1959 did the Fourth U.S. Army purchase the building for an annex to its Fort Sam Houston Quadrangle headquarters at a price of $525,000.

In July, the Board authorized Cheever to contract with the firms of Phelps and Dewees and Simmons, and Atlee B. and Robert M. Ayres for the planning, designing, engineering, and supervision of construction of the new Home Office Building for a fee of 6 percent. Both firms were local and had excellent experience. Ayres and Ayres had designed the administration buildings at Randolph Field, the Municipal Airport, the Municipal Auditorium, and an addition to the Menger Hotel. The Phelps firm had designed the San Antonio College buildings, the First National Bank, the USAF Security building at Kelly Field, and the Texas State Tuberculosis Hospital. The Board believed it would get better service and performance from proven local firms than from a firm outside of San Antonio.[10] USAA would profit from the Phelps firm's excellence in functional planning and economy, and the Ayres firm's excellence in designing beautiful exteriors, lobbies, and interiors. The two firms had written to Cheever that they had worked together well in the past and would do so on the USAA project.[11]

Following the approval to go ahead with the recommended architects, Cheever and his Second Assistant Attorney-in-Fact, Eugene Waldron, visited various new business buildings to look for features worth incorporating in USAA's new facility. These included

Modernizing The Association

the Pan American Life Building in New Orleans, the GEICO building in Washington, D.C., and the Dunn and Bradstreet Building in New York. Based on these visits, one major decision Cheever made was to add a cafeteria to the plans. At the December 1953 Board meeting, Cheever showed the architect's model of the new Home Office Building. The proposed building would be six stories high and include a wing for a cafeteria. He briefed the Board that the cafeteria's cost of $350,000 would repay itself many times over in improved efficiency. Just an increase of a conservative 5 percent in efficiency would put USAA well ahead on the investment.

In his briefing, Cheever reminded the Board that the preliminary estimate for the building was $14 per square foot. The final estimate was $15.90 per square foot or a cost of about $3.6 million. He pointed out that *"the money in the building was part of the reserves that have to be maintained anyway"* and would not be available for distribution to members whether or not USAA invested the money in the building. Further, he urged the Board to consider that rentals in new air-conditioned buildings, like the one he proposed, leased for about $4 per square foot annually. USAA would be getting a great return by building its own rather than by leasing some other company's investment.[12] The Board agreed, and authorized Cheever to proceed with the construction at a cost not to exceed $4 million. Later, the Board even briefly considered leasing office space in the new building to others as a source of income. As construction proceeded, many changes in scope increased the size to eight floors and an increased cost of the building. At last, however, the big day arrived.

In early May of 1956, Frank Kerford directed the move from Grayson Street to Broadway. It took Central Moving and Storage Company three days to move the 175 van loads of furniture and equipment. Outside hoists as well as the internal elevators moved the pieces in place over the eight stories. On Thursday, May 24,

USAA held the formal dedication and ribbon cutting of its new building, which eventually cost about $6 million.

This was followed by an open house for business associates on Friday and an open house for employees' families and friends on Saturday. The facility, constructed by the Henry Beck Construction

USAA founder William Henry Garrison Jr. and Charles Cheever at the dedication of the USAA Building.

Company of Dallas, was impressive. The *San Antonio News* published a long feature about USAA's new showplace. It started off:

> Situated on an artistically landscaped 10-acre tract adjacent to beautiful Brackenridge Park, the nine-story structure rises impressively from its quiet surroundings — a dazzling giant of glass, marble and aluminum.[13]

One of the largest air-conditioned buildings in the Southwest, the new USAA Home Office contained 264,000 square feet. It

USAA's Home Office Building on Broadway

boasted elevators and escalators that moved passengers from the ground to the seventh floor at 120 feet per minute. Electric-eye doors into the main work areas, an auditorium with seating for 218, and a cafeteria that would seat 900 people were features that excited the visitors. Two well-equipped classrooms were designed specifically for USAA training programs.

The *San Antonio News* noted that the business efficiency was matched by the decor. It pointed out that "the interior was designed with an eye to the more than 800 women who work there." Vivid coral, yellow, and turquoise blended with the soft-green and beige "in the soothing, well-planned color scheme carried throughout the building."[14] Parking for 425 and terraced gardens set off the outside of the Home Office. In the welcome brochure passed out at the opening, Cheever put the new structure in perspective:

A TRADITION OF SERVICE

As proud as we are of our new Home Office Building, we are more proud of the men and women who made it possible — our assureds and our employees.

The USAA employees were very proud of their new building. Frances Moore recalled that the building looked enormous to them. It seemed that "the employees couldn't walk the length of it without falling down with exhaustion," and it took them about two weeks to get adjusted. They loved the cafeteria and "the food was great."[15] Laverne Hanks said that the cafeteria was so lovely that many people in the city did lease it to have parties in the building.[16] (The Board had approved public use because the projected loss for the cafeteria was $25,000 in 1956.)

USAA management was very sensitive to the employees and their contributions to USAA and worked to make them happy and pro-

The cafeteria in the Broadway Building

ductive. Of great concern was employee turnover, which rose higher than 100 percent in the early fifties. Competitive salaries were critical, but the annual inflation controls placed on increasing salaries by the Federal Wage and Price Stabilization Board made it difficult. The USAA Board of Directors raised the salaries of top management to a competitive level by granting two raises at the same Board meeting — one effective on December 1, 1952, and the second on February 1, 1953. For the other employees, the Board authorized management to raise the salaries as long as the overall increases did not exceed 10 percent of the payroll.

The raises had an immediate impact on employee morale. Even though the volume of business steadily increased, the Association did not need to add new employees to the work force, and still kept up with the workload. Their positive feelings reflected in personnel statistics. The use of sick leave declined rapidly from 781 days in January 1953, before the raises went into effect, to 424 days in February, and 347 in March. In addition, employee time in the First Aid Room declined by 50 percent.[17] Incidentally, later USAA had a nurse who visited sick employees at their homes if they were out more than three days. The genuinely sick appreciated the gesture, but malingerers obviously did not like the practice.

It was evident to Cheever that he needed someone of broad experience in personnel to assist him — and he wanted a woman. He was already impressed with the women at USAA, and the Ashley Montagu book, *The Natural Superiority of Women* (1952), had a great impact on his thinking. Waldron began a search and found Jean Moye working at General Electric in New York, where Moye was the Assistant to the Manager of Employee Relations. A native of Albany, New York, she graduated from the College of St. Rose and attended the School of Labor and Industrial Relations at Cornell University. She had experience with a work force at GE that grew from 300 to over 6,000 with all the attendant problems. She loved her job, but felt that the USAA opportunity would be good for her. Also, she thought that the San Antonio weather would be good for her young son, who suffered from bronchitis. At $5,000, her new salary was slightly less than her current salary, but she thought that the long-term potential at USAA was far better.

When Moye arrived at Grayson Street for work, she felt like she "was walking backwards through time." Training, employment standards, the caliber of the work force, supervisor development, and the benefits program were way behind contemporary standards. When Moye went to the First Aid Room, she asked the Licensed Vocational Nurse how she spent most of her time assisting the employees. The reply stunned Moye. "I spend most of my time giving high colonic enemas and henna hair jobs," the LVN said.[18] If Moye had doubts before, she knew now that she had her work cut out for her. In looking around, she noted very few employees of Mexican origin. She found that supervisors often wrote on the face of the forms used for personnel hiring requisitions "no Mexicans please." She halted that practice at once and the numbers of employees of Mexican ethnic background grew rapidly.[19] With the approval of Cheever and the Board, she developed a wide range of programs including salary administration, pre-employment screening, a bi-weekly pay schedule, and orientation of new employees to improve the work force and its productivity. June Reedy received USAA's first maternity leave in 1955. In earlier years, a woman had to resign when she began to "show." Another benefits improvement was the charter of USAA's

Jean Moye

Modernizing The Association

Federal Credit Union in 1955. Beulah Frees was its first president. The two-year improvements were so impressive that the American Management Association made a paper by Waldron and Moye describing the personnel modernization the subject of a special meeting in Atlanta in 1956.

In 1955, the issue of salaries came up again. The USAA clerks earned 87½ cents per hour, but Congress raised the minimum wage to $1 per hour. Because of this and competition for employees by various federal institutions and companies throughout the city, USAA was losing a considerable number of typists, IBM machine operators, and others. The Board authorized Cheever to raise the USAA clerks' wages to $1 per hour and everyone else's wages at the same time. The raises ranged from 8 to 14.29 percent, pushing the payroll up close to another 10 percent. In addition, the Board continued to grant a half-month's salary each Christmas and gave employees half a day off to shop. It was a terrific benefit for the employees — and for the city merchants. A brief news item and cartoon in the *San Antonio Light* says it all.

Tip to San Antonio merchants: Better put on some extra clerks the afternoon of Dec. 1. That's when all those gals at the United Services Automobile assn., some 900 strong, get their annual half day off to go Christmas shopping.

San Antonio Light, November 23, 1955. *(Courtesy of San Antonio Express News)*

A Tradition Of Service

To keep up with the workload, USAA continually added new employees. Board member Colonel Edward Keyes was concerned about the number of men USAA was hiring. He noted that USAA's previous policy had been to place women in all the executive and administrative positions, except for the three attorneys-in-fact and the claims attorney. He wanted to know how many men were employed and "whether or not the morale of the women employees had been adversely affected by the employment of men." Cheever told the Board that as of March 15, 1955, USAA had less than fifteen male employees and that "in his opinion no morale problem had been created" as a result of their employment.[20] Promotion of males over females did not go down easily, however. Some managers did have a concern about productivity — perhaps with tongue-in-cheek. Maurine McFarland gave Charles Weeber his orientation after she hired him. She told him he was to go from the parking lots directly to his desk, and that he was not to go on the second or third floors. When he asked why, she told him that there were only women on those floors. And every time a man went up there, the whole floor lost ten minutes work time.[21]

Hiring more people was not enough. Exposure to modern management techniques and improved ways of handling business was critical if USAA managers were to succeed at guiding their employees. Professional associations like the National Association of Independent Insurers (NAII) and the National Association of Insurance Commissioners enabled Cheever to stay abreast of his peers in the insurance industry. He was on the NAII Board of Governors for fifteen years and president of the organization in 1956 and 1957. His fellow CEOs had great respect for him. He also attended a course for presidents held by the American Management Association at Colgate University at Hamilton, New York. On occasion he also spoke about USAA at such places as the Harvard Business School. The Association's officers attended seminars given by the Ameri-

Modernizing The Association

can Management Association in their areas of responsibility, including personnel administration, clerical standards, and the treasurer's function. Some attended technical courses on the IBM 650 computer at Endicott, New York. This was in addition to the in-house training programs for many employees begun by Moye.

When Cheever had briefed the Board in April 1953 about the need for a new building, he projected an increase of 58,000 members for 1953 and 50,000 more annually for the next five years. Based on the potential future eligibles and the growth rate in 1953, his projections looked good. In fact, 1953 turned out to be enormously successful. USAA added over 45,000 members for a growth rate of 34.31 percent. Policies in force expanded almost 34 percent and premiums written rose nearly 44 percent to almost $19 million. USAA ran half-page notices in various publications touting the Association's success. While USAA was proud of its success, the main reason for the costly notices was to counteract any adverse publicity the Association might receive because of mistaken identity with two insurers in El Paso, Texas, that had gone into receivership in 1953. The names "United Lloyd's" and "United Services Underwriters" might be close enough to confuse some members.

Possibly misleading to Cheever's growth projections was the continuing Korean War and the election of President Dwight David Eisenhower. As he was a retired general and a Republican, one might have expected increased military forces. This was not to be the case. Eisenhower had a commitment to "maintain a long view of the Cold War, hoarding national resources, and restraining militarization." He viewed disarmament as necessary because he believed that no country could advance intellectually and culturally if it had to devote everything to military buildup.[22]

Eisenhower was true to his beliefs. The total active-duty strength of 3.6 million in 1953 fell more than a million by the time Eisenhower completed his presidency. The active-duty officer

USAA member Dwight Eisenhower addressing USAA employees, October 30, 1961

strength was reduced from about 354,000 in 1953 to about 315,000 by 1961. This reduced USAA's potential pool of new members considerably and contributed to USAA's annual growth rate of less than 7 percent by 1960. The growth in the USAA employees' workload continued to climb, however. For example, in 1955 Stuart Gwyn reported to the Board that transactions in underwriting alone increased almost 26 percent over the previous year. The installation of a new IBM 650 computer eliminated operations in coding and rating, enabling the same number of employees to produce 50 percent more work. This, and the reorganization of the auto policy department into eight geographic units to simplify training, were two significant efforts to keep up with the growth.

Although the rate of growth steadily declined after the record-setting year in 1953, the numbers of new members were still very significant. Over 40,000 joined each year in 1954 and 1955, and an average of about 25,000 became members annually through the end of the decade. Those growth statistics were good and positive. Nevertheless, USAA continued to market the Association in a variety of ways.

USAA had always depended heavily, but not completely, on word-of-mouth advertising to encourage new members to join. From the earliest days, USAA advertised in several military publications, and in the 1950s, some ads included coupons for the first time. A drawing of Cheever was included in one of the ads.

In 1951, the Association also began sending letters to cadets in ROTC units. The Professors of Military Science and Tactics agreed to USAA's request and distributed the letters to the cadets in class. The Association also included a prepaid postcard with the *Annual Report* to solicit members for Household and Personal Effects World-Wide Insurance, Comprehensive Personal Liability Insurance, and Auto Insurance. Cheever reported to the Board that the effort with the 1958 *Annual Report* was "most gratifying." The Association received almost 20,000 inquiries for household goods and personal effects, over 26,000 for personal liability, and 1,367 for automobile insurance. Mixing member education and marketing, USAA mailed an updated version of McDermott's *Principles of Insurance* to all members in 1959.

USAA was always eager to sign up cadets at the service academies. Cheever told the Board that it was very important to insure the majority of the First Class upon graduation. When the West Point Class Committee Insurance Representative for the class of 1957 requested USAA send someone to talk with his class, Charlotte Hildebrandt of USAA's recently opened New York City office, and Helen Wallace, an underwriter helping her out, traveled to West Point. Wallace talked to about 100 cadets and was asked to return again. She thought these visits were advantageous to the Association because a GEICO representative had already traveled to West Point. The Naval Academy turned down a USAA offer to brief the

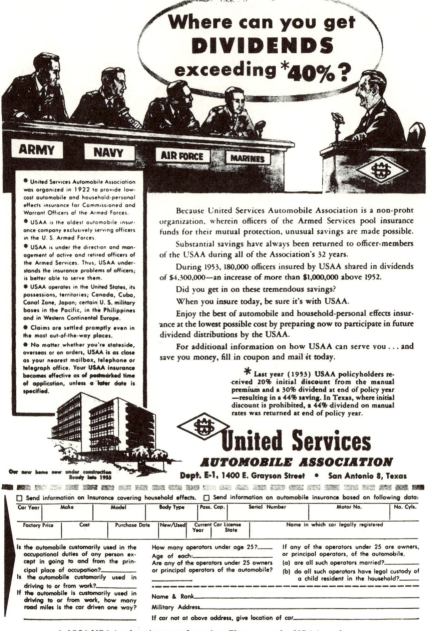

A 1954 USAA advertisement featuring Cheever as the USAA spokesman

MODERNIZING THE ASSOCIATION

Aerial view of the United States Coast Guard Academy. *(Courtesy of United States Coast Guard Academy)*

midshipmen, but the representative told Captain Waldron that "practically all the graduating midshipmen would probably insure with USAA."[23] And, when USAA received a request from the Naval Academy Athletic Association to contribute to the Navy-Marine Corps Memorial Stadium in Annapolis, it did. The Association donated $1,000 for a memorial plaque in the name of USAA and noted in the Board minutes that "this contribution be considered as advertising."[24] By 1959, USAA representatives were visiting West Point, Annapolis, and the U.S. Coast Guard Academy to try to interest the potential officers in the Association.

Marketing helped fire the growth that was pushing USAA toward modernizing its whole operation. The new USAA office building on Broadway was symbolic of changes taking place at USAA. The metamorphosis of USAA's organizational structure into that of a modern company had begun in 1954. USAA's application for a license in Maryland was held up when the Insurance Commissioner objected to USAA's practice of operating and functioning through three apparently equal attorneys-in-fact, rather than one. The Board satisfied the Commissioner by directing that "only the Secretary-Treasurer shall act as the Attorney-in-Fact for the subscribers."[25] Mert Proctor and Waldron would perform the attorney-in-fact function only when Cheever was not available, and each was to be called "Assistant General Manager."

The more dramatic structural changes had evolved out of a discussion of attorney-in-fact retirements in November 1955. Retired Army Colonel Neill E. Bailey, Board member and chairman of the committee studying retirements, made a number of recommendations. Included in the recommendations were a 2 ½ percent per year retirement income and mandatory retirement at age sixty-five, unless precluded by an existing contract. The Board concurred. Then, retired Army Brigadier General Rex E. Chandler raised a question. If it were wise to require an attorney-in-fact to retire at sixty-five because his age affected his executive capabilities, shouldn't the mandatory requirement at that age apply to directors and officers too?

After a general discussion, the Board members decided that they could not make such decisions without changes to the bylaws. The Board voted to have the president appoint a committee to look into the bylaws and to suggest any necessary revisions to the Board. Ovenshine appointed Bailey to be the chairman and two active-duty officers, Air Force Brigadier General Cecil E. Combs and Army Colonel Lawrence J. Lincoln, to assist. At the December Board meeting, the Bailey Committee reported back.

The committee proposed sweeping organizational changes through revision of the bylaws. Its first proposal was to change the existing president position to a chairman of the board position. The vice president's position would become the vice chairman's position. The president (now Ovenshine) of the Association had never held active managerial duties at the Association, but rather presided as chairman at meetings of the Board of Directors and the Executive Committee. His first and second vice presidents served in his absence.

The committee pointed out that the managing officer in most modern businesses was the president. At USAA, the general manager, and managing officer (now Cheever), was also secretary-treasurer. The proposal was to establish a new and different position of president, which would be held by Cheever as the managing officer. Further, the proposal included splitting the secretary-treasurer's position into two positions, both to be held by USAA vice presidents reporting directly to the president. The president, as the managing officer of the Association, would also be a member of the Board of Directors. The Board would appoint all Association officers, and the membership would elect the Directors.

The committee recommended that the Association eliminate the requirement that a Director reside in Bexar County, the location of the Home Office. This restriction limited the pool of potential Directors and gave USAA a provincial look. Also, it recommended that Directors no longer serve past the age of seventy. Elected Directors would serve four years, and two years upon reelection. Their tenure would be limited by allowing only 50 percent of the whole board to serve continuously. Current Board members would be grandfathered. Active-duty officers who retired could complete their terms, but could not be reelected. Their "active-duty" slots could be filled only by other active-duty officers. The committee recommended this to prevent the number of active-duty officers from falling below the current number of three out of thirteen total Directors. The Directors would elect the chairman of USAA from its own ranks. The Executive Committee then would be composed of the chairman, vice chairman, and president.

With minor revisions, the Board voted to accept the committee's report and to place the bylaws' changes before the membership. At the June 20, 1956, Annual Members' Meeting, the changes passed by a wide majority. USAA's organizational structure now reflected contemporary business practices.

Immediately after the Members' Meeting, the Board placed names and faces to titles and positions. The Board elected Bailey, eighty-one, as USAA's first Chairman of the Board and Colonel Edward A. Keyes as the initial first Vice-Chairman. The Board appointed Cheever as USAA's President, Colonel Mert Proctor as Vice President and Treasurer, and Captain Eugene M. Waldron as Vice President. It appointed Consuelo Kerford as Secretary. As such, she became USAA's first woman officer. Although she did not receive the title of vice president because she was not military, she received the same pay as Waldron.[26]

When Bailey died less than three months later, retired Army Brigadier General Rex E. Chandler was elected the new USAA Chairman by a scant margin. Born in Missouri, Chandler was a 1923 graduate from West Point. Most of his career was spent in the Artillery Branch and he served in World War II combat in the Pacific with distinction. In 1947, he received a physical disability retirement in San Antonio as a result of his service in the Pacific. A West Point classmate recalled that he was an innovator in the Army and a cartoonist whose work revealed a pointed, but light wit that conveyed a serious message. On the USAA Board, however, he was direct and to-the-point with management on a variety of issues.

The change making the president the responsible manager of USAA began a shift of power away from the Board, and Chandler did not like it. For years, the *Annual Report* had been approved by the Board of Directors in detail, but had been signed by the general manager. In February 1957, when the *Annual Report* for 1956 came up for Board review, Chandler objected to the tone. Further, he thought the report to the members should be from their elected representatives — the Board — and not from the appointed president.

MODERNIZING THE ASSOCIATION

Board member Major General John McCormick argued that in modern businesses, the annual reports were signed by the president — and that was how USAA should do it. A motion was offered to that effect and the Board voted that the report should be from the president.

At the same time USAA was making positive strides in growth, operations, and organization, something discouraging was happening. USAA losses grew rapidly — specifically, the growth of net losses to net premiums earned. The Association's record-breaking 50.63 percent in 1953 had declined in the next two years, and it was hoped things were under control. The year 1956 registered a jump to 60.87 percent and the following year to 64.47 percent. When coupled with the gradual increase in net underwriting expenses to premiums written, the numbers spelled trouble for USAA. What these figures meant was less money available to apportion to reserves and savings (dividends) to the members.

Most of USAA's reserves were governed by law or state regulation and were fixed. Behind the concept of reserves was the understanding that insurance companies must be able to meet any contingency. The Unearned Premium Reserve was to enable the company to return the money paid to USAA, but not yet committed to actual insurance. This would enable USAA to return uncommitted premiums to policyholders, even if everyone cancelled policies at the same time. The National Association of Insurance Commissioners proposed and State Insurance Departments accepted that the states require a Loss Reserve which amounted to setting aside 60 percent of Bodily Injury, Property Damage, and Medical payments for three years to cover possible claims. Unusual losses on specific cases also required a "case basis" loss reserve. The Unexpected Losses reserve account was to cover just what it said, and was required by New York as a condition of licensing there. Further, reserves had to be set up in various states where USAA held a license to guarantee payment of premium taxes. Last was the reserve for payment of savings to members. Before the Texas Insurance Department would approve payment of savings to members, all these reserve accounts had to be in order.

The 1956 loss ratio forced the Board of Directors to consider carefully the dividends that could be returned to members in 1957. The members would already receive the benefit of 20 percent lower rates than the Manual suggested. That made USAA a better bargain to begin with than all the stock companies, which charged whatever the Manual listed. At the beginning of the decade, USAA had returned to the members 32 percent on the already discounted rate. In more recent years, the dividend had been 30 percent. For 1957, and the following year as well, the dividend was set at 20 percent of the discounted rates. This was still far superior to other companies, but it caused serious concern at USAA.

Although the USAA leadership was not happy with the ultimate cost of insurance to members, its clear advantage on premiums did not sit well with other insurers competing with USAA for business. This was especially true with stock companies like Allstate. In 1936, the Commissioner of Internal Revenue ruled that USAA was exempt from paying income tax as long as it did not change how it was organized or how it operated. In 1942, the Federal Income Tax Law had been amended. Through the efforts of the American Reciprocal Association, a provision was added giving all reciprocals a $50,000 exemption on investment income. USAA's investment portfolio was principally in municipal bonds, which were exempt totally, and certain Government bonds, which were partially exempt. The net effect was that USAA paid no federal income tax.

In 1953, Allstate Insurance Company had begun a movement to amend the tax law so that stock, mutual, and reciprocal companies would all be taxed on the same basis. USAA needed help to keep track of this new potential tax problem and state regulation. It hired

MODERNIZING THE ASSOCIATION

Robert E. Joseph, retired Army Lieutenant Colonel and Staff Judge Advocate. Joseph represented USAA on a newly formed Reciprocal Inter Insurers Federal Tax Committee that had the avowed purpose of fighting any unfavorable tax changes. USAA's assessment for participating was one one-hundredth of 1 percent of net premiums for the previous year. In 1957, it amounted to nearly $2,800. Cheever told the Board the cost was "small, considering the overall benefit to the Association if adverse tax legislation is prevented."[27]

Cheever was very worried about the first dividend reduction and asked Antoinette Donohue, USAA's Chief Accountant, to discuss operating expenses with the Board. Donohue said that the main increases in operating expenses were due to inflation and the many expenses associated with moving into the new building. As part of her briefing, she compared USAA with its close competitor, GEICO. Although USAA was slightly larger in terms of premiums written and earned, GEICO's costs were much higher. GEICO's underwriting expenses to net premium written were 16.34 percent, while USAA's were only 12.94 percent. USAA's combined loss and expense ratio for 1956 was 73.81 while GEICO's was 86.0. In fact, USAA's ratio was less than any "one of the 120 stock companies selected by *Best's* as being reasonably representative of the industry as a whole."[28]

In further explaining the losses to the members, Cheever attributed them to a combination of causes. He pointed out that in 1955, based on past experience, the rate-making bureaus promulgated a substantial premium reduction in the standard rating Manuals. When the accident rates shot up again, the Manual rates did not respond quickly enough. The increasing number of accidents was a national problem and affected everyone. Not only were insurance companies not able to charge enough, but also the claims grew rapidly, intensifying the losses. The military saw the accident rates as eroding its manpower and ability to perform its mission. In the fifties, military installations made attempts to reduce accidents among their personnel by doing such things as encouraging them to sign safe driving pledges. From Andrews Air Force Base came a tougher line. The Base stated in its newspaper that:

> it didn't want to curtail weekend trips by service personnel, using their personal vehicles for transportation, but neither can it continue to experience the large toll of accidents that is being suffered by its service personnel so needlessly. Heed the warning or suffer the consequences.[29]

When the premiums did begin to rise and catch up with the accident rates, voters complained and by 1960, thirty-five states put in Safe Driver Rating Plans which penalized the accident-prone and reckless drivers. Overall, USAA members benefitted from these plans. For example, about 90 percent of USAA members qualified for the Safe Driver ratings in California.

Coupled with more accidents was the rapidly increasing costs of the accidents. Medical and hospital expenses were up sharply, as was the cost of automobile repair. Modern design of cars including "wrap-around" windshields, one-piece fenders and side panels, two-tone paint jobs, and power systems all contributed. On top of these claims, USAA paint and glass losses to windstorms were mounting in the Western and Midwestern States — almost one million dollars in the first six months of 1956 alone.

In spite of Cheever's and Donohue's explanations, Chandler felt expenses were going up abnormally. It appeared to him that no control was being exercised. This was news to Cheever, who was well aware of many cost-cutting efforts, especially a stringent one going on in office supplies. To get a new pencil, an employee had to return a completely used stub to Meta Willis, who headed the unit. Even Cheever himself was not exempt. When he stopped by the supply room on one of his walks around the building, he asked for a bottle of ink. Willis told the president of USAA "no." She told him that she had given one to Waldron recently and that Cheever would just have to share that one with him!

Nevertheless, Chandler wanted to further reduce operating expenses. When the USAA travel budget for 1957 was proposed at $30,000, Chandler moved it be reduced to $20,000. The Board turned down Chandler's bid, nine-to-two, and then approved the original budget. Using the dividend issue, at the 1957 Annual Members' Meeting Chairman Chandler made one more attempt to exert more control over USAA's operations — by running the meeting. He and Carl Schenken were both nominated to preside over the meeting, but Schenken got the nod by 8,000 votes. This vote presaged the next step. There were eleven nominees for eight Board positions. Chandler lost and left the Board to be replaced by Major General Peter C. Hains III as Chairman.

Contrary to Chandler's beliefs, USAA management was very much concerned about rising costs and sought various means to reduce them. One way to help reduce costs was to reduce losses by more careful underwriting. In part, this was being done by the National Bureau of Casualty Underwriters and the National Automobile Underwriters Association. The Bureaus developed and refined certain rating classifications so that higher risks would pay higher premiums. One example was the higher rates being charged to male drivers under twenty-five years of age.

The National Safety Council released statistics that showed that an individual who had one accident was twice as likely to have a second one and so on. Based on this theory, USAA began a systematic review of records, but set no specific rules on the number of claims that would cause a cancellation. Cheever told the members that each case would be decided on its individual merits. Members who had repeat accidents or evidence of drinking and driving frequently lost their insurance with the Association. In addition, the Association had seen "an increasing number of policyholders who are plainly dishonest," said Cheever. They were guilty of padding repair estimates to cover deductibles and committing fraud using other "ingenious ways." Cheever stressed that these "moral risks" were rare, and cancelled when discovered.[30] The totals of those cancelled for all reasons, including these moral risks, were rather small. In 1957, the Board cancelled memberships of only 158 out of over 318,000 for cause.

Even though the Executive Committee weekly was looking at accident files, reviewing more records, and terminating more memberships, it still considered each case carefully. A "playboy" with domestic problems was cancelled, and an officer under arrest was to have his policy cancelled, if the allegations were proven true. On the other hand, the Committee wrote to an officer overseas to bring his attention to the poor driving record of his daughter at the University of Texas so that he could counsel her; his policy was not cancelled. An older retired nurse's policy was not cancelled either, but the Committee cautioned her about her driving habits and suggested that she have someone drive for her. Letters were sent frequently to members to tell them that the Committee had considered cancelling them, but was giving them another chance in the hope they would improve their driving.

Another way USAA sought to reduce expenses was to reduce the Association's reliance on reinsurance. Schenken, Vice President-Treasurer, studied USAA's reinsurance experience over the years and then presented his findings to the Board. Between January 15, 1941, and May 1, 1959, USAA paid $507,000 in reinsurance premiums for automobile Physical Damage. Of this, USAA recovered only $401,000. Some years USAA recovered nothing, but following years when USAA did make a substantial recovery, it was hit immediately with comparable rate increases. Since June 1, 1946, in the Household Goods and Personal Effects reinsurance program, USAA had paid over $55,000 in premiums and had recovered nothing. The Board decided the Association was strong enough to handle the risks alone and voted to cancel the two policies with Lloyd's Underwriters effective October 1, 1959. Next, Schenken studied USAA's reinsurance on automobile Bodily Injury Liability. The situation was similar. From 1949 to 1959, USAA had paid over $900,000 in reinsurance premiums and recovered only a little over half. The Board voted to cancel the agreement with Employer's Reinsurance Corporation effective January 1, 1960. To cover all contingencies, USAA raised its reserve for Unexpected Losses to $3.5 million and kept the $500,000 reserve to guarantee USAA members that they would not be assessed to cover financial shortages.

Reducing operating costs and the ultimate cost of insurance was crucial, but there were other elements of service as well. Providing good service to military officers meant insuring them wherever they were. This included meeting licensing and other requirements of the byzantine labyrinth of state regulation. New York was particularly difficult. Just when USAA thought all was well in New York, the state legislature passed a compulsory auto insurance law effective January 1, 1957. USAA had a New York license, but beginning in 1957, the insured would have to present a New York prescribed form (FS-1) at the time of vehicle registration. USAA had a problem in getting the form to the members because of the mail lag time. Earlier, USAA had solved the mail lag time for incoming mail by dating policies effective the date of the postmark, rather than when it was received. While this was a great service, it wouldn't help this situation.

USAA's first impulse was to get the New York law amended. GEICO joined with USAA to contact Senator MacNeel Mitchell, who earlier had introduced a successful bill into the state legislature for USAA to enable reciprocals to get licensed. USAA also participated on a National Association of Independent Insurers Committee which was working with the New York legislature. Senator

A Tradition Of Service

Mitchell introduced a compromise amendment which enabled members of the Armed Services to comply more easily with the law. He urged USAA to have its New York members write their legislators. Presumably they did, and the amendment passed both houses easily. Unfortunately, however, the Governor vetoed the legislation.

While Senator Mitchell was working on the legislation, USAA decided to open an office in New York City to issue the required state certificates as a backup plan. In November 1956, Cheever reported to the Board that he had rented 200 square feet of space from USAA's New York adjuster, Crawford and Company. Located at 116 John Street, this was USAA's first office in the U.S. outside of San Antonio. Miss Charlotte Hildebrandt, formerly employed by USAA in Europe, staffed the office, which was linked to the Home Office by a TWX line. In April 1957, Mrs. Helen Wallace, an underwriter visiting New York from the Home Office, reported that the New York office received thirty-five to fifty calls per day, saw ten to fifteen insureds in the office, and issued twenty to forty FS-1 forms daily. The four employed clerks also provided considerable service to members returning from overseas through the New York port. Two years earlier, even though it was not really insurance business, Cheever had sent USAA legal counsel Robert Joseph to New York to help settle a problem that USAA members were experiencing when returning from overseas. After the officers picked up their cars at New York metropolitan area ports, police in New York and New Jersey were ticketing them for having European or military plates on their vehicles. Joseph made arrangements with authorities so that the returning officers could travel through those states to their new assignments without being stopped. This service to the members was greatly appreciated.

The complications in selling insurance in Europe were even more difficult. The Cold War Peace had settled to the ground like an early morning fog, confusing things that USAA had already set in motion. The Status of Forces Agreement (SOFA) that had been signed by the U.S. and Germany tried to define various relationships between the American forces in Germany and their host country and its citizens. About fifteen months after the opening of the Frankfurt office, the Commander-in-Chief of the Army in Europe notified USAA that, in line with SOFA, certain logistic support would be withdrawn on September 1, 1953. USAA could still operate, but the Association would have to pay for services previously provided free or at a reduced cost by the Army. This was because USAA was a private company, theoretically competing with German companies. The SOFA precluded U.S. government support for such a company. Cheever reported to the Board that all-important support had been terminated, and USAA had to vacate its requisitioned office in Frankfurt and register its company vehicles with German plates. USAA's efforts to be permanently assimilated as an official support agency with the U.S. Forces in Europe did not succeed.

While the peace made business more troublesome in some ways, it made it easier in others. The earlier reluctance to write insurance in Germany was because USAA members would likely drive to other Allied countries where a lack of court structure, claims offices, and recognition of USAA would cause problems. When USAA formally entered the German market, the International Motor Insurance Card (Green Card) system became available to use and would ultimately allay USAA's fears. The system was set up by the Motor Insurers' Bureau in line with a recommendation made by the United Nations Economic Commission for Europe. The various European governments accepted the Green Card as evidence that the bearer had insurance to meet the compulsory limits in each nation. If an individual company failed to handle a third-party claim, the Motor Insurers' Bureau guaranteed to settle the claim.

The kicker for USAA was that it was not licensed in any European country and, therefore, could not belong to the Motor Insurers' Bureau. Thus, USAA could not issue the Green Cards. After American International Underwriters turned USAA down, the Association entered into an agreement with the Zurich Insurance Company. USAA deposited $25,000 in a Swiss bank to guarantee its liabilities to Zurich. Zurich would sell the Green Cards to USAA which in turn would issue the cards to USAA members who paid a $5 fee. The solution was a very positive one because it meant USAA members could travel worry-free throughout Free Europe and be fully insured in each country. And a fringe benefit to USAA was to be its positive contribution to the American balance of payments problem.

USAA established a European Department, headed by Colonel John McComsey, that monitored all the operations there. In 1957, Tanis Jenschke began at USAA in this department as a "Green Card Clerk." Her job was to take members' requests and to type the Green Cards and mail them to the members. Like many other employees, she enjoyed working at USAA, but she did not appreciate the bells that signalled in her area when breaks were to begin and end, and

Staff members of the European Central Claims Office in Frankfurt, Germany, 1957

the idea that she had to ask permission to go to the restroom.[31]

Overall, the European program was a success. It provided service to the members and returned a profit. Cheever reported in early 1960 that the German government had given USAA a license to do business in Germany. This was contingent upon USAA depositing DM100,000 with the German government and would be effective upon the ratification of a revised Status of Forces Agreement. Welby Logan was rewarded for his outstanding efforts when the Board appointed him Resident Vice President-Europe in May 1961.

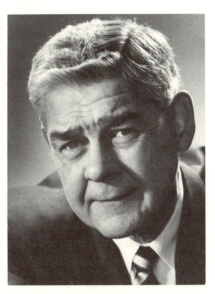

Welby Logan

In Japan, different obstacles developed in providing insurance for USAA members. In July 1955, the Japanese Diet enacted a compulsory insurance law. The law required personal liability insurance to be proven by a certificate issued by a carrier licensed in Japan.

Payments Required by Japanese Law

Yen	U.S. Dollars	Claim
Y30,000	$ 83.33	Slight Injury
Y100,000	$277.78	Serious Injury
Y300,000	$833.33	Death

The law did not apply immediately to Americans stationed in Japan, but on February 29, 1956, the U.S. Government agreed that the law would apply to American servicemen. Cheever sent Consuelo

Kerford, Helen Wallace, and Max Wier Jr. to Japan so that they could make recommendations to the Board. Incidentally, the younger Wier had started at USAA in March 1953. Born in San Antonio, Wier received his law degree from the University of Texas in 1938. He entered private law practice in San Antonio as his father's partner in the firm of Wier and Wier. During World War II, he served in the U.S. Army as a Special Agent and investigator under the Office of the Provost Marshal General. He would serve the USAA membership until 1979, retiring as Senior Vice President, Claims.

Max Wier Jr.

In May, the three made their report to the Board. They found that insureds could be held responsible for liabilities above the compulsory law limits, and most individuals in Japan carried voluntary excess insurance. For a number of reasons, the committee recommended that USAA not get a license. Taxes were prohibitive, rents were high and required a three-year lease, the cost of installing one telephone was $1,000, and no U.S. logistic support was available. USAA would be required to accept applications from anyone, American or Japanese, contrary to the Association's bylaws. In the group's view, the Japanese were highly nationalistic and did not want foreign businesses coming to Japan. As one example, the USAA team mentioned that the English-speaking Minister of Finance for Japan had not spoken a single word of English, business or social, since the peace treaty was signed in April 1952. Further, most Americans in Japan felt that all their forces would be gone within five years anyway. All things considered, the committee advised USAA to send a circular letter to the members recommending that they purchase the compulsory insurance from any of the twenty-seven carriers in the market. Even without a Japanese license, USAA could offer excess voluntary insurance which would satisfy the Provost Marshal's requirements for minimum coverage. The officers could then get base access. The Board commended the committee and the letter went out to the members a week later.[32]

USAA continued its focus on automobile insurance, but listened to the members for other needs. Cheever explained to the Board in late 1956 that because of the competitive market in insurance, it was advisable to furnish members with as much of their insurance as is possible. When Cheever finished, Vice President-Treasurer John McComsey outlined the new proposed Comprehensive Personal Liability Policy designed to meet the demand of the membership. General McCormick moved that the Association "extend its insurance service" by writing the new policy. His motion carried unanimously.[33] Only one year later, the Board measured its success and voted to pay a dividend on the new policy.

In the 1950s, the combination of more purchasing power, G.I. loans, and the availability of single homes built in tracts increased home ownership. The Levittown model of the post-World War II years spread across the country. While the percentage of owner-occupied homes was 43.6 percent in 1940, the figure rose to almost 62 percent by 1960.[34] On some military installations, there was not sufficient government family housing available for all active-duty officers, and some bought homes. Also, retired and separated officers who were no longer eligible for government housing began to buy their own. This began to impact USAA. By the mid-1950s, USAA staff and employees working with the household goods and comprehensive personal liability policy areas became aware of a growing number of cancellations. By September of 1958, the Association was losing approximately 100 household and sixty personal liability policies every month. The home-owning members found it convenient to combine these under a homeowner's policy, and USAA did not offer one.

That changed in 1960, when USAA began offering homeowners insurance. The Homeowner's Policy provided insurance on the residence, household goods and personal effects, and comprehensive liability protection — all in one package. Because of the requirement to meet the complex codes of each individual state, USAA's plan was to extend service to the entire membership gradually, on a state-by-state basis. By the end of 1960, USAA had sold over 1,800 of these policies in the four states it was licensed to do so — Texas, California, Washington, and Virginia.

USAA's first homeowners policy was issued to Captain Leslie B. Huff, USAF (Ret.). USAA President Charles Cheever presenting the policy to Captain Huff and his family at their home in San Antonio.

Modernizing The Association

Just getting licensed, of course, was only the first step. The second was to convince bankers and other lenders to approve mortgages insured by USAA — an Association few knew. It often took personal intervention by Cheever. For example, on a trip to San Francisco, Cheever called on C.H. Baumhefner, Vice President and Cashier of the Bank of America (BOA) in charge of mortgage loans. A short time later Baumhefner wrote Cheever and told him that USAA had been added to BOA's approved list. Since the BOA had over 800 branches, the news was good indeed.

On some occasions, the Association improved its service by broadening or increasing coverages at no extra cost. In 1957, Mrs. Beulah Frees, the Underwriter in charge of the Association's household and personal effects insurance line, briefed the Board. She explained in detail the new changes which the members requested for years and which had been approved by the states. The policy now applied worldwide for the first time. It covered numerous risks including fire, lightning, windstorm, hail, explosion, riot and civil commotion, smoke, theft, robbery, transportation, pilferage, holdup, burglary, and embezzlement. The maximum limits were raised to $25,000 for fire and $12,500 for theft. And all this at no increase in premium.

Beulah Frees

The new products were a positive addition to the members' financial security and increased pride in their Association. The decade's growth was strong, and even with some reduction in dividends, the members still found their insurance cheaper and better than they could get anywhere else. *Best's Insurance Reports* continued to give USAA an "A+" policyholders' rating for general reliability — its highest rating. After the Senior Examiner for the Texas Board of Insurance Commissioners spent several weeks looking at USAA's operation in detail, he reported to the Board in 1954 that he had "no recommendations or suggestions to offer which would improve the management of the Association."[35] Looking ahead to the 1960s, Cheever told the membership that the problems ahead would probably be similar to those of the 1950s. As he saw it, the challenge to management was to resolve the problems and continue "to provide sound insurance service and protection at the lowest possible net cost to the individual member."[36]

CHAPTER SIX

THE SIXTIES — MATURITY AND PROGRESS

So much of America in the Fifties seemed content, wrote John Kenneth Galbraith of the times.[1] In some ways that was true, although the Cold War tension continued under the facade of fun and prosperity. Median family income was up and, for most of the decade, unemployment was down. Cheap oil helped spur industrial and commercial growth, and corporate recruiters scoured the college campuses looking for graduates to participate in the healthy economy. The automobile, festooned with fins and chrome, had become a necessity as well as a joy, and USAA benefitted from its rise in importance. The signs of the car's influence were everywhere. The rapidly increasing number of motel rooms, malls, drive-in movies, highway construction projects, and suburbs all testified to the automobile's impact.

But the Cold War and the international instability kept the American people and their government from getting too comfortable. For a brief moment at the end of the fifties, hope emerged for a Soviet-American detente. In September of 1959, Khrushchev made a lengthy visit to the United States, and he invited Ike and his family to visit the Soviet Union after the planned 1960 Summit. The President had wanted his legacy to be a limitation of the arms race, possibly even including some type of nuclear test ban treaty, but it was not to be. In May 1960, Francis Gary Powers flew his U-2 reconnaissance plane over the USSR towards Sverdlovsk. A dull thump, followed by an orange flash that illuminated the cockpit, resulted in the destruction of the U-2 and the pilot's capture. "A genuine beginning of peace — had been shot down along with Powers."[2]

A Tradition Of Service

In the sixties, as in the past, events external to USAA brought sweeping changes to the Association. The popularity of the automobile and its necessity were reflected in new home designs that began to include two-car garages. USAA members were part of the car's popular cult following — 15 percent owned a second one by 1960. This meant an increased workload in San Antonio because each car was covered by a separate policy. To meet demands caused by changes in patterns of home ownership and higher values on personal goods, USAA added new insurance products to protect financial security that generated thousands of other policies. And the continuing Cold War tension and government actions to counter the threats increased the pool of USAA eligibles. All this would force USAA to adjust if it were to be able to handle the workload and continue to serve its membership well.

On the afternoon of June 28, 1960, Charles Cheever entered the gathering of mostly men with military bearing and haircuts to match. He moved easily among these members waiting for the Annual Membership Meeting to begin. His easy smile, good memory for names, and warm handshake made his fellow officers feel welcome and comfortable. The comradeship between the President and the members was as genuine as was his warm relationship with his employees. Promptly at 1:30 p.m. the group was seated in the auditorium. Carl Schenken chaired the formal meeting, which finished about an hour later with much accomplished.

The most important issue that came up at the meeting was a proposed bylaws change spelling out new eligibility for joining USAA. Up until the meeting, officers separating from the armed services gave up their memberships if they relinquished their commissions. This was true even if they were excellent members with superior driving and payment records. In many instances, the officer had no control of the situation, but was caught in Congressionally mandated force reductions. This USAA eligibility policy was also hurting the new Homeowner's Policy sales. Some financing agencies were reluctant to give long-term mortgages to USAA members because the Association would cancel insurance if a mortgagee lost eligibility due to change of military status. An additional difficulty was eligibility determination — it was often impossible to ascertain an officer's status unless the officer let USAA know. The bylaws change passed the membership easily and, more importantly, established the principle of "once a member always a member."[3] The Board met after the meeting and made the change retroactive to the founding of the Association.

Although the members never saw Cheever's original proposal to the Board on the bylaws change, it had included a provision to offer enlisted personnel the opportunity to join USAA. If approved, membership would have included:

> Active and retired commissioned officers, warrant officers *and the two highest grades of non-commissioned officers of the regular components of the United States Services.*[4]

Another of Cheever's proposed changes included offering membership to the two highest non-commissioned grades of the National Guard and of the Reserve components when they were called up for extended active duty. The Board discussed these proposals at length. The Directors agreed that these non-commissioned officers were superior in every respect and would be excellent risks. Several of the Directors questioned the need of extending the eligibility, however, since USAA was already growing at a steady pace. The Association had gained nearly twenty-four thousand new members in 1960 alone. Finally, Board member Rear Admiral Louis J. Kirn moved to eliminate the enlisted personnel from the proposed bylaws changes. The Board agreed unanimously.

Another issue that Cheever discussed with the members was the problem of state licensing. USAA's traditional position was to forgo state licenses unless absolutely necessary to continue to serve its members. As a result, USAA was licensed in only fourteen states, the District of Columbia, and Guam, these locations accounting for about two-thirds of the Association's policies.

Over the years, many "fly-by-night" companies that were servicing military personnel had failed or otherwise defrauded their customers. Complaints by the servicemen to their congressmen and Better Business Bureaus resulted in pressure on the Department of Defense (DOD) to do something to protect them. Cheever told the Board that the DOD had studied the problem and was considering a new directive. This proposed directive would require commanders to recognize insurance policies only from companies licensed to do business in the state where their installations were located. If the commander refused to accept the insurance of a particular company, the servicemen would be unable to bring their cars onto the base until they secured insurance that would qualify. The National Association of Independent Insurers and the Association had protested the stringency of the requirement to no avail. If approved, USAA-insured vehicles would not be permitted on military installations in thirty-six states!

In addition to this potentially serious DOD problem, other developments encouraged USAA to change its policy on state licenses. The National Association of Insurance Commissioners (NAIC) had approved a model piece of legislation which could hurt USAA badly. If passed in the state of Texas, it would require the Texas Insurance Commissioner to revoke USAA's license because the Association sold insurance in states where it was not licensed. The NAIC model bill was actually introduced in the Texas legislature, but was defeated amidst some anxious moments for USAA.

Another argument for applying for state licenses was the insurance industry's advocacy for strengthening the state Financial Responsibility Laws. Under the proposal, only licensed companies in a particular state could provide insurance certificates enabling a driver to get an operator's license in that state. The ability to issue these certificates was critical if USAA were to be able to serve its members. To suggest the stress these laws put on individuals, retired USAA employee Frances Moore told the story years later of a very agitated young officer who was driving from the East Coast to a new assignment in the southwest. He had no operator's license because he needed a financial responsibility certificate first and he had none. He stopped at the home office to try to get help. As he talked to Moore, he nervously lit up a cigarette. The next time she looked up, he was smoking two cigarettes at the same time. Fortunately, Moore was able to issue a certificate and send him on his way before he lit up a third.[5]

Other arguments in favor of getting licensed in all states included the growing interest in compulsory automobile insurance laws, and mortgage lender requirements for fire policies to be written only by companies licensed to do business in that state. The rationale against mass licensing for USAA was primarily cost. Cheever estimated that to add all the states, the cost for licensing, premium taxes, and fees would run between $500,000 and $750,000 annually. Over and above this would be overhead costs at the home office for operating and managing the state licensing programs. Previously, USAA had still been able to issue policies and certificates of financial responsibility in all states without being licensed. Times had changed, however, and Cheever announced to the annual meeting that the Association was going to move ahead and get licensed in all the states.

The Association had to overcome many obstacles to accomplish this. For example, Rhode Island and Kansas wanted a total of $56,000 in back taxes, even though the Association had never been licensed in those states. It wasn't really fair to be taxed on programs that USAA never operated, but that was the condition of getting licensed. New Hampshire required that USAA deposit $25,000 in actual securities in New Hampshire for a certificate of financial responsibility on *each* car the Association insured there. Fortunately, this requirement remained in effect for only three years.

The other major topic Cheever discussed at the annual meeting was the need to expand the home office building on Broadway because of USAA's growth. In 1953, the plans for the original building forecasted that it would serve USAA's needs until 1960. The forecast proved to be remarkably accurate, and the work force was now getting cramped. The first floor, which at first was rented out to third parties, was now fully occupied by USAA. The construction began immediately.

The five-story addition was constructed above the cafeteria. In the original architectural design, provisions had been made for the future upper floors by strengthening the foundation. The final cost was a little over $3 million. Completed in 1961, it was designed by the same architectural team that did the original building and was constructed by Henry Beck. The project increased USAA's workspace by close to 50 percent and included expansion of the cafeteria, a records room, additional air conditioning capacity, and a new bank of elevators. Cheever told the *Navy Times* that the addition would permit the Association "to keep pace with its continued growth . . . and services rendered to its membership."[6] Added to the Board room, in the main home office building about the same time, were new oil portraits of former leaders Hinds, White, and Jones. Painted by Charles J. Fox, the portraits joined one of Garrison, USAA's founder.

What the addition did not help was the parking problem. In 1958, 800 of USAA's employees registered their cars for 520 parking spaces. Incarnate Word College, across the street from USAA, had allowed the Association to use a lot with sixty spaces to help in return for $250 a month. The addition forced USAA to buy some neighboring property for parking lots, but soon the growing work force even overwhelmed this new capacity. In 1964, the Board briefly considered constructing a six-level parking garage with a tunnel

THE SIXTIES – MATURITY AND PROGRESS

USAA Broadway Building with the five-story addition completed in 1962

under Broadway connecting the building and the parking garage, but finally decided against it. By 1965, Schenken told the Board that the 1,100 parking spaces for about 1,900 employees were not enough. Something had to be done. Fewer and fewer employees were riding public buses. The Board authorized Schenken to purchase twenty-four lots on nearby Groveland Street which would accommodate four hundred cars. Even with this addition, parking continued to be a problem for USAA employees.

In the last half of 1960, the attention of Americans — and the world — focused on the presidential election. Richard Nixon, as Eisenhower's Vice President for eight years, should have had the edge. His opponent, John F. Kennedy, a young Senator from Massachusetts, was thought to be burdened by his Roman Catholic faith. In the final analysis, most historians agree that Kennedy won their nationally televised debates and the close election as a result. Kennedy's flair and style made him enormously popular, and his plea to Americans to "ask not what your country can do for you; ask what you can do for your country" was answered by thousands who joined the Peace Corps. USAA answered Kennedy's challenge as well. Cheever told the Board that Sargent Shriver, Director of the Peace Corps, had asked American business to help in the Peace Corps effort. The USAA Board decided to grant up to a two-year leave of absence to any employee who served actively in the Peace Corps, although there is no record of any takers.[7]

As the previous decade had drawn to a close, a crisis in character and ethics seemed to engulf American thought. A series of well-publicized examples suggested something was very wrong. Eisenhower's chief assistant, Sherman Adams, accepted a vicuna coat and hotel stays from a businessman currying favors from the federal government. A University of Pennsylvania study discovered that more than 40 percent of students were cheating in college. Columbia Professor Charles Van Doren drew millions of adoring fans to NBC's extremely successful quiz show, "Twenty One." The disclosure that Van Doren cheated on the show and then lied to a Grand Jury in his confession to a Congressional Committee set off seismic vibrations in the country's moral consciousness. Historian Eric Goldman wrote that "moral relativism had replaced moral certitudes."[8] This breakdown in morality prodded actions in the insurance industry.

In 1961, the National Association of Insurance Commissioners included a new interrogatory which companies had to include in the Annual Statement to states where they were licensed. The question read as follows:

> Has the company (or other appropriate term) an established procedure for disclosure to its board of directors or trustees of any material interest or affiliation on the part of any of its officers, directors, trustees or responsible employees, which is

in or is likely to conflict with the official duties of such person?

This became the genesis of USAA's first formal policy statement, "Conflict of Interests and Business Ethics." Cheever noted that there was "no doubt about the loyalty and integrity of all USAA personnel," although, "the challenges besetting our economic society today are too acute to permit half heartedness in erasing doubts about our adherence to high standards of honesty and public service."[9] The statement included warnings about personal financial interests, insider information, acceptance of gratuities, and outside business activities. Passed on December 27, 1961, the policy applied to all directors, officers, exempt employees, Purchasing Department employees, and other employees in sensitive positions. In 1963, the Board extended the policy to cover all USAA employees and those of its subsidiary companies as well. The trust and integrity between USAA and its members over the years was crucial and had to be protected.

A strong code of ethics was fundamental to Cheever's leadership. Another key element was his willingness to delegate responsibility. During his frequent and lengthy travels for the Association, he trusted that his team would keep USAA running smoothly. The Executive Committee found that some of USAA's key positions corresponded with similar positions that carried the title of vice president in other insurance companies. So when Board member Major General Robert M. Stillman suggested that heads of divisions should be vice presidents, Cheever agreed. The Board decided to bring USAA in line with other companies and appointed four additional employees as vice presidents.[10] This was a formal break in the previous USAA practice to give officer titles only to former military officers.

Miss Consuelo Kerford	Vice President-Secretary
Mrs. Stuart C. Gwyn	Vice President-Underwriting
Mrs. Meta N. Willis	Vice President-Comptroller
Mr. Max H. Wier Jr.	Vice President-Claims

USAA's officers, August 1961. Seated, left to right: Stuart Gwyn, Consuelo Kerford, Meta Willis. Standing, left to right: A.T. Leonard, Welby Logan, Max Wier Sr., Max Wier Jr., and Carlton G. Schenken.

They joined USAA's other vice presidents: Amel T. Leonard, Vice President and Attorney-in-Fact; Carlton G. Schenken, Vice President-Treasurer; and Welby C. Logan, the resident Vice President-Europe. The next month, retired Max H. Wier Sr. was appointed Vice President-Emeritus in recognition of his past service and his continuing service as General Counsel on a contractual basis. Wier had been retired mandatorily at age seventy, but he was so valued by USAA that he was continued as a contractor until he reached eighty. These promotions ratified the responsibilities already being performed and gave the USAA organization a much more modern look and structure.

In line with this was the gradual withdrawal of the Board and

The Sixties – Maturity And Progress

Executive Committee from operational decisions. During the sixties, the Board continually expanded management's responsibility in such areas as settling claims, canceling members for cause, and sale of securities from the investment portfolio. The method of Board payment was changed from per meeting to an annual retainer of $600, and Executive Committee members were to receive $2,080 in part as a reflection of USAA's modernization.[11] The Executive Committee received more because it continued to meet weekly, principally on claims matters. Beginning in 1967, out-of-town Board members were also to be reimbursed for travel, making things easier on Board members not living in San Antonio.

Another visible sign of growing maturity was the evolution of USAA's corporate good citizenship (charitable contributions) program. USAA's traditional position had been one of no charitable contributions. The only exception had been $250 donated to a General Relief fund in 1932 during the Great Depression. In the late fifties, the Board and Executive Committee discussed the issue often, usually because a Board member thought USAA should give to the United Fund. The consensus had always been "no" because the contributions would have to come from the members' savings — and members would have no say and no benefit from the contributions. The United Fund was local, and because of USAA eligibility rules, giving would be marginal as advertising because USAA could not sell insurance unless an individual was eligible. The employees were encouraged to give, however, and supported the United Fund well.

In 1961, N. E. Dunn, United Fund Campaign Chairman for San Antonio, wrote a letter to each of the Directors requesting that USAA make a "corporate contribution." General Robert Stillman recommended that USAA give $10 per employee, but the consensus of the Board was to request a study of the issue. The subsequent study noted that the National Industrial Conference Board reported in 1961 that the national average of corporate giving was seven-tenths of 1 percent of pre-tax income in 1959. "Service" companies gave .45 percent as contrasted to the .83 percent given by "industrial" companies. As to the question of whether USAA could use members' funds for charitable contributions, the New York Insurance Law specifically noted that a reciprocal could act in the name of the collective membership. This legal interpretation had a strong impact on the Board's thinking.

At the August 23, 1961, Board Meeting, the members discussed the report and concluded that because of the Association's size, USAA should begin to make corporate charitable contributions. The Board members came to the conclusion that the Association had a responsibility to the community where the home office was located and that such a contribution program would be a *"justifiable business expense."* Rear Admiral Kirn moved that USAA allocate $25,000 as a budget for health and welfare agencies such as United Fund, hospitals, national health agencies, and medical research. He also recommended that USAA's management team recommend the distribution for the Executive Committee and Board to approve. The first approved budget allocated $15,000 to the United Fund and $4,500 to local hospitals and national health agencies. The rest was spread among the relief societies of the armed services, the American Red Cross for Hurricane Carla, the Boy Scouts, and the Salvation Army. Over the next few years, the program budget remained very similar except that $400 was held back in latter years for "unanticipated requests." The first deviation from the health and welfare orientation was a special 1967 donation of $2,000 to the San Antonio Symphony. The inception of the charitable contributions program was another recognition by USAA's leadership of the Association's coming-of-age. Employees expended their volunteer time and energy too. The USAA Christmas Choir that had been organized in 1954 continued to perform over the holidays. In 1963, USAA's Christmas Cheer program began helping needy families over the holidays.

THE SIXTIES – MATURITY AND PROGRESS

The growing desire for financial security by individual members changed their needs, and USAA moved to meet them. In some cases, the Association was able to add new products as it always had. Limits were adjusted and perils added without cost to the Household Goods and Personal Effects Floater. In 1961, when a landslide into the Hudson River produced a tidal wave at West Point, USAA extended

United States Military Academy Color Guard. *(Courtesy of the United States Military Academy)*

its coverage to cover the claims. One peril added, riot and civil commotion, would have an impact later in the decade. Boatowners, ocean marine, and credit card insurance were also added. Occasionally, to provide new products and services, significant bylaws changes had to be made. The Annual Members' Meeting in June 1962 approved these changes. The first requirement was to find a way to enable the Association to still do business in locations where being a reciprocal hindered operations, such as in the state of Ohio. The attendees accomplished this when they approved a provision that permitted

USAA to organize wholly-owned subsidiary companies when it was in the best interests of the Association.

British law prohibited USAA, as a reciprocal, from being licensed. Cheever argued before the Board at the end of 1961 that if the Association could find a way to get licensed in Great Britain, then USAA could operate there at less cost. The Association could save over $70,000 annually in fees it paid to other companies in Britain to write liability insurance, provide adjusting services, and issue the Green Cards enabling members to prove they had auto insurance at international borders. Also, if USAA had a subsidiary to do this, it might have another significant benefit. It was possible that this same subsidiary could be licensed to sell casualty insurance in Ohio, Delaware, Vermont, and New Hampshire, states which still had laws forbidding a reciprocal to be licensed.

The second bylaws change that was approved at the June meeting authorized USAA to sell insurance products other than property and casualty insurance such as life insurance. A significant number of members wanted life insurance; as Cheever had argued on other occasions, USAA would be more valuable to its constituents if it could handle all their insurance needs. The change increased USAA's options by authorizing the Association to "provide such insurance coverages as the Board of Directors shall determine." The members had unlocked the door to improved service. Now it was management's job to open it.

With the approval to organize a stock company in hand, USAA management went into action. On October 1, 1962, the organizational meeting of the American Officers Insurance Company Limited (AOIC) was held in London. USAA's total investment in AOIC was $200,000. That included the purchase of all 50,000 shares of AOIC.[12] General John McCormick was elected Chairman of the Board of the new company, and Cheever was its Managing Director. Other Board members included Carl Schenken, Welby Logan, and James

THE SIXTIES – MATURITY AND PROGRESS

W.T. Crocker. Crocker was the USAA counsel in England who organized the new company. Mrs. Marion McDougall was made Assistant Secretary for AOIC to maintain corporate records in London. McDougall was originally employed by USAA in Germany in 1952 and had been in charge of a small USAA London office since its inception in 1960.

James Crocker (left), with Michael Hawker, Manager, USAA Ltd.

Marion McDougall

At first, USAA's London subsidiary was successful in helping the members in England, but it did not do well financially. The first six months of 1963 showed a deficit of $57,000 because of a small earned premium and one large claim calling for a $25,000 reserve. During this same period, two other companies writing insurance principally for U.S. Armed Forces members stationed in England failed. To preclude any questions from British officials about the financial stability of AOIC, the USAA Board transferred $60,000 to its subsidiary's capital by purchasing 15,000 additional shares. This put AOIC in the black. By 1964, USAA was issuing over 3,000 Road Traffic Certificates annually to USAA members.

American Officers Insurance Company, Ltd.

The second bylaws change gave USAA the opportunity to provide new products. In the United States between 1950 and 1960, disposable income rose 49 percent, but the dollar volume of individual life policies rose by more than 200 percent.[13] It was a growing business. In mid-1962, Carl Schenken began to look into the possibility of the Association offering life insurance. After Schenken completed his study and briefed the Board, it authorized Cheever to organize a wholly-owned life insurance stock company. Its purpose would be to serve qualified USAA members and USAA would invest $5 million in the company.

THE SIXTIES – MATURITY AND PROGRESS

Carlton G. Schenken

James Snyder

Cheever interviewed twelve candidates and selected Richard C. Roberts to be responsible for setting up the internal operations of the company. He had previously been Assistant Secretary of the Atlantic Coast Life Insurance Company of Charleston, South Carolina. Cheever pointed out to the Board that Roberts would be "the 'life technical' man and would report to a vice president of the Life Company who should be a military person."[14] This was to be retired Army Major General James L. Snyder who was raised on the former Theodore Roosevelt Ranch in North Dakota. He received his M.D. from George Washington University in Washington, D.C., in 1933 and, after his internship, went on active duty. After a career in the Army Medical Corps, he retired and went to work for USAA in 1965.

In 1963, Usaa Life Insurance Company was chartered in Texas and the Texas State Board of Insurance licensed the company on August 20, 1963. Lil Bates, Cheever's secretary, later recalled the upper and lower case "Usaa" was used in the name of the Life Company instead of "USAA" at the insistence of the Texas Insurance

Commissioner. It was to distinguish the Life Company from its parent. When the Life Company was rechartered, the USAA reverted to all capital letters like the parent company. Of great significance and special service to military officers was the absence of a war clause, standard in most life insurance policies. The first one was sold to Lieutenant Jack H. Griffith Jr., who was stationed with the 1st Armored Division at Fort Hood, Texas. In 1964, the USAA parent held an investment of $1 million in capital stock of the company and contributed $2.5 million to surplus. By the end of the first full year in 1964, Usaa Life had almost $35 million of life insurance in force.

Cheever understood the importance of members clearly associating the new Life Company with the USAA they had always known and trusted. In one action, the Board had agreed that the USAA Board of Directors and those of the new company should consist of substantially the same persons. The Board felt "it was desirable that the USAA image should be projected into the Life Company."[15] Also, the Board authorized the new company to use the trademarked USAA emblem to reinforce the USAA image.

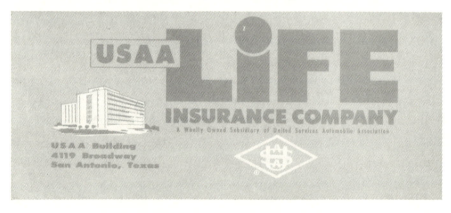

A brochure advertising USAA Life Insurance Company

At 3:45 a.m. on a cold October morning in 1962, the young Air Force lieutenant, his wife, and their two small children awakened to a series of powerful knocks on their door. The officer opened the door of his apartment in rural Turkey to two U.S. Navy Shore Patrolmen. "Be ready to evacuate with your family on one hour's notice, but we can't tell you why," they said. The officer turned on his short-wave radio to see what was going on. The Russians had jammed the British Broadcasting Corporation (BBC) and Voice of America (VOA) stations. With no information, the family was anxious, and the darkness of the early morning hour only heightened the tension.

In the United States, more information did not relieve the tension for people living there. The television pictures of the missile-bearing Russian vessel heading towards Cuba and perhaps a date with the apocalypse caused tremendous fear in the United States — and the highest alert status on all military installations. The Cuban missile crisis was the most terrifying episode in the Cold War. When the Soviet leadership backed down and the vessel turned around, the intensity decreased, but it demonstrated the fragility of the world situation and the continuing tension between Russia and the United States. President Kennedy had already suffered through the disastrous Bay of Pigs adventure in Cuba. His meetings with Nikita Khrushchev in June 1961 had not eased the anxiety. Kennedy responded by tripling the draft calls, calling up 150,000 reservists, and expanding the civil defense program to protect Americans against nuclear attack. The Soviet's reply was the Berlin Wall.

Kennedy's actions were to have an almost immediate impact on USAA. In response to the Office of Civilian Defense, Cheever agreed to permit the home office building to be designated a public fallout shelter in the event of enemy attack. Employees received the necessary training for emergency medical assistance, bringing war fears home, so to speak, to the Broadway building. The major impact was Kennedy's move to increase America's conventional military strength. Total military end-strength went from 2.5 million in 1960

A TRADITION OF SERVICE

to 2.8 million in 1962. The officer strength rose to over 343,000, matched by a rise in USAA membership and its resulting workload on Broadway.

The turmoil in foreign relations was matched by social upheaval at home. The struggle for civil rights for African-American citizens was the centerpiece of social reform in the 1960s. A series of events received wide media attention, and brought America's racial problems to the forefront. Beginning in 1960, non-violent demonstrations took place at segregated lunch counters. Freedom rides tested segregation on public transportation. In 1962, James Meredith entered the University of Mississippi under protection of 5,000 National Guard troops, but only after two citizens died and 160 were wounded. In April 1963, Martin Luther King Jr. decided to stage non-violent protests in segregated Birmingham, Alabama. Police Commissioner Eugene "Bull" Connor met these protests with high-pressure fire hoses, electric cattle prods, unleashed police attack dogs, and the jailing of over 2,200 protestors. The television cameras brought these scenes into living rooms everywhere. And that included San Antonio.

Ollie Smith

The USAA Executive Committee met for its regular weekly meeting on June 14, 1963. The committee discussed the events, which prompted a question of Cheever. The committee wanted to know what the Association's policy was with regard "to the employment of members of the Negro race." Cheever's reply was that there were only two, both porters — Ollie Smith and Romeo

Robinson. He noted that USAA had accepted applications from Negroes at various times for other positions, but none had been employed. The committee discussed the issue and then agreed that applications "of the Negro race" for employment should be considered for employment, "providing that they met the Association's established personnel standards and requirements for proper placement on the job."

This was a major step for USAA, and put it among the leaders in the business community. USAA had always been "colorblind" in regard to members — eligibility or cancellations never considered race, ethnic background, gender, or creed.[16] Opening the doors to African-American employees was long overdue. It is easy today to criticize USAA for waiting so long, but it is important to consider the action in historical context. USAA's attitude towards hiring minority employees reflected that of San Antonio and the military itself. The original design for the Broadway Building included segregated bathrooms, as required by city building code. Moye quickly had "colored" and "white" signs removed from the doors of the basement restrooms.[17] And, although President Harry Truman ordered the integration of the armed forces in 1948, it did not happen fully for many years. Great Britain and other European nations refused to accept the assignment of African Americans to American military bases within their borders. Opposition within the armed services was widespread. It wasn't until after the Korean Conflict that the last all-African-American units in the Army and Navy disappeared. As late as the early 1960s, recreational activities and various facilities on some installations still remained segregated, as did schools and civilian businesses on the fringes of the installations. Many military installation commanders believed that the civilian communities were not their responsibility, even though the segregation hurt the morale of their people. They weren't, legally — until the passage of the Civil Rights Act of 1964.[18]

A TRADITION OF SERVICE

This was the world in which the members and many of the USAA leaders had lived for decades. It was bound to affect them. To USAA's credit, it did change the USAA official policy before the Civil Rights Act of 1964, and Jean Moye and the personnel office immediately brought four new African-Americans — the first of many — into the work force in various business areas. USAA was the first private company of any size in San Antonio to break "the color line," and Moye officially notified the Texas Employment Commission (TEC) that USAA had no restrictions on applicants other than business qualifications. A year later, in an interview for the *San Antonio Evening News*, an African-American member of the TEC staff applauded "USAA's efforts in hiring Negroes."[19]

USAA was in the forefront of other employee recruitment as well that demonstrated the Association's social conscience. In 1964, Cheever announced a program designed to salvage high school dropouts. Working with the "stay-in-school" specialists at Edgewood, Harlandale, and San Antonio school districts, USAA began hiring dropouts with the proviso that they attend night school to complete high school.

High school dropouts hired by USAA

THE SIXTIES – MATURITY AND PROGRESS

Many of these employees would stay on with USAA and contribute to the Association. USAA also hired handicapped individuals who became a valuable part of the work force. In 1967, USAA received the President's Employer Merit Award, the only employer so honored to date in Texas for its efforts. At the time of the award, of 2,270 USAA employees, 200 came within the definition of the handicapped. USAA was not enlightened in every way, however. Retired employee Dorothy Wildenstein recalled that when she first applied at USAA, she did not meet weight standards. She was hired as a temporary and given six months to lose the weight. Six months later, she had not lost the weight and was told she'd have to leave. Begging for and receiving a one-month's extension, she virtually lived on coffee and cigarettes and made it.

USAA made sincere efforts to make the Association a great place to work. Posters around the building entitled "A Better Place to Work" gave suggestions on how everyone could improve the work environment. The workload was heavy and overtime frequent, but Moye worked with Cheever to keep the pay and benefits competitive or better. In the 1950s, improved pay had been the most important factor in reducing employee turnover, and the pay issue required constant attention. In 1960, management consultants from Bowles, Andres, and Towne studied the USAA pay structure. Their recommendations for separate salary plans for exempt and non-exempt (hourly wage) employees were approved by the Board to be effective June 1, 1960.[20]

Over the next few years, USAA employees received a number of salary increases. Some were in response to the increase in the Federal Minimum Wage Law of 1961 which raised the minimum wage in three increments, reaching $1.25 in 1963. All exempt salaries were raised in 1963 in response to the U.S. Department of Labor, which raised the minimums that exempt employees could be paid. In 1964, raises of 4.5 percent came to make USAA employee salaries competitive in San Antonio. The following year Benny Leonard told the Board that 34 percent of the employees leaving USAA were doing so for better-paying positions. The Board raised non-exempt salaries another 7.5 percent.

Also in 1960, USAA changed its retirement plan drastically. Under the existing plan adopted in 1948, each employee's retirement account was an individual annuity. The Board established a new USAA Retirement Plan and Trust that was to be administered by the United States Trust Company in New York. The plan included all USAA employees. All individual annuity policies were cashed in and the money passed along to the new retirement trust in New York. The full USAA benefits were explained to the employees at LaVillita Assembly Hall in San Antonio.

Employees and guests gather at La Villita Assembly Hall to learn about the revised USAA Employee Benefits Program, May 23, 1960.

The benefits provided full retirement at age sixty-five with provisions for early or late retirements. The mandatory retirement age was seventy, but Mrs. Nancy Brooks was in good health and an excellent underwriter when she reached that age. When it was pointed out that her continued employment "would not prevent a younger employee from getting promoted," the Board decided to offer her employment on a year-to-year basis.[21] Another twist occurred when Mrs. Imogene Townsend, Underwriting Director, put in for a retirement on October 1, 1966, at age sixty. She pointed out that her USAA retirement would not be sufficient to live on until her Social Security kicked in at age sixty-two. The Executive Committee decided to pay her an additional $106.20 monthly for twenty-seven months until she reached age sixty-two. That was the estimated amount of Social Security she would receive. Although the Committee stated this was not to be construed as a precedent or policy, it did set the stage later for a Social Security supplement for early retirees in future retirement plans.[22]

Later, another important part of the total retirement package to be implemented was a "Retirement Savings Supplement Plan." USAA would match $1 for each $10 saved. To qualify under Internal Revenue Service regulations, 50 percent of the employees in the lower two-thirds of the salary levels had to participate. When the employees did not sign up in the required numbers, the Board added an inducement. All employees who signed up for the plan by March 29, 1966, would be 100 percent vested after completion of one year in the plan.[23]

Cheever's daily habit of walking through various work areas and talking to employees one-on-one was an important factor in making the employees feel appreciated. Free hospitalization and free coffee twice a day also helped. In 1962, USAA began a "tuition loan" program where participating employees agreed to work at USAA one year for each year of tuition-free education. In summers, however, another problem arose that needed imagination to solve. Children were out of school and many of USAA's women had to resign to take care of their children. Most would return in the fall again, but the Association's workload was heaviest in summer, and things did fall behind.

A Tradition Of Service

In the spring of 1963, after one of the personnel staff told Moye that she was leaving to take care of her kids, Moye brought a proposal to Cheever. USAA should run a summer day camp for employees' children. The parents would bring their kids when they arrived at work and pick them up after work was over. Cheever and the Board agreed, and for less than $10,000 for a pavilion and restroom, the camp was in operation that summer. The YWCA ran the camp and the parents paid $10 per week per child.

The camp was operated on "Mira Flores," the 4.5-acre property of Doctor Aureliano Urrutia purchased by USAA the previous year as a buffer for the home office property. Dotted with pieces of Mexican and Aztec statuary and ceramics, the park-like area still exists today. This day-care program was one of the first in the country to

Opening of USAA's day camp, June 3, 1963

recognize the special needs of single and working parents and their children.

There was a very strong familial bond among the USAA employees that Lil Bates, secretary to Charles Cheever, still recalls with emotion today. The employees were proud to be there. New employee Marcella Morgan's 1961 Christmas card was a sketch of the USAA building. The employees worked hard to serve the members and some managers were overzealous in their supervision, but there was time for fun and excitement too. On November 21, 1963, the USAA employees poured out of the building to give a boisterous welcome to President and Mrs. Kennedy. San Antonio policeman Cecil Burgett was knocked off his escort motorcycle by the tide of females rushing to get close to the smiling President. Doris Dent, today a USAA vice president, and the other young people especially liked Kennedy.

President John F. Kennedy upon his arrival in San Antonio. Photograph taken at Brooks Air Force Base. *(Courtesy Institute of Texan Cultures)*

A Tradition Of Service

The next day the gunshots from the Texas School Book Depository rang out at 12:30 p.m. and by 1:00 p.m., Kennedy was dead. The news spread quickly at the USAA building, which soon resembled a tearful, emotional wake. All work stopped and, within the hour, USAA sent all its employees home for the rest of the day.

By the mid-1960s, USAA had a solid reputation as a good employer, but not everyone was happy. Rumors began to drift around the company about active pro-union activity in the claims area. What was a little surprising about this activity was that it was started by exempt or professional employees. Moye recommended USAA's first employee opinion survey that was administered in 1966 by the Psychological Corporation of New York. Bell Labs performed a computer analysis, and the results were published and given to all employees.

Overall, the news was good. About 90 percent liked the working conditions, 98 percent felt the employees got along well with each other, and 95 percent indicated friends and neighbors thought highly of the Association. Also, 85 percent would recommend it as "a fine place to work," and about 75 percent liked their work. One serious problem that emerged was the need to improve USAA's supervisors. Almost all the employees had specific criticisms about their supervisors. The Psychological Corporation set up management training programs to try to improve the supervisors and to meet the employee's complaints. Another principal finding was that about half of the USAA employees did not understand their benefits. Actuarial consultants Bowles and Tillinghast were brought in to meet this deficiency. In September 1966, all USAA employees and their spouses met in San Antonio's Municipal Auditorium to have the programs explained to them. The employees listened intently and were appreciative of the Association's efforts. About two-thirds of the employees, however, felt that improved communication was needed. To this end, Cheever started in the same month an employees' newsletter, first called *USAA Newsletter* and later with the

March 15, 1967, issue called *USAA Coverage*. Articles explained functions of various USAA agencies, and a column called "Employees Speak Out" gave employees the opportunity to present their views.

In 1968, the city of San Antonio hosted a HemisFair, today considered the city's first major push to become a tourist mecca. Cheever participated in the planning of the event for the city and encouraged USAA to participate. He opened USAA to visitors, who were guided by USAA volunteers in specially designed uniforms.

USAA employees volunteered as tour guides for the Home Office Building when San Antonio hosted the 1968 HemisFair.

Moye also planned a USAA Employees' Day at the HemisFair. It was the first USAA event for employees and all of their families. The employees paid their own way in, but the Association gave away a large number of prizes for those attending. Attending the HemisFair events was a reminder to USAA employees that their world was expanding outside USAA as well as inside USAA.

One feature of USAA service that had great appeal to military officers was the overseas coverage. The members were not always aware of the effort it took for USAA to provide continuing service from the continental United States to overseas locations and back again. In Germany, fearing loss of the right to operate there, USAA had completed a licensing agreement with the German government — contingent upon a new Status of Forces Agreement (SOFA) being signed. In the meantime, USAA worried about the Army's European headquarters canceling insurance licenses prior to a SOFA. It also turned down an offer by the Air Forces Exchange Europe to allow USAA to sell insurance in the exchanges on military installations for a percentage of the sales or income. Rather than getting licensed by Germany, USAA's preference would be to have itself included in the military forces under the new SOFA. This was not to be, however, and the SOFA signed required Army Headquarters to cancel the American automobile registrations on any car not insured by a company licensed by Germany on July 1, 1963. USAA then activated its agreement with the German government, became licensed, and began issuing policies printed in German and in English.[24]

Since opening the sales of automobile insurance in Germany in 1952, USAA's business there had grown steadily. The employee work force had grown from twelve to sixty-six and the original office was no longer adequate. Welby Logan located a new nine-floor building in Frankfurt that was available for lease for $40,000. USAA decided to take it even though the Association would need only about 60 percent of the structure. It was able to sublet the rest.

One interesting sidebar occurred in June 1965, when USAA sent one of the first commercial telex messages to Frankfurt via the COMSAT-owned Early Bird satellite.

The Sixties – Maturity And Progress

1 Siesmayerstrasse, Frankfurt, Germany.

In the spring of 1963, on the other side of the world, a new complication arose. Cheever had always been very positive about offering insurance to members in Japan because of the strong military justice system available. Thus he was disappointed when he learned that the Japanese Diet was considering a new law. This law would require all residents in Japan to buy insurance only from companies licensed in Japan. Cheever's first action was to write to the Staff Judge Advocate of the Fifth Air Force in Japan to find out the status of USAA officer-members. The reply was that effective July 1, 1963, the law would apply to all U.S. Armed Forces members stationed there. Cheever then found out that it was legal to hold a policy before arriving in Japan, but only illegal to sell one there. Cheever's solution was ingenious. All USAA policies on members rotating to Japan were endorsed "until terminated" and were billed on the anniversary date. A simple solution avoided a possible complex problem.

Besides the countries where USAA was already licensed, as the world situation changed, USAA had to make continual adjustments to follow its members. In 1962, Cheever traveled to Asia. From there he cabled USAA and began the effort to insure autos in Thailand, South Vietnam, and Taiwan. USAA members were being ordered to these locations in increasing numbers as the buildup in Southeast Asia progressed. The John Mullen Agency in Hawaii was selected to represent USAA there after USAA's existing contractor issued a demand to triple the charges for servicing USAA. In fact, USAA followed the winds of international tension to insure its members whenever their numbers in new locations began to rise. Thus, USAA began coverage in such far-flung places as Israel, Libya, and Guantanamo Bay, Cuba.

Sometimes just when it appeared that all was well, things unraveled, forcing USAA to react quickly to solve contentious and complicated problems. A good example was when President Charles De Gaulle decided to pull France out of the North Atlantic Treaty Organization. All U.S. forces had to leave France but still remain in Europe. The North Atlantic Treaty Organization headquarters and that of the Allied Forces Central Europe moved to Belgium and the Netherlands. This caused the immediate relocation of several thousand cars insured by USAA to these two countries, where USAA was not licensed. With quick action, USAA got Belgium and the Netherlands to accept the USAA-issued Green Cards, thus enabling

THE SIXTIES – MATURITY AND PROGRESS

members to relocate to these countries and to operate their vehicles there. USAA received an unfortunate surprise when an Army captain broke his back in an auto accident in Belgium. Because all policies there were written for unlimited liability, USAA had to reserve $200,000 for the loss. In 1963, as a result of the large volume of business in overseas areas, USAA named Peat, Marwick, Mitchell and Company its independent auditor because of its worldwide office locations.

Another problem occurred when the Air Force issued its directive on automobile insurance to be effective July 1, 1964. The directive required an insurance company to be licensed in any state hosting an Air Force base or its insurance would not be valid on that installation. USAA had been trying to get licensed in all states since the threat first arose, but still had no license in twelve states. In order to preserve business in those states, Cheever sent telegrams to the commanders of the Air Force bases. He asked the commanders to let their officers know that USAA was extending all policies until June 30, 1965, to give the Association more time to get licensed and to meet the Air Force regulations. That Cheever would ask and the commanders would tell their officers was a testimony to the faith in USAA.

Offering policies everywhere was great service, but handling claims in areas following a natural catastrophe was very special. In March 1962, Max Wier Jr., Vice President-Claims, sent a team of four adjusters to Virginia in response to severe storm damage. This was the first such action and the catastrophe team concept was very successful. The first really dramatic demonstration of the concept occurred in November, when four adjusters were sent to Guam in the wake of Typhoon Karen. The storm was a huge one, with wind gusts recorded up to 208 mph which inflicted tremendous damage. USAA was the first insurer on the scene, to the members' delight. Air Force Captain Henry J. Meredith summed it up: "Couldn't ask for any better service. You have a lifetime member."[25] It was things like this that bonded members to USAA — not only the single insured, but also his friends and others who heard about the service.

USAA continued to market aggressively at the service academies and ROTC units even though growth was positive. In 1962, Cheever did decide that a name change for USAA was in order to better reflect the Association's products. He proposed to the Board the name "United Services Assurance Association" which would retain

Advertisement which appeared in the 1963 *Polaris*, the United States Air Force Academy yearbook

THE SIXTIES – MATURITY AND PROGRESS

Back in 1923, only a few months after USAA was organized, this advertisement ran in the *Army and Navy Journal.*

It was an invitation to join the Association and to share in savings on automobile insurance premiums.

Today there are over 452 thousand USAA policyholders scattered all over the world who are participating in the liberal savings now offered by USAA on many forms of insurance.

When a handful of armed forces officers met in San Antonio 41 years ago to organize USAA, they had one objective in mind — to provide economical insurance especially tailored to fit military service needs.

This was to be accomplished by selling insurance at cost, since the association was to operate on a non-profit basis and be managed by retired service officers.

During these 41 years, USAA has grown to become the largest and strongest non-profit insurance organization serving the armed forces officer.

Since its organization and up to July 1, 1963, USAA has returned $117,493,512 to policyholders in dividends — savings on insurance. Last year alone, $13,528,955 was distributed to members.

In addition to AUTOMOBILE INSURANCE which was first offered, eligible members today can also save money on a WORLD-WIDE HOUSEHOLD GOODS AND PERSONAL EFFECTS FLOATER; a PERSONAL ARTICLES FLOATER; COMPREHENSIVE PERSONAL LIABILITY and in 14 states and the D. of C. on a HOMEOWNERS AND DWELLING FIRE policy.

To save costs, selling is by mail. Write today for information on policies that you are interested in.

*Total USAA membership as of July 1, 1963

August 31, 1963 *Army, Navy, Air Force Journal and Register* USAA advertisement

211

the USAA initials. The Board did not like "Assurance" and suggested substituting "Insurance." Fortunately, the state of Virginia would not approve any name change for USAA unless it contained descriptive words such as "exchange" or "reciprocal." Cheever and the Board then dropped the idea. In 1967, another marketing ploy occurred when Cheever found out that Vice President Lyndon Johnson was going to visit Guam. Cheever mailed brochures to Guam for distribution that told about USAA's service there after Typhoon Karen. In another new effort, Cheever also sent home office personnel to brief officers on insurance at the Signal Corps School at Fort Monmouth, New Jersey, and to the Naval Base Command at Pensacola, Florida. In addition, USAA continued to advertise in publications directed at officers and officer candidates.

Many numbers other than growth were also very positive. Productivity improved gradually due to a combination of training, more experienced employees, and automation. While in the early fifties, the ratio of employees to policies was about 1:290, by 1965 the ratio climbed to 1:509. In another area, the ratio of underwriting expenses to net premiums written remained reasonable — in the 13-to-15.2-percent range. This ratio placed USAA in the top rank of the nation's insurers.

All the positive numbers brought satisfaction to the Board as well as to Cheever and his staff. What did not was the rising costs of doing business reflected in the ratio of losses and adjustment expenses incurred to premiums earned. Breaking 60 percent in the year ending 1961 was considered very troubling at the time, but by 1967, the percentage rose to 70.67 percent. The result was higher premium charges to members when state approvals could be achieved, and a reduction in dividends to a record 12 percent off the manual rates. That USAA was doing considerably better than the industry as a whole was small solace to Cheever and the Board.

One new cost was generated by the Internal Revenue Act of 1962.

THE SIXTIES – MATURITY AND PROGRESS

For many years the stock companies sought federal relief for what they viewed as a taxing inequity. Reciprocals had exemptions that made them less liable for federal taxes. Beginning January 1, 1963, the new act taxed all insurance companies on the same total income basis, eliminating the former $50,000 exemption on interest income and raising USAA's taxes. The Board set up new "Subscribers Credit Accounts" to place distributions for individual members to avoid taxes. Unfortunately, USAA's cost experience was so bad in the 1960s, it was unable to make any distributions to take advantage of the law.[26]

The new taxes had been expected. The major insurance industry losses arising from the racial riots in the big city ghettos were not. Since the 1950s, African-Americans were becoming more militant, although most followed the path of non-violence preached by Martin Luther King. Many others suggested, sometimes strongly, that violence was coming if things did not change. In 1962, James Baldwin in *The Fire Next Time* quoted a slave song that suggested the violence that lay ahead:

> God gave Noah the rainbow sign
> No more water, the fire next time.[27]

The best-known episode of violence was the Watts (Los Angeles) riots of August 1965 that resulted in 34 dead, over 1,000 injured, and estimated property damage in excess of $40 million.[28] Shortly after, *Barron's* urged the insurance industry to look carefully at Watts. Whether the event was defined as a riot, civil commotion, insurrection, or revolution would mean a difference of millions to the insurance industry.[29] By the spring of 1968, 110 cities had suffered civil disorders, including Detroit, New York, and Newark. Contemporary estimates of Detroit's losses alone ranged up to $100 million. Even the nation's capitol was not immune. After King's assassination, mobs burned and looted property in the center of the city. USAA was not hurt much directly by the riots because it provided no commercial insurance, and few members were exposed to the civil disorders. New Jersey, however, required USAA to join an assigned risk plan for commercial property in that state as a result of the riots there. After the riots, the first property under this directive that USAA shared coverage on was an apartment house in Newark.

USAA shared industry concern over the riots, and worked with other insurance companies on the issue. The major part of the rising costs for USAA, however, was in settling automobile claims. The increase in accident frequency, coupled with high costs for settling claims, drove premium costs higher. Max Wier Jr. made continuing studies of claims adjusters and tried to keep costs under control, but it was not enough. Cheever reported to the members in 1963 that USAA's losses were, unfortunately, following the national trend. In statistics published in the *Army, Navy, Air Force Register,* the Air Force reported, not surprisingly, that youthful second lieutenants sustained auto accident injuries at six times the rate of colonels.[30]

In absolute numbers, the automobile accidents rose nationally by one-third in the 1960s to over fifteen million by the close of the decade. More tragic was the rise in death rates. Annual deaths rose from about 38,000 as the sixties began to nearly 56,000 at the end, an all-time high. Death rates plotted against population, numbers of vehicles registered, and miles driven all showed significant increases.

Just before the June 1965 Annual Members' Meeting *U.S. News and World Report* published an article on "The Crisis in Auto Insurance," a subject which had been discussed in depth at USAA. The article showed dramatically what the accident rates and inflation were doing to the nation's insurance companies and their customers. Underwriting losses in 1964 were over $200 million. The trends were all bad for the previous ten years; medical costs up 37 percent, court awards up 26 percent, and repair bills up 22 percent. The article gave examples of costs for parts and labor for a sample of comparably priced, but unnamed, models:[31]

Rising Costs of Auto Repair

	1954	1965
Front Fender	$44.49	$94.50
Windshield	$56.88	$110.95
Hood Assembly	$63.85	$115.85

In canvassing insurers, the article offered a gloomy forecast for conditions that were likely to make things worse. The prediction was for more than 100 million bigger, speedier, and more powerful cars driven on more congested roads in the future.

USAA did whatever it could to reduce accidents and claims expenses. It continually urged members through annual reports and other communications to avoid the principal causes of accidents. The Association focused on excessive speed for road conditions, driving while fatigued or under the influence of alcohol, disobeying traffic laws, and inattention. In 1965, in an attempt to prune losses, USAA began checking driving records of new applicants and intensified the review of accident repeaters who were already members. USAA strongly supported the Insurance Institute for Highway Safety, which worked towards research, legislation, education, and law enforcement in the field of traffic safety.

The efforts of USAA, other insurers, and national groups such as the National Association of Independent Insurers were met by criticism from a number of directions. Senator Abraham Ribicoff of Connecticut sparked the unprecedented interest of the federal government in traffic safety. In 1967, Representative Emanuel Celler (D-NY) gathered information from auto insurance companies. Unhappy with the results, he called for the Federal Trade Commission to investigate the insurance industry. In his 1968 State of the Union message, President Lyndon Johnson called attention to the problem of automobile insurance, resulting in a study by the Department of Transportation. In 1968 alone, over 6,000 bills on insurance were before the various state legislatures.

What frustrated Cheever even more than the federal intervention was the media. In June 1968, Cheever pointed out to the members that *Life* and *Time* magazines wrote editorials on the insurance problems. The thesis of these editorials was that the insurance system was inefficient and that the cost of automobile insurance had "soared" 55 percent in the previous ten years. Cheever told the members that he called the library and found out that the cost of *Life* "soared" 75 percent and *Time* 150 percent over the same period! He asked rhetorically whether these magazines were giving their readers more. Perhaps, but not double. If asked, the publishers would probably justify these costs on such things as paper, ink, transportation, and salaries. USAA's rising costs were also tied to an inflation over which the Association had no control. For USAA, the same ten-year period saw an increase of 92 percent in daily hospital charges, 39 percent in prescriptions and physicians' fees, and 60 percent in the minimum wage.

The important thing was that, in spite of the costs, USAA's insurance was the best value around. What improved the value was the personal, hands-on service that went along with the price. As Cheever put it, "USAA has been a service organization in every sense of the word and if it ever fails to fulfill this fundamental philosophy, it will have no further need of existence."[32] What was happening on the other side of the world was to play a role in a severe test of this philosophy.

CHAPTER SEVEN

HIGH ENERGY

Vietnam barely pierced American consciousness in the early days of U.S. involvement, but the war touched USAA from the beginning. When the French found themselves surrounded at Dienbienphu, American military pilots were flying in supplies from the Philippines to the beleaguered forces. USAA Personnel Director Jean Moye's brother and USAA member Lieutenant Colonel Harry Schiele was among them. The surrender of the French in May 1954 was followed by a conference at Geneva which split the country at the 17th parallel. President Eisenhower and the United States supported South Vietnam with financial aid and military advisors. In 1959, USAA member Major Dale Buis and Sergeant Chester Ovnand, advisors, were the first Americans to die at the hands of Vietnamese communist guerillas. After Kennedy's election in 1960, he increased support for South Vietnam; by mid-1962, there were 12,000 military advisors on Vietnamese soil, many of them USAA members. After Kennedy's assassination, President Johnson continued and intensified American efforts in Vietnam.

In August 1964, a Vietnamese patrol boat attacked the U.S. destroyer *Maddox* in the Tonkin Gulf. A second alleged attack prodded Johnson into sending a retaliatory raid against the North Vietnamese. Among those on the raid was Lieutenant (jg) Everett Alvarez Jr. Alvarez took off from the U.S. carrier *Lexington* and headed for a patrol boat base northeast of Hanoi. While making a firing pass, Alvarez's plane was hit. Alvarez ejected and fractured his back when he landed hard in shallow water. Captured immediately, he spent more than eight years as a prisoner of war in the

Lieutenant (jg) Everett Alvarez Jr.

communist internment facility known to the POWs as the Hanoi Hilton. USAA member Alvarez was the first aviator to become a POW of the nearly 600 American airmen captured during the conflict.

This was just one aspect of the tragic human dimension of the war, and USAA acted to try to make things easier on members and employees who became involved in rapidly increasing numbers. A special action office was set up to focus on POW and missing-in-action cases. When USAA received such a notification, this office flagged the files for special handling and contacted the family of the member to provide whatever help and assistance that it could. USAA's extraordinary efforts with these cases did not go unnoticed. In 1970, Chief of Naval Operations Admiral Elmo R. Zumwalt wrote to USAA expressing his personal appreciation. He was grateful that the Association had been, "unusually responsive to the sensitive situations of our missing in action and prisoner of war families."[1]

USAA also provided strong support to employees who were drafted or called to active duty from the Reserves. In a 1968 revision to the USAA retirement plan, employees received up to two years of credited USAA employment to count towards their re-

USAA member Admiral Elmo R. Zumwalt

tirement benefits. Those who served overseas received an additional one-third bonus for their time there. Employees who were in organized Reserve or National Guard units and who were called up received an additional benefit. For the first three months of their service, USAA paid those employees the difference between their military pay and benefits and their USAA salary.[2]

On the business side, USAA did its best to provide a balance between the needs of individual members and the membership as a whole. USAA property and casualty policies included a war clause, but it had very limited impact on the membership. And this was principally on members stationed with their families in Vietnam before the war started.

The life insurance offered by the fledgling USAA Life Insurance Company was a different matter, and USAA was supportive, but cautious. As the war expanded, the USAA Life Insurance Company gave considerable thought and study to the possible casualty exposure of the Association. Most standard life companies had a war exclusion clause in their policies, and that was the safe thing to do. But, USAA and its life subsidiary had been organized to serve military officers. To put a war clause in its life policies would seem to be a breach of trust and would tarnish USAA's image badly. The USAA Life Company Board decided on a middle ground and limited life insurance for those bound for Southeast Asia to $20,000. To further protect the membership, USAA entered into new reinsurance agreements with the Life Insurance Company of North America and American United.[3] This decision was a good one. In the first nine months of 1966, reinsurance covered nearly 60 percent of over $325,000 in claims against USAA life policies.[4]

The most serious challenge of the Vietnam War to USAA was not from bullets, however, but from paper. The growth of U.S. forces in Vietnam exceeded everyone's expectations. By the end of 1965, over 200,000 Americans were in Vietnam, and this number nearly doubled in the next two years. On January 31, 1968, the communist Tet Offensive began and American confidence was badly shaken. In response, President Lyndon Johnson announced that he would not run for reelection, but authorized a further increase in troop strength to 540,000. And, recall that most of the American military served one-year tours and returned, calling for hundreds of thousands of replacements over the war years.

Captain Thomas Draude receiving the Silver Star from General Wallace M. Greene. Draude retired from the USMC as a Brigadier General and in 1997 was serving USAA as the Regional Senior Vice President in Tampa.

This almost insatiable appetite for men and women to support the war effort had a predictable effect. Total military strength rose from 2.7 million in 1963 to 3.5 million by the end of 1968. The number of officers on active duty rose during the same time period from 334,000 to 416,000. The Reserves and National Guard units filled their authorized positions as well.

USAA's membership totals reflected the Vietnam surge, rising about 200,000 from 1963 to 1968. Cheever had often noted to the members that, while positive, growth and size were not primary objectives of USAA, but were products of USAA's service philosophy. Size did not reduce efficiency and effectiveness, but gave the Association greater financial strength. Cheever said that this enabled USAA "to render better service at less cost per member" than if USAA had remained a small organization.[5] The rapid growth did reduce USAA's effectiveness, however.

The member growth numbers alone would have strained USAA's resources, but there was more. In 1963, the average number of policies per member was 1.7. By the end of 1968, the figure was slightly more than two policies overall, and new members averaged closer to three policies each. The increase resulted from more multiple-car families as well as from other property and casualty and life products. A further complicating factor was that the workload peaked nearly 40 percent in the summer months, when more military transfers took place, making the yearlong efforts uneven. USAA was truly being overwhelmed by its very success. Besides the growing numbers, a confusion factor introduced by new members was the growing propensity for women to retain their maiden names after marriage, causing records mix-ups.

As paperwork fell quickly behind, management's first reaction was to hire more employees. From 1965 to 1968, USAA's work force climbed from 1,850 to nearly 2,400. It was difficult to find employees, and so USAA contracted for 120 employees from a U.S. Department of Labor Job Corps program for the hard-core unem-

Working conditions at USAA

ployed.[6] The available space at the Broadway building — and the employees — became more and more crowded. Cheever even submitted plans to the Board to close in the porches on the west end of the building to provide more space. Such efforts were not enough, however. In a 1968 survey of over 1,300 employees, 30 percent found the working conditions unpleasant.

Individual comments on the survey reflected the employees' frustration. "Working conditions are crowded; there just isn't enough space to work" and "desks are very close together and there are constant interruptions."[7] The crowding was only part of the dissatisfaction. A significant number of employees were unhappy about the pressure and the overtime. One employee pointed out that she had been working overtime for the previous five months. During the summer, she worked ten-hour days and even Saturdays. She was just tired out. These working conditions initiated a new rise in the employee turnover rate, which had been declining steadily since the mid 1950s.

Contributing to the pressure and the deteriorating service levels was how the work moved along at USAA. Although there were many member complaints, things were not as serious as they might have been. Members might not receive actual policies for weeks or even months. But because they knew their insurance was effective on the date of the postmark of their application, they didn't worry. They had faith and trust in their Association. Nevertheless, USAA knew it should do much better. By 1968, there were stacks of member files everywhere. A typical desk would have three or four stacks of files twelve to eighteen inches high and laundry baskets full of records by the side all waiting for action. Multiplied by the number of employees, the number of files removed from the central files area was enormous. At any given time thousands of files were missing — not lost, but whereabouts unknown.

To find these records, USAA hired night search teams of college students. During the day, lists of missing records were run off in

File locator/clocking station, 1966

terminal digit order, one column wide. The young men would then sit down at a desk and compare the files in that work area with their listings. When they found one, they would put a red tag on the file. When the regular employees arrived to work in the morning, they would call an action desk to find out where the file had to go next. Sometimes the records were never found. Employees then had to contact the members and try to reconstruct the missing files.[8] Official position titles such as "mismatch clerk" and "correction clerk" suggest the institutionalization of the problem.

One attempt to solve the problem was made during the last weekend of June 1968. Cheever agreed to a moratorium on all incoming mail to make an extensive effort to reduce the backlog and to return underwriting files to the records center. All employees in areas such as data processing, communications center, underwriting and many others were required to work both days. To make it more palatable, all employees received time-and-a-half, free coffee breaks and hot lunches, and free day camp or reimbursement for babysitting fees for children under five years of age. Jean Moye recalled that the moratorium helped over the weekend, but productivity fell off the following week.[9]

Although USAA expended enormous efforts in getting licensed everywhere, by 1968 USAA was not yet licensed to sell automobile insurance in Ohio, Vermont, and New Hampshire. For example, the state of Ohio refused to license a reciprocal to write automobile liability insurance for personal cars. Cheever recommended that the Association organize a wholly-owned multiple lines subsidiary stock company. Its purpose would be "to serve the insurance needs of qualified USAA members in those states where the Association cannot be licensed as a reciprocal insurance exchange."[10] The Board agreed, and the organizational meeting of the Board of Directors of the United Services Casualty Insurance Company (USCIC) was held on September 20. The Board authorized the new company to apply for a license in Ohio, Vermont, and New Hampshire. The state of Texas licensed USCIC three days later. At the same time, USAA Life was trying to get licensed in every state as well; a new DOD directive prohibited allotting pay for life insurance premiums in states where a company was not licensed.

* * * *

As USAA grew through the sixties, Cheever was moving through his own sixties and thinking about a successor. Although there were many suitors for the position both inside and outside of USAA, Cheever only really considered one man — Air Force Brigadier General Robert F. McDermott.[11] After Cheever's initial contact with McDermott, who was teaching at West Point, in 1953, to secure reprint permission for McDermott's *Principles of Insurance*, he saw him often. He visited him at West Point and later annually at the Air Force Academy when Cheever traveled with the USAA team to brief the cadets on insurance. Cheever asked McDermott informally about coming to USAA in the mid-sixties, but McDermott refused because he still had things he wished to do at the Academy. In 1967, Cheever decided to wait for McDermott. He renewed his five-year contract at USAA, but insisted on a sixty-day cancellation clause. Next, he cornered McDermott's wife, Alice, about the position. She wanted McDermott to retire from the Air Force, because with two children in graduate school and two more to send at least through undergraduate schools, their financial resources were dangerously low. Prodded by Alice, McDermott agreed to take her to San Antonio in December to take a look. It was then that Cheever made a formal offer to him, contingent on Board approval.[12]

The following month McDermott returned to San Antonio to be interviewed by the USAA Board of Directors. Opening the meeting, Cheever briefly discussed various successor candidates, but recommended only McDermott. He then told the Board that McDermott was interested in coming to USAA, provided he would become president on Cheever's retirement.[13] The Chairman of the Board, Air Force retired Major General John H. McCormick, recalled later that McDermott made a very strong impression. The Board appreciated his West Point education, his Harvard MBA, his book on insurance, and his leadership at the Air Force Academy. It then offered him the position effective upon his retirement from the Air Force.[14] Although he had offers from General Mills, the Educational Testing Service, and Litton Industries, he decided upon USAA. McDermott took terminal leave from the Air Force and arrived at USAA ready to sign his five-year contract and to assume his position as Executive Vice President on July 16, 1968.

McDermott was born on July 31, 1920, in Boston, Massachusetts. Along with his three sisters, he was raised in Readville, Massachusetts, a small blue-collar town. McDermott's father, Marlow, was a milkman and later manager of milk distribution. He had a beautiful Irish tenor voice and sang at most of the town's weddings and funerals. It was he who taught his son to play the trombone and gave him his love of music. His mother, "Tootie," was a warm and friendly person, and the backbone of the family. Backing up every mother in Readville were the other mothers all over town who were quick to correct any child's misbehavior and to notify the family. The "whole village to raise a child" theory was a practiced behavior in Readville. Recreation in the small town was pick-up games in baseball and ice hockey, ice cream at Solemy's, marbles, and watching trotters train at the racetrack where McDermott's grandfather was a blacksmith.[15]

An early glimpse at a facet of McDermott's character was recalled by a boyhood friend from Readville. One day, seven-year old Eddie Cox sneaked out of his house with his bag of marbles without permission. The older boys won all of Eddie's marbles and he began to cry. He knew his parents would be angry with him, and he'd lost his treasured marbles as well. McDermott, who was a little older than Eddie, observed the scene and took Eddie to his home. Although he did not really know Eddie, McDermott brought out his own marbles, counted them out, and gave the unsuccessful gambler half of his marbles. This was the beginning of a lifelong friendship between the two boys.[16]

McDermott's deep respect for education and learning began in a two-room schoolhouse. It was his teacher, Miss Hastings, who encouraged him to challenge himself to develop his mind. At twelve, he was selected to go to a Harvard University summer session taught by the brother of his former kindergarten teacher. Hastings encouraged him to enroll in and to commute forty-five minutes daily to attend Boston Latin School. He and Leonard Bernstein played in the school orchestra together and when he graduated, McDermott won the prize for the outstanding musician in his class as Bernstein had two years previously. Along with Miss Hastings' Old Testament reading in school and Sister Reparatta's instructions at St. Ann's Sunday School, his family life encouraged a strong belief in the Catholic faith.

High Energy

One of McDermott's teachers at Boston Latin School was "Itchy" Faxen, who encouraged McDermott to work for his brother during the summer as a caddie on Cape Cod. He and Ed Cox made seventy-five cents for eighteen holes. With a twenty-five cent tip, they just covered their daily boarding fee. To make any spending money, they had to caddie a second round. On one day a week, the caddies were allowed to play golf for free, and this is where the golf "vice" became a permanent part of his life. A second vice he acquired at the golf course was smoking, which he continued for years.

When he graduated from Boston Latin School, McDermott wanted a service academy education, but he did not get an appointment. Instead, he went to Norwich University in Vermont for two years and again sought an Academy appointment. At Norwich, he was fourth in his class in academics, first in military science, and class president. His father had always wanted his son to go to an Academy and was very pleased to see him enter West Point. It was at the Academy that McDermott picked up his nickname "McD" (Mack-Dee) which stuck permanently. During his first two years, he repeated courses he took at Norwich because of a set West Point curriculum and became bored, but his interest and his grades improved in his last two years. Overall, McDermott was a solid student, just missing the top quarter of his graduating class.

His West Point yearbook suggests that his class standing reflected his preference for between-class naps, fair ladies, and music to studying Newton. The yearbook described him as always amiable, with an enormous amount of natural ability. It predicted that "individuality and inventiveness will draw him to the unusual soldiers of tomorrow."[17]

Due to the pressure of World War II, his program at West Point was an unusual one. General H.H. "Hap" Arnold came to West Point in 1942 to ask for volunteers to fly with the Army Air Corps. That had always been a dream of McDermott since he watched *Talespin*

Robert F. McDermott as a West Point cadet

Tommy at the movies as a boy. The dream was reinforced when he went with his father to a parade honoring Charles Lindbergh, who then became his boyhood hero. McDermott volunteered and went to flying school the summer of 1942. In the meantime, he continued to date Alice McDermott (no relation) whom he met when she was another cadet's blind date. He had turned the same blind date down first, but quickly reversed his field once he saw her. His class graduated six months early and he was commissioned on January 20, 1943. On the day after his graduation, he married Alice at Trinity Chapel at West Point over initial opposition of his parents because he was "too young."[18]

After graduation, McDermott went to flight school and checked out in the P-38 Lockheed Lightning. Assigned to the 474th Fighter Bomber Group, McDermott flew sixty-one combat missions as the outfit moved from England through Europe and ultimately into Germany. Throughout his life, he exhibited a charisma that attracted others to his leadership. In 1990, attending his first reunion of the 474th Fighter Bomber Group, McDermott's wartime crew chief, John Perkins, said he remembered "Major Mac" very well, but did not know what happened to him after the war. (McDermott was not at the reunion.) He was surprised to hear of McDermott's postwar life. It was obvious, however, McDermott had a powerful impact on the life of his crew chief. On this day, some forty-five years after their World War II tour together, he pulled out his billfold and showed a faded picture of McDermott in his flying suit. "I've said a prayer for him every day since the war," Perkins volunteered.

After the war, McDermott was assigned to General Eisenhower's Headquarters where he helped plan the movement of dependents overseas, and then went to the Pentagon as a personnel officer. The Harvard Graduate School of Business was next, where he received his MBA in 1950. He then joined the Social Sciences faculty at West Point. McDermott had finagled a flying exchange tour with a Navy carrier to follow this assignment, but Lieutenant General Hubert Harmon, Superintendent of the Air Force Academy, got it canceled to McDermott's disappointment in favor of an assignment to the Academy in 1954.

Captain Robert F. McDermott as a fighter pilot in World War II. He named his P-38 for his first daughter.

A Tradition Of Service

McDermott joined the Air Force Academy faculty at its temporary location at Denver. In 1956, he was appointed Dean of the Faculty. He was challenged to get the Academy accredited by the North Central Association of Colleges and Schools by the time the first class (1959) graduated. Through a series of initiatives, he was successful. The reward was a rich one. In 1959, he was promoted to brigadier general at age thirty-nine, becoming the youngest flag rank officer in the country. The same year, President Dwight Eisenhower also appointed McDermott as the first Permanent Dean of the Faculty. He served in this position for the first ten graduating classes until his retirement in 1968.

Brigadier General Robert F. McDermott as Dean of Faculty at the United States Air Force Academy.

High Energy

McDermott's ten years at the Air Force Academy were very innovative ones, and established the school as one of the nation's premier academic institutions. Nevertheless, his changes generated tremendous opposition from many throughout the military establishment. In reaction to his experience at West Point where he had to repeat academic courses he had already successfully completed at Norwich, he began a curriculum enrichment program. This enabled cadets to validate courses and to move ahead as quickly as they were able. He established academic majors and began the first Department of Astronautics in the country. Then he set up cooperative Master's degree programs with such outstanding institutions as Purdue (astronautics), Georgetown (international affairs), and UCLA (management). Cadets took some graduate work at the Academy and then were able to complete their Master's degrees at the civil-

United States Air Force Academy cadets with the Cadet Chapel in the background

ian institutions eight months later. He also developed a "whole person" concept in admissions which considered a variety of measures resulting in better-qualified cadets at the Academy. Another of McDermott's beliefs was in an all-military faculty. At the time he said the faculty "teach subject matter by what they say and inspire professionalism by who they are."[19] Many of his innovations at the Air Force Academy were praised by West Point and Annapolis leaders at the time and were subsequently adopted by those service academies. Years later, then Under Secretary of the Air Force Anne Foreman called him the "Father of the U.S. Air Force Academy" and the "Father of Modern Military Education." She believed that his contributions to the Academy were as revolutionary as those Sylvanus Thayer had made to West Point in the nineteenth century, earning Thayer the honorific title of "Father of West Point."[20]

When McDermott retired, Harvard University professor Samuel Huntington wrote congratulating him on his contributions to military education. Then he continued, "Knowing what a restless creature you are, I wonder what major innovations you will soon be promoting at USAA. Does the Board of Directors really know what it is letting itself in for?"[21] The answer was "no," at first.

In July 1968, USAA was a strong, vibrant company with a solid reputation. It was the sixteenth largest writer of automobile insurance out of over 1,000 property and casualty companies in the nation. Insurance examiners representing the Insurance Commissioner of Georgia had just completed an examination of the Association's rating procedures and did not find a single error. In about the same time frame, USAA also received favorable examiners' reports from Texas, Iowa, and Virginia.[22] *Best's Insurance Reports*, 1968-1969 Edition, again gave USAA its highest "A+" rating.

In the same month, Professor Richard Norgaard of the University of Southern California, a national authority in the field of insurance, investments, and finance, testified before a U.S. Senate

Judiciary subcommittee. He reported the results of his study on the profitability of 666 U.S. business organizations, including twenty-five insurance companies, during the period 1953 to 1967. Of the 666 companies he studied, he pointed out that USAA had the best rate of return and was the "best of all my companies in the sample."[23]

In the summer of 1968, when McDermott began at USAA, Cheever told him that he did not want him to try to make any changes immediately. Rather, he wanted McDermott to spend the next few months getting oriented to the business world in general, and to USAA in particular. He also gave McDermott the responsibility to handle long-term projects that would come to fruition after he became president. Cheever shared everything with his protégé and included him in meetings inside and outside of USAA. For example, Cheever stepped down from his Board position of the NAII and made it possible for McDermott to take his place. McDermott spent time in all the operational areas, listening and observing. He also traveled to Europe with Cheever to get an insight into the European operations. The only announced change in late 1968 that McDermott initiated was that effective in January, USAA employees would no longer punch the time clock.

The most visible symptoms of USAA's troubles to McDermott were the tremendous number of files everywhere and the crowded working conditions. While USAA had firm plans for the original Broadway building and even an addition to that building years ahead, no long-range plans existed beyond that. In August 1968, for the short-term, Cheever proposed that USAA construct a three-story annex on Broadway. For the longer term, Cheever requested authority to purchase a 50-to 100-acre tract of land for a new building.[24] The Board later amended that to 250 acres and in November 1968, the Board agreed to purchase 212 acres from Marshall T. Steves that fronted on Bitters and Blanco Road in northern San Antonio.

USAA management had recognized that technology would be the key to handling the paperwork and took steps to acquire the latest equipment. It was the first company in San Antonio to purchase an IBM 650 computer and the IBM 7074 and 1401 electronic data processing systems. In 1966, electronics and data processing consultant Richard C. Canning visited USAA. After reviewing the Association's plans and progress in the field of automation, he advised USAA that it was "far ahead of most companies in the U.S. in the use and applications of electronic data processing equipment."[25] In 1967, USAA acquired two IBM 360 systems that could provide real-time confirmation of insurance coverages to claims representatives on television screens (IBM 2260 visual display units). Key punching had given way to Mohawk (magnetic tape) Data Recorders and then eventually to more efficient systems keyed directly to computers. In spite of these technological enhancements, the workload and backlog continued to increase along with a deterioration in service. In recognition of the critical and growing role of computers, the Board split the position of Vice President-Personnel and Data Processing into two separate functions. Colonel A.T. "Benny" Leonard became Vice President of the EDP function, and Jean Moye became Vice President, Personnel.[26]

In July, Clem H. Spalding, Underwriting Director, sent a memo to his boss, Colonel Jack Griffith, Vice President of Underwriting, indicating that USAA needed total automation and not piecemeal implementation. Others talked about this too, but Spalding's memo struck a sympathetic chord and McDermott called Spalding to his office. Spalding, USAA's only professional Chartered Property and Casualty Underwriter (CPCU), told McDermott that some companies were using a multi-car policy — putting all the cars of one family on one policy. It was more efficient and less costly. McDermott put Spalding on this special project immediately, and relieved him of all other duties. He also gave Spalding the authority to pick out a few people in the Association to help him. He was to report directly to McDermott.²⁷ June (Rogers) Reedy was one of Spalding's team members.

Reedy had seen a briefing on automating insurance writing by INSCO Systems Corporation, a subsidiary of Continental Insurance Company of New York, that she thought would help the Association. USAA contacted INSCO and, in mid-October, two INSCO officials came to San Antonio. As they explained their system, the USAA attendees saw the tremen-

Clem Spalding

dous opportunity it presented. When uncoded answers to a questionnaire were entered into the computer, it automatically established the rate classification and codes, printed the appropriate automobile declaration and invoice, and prepared accounting and statistical records. McDermott gave the project an enthusiastic go-ahead. When Spalding later told McDermott that the system could potentially eliminate much of the paperwork for over 282,000 separate policies and consequently reduce personnel, McDermott ordered the termination of plans for a three-story annex on Broadway at once. All USAA departments were to request their additional short-term space requirements early in 1969.²⁸

In October, Benny Leonard and Carl Schenken, Treasurer, announced their intentions to retire early in 1969, and consultant Max Wier Sr. was approaching eighty years of age. The average age of all the USAA officers was sixty-two. It was time for McDermott to start building his own team. He talked to many individuals and also called Air Force Colonel John F. "Jack" Daye Jr., a West Point classmate who was stationed in Washington, D.C. He asked Daye to check out Air Force Colonel Martin D. "Marty" Fishel Jr. for the data processing position. McDermott's Harvard Business School classmate and West Point graduate Brigadier General Walter Brinker had recommended Army Lieutenant Colonel George H. Ensley for the finance area, and Daye interviewed him also. Daye recommended both men and Moye traveled to Washington, D.C. to interview them. She ended up sending both of them, and Daye, to the Psychological Corporation in New York City for personnel testing.

In January, McDermott asked Ensley to join USAA, but Ensley had always planned on settling in California and asked for thirty days to decide. He then interviewed for the secretary-treasurer position at a San Francisco company which was offering him a higher salary than USAA had offered. During his final interview, while receiving the actual offer from the president, Ensley decided to take this San Francisco job. Then he looked out the window of the company's high-rise facing the Oakland Bay Bridge. Seeing the traffic jam on the bridge and contemplating a one-to-two-hour commute, he blurted out to the president, "This isn't for me." He left the shocked executive in his office, found a pay phone, and called McDermott to accept the USAA job.[29] All three men were to join USAA in early 1969.

Cheever, at the age of seventy, was happy that McDermott had arrived and that USAA would be in good hands. It was obvious to him that McDermott was eager to take over, and he discussed retiring immediately with some of his close associates. Most discouraged him from doing this, however. They thought that McDermott should continue his orientation and preparation.[30] But on November 26, believing that McDermott was ready, Cheever wrote a letter to the chairman of the USAA Board requesting that his retirement be approved and be made effective January 3, 1969.

HIGH ENERGY

In December, Cheever wrote a letter to Major General William W. Berg at Headquarters, USAF. He called his letter "a report of my trusteeship to the Defense Department." He noted that during his presidency, membership had grown from 134,000 to over 640,000 and that policies in force had grown from 170,000 to over 1.2 million. Further, assets had climbed from $16 million to over $200 million. Cheever was pleased with USAA's positive image and sound financial position. He also expressed his hope that at some time in the near future USAA would be able to extend membership to the enlisted force. Cheever stated that the Association had not already done so because the Association was not in the position to add categories of membership "without interfering with the service for the group for which the Association was organized."[31] This letter is striking because it shows that Cheever and USAA felt a sense of obligation to the Department of Defense that went far beyond marketing. In view of subsequent developments, his thoughts

Betty and Charles Cheever at his retirement coffee

on accommodating enlisted personnel are interesting as well.

And so Cheever walked away contentedly from USAA. McDermott talked to him often, but it was for discussions on USAA individual employees and the politics of San Antonio, and not on future plans for USAA. Cheever left USAA to McDermott and spent his remaining working years as Chairman of the Broadway National Bank. After so many years at USAA, the employees and a generation of military officers had grown accustomed to him. Member and Navy Commander Jeremiah E. Lenihan summed up the feelings of many when he wrote to Cheever after his retirement. He said that for years "your name and the outstanding service of U.S. Auto seemed to be synonymous and your signature at the end of the Association's letters was as comfortable as an old shoe."[32]

On Friday, January 3, 1969, McDermott became President and Attorney-in-Fact of USAA. It was a new environment for McDermott — a world of women. USAA was over 90 percent women at the time. It would be an adjustment for him to make, having come from a world of men. He told a reporter from the *San Antonio Evening News* that he had "never seen so many women in one place before in his life." At forty-seven, he was handsome and had the classically erect posture of a general officer. He was an immaculate dresser, his gray hair was wavy (and all there), and his golf-tanned face framed piercing blue eyes. During McDermott's first week, one female employee was heard to say, "look out, Paul Newman!" Beyond the physical differences, other changes were immediately evident to the employees. McDermott tended to stay in his office and not walk the floors and engage in casual conversations with the employees as Cheever had been accustomed to doing. After years of Cheever's easy warmth, McDermott's apparent cool demeanor unsettled them.

On January 12, in his first interview with the San Antonio *Express-News*, McDermott tipped his hand on some of the things on his mind. He mused that a subsidiary company for non-commissioned officers might be a possibility, and said that he wanted to reduce personnel turnover. He questioned whether USAA could be more efficient with its mail, and thought that USAA should do more with its life insurance business.[33] These were in addition to the things McDermott was already working on at the Home Office.

His statements were not idle talk. Over the next three years, McDermott led the Association through sweeping changes in virtually every area. No problem was too large or too small, too complex or too simple to attack. Based on his own vision, input from his employees, and practical necessity, the changes laid the foundation for the future direction of the Association. McDermott's intelligence, energy, intensity, and workaholic nature were keys to the transformation. Lil Bates, Cheever's former secretary and then McDermott's during this period, was amazed then and now. McDermott arrived at 8 a.m. When she left for home to cook supper for her family, he was still at his desk. She returned a couple hours later and they worked until somewhere between 11 p.m. and 2 a.m. He then followed her car home to make sure that she was safe. Usually he went home, but occasionally he returned to the office and was at his desk when she arrived in the morning. In any case, this level of effort continued month after month, stretching into 1972.[34]

From the beginning, he believed that the key to success was the employees. In his supervisor's meeting on September 25, 1968, he spelled out his beliefs. What did not concern him was getting needed changes accomplished — he knew this was already being done. He went on to say that his principal concern was that in directing attention to operational matters, "we may lose sight of the fact that in the final analysis we will accomplish the desired results and reach our goals" only through people — our non-exempt employees. He urged his supervisors to develop good communications with their

Martin Fishel

employees. His belief in the importance of the USAA employees would guide his actions over his tenure. His management team fully supported McDermott in his efforts with them.

The first of McDermott's new management team to arrive was Marty Fishel. Fishel had been a career Air Force officer, retiring with the rank of colonel. Beginning as an aviation cadet in 1943, he earned the Distinguished Flying Cross during combat in World War II. In his subsequent Air Force career, he had assignments in automatic data processing, statistics, and systems development, making him a valuable asset to USAA. His intelligence, vitality, and organizational skills were critical in his position as Vice President, Computer Services, in McDermott's first years at USAA.

Next to arrive was George Ensley, a native of Hemet, California. After serving a hitch as an enlisted man in the Army, he got out and worked his way through the University of California at Berkeley. While waiting for a blind date in the parlor of a boarding house, he spotted Lucille Lichens visiting a friend. He found out who she was and where she lived. He took his blind date out for a milkshake and took her home, then headed for Lucille's boarding house, where he introduced himself. According to Lucille, his "beautiful blue eyes" caught her interest at once. Within three weeks the couple was engaged, and three months later they were married in August 1949.

The Phi Beta Kappa graduate received a regular Army commission in June 1950 in the Finance Corps, but was detailed to the Armor Branch. When the Korean War broke out, he was assigned

High Energy

Lieutenant George Ensley, 1950. His tank, pictured above, had been hit and disabled.

as a tank platoon leader with the 2nd Infantry Division in Korea. During his year there, the 2nd Division sustained tremendous casualties. S.L.A. Marshall's *The River and the Gauntlet* described the Division's struggles while it was close to the Yalu River which separates Korea and China. When the Chinese troops staged a twilight mass attack, Ensley's reinforced tank platoon helped repel the enemy forces. Wounded in the action, Ensley later received the Purple Heart and the Silver Star for gallantry.

In 1951, Ensley returned to the United States and in 1952 was assigned to the Finance Corps. He had a superb mind for finance. He stood near the top of his class at the Army's Finance School, and he tied for first out of 200 while getting his MBA at Stanford University. His military career included finance, comptroller, and plans assignments. His final tour was as a budget officer for the Deputy Chief of Personnel of the Department of the Army in Wash-

A Tradition Of Service

George Ensley, 1969

ington, D.C. Ensley became USAA's Vice President-Treasurer on May 1, 1969. His first assignments, to review USAA's investment portfolio and to prepare a twenty-year forecast, were most valuable and presaged an outstanding career at USAA.

The third critical hire for McDermott was Colonel "Jack" Daye. Daye was an Army brat born in the Philippines. He entered West Point as a classmate of McDermott's, and for a brief time they were roommates. Daye commanded a photo reconnaissance squadron in World War II and served on the staff of the Far East Air Material Command during the Korean War. He also commanded a fighter interceptor squadron and an air defense group. After serving as Deputy Director for Advanced Plans and Future Developments at Air Defense Command, he became

Jack Daye as a pilot in World War II

Deputy Commandant for cadets at the Air Force Academy while McDermott was Dean. Daye's final tour was with Headquarters Air Force at the Pentagon. McDermott talked to Daye at the Pentagon and asked him to come to USAA to set up a plans operation. Daye arrived July 1, 1969 and became USAA's Vice President, Plans and Programs.

In August of 1969, McDermott sent Ensley to Washington, D.C. He was to explore the feasibility of USAA acquiring a national savings bank, a savings and loan association, and a mutual fund. Ensley consulted with numerous congressional staffers from the Banking and Currency Committees and Texas legislators as well as representatives of the Federal Reserve Bank, Federal Deposit Insurance Corporation, and the Security and Exchange Commission. The suggestions Ensley received helped McDermott plan USAA's expansion into financial services. Knowing what might be done, McDermott wanted an input from the membership on what they wanted.[35]

One of Daye's first tasks was to survey USAA's members to find out what they wanted and expected from the Association. The results of the Gelb Marketing Research survey showed significant member interest in new products and services beyond insurance:[36]

Gelb Marketing Research Survey Results

Automobile Financing	76%	Mutual Funds	65%
Home Mortgages	78%	Savings Accounts	47%
Signature Loans	66%	Automobile Leasing	41%

At the same meeting, Gary Wilson, Director of Plans, outlined a new automobile purchasing program which the Board returned to management for further study. To enable USAA to offer these new services, Daye's recommendation was to change the bylaws.[37]

At the first USAA Board meeting in January 1970, McDermott proposed the bylaws change. He wanted it changed to read: "The purpose of the exchange is to afford such insurance coverages *and other products and services* as the Board of Directors shall determine." (Proposed change in italics). The Board questioned the wisdom of changing the basic philosophy, diluting present services, becoming a conglomerate, and dissipating the talents of the staff.[38] McDermott saw he did not have and probably would not get the needed votes, and discussed withdrawing the proposal from the agenda of the February meeting himself. The Board considered it nonetheless, but then decided to withdraw the proposed amendment from consideration.[39]

Instead of arguing with the USAA Board with a change in purpose to allow USAA to establish a no-load mutual fund, McDermott decided to try a different tack. In February 1970, he had his Director of Planning brief the Life Company Board on the need for an open-end mutual fund to provide the military man with a "savings package" in connection with his life insurance. In the Gelb survey, 65 percent of the members had indicated an interest. Although the Life Company Board had essentially the same members as USAA's Board, it agreed that the concept of a mutual fund as a subsidiary of the Life Company could be explored further. William Camp, U.S. Comptroller of the Currency, had advised placing any mutual fund under the Life Company.[40] Two months later the Association's Board agreed that the Life Company could organize a mutual fund as a "proper adjunct" to insurance coverages under the USAA bylaws. Some Board members who had believed that a reciprocal could not sell life products agreed that Life Company, as a stock company, could do so.[41] And so, in June 1970, the Life Company organized its first subsidiary — the USAA Fund Management Company, under the leadership of retired Army Major General Walter E. Brinker. USAA's first no-load mutual fund, the USAA Capital Growth Fund, was approved by the Securities Exchange Commission on March 30, 1971. Sales to members began the following week.

When USAA was in the midst of planning for a mutual fund, it did have a competitor in place in San Antonio. The United Services Fund, Inc. began in 1958 as the Ventures Investment Club founded by Clark Aylsworth while he was stationed at Randolph Air Force Base in San Antonio. From 1965 to 1968, while stationed at the Pentagon, Aylsworth took the necessary steps to initiate the new fund issued by the Military Services Investment Advisors, Inc. (MSIA). In August 1969, members of the Ventures Club exchanged their shares for shares of the United Services Fund. The shares were first offered to the public on July 1, 1970.

In July 1969, Aylsworth met with McDermott. Aylsworth offered MSIA, along with its mutual fund designed for servicemen, for an initial cost of almost $288,000 or $10 per share. The sale proposed was not a clean one, however. Aylsworth wanted a job and to sell his shares over four years, with a bonus payment of $4,000 for each $1 million of net asset value of the fund each year. All the MSIA stockholders wanted an opportunity to participate in the growth and success of the fund. The probability of name confusion of the United Services Fund with United Services Automobile Association was a consideration for McDermott because of USAA's name identification problems with United Services Life Insurance Company. Nevertheless, McDermott turned down the offer and MSIA eventually became United Services Funds, Inc.[42]

* * * *

From the time he arrived at USAA, McDermott was not comfortable with the USAA Board of Directors and its role in the Association. The Board members were principally active-duty officers who were stationed in San Antonio, with the exception of an occasional naval officer based at Corpus Christi, Texas, or New Orleans. As all Board members retired or moved to new duty assignments, their military replacements normally took their places on the Board. Because of their short tenure, the real power resided in the retired military members on the Board who made up the Executive Committee. This committee met weekly at the home office, deciding on larger claims cases and meddling in other matters that most would construe as the business of management. In addition to the Executive Committee meetings in the USAA building weekly, the regular Board met there monthly — and all were ready to discuss and ask questions on USAA matters and rumors about USAA that they heard in the community.

Over his early years, McDermott worked to change the composition and philosophy of the Board. The newly elected members were to come from outside of San Antonio, and he eased scheduled Board meetings from monthly to quarterly. The Board increased in size to fifteen enabling more McDermott appointees and a formula for representation developed eventually — five Army, five Air Force, and five sea services representatives. Mandatory retirements at seventy forced conservative members off as time passed and a term limit of three terms of two years was imposed. By 1972, only three of the fifteen 1969 Board members were left, and the entire Executive Committee was new. The final step in McDermott's quest occurred on March 22, 1972, when the weekly meetings of the Executive Committee were discontinued; it was to meet henceforth only on emergency business. The full Board directed routine business previously referred to the Executive Committee to the President of USAA. McDermott now had a Board that would support, or at least seriously consider, his proposed changes.

McDermott also made changes to the organizational structure of USAA management as USAA continued to grow, and as he built his own management team. He added many officer positions, and to keep from having so many direct reports, received Board approval for four senior vice president positions. The first two in 1969 had responsibility for fire and casualty (Fishel) and claims (Wier). These were followed by another in 1970 for treasurer (Ensley) and one the next year in underwriting (Jefferis). McDermott hired Clifford Jefferis, originally at GEICO, to replace Welby Logan in Europe. Jefferis returned to San Antonio to take this promotion.

USAA's head also wanted other changes to make the Association better prepared to handle the challenges posed by the 1970s. Ensley chaired a committee to coordinate the development of a management control system, which was in place by the beginning of 1970. The system provided a means for management to plan, control, and measure resources. This included the first full budget, cost accounting procedures, personnel authorizations, and performance measurement. Publications such as the "USAA Pocket Scoreboard" disseminated statistics to the Association's managers. And two new staff officer positions were added. William McCrae, an Assistant Counsel for State Farm, became USAA's General Counsel and Charles F. Cook, an actuary with General Accident Group of Philadelphia, became USAA's Chief Actuary.

Bill McCrae

Additional space for insurance operations was top priority. McDermott had already decided against expansion at the Broadway location. The question was, where? The early plan to build on the 212-acre Marshall Steves property at Bitters and Blanco had collapsed. Part of the property turned out to be in a flood plain, and public plans for highway and sewage service were inadequate. USAA was able to shed the contract legally when Steves sued and the Texas Supreme Court ruled in USAA's favor.[43]

At his first Board meeting in January, McDermott had discussed construction of a new building with the Board members. He had already hired a consulting landscape architect, and he wanted amenities that would help reduce turnover and training costs. His preliminary thoughts included efficiency apartments for "unmarried girls," a service station, swimming pool, bowling alley, nursery, summer day camp, employee club house, and a golf course. He was already thinking about the unbuilt northwest sector of San Antonio, and some of these amenities would help induce employees to move with the company.

Ensley's twenty-year forecast for USAA provided a strong rationale for a new building with potential for expansion. He forecast that, by 1989, USAA would boast a membership of 2.6 million members, over 12,000 employees and a space requirement of over 1.2 million square feet.[44] (USAA's actual 1989 totals were 12,515 employees and nearly two million members.) These projections included contingencies such as continuation of the Vietnam War, expansion of USAA eligibility to other groups, expansion into new lines of business, and reduction of the forty-hour work week to thirty-five hours.

Daye, in his role as Director of Plans and Programs, studied the issue and reported to the Board in June that only two options for a new home office existed outside of the Broadway expansion. The San Antonio Urban Renewal Authority wanted USAA to move downtown to a 13.2-acre site it would make available. This would have meant a high-rise with expensive parking and limited long-term expansion possibilities. Daye then explained McDermott's preference to situate the new office building further outside the city.

The Board concurred with Daye's presentation and authorized purchase of up to 200 acres at a total price not to exceed $1.6 million.[45] By August, USAA had already purchased options on three tracts at the proposed northwest San Antonio site totaling 161 acres. Pleased with these results, the Board expanded management's authority to purchase up to 300 acres.[46] Eventually USAA bought seven tracts totaling about 287 acres.[47]

While plans were moving ahead for a new building, USAA had to make more space until it was ready. Beginning with the Rand building, in downtown San Antonio, the Association leased space for various operations. About 400 employees in Claims moved to the Rand location. Eventually more than 1,200 USAA employees used seven different leased locations up to fourteen miles from the Home Office building. This made things very inefficient. The Association also purchased the Salvation Army Home for Unwed Mothers and Hospital next to the Broadway building for additional office space.[48] Some employees, such as actuaries Steve Goldberg and Alice Gannon who worked at the former Salvation Army facility, wryly and humorously contemplated why their offices were located there.

Another top priority that required immediate action was to improve automobile insurance operations. The answer was not simply procuring automation equipment — that had already been done. When Fishel visited USAA for an interview in 1968, McDermott had shown the paperwork disaster to him. Fishel pointed out at the time that the business flow had to be straightened out first. Only then could the computers help. Upon Fishel's arrival, McDermott assigned this as his first priority and he chose June Reedy for his team. After studying the existing workflow, she found that to process a single auto policy required fifty-five steps, through fourteen units, and requiring the file to move thirty-two times over four floors![49] On average, over 100,000 files floated daily in this system

June Rogers Reedy

and the number was growing. On January 15, 1968, 83,000 files were out; the same day a year later, 117,000.

McDermott directed a reorganization of the entire process in a plan called Project 1969. The work distribution was changed to terminal digits of membership numbers assigned to five major units. The members' files would reside in each unit assigned those numbers. To do this, virtually everyone in the building had to move. Fishel was put in charge and he directed the changes from an office dubbed "Marty's War Room." Moving electrical wiring and telephones was exceedingly difficult because of the tens of thousands of holes to be drilled in concrete, steel, and wood.[50] The changes in productivity were dramatic. From April until December 1969, policies in force per employee rose from 649 to 1,149 and employees in automobile policy production went from 1,498 to 929. Overall there were 144 fewer total employees at USAA than in the previous year.[51]

The improvement in productivity helped offset the unfavorable financial news stemming from increasing claims losses. In October 1968, Vice President-Comptroller Wade Gring predicted a profit of over $30 million and recommended that the auto dividend be raised to 21 percent.[52] Deterioration of finances in the last quarter of 1968, however, reduced the actual underwriting gain to $22.2 million as opposed to the projected $24.9 million. Using the 21 percent dividend rate would cut deeply into the surplus in mid-1969. Fearing an adverse ratings reaction by *A.M. Best*, McDermott recommended a reduction in the auto dividend from 21 percent to 15 percent effective October 1. The Board concurred with McDermott's request.[53] The dividend was further reduced to 12 percent in 1970.

As 1969 progressed, the economic losses from automobile accidents mounted rapidly. By October, the Insurance Information Institute reported hundreds of millions of dollars in losses greater than in 1968 for the industry. The NAII reported that while the most popular 1969 new car models had risen about 10 percent in cost, replacement parts for a Ford, for example, went up over 36 percent. As a rule of thumb, a car 25 percent damaged was written off as a total loss. Testimony before a Senate subcommittee reported that

Muscle car – 1958 Corvette

super-powered or "muscle cars" were producing 56 percent more losses than standard-powered cars.

For USAA, the 1969 loss ratio was 74.62 percent, the highest in USAA's history. Claims frequency remained at thirty-two vehicles per 100, but costs for each accident rose. McDermott asked the USAA policyholders for more careful driving and used *Aide Magazine* as a safety forum. In fact, the first issue of *Aide Magazine* featured an article on the problems with muscle cars.

McDermott also won Board support to join the National Safety Council even though it would not benefit USAA directly. In 1970, he and other insurance company leaders met with General Motors officials in Detroit to discuss national safety standards. John DeLorean, a top Chevrolet executive, commented on safety features in the August 25, 1970, issue of *Look* magazine. He said that General Motors believed that "the auto industry is basically a fashion industry" and would add safety features only when forced to by competition or by a government edict. By early 1972, however, General Motors invited McDermott along with thirty other insurance company presidents to give them a progress report on their safety research. Nevertheless, it would be a long time until safety approached fashion as a factor in the sales of cars.[54]

Besides safety, many other issues came up that were outside USAA's control, but had the power to impact the bottom line. In these cases, McDermott entered into and initiated many cooperative efforts with insurance industry partners. For example, fraud was a relatively minor problem for USAA. The Association trusted its members and the trust was returned. When members requested reimbursement for telephone calls necessitated by unsatisfactory service, at first USAA requested a copy of the telephone bill. When an employee finally questioned the practice, June Reedy told the employees to accept a member's word for the expense incurred from that time on.[55] In spite of USAA's positive experience with its own policyholders, the Association became a charter member of the Insurance Crime Prevention Institute in 1976. The main purpose of this organization was to investigate insurance fraud. When the "accept-all-comers" movement gained momentum, McDermott chaired a NAII committee to fight the issue. He also worked with NAII on "no fault" insurance, which was spreading rapidly in the face of a Congressional threat to take over automobile insurance from state control if states did not adopt the new coverage.

Complicating the financial picture was a significant weakness in investment income. Ensley's recommendation to move USAA investments from United Trust Company of New York to the Republic Bank of Dallas under financial wizard Dr. Edmund A. Mennis in 1969 produced a turnaround. The move to common stock and away from preferred stock investments played a significant role. By 1970, the net investment income included a record high rate of return of 6.2 percent and over $9 million. Establishing lines of credit at two local banks eliminated USAA's need to sell investment securities at unfavorable prices to meet short-term claims losses. This also helped stabilize the investment picture. Thus, when a postal strike and computer problems related to the extended pay plan constricted USAA's cash flow in the spring of 1970, the lines of credit provided the necessary cushion. Another wrinkle in investments was the purchase of $2 million in Deutschmarks as a hedge against reevaluation of the Deutschmark.

Even with the reduction in dividend, USAA's surplus-to-written-premiums were dangerously low. While a ratio of 50 percent was considered prudent, and 30 percent the minimum for fiscal soundness; USAA's fell to 33 percent. In 1970, USAA had net earnings of $37 million. Ordinarily, USAA would have allocated $10 million to dividends, $12 million to federal income tax, and $15 million to surplus. But not this time. Thanks to extensive lobbying in the previous decade by USAA President Cheever and other reciprocal heads, the Internal Revenue Act of 1962 provided a way for reciprocals to build capital by placing tax-free allocations in a Subscribers' Savings Account (SSA). USAA had established such an account, but had never made a distribution to it because operating losses precluded it from having to pay any income tax.[56] McDermott approved allocations of $22 million to dividends, $3 million to free surplus, and $12 million to the SSA (a sub account of surplus) encouraged by Ensley and in accordance with a formula developed by new USAA actuary Charles Cook. By using the SSA, USAA paid no income tax in 1970 and increased the dividend to members by $12 million. Because of benefits to the members and the great financial strength it affords the Association, USAA has continued the practice.

Project 1970, under the overall leadership of Jack Griffith, was to effect further and significant improvements in servicing USAA's membership. This involved the introduction of the multi-car policy

Reuben Machado

and the conversion of USAA's policy writing to the new INSCO system. The conversion was difficult, and problems centered around interfacing USAA programs to accommodate the new extended payment plan. When the conversion faltered and stopped, McDermott passed the responsibility to make it work to Reuben Machado. From July 12 through October 4, employees put in enormous overtime. McDermott specifically praised the dedicated Machado and Richard Costello, who each worked 430 hours of uncompensated overtime. Many other employees contributed as well.

Following intensive training on Frieden Flexowriters by Mary Pieper and others, the conversion began. Employees entered uncoded application answers into the program, which transcribed the application onto paper tape. Data on this tape was then transcribed onto magnetic tape and fed into the computer. Production of new policies was reduced to three to four days instead of weeks. The system also generated the majority of renewals automatically. Putting all members' cars on one policy meant that employees had to handle 42 percent of the total membership only once a year under ordinary circumstances. Another significant benefit was to level out the workload over the year by changing permanent renewal dates to the month with the lowest workload. The summer months' renewals were deliberately lowered to provide for employee vacation times.

Since members would have to pay insurance premiums for all cars at once, USAA introduced a nine-month extended pay plan. In addition to the savings to the Association, multi-car discounts went into effect in states like Texas that did not allow such discounts unless all autos were on a single policy. The completion of Projects 1969 and 1970 resulted in dramatic service improvements and lowered stress levels on the employees trying to provide good service. Service and error complaints from members for all of 1971 were down 39 percent for automobile policies. McDermott's Project 1971 under the direction of Fishel had the goal of designing a new USAA multi-car system with a target date of January 1, 1974.

Another element of service was to provide products and services that members would find useful and still would benefit the Association as a whole. For example, when members had accidents, they were without transportation if the repairs took a few days or longer. In some areas, a car rental was the only solution, but this was often an expensive one. In 1972, USAA began offering optional rental car reimbursement insurance. It became popular and offered a relatively inexpensive service to the policyholders.[57] In some cases, however, not offering products was to the benefit of the membership. USAA discontinued offering Farm Fire, Farmowners, and Farmers Comprehensive Insurance policies because of low use and net losses. A study of accident and health insurance resulted in the Board's decision in 1972 to stay out of this field because of other programs members could use.[58]

* * * *

From the first, McDermott knew one of USAA's serious shortcomings was in long-range planning. After he arrived at USAA, Daye discussed the issue with Jean Moye. Daye had great respect for Moye's business acumen, calling her the "modern business person" in the whole company with "more damn ideas" and someone who read everything there was to be read in business.[59] Moye recommended the American Management Association (AMA) Company Program. After Daye brought in an AMA representative, McDermott jumped on the idea. In January 1970, he and a few others including Daye, Fishel, Ensley, Kerford, Wier, and Moye went to Hamilton, New York, where the AMA helped USAA develop a draft mission statement, creed, and long-range plan. It was here that McDermott first expressed his long-term goal, which in the light of USAA's overwhelming paper problem seemed quixotic. He wanted to make USAA a "paperless" insurance company. To Max Wier's memory, it was USAA's first real planning meeting.[60] The team returned to San Antonio with homework assignments, then returned to Hamilton in April to put everything in final form. Now USAA had a plan, and a good idea where it was going and how to get there. Especially important, the plan established four "Key Result Areas" — service, profitability, financial strength, and growth. Each had continuing objectives and specific objectives. Some specific objectives included quicker policy turnaround, underwriting gain over 15 percent annually, loss ratio under 70 percent, a surplus ratio of .5 by 1974, and 1.2 million members by 1980. This enabled the Board and management to measure USAA's progress.[61]

When the plan was published, McDermott told the employees that they were the key to accomplishing these goals. Every employee was needed "in the continuing effort to upgrade our service to members."[62] The many changes at USAA caused some tension. McDermott brought in Dr. Alvin Burstein from the University of Texas Medical School at San Antonio to hold focus groups with 250 supervisors. In April 1971, he reported to McDermott a type of "culture shock" that could be blamed mostly on a lack of communications. There was work to do. A series of initiatives helped reduce the personnel turnover, which had climbed to a recent high of 38 percent (44 percent among non-exempt females). By the end of 1971, it stood at 27 percent and continued falling.[63] In Operation: How Are We Doing? the personnel department interviewed employees after their first six months at USAA to identify possible problems. In response to employee requests, McDermott issued a management directive in April 1971 authorizing pregnant employees to work until the date of delivery assuming physician's written approval and satisfactory job performance. Fundamental to morale was good pay, and Moye worked to make USAA's structure attractive. Very important in inflationary times was the introduction of a quarterly reassessment of the cost of living, and raises to keep up. The total personnel cost objective had been set at 11.7 percent of earned premium. When the 1972 actual level turned out to be 10.67 percent, USAA revised the benefits package upwards to reach the 11.7 percent level by including such things as a waiver of pre-existing medical conditions on employees' health policies.[64] To add new employees, USAA instituted a bonus referral program for six months in 1971 — $50 on hiring, $50 after three months employment, and $50 more after six. These efforts didn't mean USAA wasn't frugal. Retired employee Bob Breitenkamp recalled that when he completed jury duty, he had to turn his jury paycheck stub in to payroll where his jury pay was deducted from his USAA paycheck.

The most dramatic new benefit of McDermott's initial years at USAA was the introduction of the four-day work week in November 1971. In anticipation of his new position at Life Company, Daye had been studying to receive the CLU (Chartered Life Underwriter) professional designation. As part of his reading, he ran across a study on the four-day work week which claimed dramatic improvements in employee retention and turnover. Daye marked it up in red and forwarded it to USAA's head. McDermott found it interesting and tasked his Vice President of Plans and Programs to take a hard look at it.[65] McDermott insisted that a plan must guarantee undiminished service and productivity and be of benefit to the employees and the Association. In July, McDermott related to the Board the results of the Plans Department's study. Advantages included McDermott's charge to the Plans' study group and more. It provided for increased member contact hours to fifty, increased productivity, decreased absenteeism (fifth day free for personal business), and Personnel's assurance that the three-day weekends would have a positive impact on recruiting. (The way it was scheduled initially was to have 2,800 employees work a Monday through Thursday schedule and 200 work Tuesday through Friday.) Shortly thereafter, the Board approved a twelve-week trial for the program beginning October 4, 1971. Employees' glee met the announcement, and media representatives from *Business Week* and other publications across the country interviewed USAA employees.[66]

Reporter Sean McNulty, of the *San Antonio Light,* said the introduction of the four-day work week was characteristic of USAA and its "mercurial president" to assume the "role of pioneer." Although about 500 companies in the U.S. were then gearing up to try short-week experiments, USAA was "by far the largest major company" to do so.[67] The test was a resounding success and met all objectives. Most important, a survey of employees found the employees thought the new schedule was a good idea (96%), liked their jobs more (94%), and the longer day was not too tiring (93%).[68] One husband, with a USAA employee wife, told a reporter that he loved the idea — his wife could cut the grass now instead of him on her free day![69] The Board approved the four-day work week on a permanent basis in February 1972.

The Association also tried other special events and activities to make the work force feel appreciated. McDermott continued a custom of the armed services and held a New Year's Day reception scheduled carefully to avoid football bowl games on television. The Association budgeted $10 per employee to support approved group activities like bowling. As was the custom of the day, large numbers of USAA female employees competed to be "Queen" of various activities such as the U.S. Savings Bond drives and the United Fund. Awards commemorating years of service points at USAA were introduced. Member letters of praise for specific employees were put in a display case in the main lobby for all to see, and McDermott sent these employees a note as well. USAA did have its employee activity limits, however, and good taste too. In 1971, when the Randolph Air Base Special Services Officer asked USAA to ship a busload of women to Randolph for Happy Hour each Friday, the Association refused the request.

Debbie Broussard, Runner-up in Miss Fair Share Contest, Robert McDermott, and Tracie Martin, Miss Fair Share.

For the long-term satisfaction of employees, and benefit of USAA, new educational opportunities opened up. McDermott encouraged professional development, and employees began participating in the Insurance Institute of America certification programs. Each one who completed received a $50 savings bond. Instructor Shirley Markette taught CPCU classes to interested employees. The program took hold quickly. McDermott attended a Houston luncheon in 1971 where twelve USAA employees received their CPCU designations. In a related program to increase education levels of employees that year, McDermott had Irene Florida begin a management intern program for ten to fifteen college graduates and summer employment jobs for ten to fifteen students each summer.

McDermott wanted USAA's rapidly growing educational and training efforts in the hands of someone he knew would make them successful. That man was Victor J. Ferrari. Colonel Ferrari was still on active duty as the Vice Commander for the Air Force Institute of Technology. McDermott told Ferrari he needed him to take over USAA's management development program to train mid-level managers. Ferrari agreed, put in his retirement papers, and arrived at USAA in September 1971.[70]

Ferrari was born in Marion Heights, Pennsylvania, in 1916 and went to a new consolidated high school in Kulpmont, Pennsylvania. The students selected him as the most popular in his class, and he was the captain of his high school football team. He majored in education at Bloomsbury (PA) State College and graduated in 1939. He joined the Air Force and became a navigator.

On Friday, November 12, 1943, while returning from a bombing mission to Bremen, Germany, his B-24 was shot down over Holland. Ferrari and the bombadier, Eddie Roberts, bailed out together, Roberts breaking his shoulder upon hitting the ground. People approached them immediately and offered them bikes, but at 5' 5", Ferrari couldn't reach the pedals and Roberts could not ride because of his injury. So began a harrowing journey of escape to the Rock of Gibraltar. It started with five hours in the icy water of a duck pond, and saw the two escapees on buses, trains, and walking from safe house through public areas to safe house for over six months. They learned to fear the S.S. and Gestapo, who continually checked passersby but somehow missed them. But eventually they made it to Spain — and home.

After intervening assignments, Ferrari was assigned to the Psychology department at the Air Force Academy. He knew McDermott only casually there, and moved on to the University of Denver to pursue a doctoral degree under Air Force sponsorship. After only a short time at Denver, he received a call from McDermott asking him to return to the Academy to become his assistant. McDermott had been reviewing prospective candidates, and one of Ferrari's Officer Effectiveness Reports caught his eye. Ferrari had reduced navigator training dropouts to near zero, and his rater said that Ferrari had "more leadership in his little finger than most of us have in our whole body." After reading this comment, McDermott decided that he wanted Ferrari. Ferrari recited all the arguments against, but McDermott told him he would take care of everything. He dropped out of school and became McDermott's right-hand man at the Academy until 1965. A lifelong bachelor, Ferrari spent almost every night until one or two in the morning in the office with McDermott and weekends at McDermott's house. He soon became "Uncle Vic" to the kids. When McDermott called him to come to USAA, his acceptance was not a surprise.

Vic Ferrari

Ferrari was intensely loyal and a close friend to McDermott during his decade at the Academy and his more than twenty years at USAA. More important, Ferrari's naturally gregarious personality made him the heart of the front office, balancing McDermott's perceived more aloof New England nature. He was weak on names, but strong on remembering faces, and his warmth to the employees was genuine and reciprocated. In his later years, his hugs were as natural a greeting from him as a "hello" would have been from someone else. Demanding and tough on those around him, he was still respected and liked. He was to play an important role at USAA over the years because of his dominant personality and his close relationship with McDermott.

At his November 4, 1971, Management Meeting, McDermott encouraged his managers to "talk up" insurance education. USAA provided incentives such as free class time, books, and fees, monetary awards, and trips to conferment ceremonies. It was important, McDermott stressed, that managers participate also and to reward these employees who tied educational accomplishments to job performance. Another educational benefit was Project Campus, begun in 1972. In this program St. Mary's University offered classes at the USAA home office to MBA graduate students and undergraduates working on Bachelors of Business Administration.

The most important of the management program initiatives was the Managerial Insurance Seminar (MIS) begun on November 21, 1971. McDermott's initiative had the purpose of improving interdepartmental communications, improving and increasing decision-making at lower levels of management, and the building of a team effort at USAA. Two weeks in length, the small classes were exposed to issues and operations across the company. For those who said they didn't have time to take it, McDermott had this to say. "If you feel you can't leave your office behind for these two weeks, you need this course more than you know."[71] The program was to be very successful over the years.

All of Ferrari's educational and training programs would play an important role in a McDermott-initiated program entitled the USAA Organizational Development Program. Its purpose was to identify, assess, and develop the executive talent that USAA would require over the next decade. To participate, middle-management employees had to volunteer and be nominated by an officer of the company. After testing by the Psychological Corporation, the nominating officers would use the results to counsel their nominees on suggested training and education. Each year, up to 100 employees would be included in the program. This formal link between education, training, and career advancement gave the self-development program a solid endorsement.[72] At the same time, McDermott directed combining jobs to make them more interesting and challenging. This made better use of the employees' recent education.

One interesting program for the employees and the Association was called "Career Fashions." In 1970, in response to employee

USAA employees modeling miniskirts

requests to be allowed to wear pants to work, the female employees were surveyed about their preferences. Of the 2,000-plus respondents, 54 percent voted for pantsuits, 41 percent favored the mini skirt, and 5 percent wanted the longer midi skirt. While USAA management authorized the pants, it was with the understanding that only actual pantsuits were to be allowed — two- or three-piece matching outfits with tunics coming to the bottom of the hip. A San Antonio newspaper columnist, Paul Thompson, received lots of mail on the subject. One USAA employee wrote that it was a good idea

USAA employees wearing career fashions, Spring 1972, left to right: Wendy Rossman, Bob Rennie, Angie Jones.

because you could move more freely: "You don't have to worry about bending, sitting, or your girdle showing." Another who wrote to Thompson borrowed from Ogden Nash on pants: "You look divine as you advance — have you seen yourself retreating?" In any case, pants were at USAA to stay.[73] To help guide employees' dress for work, McDermott introduced the Career Fashions concept at his September 1971 management meeting. He told the employees that he was justifiably proud of USAA's image and felt that the new program would further enhance it. At the same time, employees who wanted to participate in this voluntary program would find the fashions about one-half the comparable prices in department stores. That said, he turned over the management meeting to Irene Florida and her employee committee that had developed the concept.

Various USAA employees including McDermott modeled the fashions, which could be ordered from a catalog with prices ranging from $17.75 to $36.50. By the close of 1972, employees had spent over $50,000 for the new fashions. USAA provided free clothing for some employees who were in constant contact with members, but most paid for their own. While the program eventually disappeared, it played a key role in emphasizing to employees McDermott's view of the importance of dressing as a professional at USAA. With the president's constant reinforcement, professional dress became part of the corporate culture. Although, occasionally, employees objected in the employee "Speak Out" columns in *Coverage* later on in the decade.

To continue to be successful, USAA had to improve its relationship with its members as well as its employees. Confirming McDermott's own intuition and that of his staff, the Gelb member survey results suggested that USAA needed to modernize its image. He created a marketing department and hired Baxter and Korge, a creative services firm in Houston, to develop a new logo design. McDermott had long felt the old logo looked too much like a dollar sign.

A Tradition Of Service

USAA diamond logo

Based on interviews with USAA members to determine their attitudes towards the Association, Baxter and Korge developed three new logos and submitted them to USAA. McDermott had the three sent to the USAA members who participated in the Gelb study as well as to groups of students in ROTC programs and at the service academies. Over 80 percent chose USAA's eagle logo.

While praise for the new logo was virtually unanimous, one USAA member included a note with a check to pay his bill. With tongue-in-cheek, the member compared the new logo to a vulture rather than an eagle. Nonetheless, he said, "I'm curious of the changes, marvel at the balance due, but with blind faith, remittance in full."[74]

USAA eagle logo adopted in 1970

The second outcome of the survey to improve USAA's image was better communications. After Daye's arrival, one of June Reedy's employees, Bob Carrington, showed him a flyer-newsletter sent to customers by the Automobile Club of Southern California and suggested USAA could do the same. Daye took Carrington's idea to McDermott, who said "let's do it!" Daye contacted Fred Korge in Houston, who designed the concept that became *Aide Magazine*.[75] The name was preferred by members in a survey administered by Gelb.

McDermott wanted this magazine to keep members informed of such things as new products and explanations of rate increases. In March 1970, Daye proposed to the Board that a magazine be approved for one issue in 1970 and three in 1971. For 1971, the total cost of the Annual Report, the adjusters list, and the three issues would only be 43¢ a member. The Board approved the concept contingent on the first issue (Fall 1970) being a success.[76] And a success it was. Edited by Edward Dunn, the first issue elicited over 10,000 inquiries for new insurance. Gabriel Gelb later praised USAA's use of market research before making major changes in relationships with its customers.[77]

Opening of offices outside of San Antonio also helped to improve communications with members. In 1970, McDermott proposed to the Board to move its existing New York City office in the Chrysler Building to Highland Falls, a town just outside the gates of West Point. This August 1971 move still satisfied the New York State Insurance Department, but also helped marketing and other service efforts because of the concentration of members around the Academy. On September 7, 1971, another office opened at Seven Corners in Falls Church, Fairfax County, Virginia. First headed by retired Army Colonel Samuel W. Pinnell, the office was required by the state of Virginia as a condition of licensing the USAA Fund Management Company.[78] In a related development, the Board approved the construction of a test "Drive-In Claims Facility" in San

Antonio at the site of the new office building. If successful, the Board decided it would consider such facilities in places like San Diego and Colorado Springs.[79] All of these developments were precursors to regionalization, and also contrary to how USAA had always been run — from San Antonio.

McDermott believed that growth was important for success. Since the pool of individuals eligible for USAA insurance was limited and diminishing, it was important to sign up as many as possible. At the Hamilton conference, McDermott made a point that USAA membership included only 70 percent of the active-duty members. He felt that USAA could do much better. He introduced advertisements with limited and bold copy claiming, for example, that eight out of ten officers had USAA insurance. Subsequent ads heralding improved numbers holding USAA insurance proved to be very effective, as did the use of coupons. USAA received almost 29,000 coupons from ads in 1970, a four-fold increase over 1969.

Typical 1970s USAA advertisement

Other marketing changes and innovations helped. Confusion with other companies including the words "United Services" forced USAA to rename its subsidiaries by eventually including "USAA" in all names. For example, the United Services Casualty Insurance Company was changed to USAA Casualty Insurance Company.[80]

HIGH ENERGY

Besides advertising in media with military readership, USAA began using a "ripple plan" whereby flyers for USAA subsidiaries were mailed to current USAA members along with their bills. For policyholders who allowed their membership to lapse, plans were developed to follow up sixty days prior to the date they would likely renew and try to return them to the fold. Even USAA matchbooks were distributed to Officers Clubs on military installations with large numbers of newly commissioned officers. Also, the Board extended eligibility for USAA membership to officers for 120 days after their release from active duty to give the Association more time to commit them to membership. Another innovation was a Members' Relations Team composed of a retired officer from each service which went to areas of member concentrations to market USAA.

McDermott saw the weak growth in the Life Company as more than a problem in marketing. USAA Life had to become more competitive in pricing policies if it were to compete with its chief competition, United Services Life Insurance Company. When USAA's existing consulting actuary could not develop an offering to beat the costs on all other competing policies, McDermott hired a new consulting actuary. Waid J. Davidson of Bowles and Tillinghast developed plans that were cheaper than all others and tailored to USAA's clientele. McDermott was delighted.

To give added impetus to growth of the Life Company, he appointed Jack Daye as Vice President in the Life Company on January 1, 1970, to become president in April. Daye began active solicitations at once. Hundreds of members responded, informing the Association that when they bought United Services Life Insurance, they thought that they were buying from USAA. An article in *Aide Magazine* and advertisements helped correct the problem. Next, USAA transferred its employees' group life insurance benefit to USAA Life effective September 30, 1976. USAA Life raised policy limits for most military officers and specifically designed a policy for newly commissioned officers. The results of these combined efforts were spectacular. In 1970, the net operating income before taxes doubled, and there was more than a 35-percent increase of insurance in force. In 1971, new business rose 118 percent, and the value of insurance in force climbed to half a billion dollars. The next year, policies in force and premium income rose 28 percent. Investment income continued to climb as well, averaging over 30 percent per year from 1970 to 1973. In recognition of the Life Company's success, A.M. Best gave USAA its respected "Policyholder's Recommendation," awarded to only about 450 of the 1,818 legal reserve life insurance companies.[81]

But all of USAA's growth was not positive. Of the total property and casualty membership growth in 1970 of 64,000, over 12,000 were assigned risks. These individuals were those who were refused insurance in the open marketplace for cause by other insurance companies. They entered state pools and then were assigned by percentage to companies according to the number of customers the companies serviced in that state. The following year, USAA had to insure more than 77,000 of these marginal drivers, a rise of 123 percent since 1968. For every dollar of premium earned from these individuals, USAA paid out $1.41 in claims, a loss of about $3 million in 1970. In addition, USAA had to pay agent commissions of 10 percent plus high administrative expenses because changes were handled manually for the assigned risk policyholders. This rise in assigned risks was attributed to increasingly selective underwriting by all companies since the losses of 1969, the failure of some companies, and the refusal of others to write insurance in states where they had catastrophic losses.[82] Early in 1972 McDermott appointed a task force to study the use of USAA CIC as a carrier for the assigned risk business. At the time he asked for the study, these assigned risks were legally regular members and entitled to vote on Association matters according to a bylaws provision forced on USAA by state insurance commissioners.[83] McDermott did not like this.

Also of concern in 1970 was USAA's disproportionate number of youthful drivers. The imbalance was caused, in part, by the teenage children of officers who joined during USAA's tremendous growth spurt from 1949-1955. The remainder included the huge numbers of junior officers joining the Association during the war in Southeast Asia. McDermott briefed the Board on a study published by the New York State Department of Vehicles. The study asserted that male drivers aged sixty and over had the lowest percentage of involvement in accidents. Male drivers aged twenty and under had the highest percentage — 38.3 percent. Those twenty to twenty-nine had a 12.5 percent involvement, still more than double those over sixty. Using these statistics, McDermott convinced the Board to support a bylaws amendment to open eligibility to Reserve and National Guard officers who had served on active duty, retained their commissions, were entitled to draw retirement pay from the government, and who had not established membership while on active duty. The pool of eligibles was estimated at about 200,000, and those older newcomers who joined would partially balance the risk of youthful drivers. The membership approved the bylaws change at the June 24, 1970 annual members' meeting. An apparent contradiction occurred when McDermott pressed the Board to offer membership to ROTC candidates within twenty-four months of commissioning (service academy cadets and midshipmen could not own cars until their final year so this did not apply to them). While this was adding youthful drivers, forty-three states agreed to count them in lieu of assigned risks on a one-for-one basis. McDermott believed that in the short-term USAA would be no better off but that the long-term prognosis was good for these officer candidates to become members in good standing.[84]

Often USAA employees in the claims areas shared the sadness

and tragedies of the members and provided support and comfort. At other times, employees shared happiness with members who called to talk of new children and grandchildren and sought advice for financial security for them. And all USAA employees shared pride in USAA members who served the nation — in peacetime activities, as well as in war. In July 1969, USAA employees joined the nation in watching with awe as Colonel Edwin E. "Buzz" Aldrin walked upon the moon. He was USAA's first active member on the moon, and "Highlights of the Week" shared the happy news with them on member #13-61-41. In fact, every man who walked on the moon was or had been a member of USAA. And, although the traffic was light, and the risks few, the Association did not offer to insure the government-owned lunar rovers.

McDermott and the USAA employees continued the Association's dedication to service. That "service" was the number-one Key Re-

USAA member and *Apollo 11* Astronaut Edwin E. "Buzz" Aldrin on the moon, July 20, 1969

sult Area in the long-range plan was no accident and no paper exercise. After he first became president, he learned that naval officers with the carrier USS *Enterprise* were uncertain of insurance for their rental cars. McDermott sent a telex to the Commanding Officer asking him to notify his officer-members that they were all covered. By early 1971, he had added twenty-three WATS (wide area telephone service) lines so employees could call members long distance on insurance problems. The employees who used the phones were specially trained on techniques designed to please the members — and they did. Inez Eversole, the Director of Communications at the time, calculated that in addition to the outgoing lines, USAA was receiving an average of 3,300 calls a day, 90 percent of them long distance and paid for by the members. She told a writer that the telephone along with the computer would help achieve top management's interest in becoming a nearly "paperless company."[85]

There were other services added as well. One was USAA's arrangement with Hertz to get USAA members a 20-percent discount on posted rates. Each service like this that was added was an additional inducement to be part of the Association. An outstanding example of service that might potentially hurt the bottom line occurred when Congress enacted the Survivor's Benefit Plan (SBP) for the military in 1972. The Life Company analyzed the plan, and then sent a letter advising all retired members of its pros and cons. The only negative was an unfavorable tax problem, which was soon removed by the Internal Revenue Service. When this occurred, McDermott pointed out that from a cost benefit viewpoint, the SBP could not be matched by any private insurer. He directed that this information be included in a special issue of the next *Aide Magazine,* and because of its importance, advance-mailed the article to all active duty and retired members of USAA.[86] He even had advertisements placed in publications read by officers to tell them that the SBP was positive for them and their families. What was lost in sales was more than gained by the members' increase in trust.

A TRADITION OF SERVICE

The most important and most visible improvement in service was the prompt and fair payment of claims. And catastrophic natural disasters provided the most important test for USAA. In the middle of the night on August 17, 1969, Hurricane Camille slammed into the Gulf Coast. Winds exceeding 205 miles per hour pushed a wall of water twenty to thirty feet high miles inland in some places. More than 500 died that night. It was not until three days later that USAA's claims team, led by Frank Spencer, was allowed in the devastated area. The Keesler Air Force Base Commander provided space for the team and publicized its arrival. By the end of the year, USAA had expended over $1 million on the approximately 900 claims. The numbers are small by today's standards, but the members appreciated USAA's on-the-spot service. Member Lieutenant Colonel Andrew Winter said his spirits were lifted by just seeing the whole USAA team in action, and he was very pleased to receive a check in record time: "How can I say how great it really is to belong?"[87] The following year, Hurricane Celia hit South Texas and was the third-largest catastrophe in modern history up to that time. USAA's loss was $2.6 million. A USAA disaster team opened its doors at Corpus Christi Naval Air Station, where more than 1,000 cars were damaged. The Honorable James D. Hittle, Assistant Secretary of the Navy, wrote a letter of thanks to USAA for the speed and genuine aid given to military members. Because of the hurricanes, reinsurance rates for catastrophes climbed rapidly and reinsurance was no longer cost-effective for USAA. The rate was to go from $122,000 annually to over $625,000. In 1971, the Board decided to allow USAA's last reinsurance policy of any kind to lapse and to self insure for catastrophes, although, it was later reinstated.[88]

One fascinating aspect of USAA's service philosophy is that it works both ways. The employees serve the members, but often the members go out of their way to serve the Association. As always, USAA's best marketing device was satisfied members who recruited other members. Some went further. One USAA member in Athens, Greece, learned of a concerted effort by local Greek agents to tell potential American customers that companies with home offices in the U.S. might be barred from doing business in Greece. At issue were not only officers assigned to Greece, but also Sixth Fleet vessels that would berth there. He wrote to McDermott and suggested that USAA review its situation and "stress to its many satisfied customers that all remains A-okay." McDermott was able to do so and thanked the officer for his interest in USAA.[89]

In another example, the Southern California Savings and Loan (S&L) Association refused to grant a mortgage because General of the Army Omar N. Bradley had offered homeowner's insurance from USAA — a reciprocal. Bradley could have easily bought another policy. Instead, he decided to wage a personal war on the S&L. Without USAA's knowledge that a problem even existed, he wrote to the S&L and asked for an exception to the institution's policies on reciprocals for USAA. He pointed out that the S&L's policy actually discriminated against individuals of character and integrity who belonged to USAA, an institution that deserved support. He also cited USAA's A.M. Best ratings. As an active-duty officer and Chairman of the Board of the Bulova Watch Company, he requested the privilege of addressing the S&L Board about USAA. The President of the Association replied to General Bradley that such a meeting would not be necessary because the Board had al-

General of the Army Omar Bradley

ready decided to grant USAA the special exemption. He thanked Bradley for his intercession. Bradley then forwarded copies of the correspondence to McDermott.[90]

In June 1970, *Consumer Reports* included an article on automobile insurance. The Consumers Union's careful and frank analysis of thousands of products and services had won it a reputation for unbiased honesty. That is why it was so pleasing to USAA employees and members alike when the article discussed twenty-five companies — and identified the "two companies that stood above the rest, State Farm Mutual and United Services Automobile Association." In the settlement of first-party claims, USAA was ranked in the top four, with the comment "if one had to choose among them, we would single out United Services."[91] USAA's great service was no longer a secret between its employees and members — it was now a national headline.

CHAPTER EIGHT

TURBULENT TIMES

February 10, 1973. You could hardly hear a sound from the hundreds of officers in the darkened Officers' Club at Tan Son Nhut Air Base in South Vietnam. On stage was a Vietnamese band called The Dreamers featuring a singer named Julie Quang. She was singing "The First Time Ever I Saw Your Face." Her beautiful voice and the haunting melody reminded many officers of their sweethearts at home. Standing applause and cheers punctuated her finish. Next on the Dreamers' playlist was "Country Roads." As the band and singers began, "Take me home . . . ," the huge room became a bedlam of singing, of clapping, of men standing on tables and chairs. The war was close to over for them, and the words of this anthem reflected the feelings of every officer in the room. To these officers, the wartime images conjured up by "Puff the Magic Dragon" and "Where Have All the Flowers Gone" had faded as surely as the Viet Cong had disappeared into the tunnels at Cu Chi. They were ready to go home.

Certain events in the year 1972 had suggested that the end of the war was impending. President Nixon revealed that Henry Kissinger had been negotiating with the North Vietnamese in Paris. The North Vietnamese Army's successful Easter Offensive had driven most of the American troops back into the fortified "Pearl of the Orient," Saigon. American aircraft intensified the bombing of North Vietnam, but it would not break the will of the communists. An illustration of the fervor and dedication of the communists was revealed in the questioning of a prisoner captured by the South Vietnamese. This youthful believer and another were given two B-40 mortar

A Tradition Of Service

rounds and one pound of rice each in Cambodia. They were ordered to walk and carry their mortar rounds (about half of their own body weight) to a point outside a South Vietnamese installation. They were told that in ninety days other supporters of the North Vietnamese cause would be there with shells, including one with a mortar tube. Sick and malnourished, but living on faith, they made it. Three met them and with the total of four mortar rounds fired, the two began their trek back to Cambodia for two more shells when they were captured. The field report noting that the four shells were fired provoked a "no big deal." How the shells got there, however, was the stuff of defeat for the United States when coupled with the unraveling of the South Vietnamese Army and government. On March 29, 1973, the last American troops left Vietnam, and Hanoi released the last American POWs two days later.

Former POW Lieutenant Richard L. Bates being welcomed home at Minot International Airport. *(Courtesy of the National Archives)*

The happiest of all the Americans to return home were those who had festered in North Vietnamese camps and prisons. Many of their comrades who died in captivity showed tremendous courage. A prime example was Air Force Academy graduate and USAA member Captain Lance P. Sijan, class of 1965, who won the Congressional Medal of Honor posthumously for his bravery. Shot down over North Vietnam, he evaded capture for more than six weeks. Suffering serious injuries, he was finally captured. He escaped and was recaptured, tortured, and interrogated. He never divulged information and served as an inspiration to his fellow prisoners.

Captain Lance P. Sijan. *(Courtesy of the United States Air Force Academy)*

Because of Americans like him and their families, the Association supported various efforts for the POWs throughout the war. For example, it assisted the League of Families of American POW and MIA by including a plea for the POWs on USAA's postage meter. And the USAA employees supported the POW and MIA families as best they could throughout the war, many wearing bracelets with names of POWs inscribed.

When the war ended, the employees scanned the lists for member returnees. McDermott sent letters to the returning POWs along with USAA's incoming free (WATS) long distance number. They were the first members to be able to use it.

A Tradition Of Service

Vietnam War POW list

Most rewarding to the employees was seeing or hearing from these returning Americans. One example was a letter from a former POW, Air Force Captain Howard J. Hill. "This is to notify you that I have returned," he began. He asked to be added to the family policy as a driver and thanked USAA for the excellent service given to his wife while he was gone. A postscript from Hill's wife on the letter told how much USAA's caring employees had helped. "How does one thank a whole company?" she wrote. She related that when she forgot to pay a premium, a USAA representative called, gently reminded her, and extended the payment deadline. When she had a minor accident, a USAA employee in the Virginia office told her the accident was his problem and not hers — not to worry about it and that he would take care of everything. She didn't and he did, to her everlasting gratitude. She concluded, "There are so many things to thank USAA for doing — but how can I? I can only send special love to all there."[1]

The human impact of the end of the Vietnam War affected all the employees — it was great to have everyone home. For some time, McDermott and his staff had been carefully watching, as the war wound down, for the business impact as well. After his election in 1968, President Richard Nixon wanted to end the conflict in Southeast Asia and embarked on a strategy called Vietnamization. The plan was to remove American military as the South Vietnamese, in theory, were able to take over their own defense. Secretary of Defense Melvin Laird wanted to move quickly, but Henry Kissinger did not, because keeping the troops in Vietnam helped his bargaining position with the North Vietnamese in Paris. Nevertheless, by December 1969 Nixon had removed the first 60,000. American troop strength in Vietnam was at 280,000 at the end of 1970 and half of that in 1971. The total number of officers on active duty fell from about 419,000 in 1969 to 336,000 in 1972, with further severe cuts to follow.

The removal of troops from Vietnam and reduction in the active force were coupled with other changes in defense policy that would also impact on USAA. Years of protest and dissatisfaction with the draft led to a decision. On March 27, 1969, President Nixon announced that he had appointed an Advisory Commission on an All-Volunteer Armed Force under the chairmanship of former Secretary of Defense Thomas S. Gates Jr. In February 1970, the Gates Commission's principal finding was that "the nation's interests will be better served by an all-volunteer force" and the elimination of the draft when the Selective Service Act expired on June 30, 1971.[2] Laird announced that effective January 27, 1973, the armed forces would depend exclusively on volunteer enlistments, although the Selective Service System would remain intact. While this debate was going on, the Department of Defense's reaction was to move towards the direction of a Total Force Concept. This 1970 decision mandated the interweaving of active and reserve forces, reducing the active forces and increasing the dependence on the reserves. This was necessary if the all-volunteer force were to be effective.[3]

McDermott believed that growth in membership was necessary to assure USAA's future success. It was not going to be as easy as the one call policy service representative Hattie Brock handled. During one telephone call from a pay phone at the Air Force Academy that lasted from about 10 a.m. to 3 p.m., she enrolled twenty-one new USAA members.[4]

On the more serious side, with the changes in defense policy coming out of the Vietnam War experience, USAA had to change if it were to continue to be viable. On March 12, 1973, McDermott wrote a memo entitled "USAA Capacity Gap, 1 January 1973-31 December '82." After looking at the Master Plan for the new proposed USAA Home Office building, the underestimated USAA productivity gains, and the opening of field offices, he estimated that USAA could accommodate at least double the more than over 3,000 current employees and handle five million policies in San Antonio. He asked the Plans Department to present a conceptual plan to see how the gap could be filled by 1982 by changing eligibility rules to accommodate the Reserves and ex-dependents of USAA members.

Military reservists in the Ready Reserve played a key role in the Total Force Concept and had long wanted to be eligible for USAA membership. The reservists on active duty had already been included, and so had those who had retired, but not those in the Ready Reserve. One reason had been USAA's fear that it did "not have the capacity to handle large numbers of new policyholders competently and efficiently."[5] On March 17, five days after receiving

McDermott's memo, Al Kirsling, Director of Plans and Programs, briefed the Board on the issue. The recommendation was to extend eligibility for USAA membership to Ready Reserve Officers, including the National Guard and the U.S. Coast Guard. While 85 percent of the officers on active duty were members, only 27 percent of the 250,000 Ready Reserve Officers were. The Board concurred with the recommendation.

Virginia National Guard 192nd Fighter Wing. *(Courtesy of Historical Society of the Militia and National Guard)*

Two months later McDermott wrote a memo to the Board. Extending eligibility to the Ready Reserve officers raised questions by Reserve officers in Standby and Unpaid Retired Reserve status. As the individual reservists shifted from category to category, their eligibility for USAA changed, although their insurability was never in question. This posed difficulties for the prospective members as well as for USAA employees who had to make technical determinations on complex military status changes. McDermott wanted the rules simplified. The Board concurred and, at its May 19, 1973, meeting, extended membership to include all officers in the Reserve Forces of the United States, regardless of status. USAA had made the Total Force Concept its own. And, as always, members were ready to help the Association. Retired Navy Captain John Riner wrote to McDermott that he had included the new eligibility information in the California Reserve Officer Association newsletter.[6]

Inclusion of the Reserve Officers would help, but it would not be enough to sustain growth in USAA. When he first came to USAA, McDermott briefly entertained extending eligibility to the enlisted force and asked for a special USAA study on the issue. When he obtained reports from the Air Force Inspector General's office detailing motor vehicle accidents, he found that the top two enlisted ranks of the Air Force had better records than the lowest two officer ranks. For the rest of the enlisted, however, the accident rate was higher than that of the officer population. He felt it was not politically feasible to insure just the upper ranks — that state insurance commissioners would not approve of the discrimination. Further, he disapproved a proposal to set up a new reciprocal just for the enlisted.[7]

While the discussions on enlisted eligibility were going on, the Association was also looking closely at the ex-dependent market. For years, hundreds of USAA members had petitioned the Association on behalf of their children who were becoming of age and moving away from home. On March 11, 1969, retired Rear Admiral Walter J. Whipple wrote to McDermott to congratulate him on becoming president of USAA. He also had another purpose — to suggest membership for the children of members. It didn't make sense to Whipple that USAA would insure dependents from age sixteen to twenty-one or so, when they posed the highest risk, and then let them go somewhere else when they gained experience and maturity. His son was already gone, he wrote, but "p.s. my daughter awaits your reply with keen interest!" McDermott gave him a noncommittal reply; the Admiral wrote again. He told McDermott that he now realized the difficulty of selling this idea to the Board. He then suggested that USAA form a subsidiary company with different criteria for membership — like the offspring of long-time members.[8]

Another case that interested USAA management came in the form of a telephone call from USAA founder Garrison's widow. In spite of her special status, USAA denied her request to insure the Garrisons' youngest daughter, Patricia. Vice President Cliff Jefferis forwarded the notes from the telephone call to McDermott with his own note — "another good example of a candidate for our dependent coverage."9

Soon afterwards, McDermott sided with heredity. He decided to insure ex-dependents in a separate company and asked his team to make it happen, at the same time dropping the proposals to include enlisted. Clem Spalding, Vice President for Insurance Operations, and Charlie Cook, Actuary, recommended placing them in the USAA General Indemnity Company (GIC). This company had been licensed by the state of Texas on August 2, 1972, to write automobile insurance, so a vehicle was already in place. In April 1973, Al Kirsling, Director of Plans, recommended to the Board of the USAA GIC that it provide insurance to non-dependent children and spouses of present and former USAA members. The Board concurred and authorized the President to take the necessary actions to make this insurance available through GIC.10

Al Kirsling

The original purpose of GIC had been to insure USAA members in the state of Ohio. Ohio had a law against licensing reciprocals to sell automobile insurance. USAA thought it had this problem solved earlier by insuring members in Ohio with the USAA Casualty Insurance Company (CIC), which was also created primarily for this purpose. Because USAA was reinsuring CIC and for other reasons, the state insurance commissioner declared this CIC-USAA arrangement no longer acceptable. After receiving its Texas license, GIC applied for a license to do business in Ohio according to plan.

The decision to insure ex-dependents using GIC made, McDermott was not satisfied. He wanted to access the approximately 40,000 dependents who became emancipated annually as quickly as possible. GIC was licensed in only one state. On the other hand, CIC was already licensed in twenty-seven. McDermott asked for General Counsel Bill McCrae's thoughts. McCrae pointed out that besides the original solution to the Ohio problem, CIC's intended role was to take all the assigned risks and cadets and midshipmen in basic ROTC. In CIC, the assigned risks could be charged higher rates than in the parent company, and the non-military affiliated drivers would no longer have member voting privileges. As of June 30, 1973, about 25 percent of USAA's approximately 60,000 assigned risks had already been moved into CIC. In addition, CIC was looked at as a possible repository for insureds forced on USAA by state "take all comers" provisions. (Although five states had such provisions, USAA had insured only about seventy individuals in the past five years.) In spite of all this, McCrae pointed out that using CIC would provide a "faster track" than GIC to penetrate the non-dependent market.[11] On the next day, McDermott announced to his staff that he had decided to have the Association insure dependents through CIC. At the next GIC Board meeting, McDermott had the Board rescind its decision to insure former dependents and to focus only on Ohio.[12] As a stock company, USAA GIC was licensed by Ohio in September and began writing new policies there November 1, 1973.

At the CIC Board meeting held on the same day, McDermott received the authority to make insurance available to former dependents through CIC.[13] On October 8, 1973, the first automobile policy was issued. Three weeks later, the CIC Board voted to include former spouses of USAA members as well. It recognized McDermott's arguments that the unsung hero of a military officer's career was often a hardworking spouse. Divorced spouses lost military benefits immediately, but in this traumatic period they needed help and support rather than the cold shoulder. McDermott estimated that this would amount to about 5,000 eligibles per year.[14] By the end of 1973, over 76,000 former dependents had joined USAA through CIC.

The rapid growth demonstrated that family ties were an important factor in bringing ex-dependents into the USAA family in their own right. Satisfied USAA parent members steered their children into the Association. In later years, retired Air Force Lieutenant Colonel David Kahne forwarded to McDermott a four-page letter he and his wife Shirley had written to their two ex-dependent children. The parents had listed all the arguments why their children should join USAA. They concluded with "it's a class outfit that gives superb service."[15] Intensive marketing also added solid results. By the end of 1974, USAA insured over 36,000 vehicles for ex-dependents, and this number more than doubled by the end of 1975. Rapidly increasing losses, however, confirmed once again that naturalist Jean Lamarck's theory of inheritance of acquired characteristics was wrong. The favorable book of business for USAA members was not automatically reflected in the business for CIC.

In the meantime, on the morning of October 6, 1973 — Yom Kippur — Egyptian and Syrian forces attacked Israel, catching the nation by surprise. About the same time, Arab oil ministers demanded a price increase from $3.01 to $5.12 a barrel from oil company representatives, who refused the demand. A week later the oil ministers announced a unilateral price increase. Coupled with this were production cuts and announcements of oil embargoes against the

U.S. by various Arab states. On December 22, the Organization of Petroleum Exporting Countries (OPEC) raised the price of oil to $11.65 per barrel. Using the "oil weapon," Saudi Arabia's financial reserves rose from $3.9 billion in 1973 to $49.6 billion at the end of 1976. The sharply rising oil prices were a serious threat to the American lifestyle. The U.S. consumed a third of the oil produced worldwide in 1973, with only 6 percent of the world's population.[16]

At the Annual Meeting of the National Association of Independent Insurers (NAII) in 1973, the energy crisis was the principal topic of discussion. McDermott reported to the USAA Board that the factors the insurers believed would have the biggest impact on automobile insurance were the reduction of speed limits, a trend towards smaller cars, car pooling, and gas rationing.[17] At the USAA Home Office Building, heating, air conditioning, and lighting were reduced to conserve fuel — about a 25 percent reduction over 1972's figures. USAA encouraged car pooling through preferred reserved parking and other incentives. By the end of 1973, USAA had over 600 car pools. In August 1977, a pilot van pool program began at USAA and, by the end of the decade, over ninety vans were in operation. Members reporting participation in car pools received $1.4 million in refunds on their policies because they had reduced driving days and mileage. USAA's overall energy program received a positive mention on the ABC *Evening News*.[18] In 1979, McDermott reported to the members in *Aide Magazine* that by the end of the year, 40 percent of USAA's employees would be participating in some type of ride sharing.[19]

The impact of oil shortages and other structural flaws in the economy resulted in unsettled economic times that lasted a decade. The NAII reported that shortages of gasoline and the nationwide speed limit of 55 mph contributed to a decreased claims frequency (minus 6.8 percent), but inflation caused the average claim cost to jump 7.1 percent. By the end of the decade, a "stagflation" developed, featuring double-digit inflation and unemployment.[20] All these economic factors were to impact on America's insurance industry and USAA in the 1970s, but McDermott regarded inflation as the "number one problem of the insurance industry."[21]

Inflation Rates 1970-1980 by Percentage Increase

1970	5.6	1975	7.0
1971	3.4	1976	4.8
1972	3.4	1977	6.8
1973	8.8	1978	9.0
1974	12.2	1979	13.3

USAA took a number of general actions in an attempt to reduce the impact of the inflationary years on USAA and its membership. Bob Brakey, then a regional vice president, recalled that McDermott pushed very hard for a six-month instead of an annual auto policy. In this way, USAA could charge proper rates to customers to keep pace with inflation. Many at USAA fought the idea because it would double the number of policies issued and increase phone-call volume. Nevertheless, McDermott had his way, and the six-month policies went into effect.[22] As home construction costs escalated 30 percent or better, USAA introduced an Adjusted Building Cost (ABC) endorsement to make sure members could replace their homes in the event of fire or other disaster. McDermott also discussed in *Aide Magazine* various ways members could help themselves and the Association cope with inflation, such as by increasing deductibles and practicing auto and home safety. In spite of all the actions USAA was able to take, inflation had an impact on all USAA operations throughout the decade.

Assuming ideal conditions, USAA management's initial prognosis for CIC was for losses at first, but for profitability by July 1978. In retrospect, the decision to enter the ex-dependent market in 1973 was not propitiously timed. The years 1974 and 1975 were the most disastrous for losses in the automobile insurance industry up until that time. In early 1976, the *Washington Post* reported 1975 losses totaled $4.5 billion with thirty insurance company failures.[23] Price controls, premium rollbacks resulting from the energy crisis, rate reductions mandated by no-fault laws, runaway inflation in auto repair costs, and medical costs all played a role. While the Consumer Price Index rose 19 percent, auto insurance rates increased only 9 percent. Nevertheless, USAA did fairly well during this period. It moved from twelfth to tenth place among companies writing private automobile insurance. USAA's loss ratio of 82.8 percent was sixth among the eighteen largest automobile insurers, but its combined ratio of 98.2 percent placed it first among the eighteen.[24]

Clifford Jefferis

The story was not so positive with the CIC subsidiary. With two years' experience behind it, USAA found that CIC losses were much worse than expected, and this caused consternation in the Association. In 1975, the CIC loss to earned premium ratio was 129.64 percent.

The focus on growth for CIC had been successful, but it was clear that USAA would have to take action to stem the flow of red ink onto the CIC books. McDermott appointed a committee chaired by Clifford Jefferis to examine CIC results, problems, and trends. It was to recommend specific actions to be taken to assure McDermott's goal of profitability by July 1978. Some of the committee's observations were expected. The age distribution of CIC policyholders was skewed towards drivers under thirty, and this group was more accident-prone. The percentage of USAA drivers under thirty was 20.7, while the same figure in CIC was 84.4 percent, with over 50 percent of these under twenty-five. When driving records for 1975 were compared in an internal audit, 63 percent of CIC policyholders had an accident or a violation conviction while only 23 percent of new USAA members had. When the CIC pricing policy had been established in 1973, it was assumed that CIC's loss ratios would exceed those of USAA by 12 percent. The actual figure was about 25 percent.

Since the explosive growth in CIC was turning out negatively for the Association, McDermott took action to slow it down. All active solicitation for CIC ceased, and the company accepted no new applicants from New York, New Jersey, Pennsylvania, and Connecticut. The In-WATS lines established for CIC applicants were terminated. In addition, USAA tightened underwriting standards considerably. It ordered motor vehicle driving records routinely and reviewed them before accepting new applicants or renewing existing policyholders. In 1973, CIC accepted 95 percent of new applicants, but in 1976 it accepted only about 50 percent. It also refused to renew about 20 percent of existing policyholders. CIC increased the deductibles and petitioned states for rate increases. Finally, in early 1976, McDermott decided to raise CIC rates from "USAA prices" to "full bureau prices." The sum of these management actions proved successful. In 1976, CIC had a net gain of only 2,020 policyholders as opposed to over 35,000 the previous year. By the beginning of 1977, McDermott told the CIC Board that no further dramatic actions would be necessary, and he announced an underwriting gain.[25] From this point on, USAA's CIC gradually began to show increasing profitability. In 1979, when Bob Brakey became the head of underwriting, he pushed to market CIC, which grew into a profitable and successful venture.[26]

Through prompt action and correct management decisions, USAA's CIC survived the problems created, in part, by the energy crisis and inflation. Management at the Government Employees Insurance Company (GEICO) was not as astute, and its problems could have hurt USAA in the long term. GEICO's founder, former USAA executive Leo Goodwin, had passed away in 1971 and did not get to witness the coming debacle. The management team at GEICO was obsessed by growth as a panacea for poor performance, and removed previous eligibility restrictions. Underwriting standards deteriorated badly, and poor business filled the growth goals. Inflation drove costs upward, but GEICO management's reaction was to keep premium rates stable to assist marketing. Predictably, severe operating losses followed — reaching $124 million in 1975. Its ratio of premiums to capital surplus was 13.4 to 1, four times the industry average.[27]

Max Wallach, Superintendent of Insurance, Washington, D.C., believed that GEICO was on the verge of insolvency. Wallach called a meeting of more than a dozen property and casualty company heads, including McDermott, to seek a way to save GEICO. McDermott asked Ensley to collect staff recommendations on USAA's participation in any bailout proposal. The staff recommended that USAA participate for a number of reasons. These included possible federal intervention, adverse publicity and legislation, massive increases in new assigned risks and, if GEICO failed, exposure for USAA as the major remaining mail order insurer. Even if USAA did not participate and GEICO failed, state assessments for USAA would exceed $8 million.[28] Also, McDermott emphasized to the USAA Board that GEICO likely insured most congressmen and senators and their staffs, as well as many state officials. The loss of GEICO might influence these policyholders to favor the agent system, with possible long-term damage to USAA.[29] The industry and the USAA Board finally agreed on a reinsurance program for GEICO. USAA's enlightened self-interest in supporting the GEICO bailout paid off. USAA made a net profit of $1.6 million by the time GEICO returned to financial health in 1978 and after the reinsurance program was terminated.[30]

While the energy shortage and inflation rate produced tremors in CIC, they also caused an unexpected casualty at USAA. In December 1972, USAA sent a survey to over 7,000 members asking about their level of interest in group charter flights. Of those returning the survey, 84.5 percent indicated that they were "very interested" or "interested," and of these, over 75 percent indicated that they would participate.[31] The USAA Special Services Company was incorporated with a broad charter on March 21, 1973, and began negotiating with airlines. The first European tour with the "Black Eagle" took off on September 17, 1973. In spite of the expressed member interest, USAA membership participation in subsequent charter flights was much lower than expected. The USAA Board met in early 1975 and found that energy problems and economic conditions drove up costs to members, and that the members severely curtailed their vacation travel. This made the group charter operations of the USAA Special Services Company unprofitable. The final blow occurred when the Civil Aeronautics Board deregulated charters and eliminated the affinity group requirement. The Board then directed that the overseas charter travel business be terminated by September 1975, with the Special Services Company still running the travel agency begun on November 1, 1974, the company store, and the van pool.[32]

McDermott had believed from the first that an important element of service was to provide new products and services that the membership desired. The problems with the group charter program did not change his mind. In fact, in 1974, he established a Group Research Department and upgraded the marketing division to help improve USAA's service. That same year USAA introduced its first Personal Catastrophe Liability (umbrella) policy and a new Mobile Homeowner's policy. In 1975, USAA added a policy for yachts, and an all-risk endorsement to the homeowner's policies. Life Company studied disability insurance, and USAA Special Services Company entertained proposals from Diners Club to begin offering its card to members.

In the financial services area, the USAA mutual fund program gained enthusiastic acceptance among the members. After its first full year in 1972, the USAA Capital Growth Fund had over 18,000 stockholders and $26 million in assets. In mid-1973, McDermott reported to the members that the value of the fund's shares had risen 28.5 percent over the previous year. This was compared to the Dow Jones Industrial Average, which was up 14.6 percent.[33]

Many older USAA members were looking for an income fund to supplement their retirements, but starting such a fund meant another large infusion of capital not available in the Life Company. At the 1972 Annual Members' Meeting, McDermott had been successful in getting the bylaws provision outlining the purpose of the Association changed to enable USAA to provide not only insurance coverage, but also to "engage in other activities for the benefit of the membership, as authorized by the Board of Directors."[34] The way was now open to offer a wide variety of financial services to the membership. In July 1973, the USAA Board authorized the president to purchase the capital stock of the USAA Fund Management Company from the USAA Life Insurance Company.[35] That completed, USAA was now directly involved in the mutual fund business and began the USAA Income Fund shortly thereafter.

For various reasons, the USAA Capital Growth Fund began to falter. After the third quarter of 1973, it fell below various yardsticks, such as the Dow Jones Industrial Average, that McDermott used to track progress. Beginning in 1974, members began writing to USAA about the falling fund value. With no improvement, shareholders began selling. By July 1976, the shareholder redemptions had exceeded new sales for thirteen months in a row. McDermott named Al Illig, fund manager of the USAA Income Fund, to also become new fund manager for the USAA Capital Growth Fund.

George Sykes

On October 1, 1976, the USAA Fund Management Company was changed to the USAA Investment Management Company (IMCO), headed by retired Air Force Brigadier General George K. Sykes. This was to reflect the new broader responsibilities of this company, which included managing the investment portfolio for USAA's operating companies in addition to the portfolio of the mutual funds, a total of $575 million.[36] USAA's Investment Division was discontinued, with most of the personnel integrated into IMCO. Soon IMCO was playing a key role in building USAA's financial strength. In September 1978, IMCO's owned and managed assets reached $1 billion and, in 1980, the Property and Casualty Company received 73 percent of its net income from IMCO investments.

Under the leadership of Jack Daye, the USAA Life Insurance Company began to fulfill the promise that McDermott had for it. Daye had McDermott's full confidence and shared his vision for rapid growth, but Daye owned a streak of independence. He built a strong team, and when the Broadway Building became too crowded, he eagerly volunteered to take his company to the Woodcock Building in San Antonio. He had a Board of Directors of his own, held planning meetings outside of USAA, for all practical purposes had his own actuary, and even insisted on a computer in a non-standard blue color. When he hired retired Air Force Brigadier General Charles Bishop from the Property and Casualty Company to come to the Life Company, he explained his philosophy to Bishop. The USAA Company in the home office building, he said, was like a Strategic Air Command bomb group. The Life Company was like a fighter squadron. "We are different. You'll like it better — we wear different baseball hats, and it's more fun over here."[37]

To help improve Life Marketing, Daye hired Dennis Cross with McDermott's enthusiastic blessing. Cross had been a USAA member since 1968 and worked for the Life Insurance Marketing and Research Association (LIMRA). While reading *Aide Magazine*, Cross's wife asked him if USAA was a member of LIMRA. Cross said it was not, but decided to stop in and talk to Daye on his next visit to San Antonio. Daye took a liking to the brash Cross and talked him into leaving LIMRA and joining the Life Company as head of Marketing.[38] Day, Cross, and the Life team worked together in improving the products, their prices, and how they marketed them. In 1979, when annuities became popular, the Life Company added a subsidiary to market and service them.

Key to the marketing efforts were service and honesty with the potential policy purchaser. A special program was developed to assist widows. The Life sales force often steered members to the Armed Forces Relief and Benefit Association for a $50,000 term life policy that was available for $35 a year. McDermott strongly believed that members should take the Survivors' Benefit Plan offered by the services in preference to any life insurance option. Why would they do this? Dennis Cross explained it was good ethics, good service, and the goodwill that would serve USAA in the form of long-term relationships.³⁹ The philosophy had overtones of Kris Kringle's in the movie *Miracle on 34th Street*, when he advised Macy's customers to go to Gimbels for better prices. The result was more sales than ever for Macy's.

The esprit de corps that Daye built was soon reflected in the bottom line. On December 16, 1973, Life Company reached the milestone of $1 billion of insurance in force when it sold a policy to Army Captain Robert J. Lifsey. In 1976, it reached $2 billion and in 1979, $4 billion, with $1 billion written in 1979 alone. In 1978, employees Sharon Patterson, Guy Covington, and Roy Morgan sold $158 million in policies, more than any of USAA's principal competitors for the military market sold in 1977.⁴⁰ The year 1980 found the Life Company among the 100 largest in the country. Along with the sales were consistent A+ ratings from *A.M. Best*. Daye exuded confidence in his operation and briefed the USAA Board of Directors in 1979 that the Life Company would "some day be stronger than the parent company."⁴¹

Part of McDermott's service thrust was to provide education and information through such vehicles as *Aide Magazine*. In late 1972, McDermott suggested that members review their automobile liability insurance and consider raising the limits to protect themselves against rising court awards. To illustrate the faith of USAA members in the Association, about 10 percent of the membership raised their limits in the first six months of 1973, even though it raised their own rates.⁴²

By the summer of 1975, USAA's membership had climbed to nearly one million members, and good service would have been impossible without technology. The outcome of Project 1971 was the new Auto Issue and Maintenance System (AIMS). Installed in 1975, it performed all previous system functions plus 111 improvements, such as on-line data entry and an error-detection feature. It enabled USAA to put up to twelve vehicles on one policy and did such things as automatic premium comparisons. At that time, USAA's most modern piece of computer equipment was the IBM 370 Model 168. It had a virtual storage capacity of up to sixteen million bytes. The overall Information Management System provided management of the USAA customer database containing 4.8 billion characters. About 350 Courier and IBM CRT display terminals initiated 110,000 transactions daily.[43] (Compare that with an average of sixteen million transactions daily in 1996.) The overall AIMS was claimed to be "the most sophisticated and efficient computerized system in the insurance industry for issuing and maintaining auto policies."[44]

The types of problems experienced in computer services in the 1970s still have echoes as business approaches the 21st century. McDermott believed in centralized services and opposed decentralization. This resulted in the necessity for systems personnel to develop an understanding of the users' needs and ways of doing business. Development of priorities across USAA was also a problem. To help with this, McDermott established and chaired an Automated Data Processing Council. This helped in both problem areas. Marty Fishel, Senior Vice President, Computer Services, pointed out a third problem. This was the recruiting of USAA's experienced computer programmers, analysts, and IMS on-line specialists by headhunters. In the first ten months of 1976, USAA lost nineteen of its best to companies such as Occidental Petroleum, McDonnell Douglas, and Boeing. Stung by the losses, USAA began reviewing jobs and grades with the intention of raising grades and salaries to retard losses.[45]

Technical advances in mail handling also helped to improve service levels. Mail volume in 1973 was considerable. USAA used pre-coded business reply envelopes and automated equipment that opened and sorted at the rate of about five per second. Procedures for handling correspondence requiring only one action, such as check deposits and requests for literature, enabled speedy mail processing. Sometimes, however, correspondence required multiple actions. To solve this, USAA procured a Xerox 7000 duplicator, which reduced the correspondence and envelope to fit on one page and made as many copies as necessary for action agencies. *Best's Review* praised the actions, which improved productivity and reduced costs.[46] Another innovation was a test that USAA's Senior Vice President, Administration, Bill Starnes agreed to run in 1974 with a new overnight package service called Federal Express. A senior officer with that fledgling company told Starnes he hoped that his company would get into the black for the first time that July.[47]

After five decades of conducting all USAA business from the home office in San Antonio, the development of regional offices in the 1970s was a portent for the future. The West Point and Falls Church, Virginia, offices were opened to meet state regulatory requirements. The Mid-Atlantic Regional Services Office (MARSO) in Virginia quickly expanded beyond its original charter as members sought out USAA services at this regional location. Retired Colonel Samuel W. Pinnell was the general manager and actively encouraged the expanded role. Underwriting services, marketing,

Mid-Atlantic Regional Services Office in Virginia

and a claims facility ultimately served the 7 percent of the USAA members residing in the Washington, D.C., area.

Regional offices in Florida and Colorado were opened to provide member service and to gain special tax benefits in those states. In Florida, the establishment of a Regional Home Office produced an annual premium tax savings of $500,000. This Southeast Regional Service Office (SERSO) opened for business in a leased building in Tampa on June 18, 1973, under the leadership of General Manager Colonel C. K. Charbonneau. This office received more authority and responsibility for claims than the one in Virginia, qualifying it for "home" office status.[48] It was a busy office and, by 1975, was handling 150 new claims every week and had opened a satellite office in Pensacola, Florida, to provide service to U.S. Navy officers in training at that location.

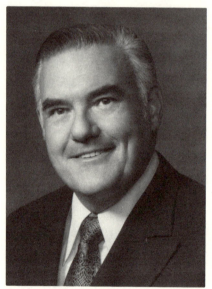
Bill Mahon

On February 4, 1974, the Rocky Mountain Regional Service Office (RMRSO) opened in a purchased building with retired Air Force Colonel William J. Mahon as general manager. As in Virginia, the Colorado Springs office experienced considerable local member interest. By the spring of 1974, the office was saving $5,000 per month by direct handling of claims. In 1977, it achieved recognition as a Regional Home Office by the Colorado State Insurance Commissioner, and the premium tax rate dropped from 3.85 percent to 1 percent at a significant savings — $377,000 the first year. Another regional office was opened in San Diego in April 1975, and in April 1977, a satellite opened in Cupertino, California, to serve the Bay area. Theodore James "Ted" Michel at the San Antonio home office supervised all these regional offices, and was promoted to assistant vice president in 1973, and vice president in 1974.

McDermott had known Michel from their days at the United States Military Academy. Michel was born in 1919 to a close-knit German Catholic family in St. Paul, Minnesota. After graduating from high school as valedictorian, he briefly attended St. Thomas College and was selected to enter the class of 1942 at West Point. He was a natural athlete and played football and lacrosse at the Academy. His handsome features and rugged physique won him selection to ice skater Sonja Heinie's All American Adonis Team. That prompted intense kidding at the Point, but Michel took it in stride. Although very busy at the Academy, he found time to attend early morning Catholic mass often. It was here that McDermott first met Michel and developed a lifelong admiration for the man and his faith.

After commissioning, Michel entered the Air Corps and married Joan Birder during flying training. In May 1943, he was reassigned to the Far East and left new bride "Jo-Ahn," as he called her, at home. He flew B-25s in India and China. Following World War II, he held a wide variety of command and staff jobs in the U.S. and overseas in Korea and Italy. He retired from the Air Force in 1970, and McDermott hired him to head USAA's office at West Point. He was next brought into the San Antonio home office to supervise the regional offices. He remained a deeply religious man and often held forth after family dinners on such topics as honesty, frugality, and other virtues. "With proper disrespect," his seven children numbered his talks; "honesty and integrity," for example, became number thirty-seven.[49] He served at USAA until he retired again in 1986. His efforts were critical in making the regionalization at the Association a success.

The establishment of these regional offices was the precursor to organizing USAA's insurance operations along regional lines. In

A Tradition Of Service

McDermott's first organizational move at USAA, he had reorganized the company into branches divided by terminal digits. The increasing activity of states in such areas as passing no-fault laws, take-all-comers provisions, and the residual (assigned risk) market made the situation exceedingly complex. No one could expect a USAA employee to be familiar with the vagaries of all fifty states. McDermott settled on dividing the insureds initially into six regions of approximately equal numbers of customers. A regional vice president was accountable for policy service, claims, and everything else that pertained to the members assigned to that particular region. Later the regions were reduced to four to service different time zones. The various alignments in regions that have occurred over the years are not important in themselves. What is important is that USAA continually tinkered with the regional alignments in an effort to best serve its customers. The regionalization concept became fully operational in 1978 after extensive testing in 1977.[50]

An important corollary to the regional development was the establishment of toll-free (In-WATS) telephone lines that the members could use to contact USAA. In the early 1970s, members had been increasingly upset by the refusal of USAA to accept collect calls in doing business. In some cases, members complained that the employees were unpleasant or curt to them. At first, McDermott had not authorized beginning In-WATS service because most calls would require the members' record to be pulled — and with over 800,000 members, it would be too time consuming and costly. When one member called, he asked about USAA getting "800" service, and the employee told him it was too expensive. The next day, this same member received an advertisement from Life Company with an "800" number to call, if he were interested. In August 1976, the member wrote to McDermott that it was "manifestly unfair to use company funds to attract new business while refusing to do so to retain company business."[51]

In a highly significant and far-reaching decision, McDermott ordered operational In-WATS testing for members to begin. On May 30, 1977, the lines were opened from New Jersey. On October 3, an experimental system was implemented in New England, and the full system was phased in during 1978 as each region was organized. The first was the Southeast Region in February 1978 under Bob Brakey. When the Northeast Region opened in June, Brakey moved there and Dale Calvert took his place in the Southeast. The next was the North Central Region under Al Kirsling. One unexpected result of In-WATS was that McDermott found that the policy service functions were more efficiently performed in the home office and claims in the field offices.[52]

Bob Brakey

With the In-WATS capability in place, USAA completed its conversion to direct claims handling in 1978. Prior to this, the Association depended on a network of more than 1,000 adjusters throughout the country to handle the majority of the claims. To save costs and to provide better service, McDermott converted the claims process from independent adjusters to USAA home or regional office employees handling the claims. He believed that USAA employees could better serve the members than contract employees. As part of this change, USAA distributed the new toll-free claims numbers to the members. The combined results of the regionalization, In-WATS toll-free lines, and USAA employee-adjusters greatly improved USAA's service.

Even as USAA continued to grow and technology improved, the

members still maintained a warm and personal view of their Association. On January 25, 1975, eighty-three-year-old World War I veteran Roberts Williams wrote a fascinating twelve-page personal letter to McDermott. He described his combat experiences as a chaplain and his life after the war. He hoped McDermott would reply in kind, but he "must do it soon," because with all his medical problems, "Taps will be blown sooner over me than I care for." McDermott replied immediately and concluded that when "Taps are blown over you, there will be many in Heaven and on earth who will say — well done." Service comes in many forms.

Each year McDermott announced an annual theme to the employees. In 1977 it was "The Year of Service"; and 1978's was "Service Through Teamwork." The significant changes noted above permanently improved USAA's opportunity to take care of its members. Stories of service are part of USAA's oral tradition — and reinforce the Association's tradition of service. When one Pennsylvania member's apartment was burglarized, he didn't notice a camera was missing. Two months later the member wrote and asked if USAA would still honor the claim for the camera. In eight days, he had a check without filing a form. He wrote that although he was surprised, he shouldn't have been. He recalled that *The Washington Post* had interviewed Pennsylvania's consumer-oriented Insurance Commissioner, Herbert S. Denenberg. When he was asked what company he used, Denenberg said, "USAA" and praised it for providing "good service at low cost."[53]

Often employees went way beyond their job descriptions to help out a member. When service representative Jeanette Carpenter called an Alabama member to check on a boat owner policy, the member's wife apologized for not providing the needed information earlier. She explained that her husband was critically ill and her son had just been medically evacuated for a hand injury to Wilford Hall Air Force Hospital in San Antonio. She was upset that she couldn't be with her son. Carpenter, a mother of two, called the hospital and made arrangements to spend a day with the member's son as soon as he was able. Following his day with Carpenter touring San Antonio, he and his mother could not believe how thoughtful this USAA employee had been to them.[54]

Especially touching were the strong links that lifetime members had with USAA. Employee Kay Prosk corresponded often with an eighty-one-year-old widow, who jokingly asked Prosk to "find her a nice, rich old man." Joe Massett recalled calming a new widow who then called him often for help. An eighty-four-year-old member, Mrs. Clayton Bissell from Signal Mountain, Tennessee, wrote to USAA. Her eyes were bad, so she had given away her car, and she no longer needed USAA's help and guidance on insurance. But she thanked USAA "for your help and protection" for her husband and herself while he was alive, and for herself after his death. Retired Second Lieutenant and nurse Ethel Knapp wrote to USAA from a nursing home. She returned, *at her own expense,* unused USAA forms, envelopes, and advertising mailings which she said she knew were an expense to the Association. She wrote that she was "on limited time due to a bad heart," and no longer needed automobile insurance. She was grateful for the "many blessings by being insured" with USAA, and she wanted to thank everyone and to say goodbye. When a retired admiral and his wife were struck by a car and killed in Argentina, their son sent USAA President McDermott the same personal note that he had sent to friends and relatives. With caring employees and members like these, it is easy to see why USAA continued to be successful in the 1970s.[55]

Insuring and serving members overseas was much more difficult than in the United States and was deeply appreciated by the membership. In 1975, Ted Michel reported that USAA was insuring over 37,000 vehicles in overseas areas. When Typhoon Pamela hit Guam in the summer of 1976, USAA's fast-response claims team was there in days. Supported by Navy and Air Force commanders, the team worked fifteen to seventeen hours daily for twenty days in processing over 1,100 claims, many in the absence of electricity. One Air Force captain wrote that all insurance companies say that they are responsive — but "not one other company responds as you do."[56]

A catastrophe may produce 1,100 claims, but if you have an accident — that's a catastrophe for you. General of the Army Omar Bradley wrote to McDermott and told him that he had long been an ardent supporter of USAA, but recently had a ringside opportunity to watch dedicated USAA employees at work. Mrs. Bradley had an accident which was emotional and traumatic for both of them. The General was grateful for USAA's great service. He was not only appreciative for themselves, but "comforting" to him and his wife was "the knowledge that USAA will always be there for the fine young officers serving our nation today."[57]

In another example, in the summer of 1978, an Air Force officer member was driving at a high rate of speed between Aviano and Venice, Italy. He fell asleep, went through a fence, crashed into a culvert, and totaled his station wagon. His wife and five children, who were passengers, had minor injuries and were taken to a local hospital. The vehicle was towed to an unknown location. The officer and his family took a train back to his base in Germany and reported the accident to USAA's Frankfurt office, where the employees had the capability of settling claims in nineteen different languages, including Italian. A week later he had a check for the station wagon. Painless? Yes, for the officer, but not for USAA. The Association had to find the vehicle, get customs clearance to "import" it legally into Italy so it could be junked there, find the accident site and the owner of the fence and pay for it, and reimburse the ambulance, wrecker, and hospital with no information on locations or names available. The great difficulty for the company was invisible to the happy and satisfied USAA member.

Sometimes USAA was not able to pay claims for sound reasons

even though management and employees agonized over the necessary decision. One example was the Iranian Revolution. In 1976, Jimmy Carter was elected President of the United States. As a graduate of the U.S. Naval Academy and a regular officer who had served on a nuclear submarine, his background suggested military support. He did reduce military strength somewhat, however. Rather than favoring pure might and possible abuse of American power, he believed that the "soul" of American foreign policy should be guided by human rights for people everywhere. Nevertheless, Carter supported the dictatorial Shah of Iran and when the President visited Teheran in late 1977, he hinted at U.S. backing despite internal critics. What he did not know was that the Shah was dying of cancer.

In February of 1978, the Tabriz riots occurred. Again in August 1978, anti-government riots broke out and martial law was declared in September. The radicals wanted to replace Shah Mohammed Palavi with an Islamic government under the leadership of the Ayatollah Khomeni, who was in exile. By November, USAA members in Iran, concerned about their coverage, were writing to the Association. On January 3, 1979, McDermott wrote to all 660 members who had addresses in Iran or policies based there. He pointed out that like all insurance companies, USAA's household goods and personal floater policies had war, rebellion, and revolution clauses precluding paying claims that might result from these traumatic events. McDermott urged the members to protect items valuable to them and their families. If claims did arise in Iran under these circumstances, USAA would have to deny the claims. He pointed out that this decision was necessary to strike a balance between individual members and the membership as a whole. Conditions continued to deteriorate and many American dependents began returning to the United States. When Carter gave the Shah clearance in October to enter New York City for cancer treatment, Iran erupted. On November 4, 1979, revolutionaries overran the American Embassy and took sixty-six hostages, about fifteen of them USAA members. The hostages would languish in captivity for 444 days, hands and feet bound at first, enduring sleeping in soiled clothes, abusive interrogations, and mock executions. By January, all non-essential personnel were ordered out of Iran and the remaining thousands soon followed. Personal goods remained in apartments and warehouses, where extensive looting occurred. Abandoned goods were not eligible for reimbursement either. Bolstering USAA's position on refusal to pay claims was the State Department's ruling that the event was a revolution.[58]

By August 1979, USAA had 243 claims losses recorded. The reaction of USAA members in Iran to the denial of claims was mixed. Chris Head, Claims Supervisor for the Northeast Region, had the difficult duty of handling hostile members. Responding to letters was tough enough, but on one occasion he had the opportunity to have one bitter member personally confront him in the USAA lobby. (The member parted peacefully.) Surprisingly, most members contacting USAA said that they understood the exclusion for Iran written into the USAA policies.[59] Air Force Lieutenant Colonel Raymond Hengel wrote to McDermott suggesting that USAA write the membership and see if they would take reduced dividends to pay the Iran claims. Even if the answer were no (and it was), Hengel said he would stay with USAA because it was "the best insurance company in the world."[60]

USAA did what it could within the boundaries of the war exclusion clause interpretations. McDermott asked his staff to look into the feasibility of paying off all the claims in spite of the clause. His staff and USAA's legal advisors advised him not to in the strongest terms, and USAA did not pay the claims. When the Department of Defense got a bill introduced into Congress to increase the maximum dollar limits for federal reimbursement from $15,000 to $35,000, USAA gave it strong support.[61] The Association lobbied Congress, and USAA members who sustained losses testified before congressional committees. As in other similar situations, such as during World War II, USAA held to the war exclusion clauses on property to serve the membership as a whole.

Fortunately, every overseas claim was not traumatic. In July 1976, Marine Lieutenant Kevin A. Garvey and his wife were visiting a religious shrine on a small island off the coast of Japan. A monkey stole the Garvey's camera bag, which the couple recovered with one lens lost. USAA disallowed the claim because it was a "loss" and not really a "theft." A monkey, USAA determined, could not "steal." So began a series of letters between the lieutenant and USAA's claims staff which finally ended when Senior Vice President Max Wier Jr. denied his claim. The series of letters was great fun to the marines of Fighter Attack Squadron 115. As Garvey related years later, he used the Uniform Code of Military Justice and believed his position unshakable. He wrote, "The use of *Black's Law Dictionary* by USAA was as dark a tactic as its very name suggests." While his claim was sincere, he enjoyed tasting the humor and folly of what life in the armed services overseas sometimes brought. He concluded by writing that he hoped his continuing membership told what he really thought of USAA.[62]

Another whimsical claim arrived from a member who put in to replace a broken windshield on his Volkswagen. This note was enclosed with the claim. "My daughter's beau smashed it with his elbow as he was turning from giving her a kiss. Must have been some kiss! Please let me know." You can't fault USAA for having no sense of romance — it paid the claim under the comprehensive portion of his policy.[63]

Providing sincere service is a reflection of employees' personal beliefs and how they feel they are themselves treated by their employer. McDermott's religious beliefs and upbringing underlined the importance of the individual and the capacity and desire of each individual to improve. His decisions on creating a superior working environment for USAA employees set a standard for USAA, but also one for other companies to try to emulate.

McDermott's familiarity with academic campuses at West Point and the Air Force Academy led him to the idea of creating a campus-like setting for USAA's new home office building. The purchase of 287 acres between two major highways provided the stage and setting. The utilities infrastructure was available or quickly developed by the servicing companies. The four existing water wells on the property would supplement the water provided by the San Antonio City Water Department. The moist-clay soils required more effort in foundation design, but this was overcome. Test borings also discovered a layer of oil-bearing shale. To prevent the foundation from shifting, the original building was set on 1,388 reinforced concrete pilings between five and six feet wide and set sixty feet deep. The natural inheritance of the USAA property was a rich one — twenty-nine varieties of trees and shrubs, twelve species of animal life, and countless birds and wildflowers. It was a rare opportunity to develop this inheritance for USAA's employees and members that McDermott eagerly seized.

McDermott selected Benham-Blair and Affiliates of Oklahoma City as the architects and Neuhaus and Taylor of Houston as the interior designers. The basic design was a low-profile structure in multiple connected buildings blending with the Texas landscape. Color was added to the concrete to help the structure match the countryside's hues. He told the architects that the building was for the employees, and that's where he wanted the emphasis. He told the architects that he wanted the money concentrated on the building's interior for the employees, and not on the outside as a monument to the architects. The employees would be spending more working hours in the building than anywhere else. McDermott wanted it to be as attractive as possible to make the employees proud and happy to come to work there. Although the work force would be large, he did not want the building to have a crowded feel to it. Installation of computer flooring also helped. Wires and cables serving the employees ran under the floor — out of sight and easily moved to accommodate desk moves. He had one other suggestion. While visiting Mexico City, he had toured the Camino Real Hotel and wanted the home office interior to follow the basic principles he had seen there. He liked the way the central spine corridors opened periodically into courtyards of varied design.

Groundbreaking for USAA's new Home Office Building, June 28, 1971.
Robert McDermott (left) and Chairman of the Board John H. McCormick (right).

A TRADITION OF SERVICE

The architectural design and the projected costs pleased McDermott and the Board, and the groundbreaking was held on June 28, 1971. Henry C. Beck Inc. of Dallas, who had previously built USAA's Broadway Building, was selected as the general contractor. By 1973, the project was in difficulty — over budget and seriously delayed. McDermott hired Cushman and Wakefield to assess the overall situation. Cushman's representative, Jim Turner, reported that the original Benham-Blair estimate of 2.7 million square feet at $18.83 per square foot for a total cost of $51.9 million was vastly understated. Turner's estimate was almost 3 million square feet required at $29.03 per square foot, or almost $100 million dollars and, the building would not be completed until eighteen months after the original estimate![64] At the next Board meeting, a Benham-Blair representative concurred in Turner's projection of an overrun, but stated that the total cost would run closer to $83 million. In either case, the project was in trouble. The Board decided it needed a new project management team, separate from Benham-Blair, and selected Project Administration Services. McDermott decided something else. He wanted someone on his staff who was familiar with large concrete and steel projects to oversee the construction.

McDermott sought help in finding the right man from West Point classmate Major General William L. Starnes. Starnes recommended a few candidates who turned out to be unavailable or unwilling. Finally, Starnes agreed to retire from the Army and come to USAA, arriving on July 1, 1973. Starnes had considerable experience with huge construction projects with the Corps of Engineers during his Army career. He had served as a combat engineer in both World War II, where he was wounded, and in Vietnam directing construction of the port and other facilities in the Cam Ranh Bay area. He also headed the construction of the Vehicle Assembly Building and launch facilities for the National Aeronautics and Space Administration at Cape Canaveral that were used successfully in the moon landing program in 1969.

Starnes found a number of problems, got them corrected, and got the project back on track. He had a critical path developed for the building so that he and project managers would have guidelines. Weekly meetings enabled him to make timely decisions on construction snags. He also reviewed the designs for cost savings. For example, all the concrete work was to be hand-chipped by hammer and chisel. Starnes saved considerable dollars by reducing the amount of chipping to visible public areas. Starnes briefed the Board routinely on the progress, and his experience and confidence reassured the Board members.[65]

William L. Starnes

Another important decision made by McDermott at this juncture was to hire James E. Keeter as landscape architect for the home office building. McDermott was very impressed with Keeter's landscaping projects, including the development of the 160-acre Hemisfair Park, the San Antonio Main Library and Marina, and the creation of an extension of the San Antonio River and Riverwalk to the Civic Center and Hemisfair complex. Keeter was instrumental in making the grounds fit the USAA building. He developed three lakes, left what trees he could in place, and moved others that had to be moved for construction reasons. He also planted 400 new trees, including 250 large live oaks, and added thousands of native plants as well as buffalo grass to the landscape.

In addition to man-made errors that caused delays and higher costs, nature also contributed. In the early stages, the weather was bad, and seventeen consecutive days of rain filled the cavernous

A Tradition Of Service

USAA Home Office Building under construction, 1973

excavation site and created a huge "swimming pool." In September 1974, with construction well along, air conditioning began breaking down. After some investigation, it was discovered that large numbers of raccoons had invaded the partly completed home office building and were chewing through pneumatic tubing and various types of wiring. USAA finally had to hire bounty hunter Carl Skaggs with his dogs to trap raccoons every night for several months. While the computer flooring was to eventually be a boon for the Association, many raccoons got into the space, which was too small even for most dogs. Skaggs had one small mutt named Scrap Iron, however, that was as tough as its name suggested and it succeeded in driving the coons out of the computer flooring. Even one wildcat took up residence in the nearly completed "D" Courtyard until the dogs finally chased it out. And all this was to the accompaniment of coyotes that howled throughout the night.[66]

TURBULENT TIMES

Whatever the financial, planning, and labor problems that occurred during the construction, the final product exceeded everyone's expectations and won numerous professional awards as well as plaudits from employees and members. As each section was completed, employees moved in beginning in the fall of 1974. In October 1975, the last of the USAA employees moved from the Broadway Building to the new home office.[67] The remaining USAA employees from other San Antonio locations moved in over the next three months.

One unusual feature of USAA's new campus was the creation of an official residence for the president of USAA. Built in 1923, a limestone house on the USAA property had been occupied by the Ernest J. and Mary (Heard) Altgelt family until 1937. Altgelt, son of the founder of Comfort, Texas, sold the house and property to Joseph R. and Emilie Straus Sr., who occupied the house with their two sons until 1971. The project manager of the construction project next resided in the house until October 1975 when McDermott and his wife Alice moved into the house.[68]

The President's house on the USAA campus

A TRADITION OF SERVICE

On May 1, 1976, USAA held the formal dedication of the now over $100-million, 3.1-million-square-foot structure. Over 700 attended and applauded when San Antonio Mayor Lila Cockrell proclaimed the whole week "USAA Week in San Antonio." Board member and Navy Captain Robin Quigley dedicated a time capsule to be opened in 2022 and World War II P-51 aircraft did a flyby to end the formal ceremony. The 1925 Elcar made its last drive before installation in the "D" Courtyard. Following this were building tours and refreshments.

The building was more than one-third of a mile long, with three levels above ground and four below. Along the central spine were

USAA Home Office Building

five courts decorated in different themes. Besides the entry court, there were four others, one for each lettered building: Southwestern (A), San Antonio (B), Commercial (C), and USAA (D) Courts. While the beautiful building awed visitors, the "people" features built into the home office awed the employees. The title of the brief-

San Antonio ("B") Courtyard

ing for visitors was called "People Come First." And that's the way the employees felt.

The building included employee lounges, two cafeterias, a U.S. Post Office, a library, an employee convenience store, a credit union, a travel agency, and a physical fitness facility (ARA received the USAA contract to operate the cafeteria in 1974). Free covered parking for 2,600 employee cars was especially prized, as was the health center and classrooms equipped with the latest audiovisual aids assisting in self-development. Also included were high-speed escalators, seven elevators, an auditorium, a computer center, and an automated mail operation. Bell installed a modern Centrex II System with 2,300 instruments and internal mail traveled via a Mosler Telelift System (self-contained cars on monorail).

While the new home office had gone over budget, it was a bargain. Benham-Blair reported the cost of the entire structure, including the interior parking areas, as $34 per square foot. Other corporate complexes completed in 1974 cost considerably more — General Electric's was $85 per square foot and American Can's was $80, although these higher figures did not include much cheaper parking areas. The *Engineering News-Record* reported that all office buildings completed in 1976 cost between $75 and $80 per square foot. Most important, in 1979 George Ensley, Senior Vice President, Finance and Treasurer, reported to the Board that after the employees moved in, morale and productivity had gone up and absenteeism and turnover were down.[69]

In addition to their new work environment, the employees enjoyed many positive benefits. They continued to take advantage of the free-tuition, self-development program under Project Campus. In early 1975, David Laird, Assistant to Jack Daye at the Life Company, completed his MBA at St. Mary's University, as did Charles Cook, USAA's Actuary. Employee Bernie Tallerico praised USAA for providing the opportunity for him to complete his MBA. As a plus to helping with the tuition, he noted that "the four-day workweek really helped. It gave me more time to study."[70] They were to be the first of dozens of new MBAs to follow. In 1978 Bob Drumm, USAA Education and Training Consultant, announced that St. Mary's University had decided to accept credit hours from San Antonio College's Mid-Management Program towards its four-year Bachelor of Applied Science in Occupational Management. Now USAA employees could earn a four-year college degree at no tuition cost without even leaving the building. USAA's encouragement applied to professional designations as well. In May 1975, employees Susan Evers and Jim Schmidt successfully completed their Certified Public Accountant examination under USAA sponsorship. Dozens of others passed Insurance Institute of America classes and Chartered Financial Analyst (CFA) examinations. In 1975, for the first time, USAA used its own CFAs to teach the courses passed by Jack Saunders, Dennis Telzrow, and Shack

TURBULENT TIMES

Cashen. McDermott's emphasis on self-development programs was a major plus for the employees — and the Association. In 1979, McDermott praised the employees who took advantage of the program. Better qualified employees resulted in almost 90 percent of vacancies being filled from within.

Janice Marshall took full advantage of the educational opportunities at USAA. Born in Utica, New York, her father was a military officer and hospital administrator. As service brats, she and her two sisters lived in a number of places in the continental United States as well as in Hawaii and Munich, Germany. She attended eleven different schools in the process. Marshall graduated from MacArthur High School in San Antonio. In 1967, Marshall started working at USAA in a quest for a second car for her family. After passing through a number of administrative positions, she became a supervisor in 1971.

David Laird, who worked for Ferrari, talked Marshall into enrolling in the San Antonio College Mid-Management program. After putting together sixty-three credit hours, she transferred to Southwest Texas State University and took the courses it offered on local military installations. It took her thirteen years to complete her degree — all reimbursed by USAA's educational program.

Janice Marshall

The education program was a positive benefit to Marshall. She continued to get promoted in the USAA Property and Casualty Company, becoming Senior Vice President, Central Region and Regional Services. In March 1996, Marshall was promoted to President of USAA Buying Services. As such, she was the first woman to serve on the Executive Council.

To help employees get ahead and to assist USAA at the same time, USAA began its Annual Organizational Review Program (AOR) in 1976. Its development followed visits to Standard Oil of Ohio, State Farm, and Nationwide Insurance Company. The AOR reviewed key management positions and identified successor candidates to fill these positions. It also identified developmental needs for individual employees to improve their qualifications to fill these jobs. By 1979, 5,000 employees were taking technical training classes annually, and an average of 2,000 were taking courses in management development. Chaired by the president, the administration of the AOR was handled by Management Development and Training.[71] Another tool used by Personnel to identify potential managers was the "Annual Peer Ratings" system. Along with regular performance evaluations by supervisors, Marie Kelleher, Vice President of Personnel, briefed the Board that these ratings helped give a better overall picture of an individual.[72]

In 1974, in another effort to improve employees' development and USAA's productivity, McDermott directed Starnes to start an Organizational Development function in concert with Training and Personnel. His idea was for a team of specialists to serve as catalysts to seek new and better ways of getting things done. He likened the process to the way workers painted the George Washington Bridge in New York City — starting at one end from bottom to top and across the bridge and to begin again. Hence, the nickname of the USAA organizational development process as "paint the bridge." During the process, McDermott expected to have Organizational Development head Jim Patterson and his painters clarify the unit's mission, check its structure, staffing, and procedures, eliminate or redistribute marginal value efforts, and see if employees within the unit were being developed to their maximum potential.[73] Over the years, this program would help harness manpower growth and increase productivity through organizational realignments.

During the 1970s, USAA increased pay and benefits to keep pace with inflation. The Board looked carefully at the Consumer Price Index and used the Cost of Living Allowances to help match inflation. After the passage of the Employee Retirement Security Act of 1974, the Board changed the name of the retirement savings program in 1975. It was now called the "USAA Savings and Investment Plan" (SIP) and it committed the Association to match up to 6 percent of the employees' base salary. In 1978, the Association's SIP contributions were expanded when the USAA contribution was figured against total compensation instead of base salary. The stated purpose of the SIP plan was to reward employees, stimulate their interest in the success of the business, and "to provide supplementary benefits to employees at retirement."[74] Another dramatic improvement was the creation, in 1976, of the Employee Benefit Association designed by George Ensley as a trust to provide health benefits for the employees. In addition, he rewrote the retirement plan, reducing vesting from ten to five years. The Association also added free life insurance for spouses and dependent children and long-term disability insurance during the decade. And, effective August 1, 1976, those who left USAA employment were no longer eligible for USAA membership — a benefit that USAA employees prized. The departing employees were allowed to apply for CIC insurance, however.[75]

McDermott encouraged retiring USAA employees to stay as part of the family. On November 22, 1977, sixty-nine USAA retirees sat down for lunch in the home office building's "C" cafeteria. Comprising over 40 percent of USAA's retired employees, the group formed a retiree club that it called the "Golden Eagles," with Bill Ward as its first president. It became a permanent addition to USAA.

The retirees met quarterly, enjoyed each other's company, swapped stories, and received updates on USAA from McDermott and other senior officers.[76]

USAA Golden Eagles, May 19, 1978

Management was pleased at how well things seemed to be going with the employees. The new building provided an outstanding work environment. Amenities such as a physical exercise facility, outdoor recreational features, and beautiful cafeterias were much appreciated. Salaries and other employee benefits were considered very generous. In light of all of this, McDermott, his staff, and the USAA Board were shocked when a union-organizing drive began in February 1978.

It began with a pro-union "petition" circulated by a few USAA employees on behalf of the Office and Professional Employees International Union (OPEIU). USAA hired Chicago's Herb Melnick, a consultant, for advice on resisting the unionization attempt. Under his guidance, Marie Kelleher, Vice President, Personnel, and

Turbulent Times

Bill McCrae, General Counsel, met with small groups of managerial employees to let them know what they legally could and could not do. In the next development, all non-managerial USAA employees were invited by union organizers to attend a meeting at a local motel; about 150 showed up. On the morning of March 20, OPEIU representatives outside the USAA gates attempted to distribute handbills with authorization cards attached.

Over the next couple of weeks, the pro-union employees attempted to get employees to sign union authorization cards during breaks and non-business hours. At the same time, USAA management discussed the pros and cons of unionization with employees. An anti-union campaign was also begun by employees who circulated petitions. One employee purchased yellow sticker dots and suggested that employees wear them if they didn't want a union. An anti-union group of employees encouraged fellow workers to wear yellow symbols. Many wore the yellow dots, and after one female employee wore a yellow ribbon, others did also on succeeding days. When Vic Ferrari asked the pro-unionists "why?", they said it wasn't the benefits — it was the supervisors. They believed that half of them were poor managers. Shortly thereafter, the pro-unionists abandoned their petition drive.

McDermott responded to the attempt, nonetheless, and had Melnick bring in trainers to give a course in management and human relations to USAA's supervisors, including himself and the other USAA managers.[77] Earl King, now a Senior Vice President at USAA, recalled that the employees nicknamed the course "charm school." Held one-half day a week for several weeks, the course covered many areas including sensitivity training that made King and others more conscious of the aspirations and feelings of females and minorities.[78] McDermott also asked Kelleher to review all employees' pay. When the review revealed that some females and minorities were being paid less than others for equivalent jobs, McDermott ordered the pay equalized for the same or similar jobs by raising those salaries that were lower.[79] He also reminded USAA officers to express time in "civilian" time rather than in the military custom of expressing time using a twenty-four-hour clock to eliminate another irritant.

Prior to this, USAA had made efforts to increase opportunities for minority and female employees. In 1972, George Ensley wrote to USAA senior officers and pointed out that not a single minority employee was included among the executive management group employees. He said it was one of "the most serious problems facing us."[80] USAA Personnel took actions to improve the situation. Also, USAA began supporting the United Negro College Fund and other minority programs with its corporate contributions. Bill Starnes set up a seminar in 1974 to strengthen ways women could achieve at USAA and still have time to take care of responsibilities at home at the same time. He was especially concerned because large numbers of women were not taking advantage of education courses. For example, of fifty-four employees in Project Campus, only four were women, although women were by far the majority in Insurance Institute of America (IIA) and Associate Degree Programs.[81] Improvements came steadily. By 1975, about 35 percent of the work force was made up of ethnic and racial minorities, and women used the educational opportunities in increasing numbers. In 1978, USAA established a special office to assist minorities and women under manager Barbara Knight. Overall, USAA continued to make progress in this sensitive area.

In the middle seventies, the sweeping changes at USAA led to changes in the Board of Directors and its relationships with USAA management. In 1975, USAA Chairman, retired Army Lieutenant General Patrick F. Cassiday, declined to stand for reelection. Elected in his place was retired Air Force General Samuel C. Phillips. Phillips, like McDermott, had also been a P-38 pilot in World War II, and they got to know each other while working in General Dwight

Eisenhower's headquarters in Europe after the war. They became close friends, as did their families, and they kept in touch over the years.

Phillips was to bring a new perspective to the Board. After his retirement from the Air Force as the Commander of Air Force Systems Command, he went to work for TRW. He was the general manager of a significant part of its operations, a vice president, and a member of its board of directors. He became a student of private industry organizational management structure there and brought his ideas to USAA.[82]

General Samuel C. Phillips
Chairman of the Board

After five years on the Board and three years as Chairman, in June 1978, Phillips proposed a series of recommendations to the Board. In the most important of these, he recommended that McDermott be elected Chairman of USAA. Phillips acknowledged that from the beginning, an outside Director had been the Chairman. This had become a matter of tradition, however, and was not included in the bylaws. The bylaws did specify the duties of the chairman. In Phillips' view, however, because of USAA's size and complexity, they were impossible to carry out without the help of the president. He also noted that a 1977 Conference Board study pointed out that a company's chairman was invariably one of the company's top two management people.[83]

While this part of the proposal was the most dramatic one, there was more. Phillips recommended the creation of an Audit Committee on the Board. In support, he cited a Korn/Ferry International

Study that reported that 94 percent of all insurance companies had one. He also recommended that the Board redesignate the existing Compensation Committee as the Personnel Policy Committee. He had drawn these ideas from his civilian experience at TRW. He also recommended that USAA directors no longer serve on the boards of USAA subsidiaries. He believed that the directors did not have the time, and that their focus should be on the parent company.[84] When Phillips passed out his memo at the Board meeting, McDermott was excused from the meeting. A lengthy discussion followed. The Board agreed with Phillips' recommendation on the chairmanship, accepted his resignation as chairman, and elected McDermott for a two-year term effective that day, June 17, 1978. The Board concurred with Phillips' recommendations on Board committees and subsidiary Board membership as well.[85]

Phillips made one more important contribution. In August 1976, McDermott had become very ill at an NAII meeting called to discuss the potential GEICO insolvency. It turned out that he had suffered an aortic aneurism and required very serious surgery. Although he did not return to the office for twelve weeks, the Association did not name anyone to replace him temporarily. The senior management team ran the organization. This situation concerned Phillips a great deal because USAA had no contingency plan, such as he had seen at TRW and in the government, if its leader were unable to serve. In February 1979, Phillips presented a contingency plan which won Board approval. In essence, each year McDermott (the president) would recommend to the Board an individual to serve as acting president and attorney-in-fact in the eventuality that the president could not. This individual would then serve until the Board selected a new president. Ted Michel was the first individual designated to serve in USAA's corporate bullpen.[86]

Three other significant changes affecting the USAA Board and its members were put in place in the 1970s. First, in 1973,

McDermott spoke to a Board member about the possibility of that individual joining USAA's management team. The Board member turned it down because he told McDermott that the offer could be interpreted as a conflict of interest by other Board members and the USAA membership. In April 1973, McDermott briefed the Board about this offer and mentioned that three other unnamed Board members had recently approached him about the possibility of employment at USAA's regional offices. McDermott recom-

Ted Michel

mended that the Board take a position precluding this. The Board agreed and forbade management from approaching Directors while they served and until six months after they left the Board.[87] Second, in 1979 at the Annual Members' Meeting, the members voted to change the tenure of Directors from three two-year terms to five two-year terms. Implemented in 1972 to keep Board members from being entrenched, the shorter tenure had resulted in too much turnover. After the vote for Directors at the 1978 Annual Members' Meeting, the average tenure was only 2.3 years.[88] Phillips noted years later that the tenure question was important and led to much serious debate. Ten years was a good figure to retain experience to benefit the Association. More than that would hurt the Association because it was necessary to add new Board members with the expertise and know-how to grapple with the changing business thrusts of USAA.[89]

The third issue was that of fees for directors. McDermott believed that USAA directors should serve USAA in leave status and should be paid fees commensurate with their fiduciary responsibilities and in line with directors of other corporations. He asked Bill McCrae, USAA's Senior Vice President, General Counsel, and Board Secretary, to study the issue. McCrae reported Korn/Ferry, Arthur Young and Company, and The Conference Board surveys indicated the average annual compensation was between $9,000 and $11,500, with stock insurance company directors about $10,000. USAA's directors were receiving $4,800. McCrae recommended a hike to 15 percent of the government employee's annual salary authorized under the federal Ethics in Government Act. As USAA used the base of a major general's salary, the Directors' new annual compensation would rise to $7,000.[90] This compensation would continue to rise over the next two decades as it would in the nation's other major companies.

As the seventies moved on, McDermott led USAA to increasingly look beyond its own business and into the community. McDermott demonstrated early in his tenure his belief in corporate good citizenship. As part of this, USAA's corporate contributions budget grew rapidly under his stewardship. In 1973, McDermott argued before the Board that USAA and other private businesses had to do more in civilian-military communities like San Antonio as the military reduced its forces. The Board agreed to fix USAA's contributions budget at an amount equal to what employees gave each year to United Way. Of this total budget amount, half went as a corporate contribution to United Way, the rest disbursed to other charitable, cultural, and civic activities. That decision more than tripled USAA's contributions budget by McDermott's fifth year at USAA's helm.[91]

Personally, McDermott got involved in the Greater San Antonio Chamber of Commerce shortly after his arrival. In 1972, under Chamber President Pat Legan, he served as the vice president for long-range planning and public relations. He took a group of business leaders to the American Management Association at Hamilton,

New York, to build a long-range plan for the community. Since most of the participants were "outlanders" or newcomers to San Antonio, like himself, the plan was drawn, but implementation dragged. He was elected President of the Chamber in 1974.

Hearing of the "Forward Atlanta" movement for economic development, McDermott brought in the Atlanta office of Manning, Selvage, and Lee to help San Antonio. The firm hired Jim Dublin as its local representative, and the result was the Economic Development Foundation (EDF), which McDermott helped found in 1974. McDermott petitioned the USAA Board to participate in the EDF. As its purpose was to promote economic growth in San Antonio, he believed that it was in USAA's best interest to support the new foundation. He felt that the well-being of USAA employees and their families — resulting from living, working, and playing in a good environment — would contribute to the greater efficiency and higher caliber of the work force. The Board agreed to donate $40,000 to the EDF with $10,000 additional being donated by the Life Company. This gave USAA five votes on the EDF Board of Directors and made USAA a prime player in the community.[92]

The EDF ran advertisements about the city, and McDermott worked hard to bring new business to San Antonio. In the fall of 1977, it looked like McDermott would be successful in bringing in an Allen Bradley Incorporated electronics factory with 400 jobs. In October, an organization called Communities Organized for Public Service (COPS) confronted McDermott in the Community Center of the Immaculate Heart of Mary Church. Bathed in the principles of radical community organizer Saul Alinski, and led by Father Albert Benavides, the volatile community meeting of about 300 condemned McDermott for trying to bring in jobs that paid lower than $15,000 per year.[93] *Forbes* magazine and other media picked up on the protest and potential San Antonio-bound business, like Texas Instruments, went elsewhere. In 1980, to bring the Mexican-

A TRADITION OF SERVICE

American community and the business communities together, McDermott helped found United San Antonio. Led by tri-chairmen, City Councilman Henry Cisneros, later to be San Antonio Mayor and Secretary of Housing and Urban Development under President Bill Clinton; Dr. Jose San Martin, former San Antonio city councilman; and McDermott, United San Antonio helped pull all elements of the diverse community together to support economic development. While COPS did not join directly with USAA, it did work with private business for the community. [94] McDermott's personal high visibility in community efforts such as these put USAA in the public spotlight as well.

Beyond San Antonio, McDermott worked to improve automobile safety for USAA members and the national community of citizens. Automobile and driver safety issues remained a concern at USAA. Although national traffic deaths trailed off in the middle 1970s, due perhaps to the energy crisis and lowered speed limits, in the best year deaths still exceeded 45,000. Inflation continued to drive up the average cost of claims because of rising costs of auto parts, labor, and medical services. The National Safety Council reported that in at least half of the 55,000 traffic deaths in 1973, alcohol was a factor. At USAA, the most frequent cause of insurance termination was alcohol-related. The interest was humanitarian — and business related.[95] *Aide Magazine* was a frequent forum used by the Association for safety messages from the President and informational articles for the membership. In 1977, McDermott's personal and early interest in auto safety was focused on the air bag. He encouraged the rating agency to adopt discounts for air-bag-equipped vehicles, led lobbying efforts to deter congressional opposition to U.S. Department of Transportation proposals for air-bag installation on new cars, and wrote letters to the editors of newspapers.

Under the adverse conditions of the seventies, USAA had reasons to be proud of its progress. It had succeeded in spite of inflation, a decline in active-duty-officer strength, rising claims costs, and the potential disaster in welcoming dependents to USAA. Even the catastrophes of 1979, such as Hurricane Frederic, did not deter the Association. A glance at the decade's statistics clearly demonstrates USAA's success. Contributing was USAA's falling combined ratio (83.4 in 1979) and a productivity increase of 17 percent over the last five years of the decade as compared to a 7.2 percent average nationally.

USAA Growth in the Seventies

	January 1, 1970	**December 31, 1979**
Military on Active Duty	3 million	2 million
Active Duty Officers	403,000	273,000
Members	701,000	1.2 million
Active Duty Members	4 of 5	9 of 10
Assets	$356,000	$1.4 billion
Surplus to Premium Ratio	32.7%	71.5%
SSA	$2 million	$475 million

Most important of all to USAA's success was its continuing focus on providing outstanding service. The members let USAA know when they were pleased or displeased with their service, and Living Sample and other surveys helped the Association stay in touch. Outside agencies' confirmation was welcome and encouraged the employees to faithfully serve their members. The Minnesota Insurance Commissioner notified USAA that it had received the fewest complaints of the thirty largest insurers in that state. The *Washington Consumer's Checkbook* gave USAA its outstanding rating, and the 1977 *Consumer Reports* lauded USAA's service.

A Tradition Of Service

The national insurance outlook for the 1980s was not so good. Predicted was high inflation followed by a recession, higher interest rates, stronger regulatory practices, and increased consumerism. The prognosis for military appropriations was flat at best. All this notwithstanding, USAA looked forward to the eighties with anticipation and confidence. McDermott advised the membership in the 1979 *Annual Report* that no one could predict with certainty what lay ahead. He noted, however, that USAA had always attached great importance to being prepared for every reasonable contingency. In any case, he emphasized that service would continue to be USAA's bedrock, and announced USAA's new slogan: "Serving you best because we know you better." And to illustrate his commitment to the service ethic, he continued to follow the precedent of Cheever and other USAA CEOs by keeping his home telephone number listed in the San Antonio phone book.

CHAPTER NINE

EXPANDING, SAFETY, AND SUCCESSION

In December 1979, fierce Afghan guerilla fighters watched intently and prepared to fight as thousands of Russian troops rolled into their mountainous kingdom. The Afghans were ferocious warriors who traced their lineage through many different tribes back into the shadows of history before the birth of Christ. The Soviet goal was to support a client who was being challenged by Islamic rebels and to maintain Afghanistan as a buffer against the rising tide of Islamic fundamentalism in central Asia.[1] The Soviet action had two disastrous results. The invading forces would become entrapped in a strange war in a strange land that would tear Soviet society apart. Echoes of the American experience in Vietnam could be heard in Afghanistan's forbidding mountain passes. In addition, world opinion lined up against the Russians and "The New Cold War" began.[2]

In the American presidential election year of 1980, the Soviet behavior provoked actions by both President Jimmy Carter and his Republican Party opponent Ronald Reagan. Carter pulled the SALT II treaty back from the Senate and withdrew the U.S. Olympic Team from the Moscow Summer Olympic Games. He took numerous other actions against the Soviets as well. Many of Carter's foreign policy decisions on the Russians, human rights violators, and the Iranians, who still held American hostages, led candidate Reagan to attack Carter's leadership. To Reagan, the Russian adventure in Afghanistan was just the latest example of the Soviet's expansionism — stirring up hot spots throughout the world. Even more troublesome than this were America's economic troubles. Rallying to Reagan's

USAA's West Point office employees and their families welcome the Iranian hostages home

cry to make America great again, the nation's voters gave him 59 percent of the popular ballot. On inauguration day, the Iranians freed the hostages and America had a new Republican president.

Reagan and his allies believed that the Russians were the source of much of the world's unrest. It was a devil theory; the world in black and white, Russia as the "evil empire."[3] Tom Clancy's new Cold War techno-thrillers became administration favorites. In 1981, Reagan believed that Carter had allowed a window of vulnerability to open that the Soviets could exploit. Because the U.S. cut back on military appropriations, the Soviets had forged ahead and threatened U.S. missile dominance. Reagan officials thought that a U.S. military buildup would deter the Soviet threat. "Defense is not a budget item," Reagan told the Pentagon leaders. "Spend what you need."[4] And spend they did. The Pentagon program called for expanding the Navy from 450 to 600 ships. It also continued programs for many weapon systems, including the B-1 bomber, the cruise missile, and the stealth bomber. In his first five years, Reagan more than doubled the defense budget with the Pentagon spending $28 million per hour, twenty-four hours a day, seven days a week.[5] The increase in defense spending translated into more officers entering active duty and increased marketing opportunities for USAA. Under Carter, officer strength had fallen from 282,000 to 273,000. By 1986, Reagan had increased officer strength by nearly 15 percent to 311,000.

USAA Chairman Robert McDermott continued to believe in the importance of growth for USAA and urged his staff to exploit the expanding pre-commissioning market. Encouraging newly commissioned officers to join USAA would enable USAA to continue to insure over 90 percent of the active-duty officers. He was successful in this, but he looked at other possibilities for growth as well. One broad category of officers that probably would have been better insurance risks than ex-dependents in the short run were not included in the USAA family in 1981— former officers who had never been USAA members. McDermott had not included them earlier because of a rumored possible takeover of USAA led by a multi-billionaire separated officer. The billionaire had gone bankrupt, however, and the takeover threat disappeared. McDermott then called for a study of growth possibilities — including these former officers, or "missed eligibles" as they were now called. Also to be considered were analogous groups such as doctors and lawyers, and FBI agents.[6]

At the May 15, 1982, Board of Directors' meeting, USAA management presented its eligibility recommendations to the Board. It recommended that the Board extend eligibility to former officers by using the 1972 Board resolution that permitted the Board to define who could be included in the "commissioned and warrant officers" eligibility. The Board agreed. The study did have one caveat, however. Seventy-eight percent of this group of approximately 1.1

A TRADITION OF SERVICE

million persons were age sixty or above. Because of this age factor and the difficulty of reaching them at all, the study advised not to market aggressively to them. McDermott decided to try anyway. The February 1983 issue of *Aide Magazine* announced the change and asked members to send along names of possible eligibles on a postcard enclosed in the magazine. In 1986, USAA began a new advertising campaign to capture the missed eligibles. Featuring World War II U.S. Marine Corps veteran Major Francis Edwin Pierce Jr., the advertisement called for members to refer their friends to USAA.

USAA advertisement from the 1980s on missed eligibles

Also discussed at the May 1982 Board meeting was eligibility for other analogous groups — specifically FBI Special Agents. The Board listened to management's rationale that the FBI Special Agents' service was an integral part of the nation's defense establishment. Further, these agents were precluded from joining the Reserves, or otherwise they might have become eligible for USAA through service in the military. The Board agreed to extend eligibility to the FBI Special Agents, and within a year over 1,100 had joined USAA. This apparent exception of offering membership to a group other than commissioned officers elicited requests for eligibility from many other federal agencies. In 1983, of all those that applied, the Board approved only U.S. Secret Service Agents for membership at the time. The following year the Board also extended eligibility to Special Agents of the Naval Investigative Service.[7]

One other change in eligibility in the 1980s came about as a result of Congressional legislation. In 1985, Senior Vice President-Underwriting Bob Brakey briefed the Board about a federal spouses' protection act that had become law in 1983. This act provided full federal benefits to divorced spouses who met a 20/20/20 rule — married to a career service person for at least twenty years, the service person having served twenty years, and the marriage and service career overlapping twenty years. The USAA Board decided to make divorced spouses who met this criteria eligible for USAA membership in their own right.[8]

In 1986, the Board sent an important message to the membership and employees. USAA had always recognized the importance of ex-dependents for its future, but the Association referred to them only as policyholders. The Board believed that this did not make them feel like a part of the USAA family. To correct this, the Board adopted a resolution extending the honorary designation of "associate member" to the voluntary insureds of the USAA Casualty Insurance Company. This resolution ratified what USAA employees

A Tradition Of Service

had already been doing — serving the ex-dependents in the same way as they had been serving the officers who were members.[9]

The other part of Reagan's program that would have even more impact on USAA than the increased military spending was in the area of economics. On February 5, 1981, he gave a nationally televised speech describing the problems facing the nation. He cited the first back-to-back years of double-digit inflation since World War I. Then he noted the dramatic changes over the past twenty years — mortgage rates more than doubled, a 1981 dollar worth only thirty-six cents, and a 100 percent increase in federal taxes before earnings.[10]

His proposed solution, later dubbed "Reaganomics," included a reduction in government spending while maintaining a social safety net. In addition, he proposed a 30-percent across-the-board tax cut over three years, and a reduction in government regulatory agencies and regulations. In a poll taken after the speech, more than two-thirds of Americans approved of his economic program. After the assassination attempt on his life, Reagan's sky-high popularity ratings helped him push his program through Congress, including a 25-percent personal income tax cut over three years. He also began his program of deregulation for America's business beginning on January 22, 1981, when he appointed Vice President George Bush to head a task force to target areas for deregulation. The individual and corporate tax cuts and other policies resulted in a recession in 1981-82, but then kept the inflation rate at a manageable level.[11] The overall economic climate that he created and the deregulation made it possible for USAA to become a full financial services provider as McDermott had envisioned. The resulting economic boom was, in effect, financed by deficit spending — money borrowed from the future.[12]

Besides the policies emanating from Washington, two management experts' ideas influenced McDermott's thinking in the 1980s. The first were included in a speech delivered at USAA in 1980 by a relative unknown, John Naisbitt, who would later spell out his ideas in detail in his 1982 blockbuster book, *Megatrends*. Cliff Jefferis, Vice President-Group Planning and Development, knew Naisbitt and invited him to speak to the employees in the USAA auditorium. USAA reprinted his entire San Antonio speech in the Fall 1980 issue of *Aide Magazine* and McDermott discussed it in his letter to the members in the same issue. Naisbitt warned institutions that when they introduced new technology to customers or employees they should build in "a high touch component" or people would reject the technology. USAA's theme for 1982 was Naisbitt's idea of "High Tech, High Touch."[13] Other Naisbitt points that McDermott stressed were the need for productivity and the control of expenses to fight inflation.

The second influence was Peter Drucker's book *Managing in Turbulent Times*. McDermott was so taken by Drucker's ideas that he ordered a copy of the book for each USAA officer and asked Executive Vice President and Treasurer George Ensley to discuss the book with the Executive Management Group (EMG). Ensley talked to the EMG about applying Drucker's Fundamentals of Liquidity, Productivities, and Cost of the Future to USAA in the 1970s and the 1980s. For liquidity in the 1980s, Ensley said USAA would continue to work towards a surplus of 100 percent of a year's earned premium, give financial strength priority over growth, and diversify geographically and by lines of business. For 1980's productivities, Ensley mentioned setting productivity goals, encouraging employee participation in Simplification and Quality Circles, and improving the use of data. He underlined the importance of Drucker's "knowledge worker" for USAA and the need for continuing professional and self development. He finished with the promise that USAA would take measures to ensure it was prepared to meet the costs in the future in spite of economic turbulence.[14] Ensley used Drucker's philosophy in practice. When he faced a problem in one of the areas under him, he sent a letter to the manager and reminded him of Drucker's ideas. He told the manager to ask when working with other units, "What do we do that helps you in your work and what do we do that hampers you?"[15]

Productivity is the result of many things, including technology, organization, and people. In 1980, McDermott ordered the development of a Long Range Systems Plan to guide automated systems development to support USAA's business objectives. Completed in April 1981, with the assistance of consultants from Arthur Anderson and Company, the five-year plan included fifty-eight different systems projects involving all areas of USAA. The first project completed put routine correspondence online to replace employees' handwritten notes or letters requested from the Word Processing Center. Also operational in 1980 was the Automated Claims Environment (ACE), which made all claims information instantly available on computer terminals. ACE II, a pilot program and USAA's first step in distributive processing, began the same year.

The USAA employees also made significant contributions to USAA's productivity through more than doing just their own job everyday. In 1979, USAA's annual theme was "Simplicity is the Key." Employees were encouraged to suggest ideas on how to make USAA more efficient. By the fall, many suggestions had come in, and Senior Vice President Human Resources and Services Vic Ferrari and Vice President, Southeast Region June Reedy decided to make the program permanent. Cape Caperton, the Executive Director of Training, called Bob Gaylor in and asked him to set up the program.

Gaylor had joined USAA as an employee that September after a highly successfully thirty-one-year Air Force career. His final Air Force assignment was as Chief Master Sergeant of the Air Force. He often gave talks on leadership, management, and professionalism in a witty, folksy style that made him much in demand as a public speaker. It was on one of these occasions when he was speaking at a management seminar to Air Force medical personnel in Kerrville, Texas, that he met McDermott. McDermott was very impressed with Gaylor and when Gaylor was ready to retire three years later, he accepted McDermott's offer to join USAA to teach leadership in Management Development and Training.

Chief Master Sergeant of the Air Force Bob Gaylor

Gaylor enthusiastically worked with programs that drew on employees' experience, and he encouraged their participation in making USAA better. The new suggestion program was called "Simplification," and in the first year, it garnered almost 500 approved ideas. A familiar sight over the years was Gaylor walking through work areas passing out awards to employees from a large box. Another responsibility of Gaylor's was the Quality Circles. In 1980, Vic Ferrari read a *Wall Street Journal* article on Quality Circles at Westinghouse. Ferrari sent Gaylor a note and asked him if they would work at USAA. Begun in Japan, the idea of Quality Circles was beginning to take root in California. Gaylor learned all he could about them and briefed the USAA Executive Council on the innovation in October 1980. Instead of a "Thank you, Bob," or "Let's study it some more," to Gaylor's surprise, McDermott told him, "Looks good, let's do it!"[16]

After attending a seminar on Quality Circles in California, Gaylor gave over sixty briefings throughout USAA. In January 1981, USAA had its first four circles under the leadership of Bob Wheelus, Patti McWilliams, Kathie Panek, and Gladys Real. Gloria (Patterson) Craven and Ric Saucedo helped Gaylor as facilitators at the meetings. By the end of the year, eleven were functioning, and two years later,

Quality Circle at work

forty-four. These circles consisted of seven to twelve volunteers from a common work area who met to identify, analyze, and solve problems related to their work. While the ideas coming out of the circles saved hundreds of thousands of dollars, the circles could not be judged simply in terms of these dollar savings. The personal development of individual employees and the experience of working together on a team benefitted USAA as well. As one participating manager put it, "We all seem to work together better now — to share the same goals."[17] The Quality Circles spread to the regional offices and found success there too. For example, the Washington, D.C., Area Office's (WDCAO) circle "Casual-T-QC" under leader Larry Garletts, solved a difficult problem of file flow and lost files.[18]

* * * *

As the USAA membership grew steadily and took advantage of new products and services, the number of employees climbed too.

EXPANDING, SAFETY, AND SUCCESSION

In 1980, USAA had about 5,200 employees, and almost 4,800 were in San Antonio. Projections of double the numbers of employees by the end of the decade demanded expansion of San Antonio facilities or decentralization of some USAA functions, or both. McDermott directed a study on centralization versus decentralization of USAA operations. Terry Shea, Assistant Vice President-Methods, briefed the Board in October 1982. He believed that three major regional offices outside of San Antonio could be supported, and recommended West Coast, Northeast, and Southeast locations. Claims functions should continue to be moved to the field with smaller claims offices reporting to the three proposed regional offices. Shea told the Board that although there was time to develop alternatives to solve the space situation at the San Antonio Home Office, space at Tampa was critical. The Board decided to keep policy service centralized in San Antonio and asked management to develop plans to move additional claims people to the field in coordination with space planning in San Antonio. Retired Air Force Major General Herb Emanuel joined USAA as Vice President for Personnel in 1983 and played a key role in the personnel movements in the realignment process. Emanuel was in the initial cadre that helped set up the Air Force Academy and had known McDermott there. He held a number of important positions in the Air Force personnel area including the Vice Commander of the Air Force Military Personnel Center located on Randolph Air Force Base in San Antonio. He would ultimately become USAA's Chief Administrative Officer.

Herb Emanuel

Over the next few years, the Board authorized management to proceed with building USAA-owned facilities in the regional areas to accommodate the move of claims. The first region to get a new building was the Southeast Regional Home Office (SERHO) in Tampa. Terry Thompson, Senior Vice President of the USAA Development Company, recommended that USAA purchase one of a three-building planned development in Tampa. The building would be owned 50/50 by USAA and USAA CIC, enabling both companies to meet the requirements for the Florida premium tax reduction. Long-term, the entire development would provide for future expansion.[19] On November 29, 1983, the new SERHO opened for business in one of the buildings in The Corporate Oaks Park with 160 employees, and with Joe House as Assistant Vice President and General Manager. By the end of 1984, southeast claims functions were all consolidated in Tampa.

In late 1983, McDermott decided to consolidate USAA California activities in Sacramento. Besides servicing a large number of members, this office would be close to legislative activity in the state capital. Another perceived benefit was that Sacramento and California were often bellwethers for the nation on a variety of programs and issues. On January 23, 1984, most Cupertino employees moved into a leased building in Sacramento. As in each region, many new local employees were hired. Extending USAA's corporate culture and technical training to these new employees fell to the centralized training department in San Antonio. In this case, San Antonio employees George Allen, Val Norrgran, Patsy Sinclair, and Peter Braeuler developed a special training course highly praised by lo-

Joe House

Expanding, Safety, And Succession

USAA's Sacramento building (above) and Joe Meyer (right)

cal USAA management. By September, the move to Sacramento was complete and USAA held a groundbreaking for its California office in July 1986. McDermott insisted on extending the successful formula of superior work environments and amenities for the employees. The Board agreed. In May 1987, McDermott presided at the dedication of the new building. He lauded the Sacramento operation as USAA's first fully stand-alone decentralized region.[20] Retired Navy Captain Joe Meyer became Senior Vice President of this Western Region in August 1987.

In Colorado, Bill Mahon, the regional general manager, and McDermott selected a site for a new building. The site was a beautiful one, with famous Pike's Peak in view and the Air Force Academy close by. The building was planned to provide workspace for 500 employees who would serve over 100,000 members in Colorado and other states in the mountain time zone. The new building opened for business on October 17, 1988, and included a drive-in claims garage.

Colorado Springs office with Pike's Peak in background

USAA had also been looking for office space in Virginia. On April 7, 1986, USAA purchased a six-story, 120,000-square-foot building in Reston, Virginia, to service the Mid-Atlantic Region. In February 1987, 320 employees moved in to service over 85,000 members within a twenty-five-mile radius. USAA also opened a small office that year in Annapolis to service the United States Naval Academy, and in 1988, USAA European operations moved into a building purchased by USAA in Frankfurt. The European office was under the leadership of Rolf E. Metzen, a German attorney and former Fulbright Scholar to Duke University.

Rolf E. Metzen

By the mid-1980s, USAA began shifting its policy on regionalization, and the term "migration" crept into position papers and announcements. Migration came to mean home office employees moving to the regional offices, but functions began moving also. The original emphasis on claims only evolved into the development of full-service regional offices as policy service responsibilities moved to the regions too. This greatly expanded the regional offices' responsibilities, and their size. At the same time, member service capabilities improved.

In 1987, to assist in determining the best balance of employees between the home office and the regional offices, McDermott asked Strategic Planning Vice President Bill Flynn for a Long-Range Basing Plan Study. Born in Virginia, Flynn had graduated from the University of Dallas and was commissioned through the ROTC program. In 1974, Flynn had just completed serving a three-year tour as a chief of data processing at the Berlin Brigade and had completed his service commitment to the Army. While visiting his parents in San Antonio prior to seeking employment in Dallas, Flynn was encouraged by his mother to apply to USAA. He started work as a programmer at USAA in January 1975. Delivered in October 1987, the strategic planning study was a comprehensive look at space planning through 2002. It assumed employee growth from about 9,600 in 1987 to over 23,000 in 2002. It recommended increased migration as greatly increased growth in San Antonio would tax home office site capacity. Increasing the work force outside of San Antonio would maintain a "human scale" in the workplace. The study suggested a maximum regional office size should be 2,500 employees, with about 600,000 square feet of building space on twenty-five acres.

Bill Flynn

For San Antonio, the study recommended construction of buildings E and F, a backup computer site, an employment center, and a bank operations building over the next seven years. It also recommended land purchases in Tampa, the Mid-Atlantic area (Norfolk was one option), Tulsa, and for the Northeast and Overseas Region on the East Coast. In addition, it recommended new buildings for the Mid-Atlantic area, Colorado Springs, Tampa, and Sacramento. Long-term, the plan proposed that 42 percent of USAA employees be based outside of San Antonio by 2002.[21]

The movement of employees and responsibilities outside of San Antonio increased the problems of training and of maintaining USAA's corporate culture. USAA management counted on home office employees moving to the regions to help. In 1987, USAA opened a migration center in San Antonio's home office building to encourage and assist San Antonio employees and their families to move permanently to the regional office locations. Especially sought after were experienced managers in all operational areas who could bring technical expertise and the corporate culture with them. Sponsorship programs were set up at the regional offices to make the moves as smooth as possible. On occasion, even USAA members helped. Tammy Mir and her husband migrated to Tampa in 1988. Their landlord was a twenty-seven-year member, and when he found out Mir was a USAA employee, he went out of his way to assist. Mir reported that the landlord-member saved them over $600. He gave them a half-month's rent free, did not charge them for a pet deposit, and didn't require any money until they actually moved in. Besides that, he stocked the refrigerator with food and drinks for when they arrived — not standard service by any landlord.[22] As had often happened over USAA's history, service went both ways.

While most formal migration of employees was completed by the end of the decade, USAA was still making adjustments to the regionalization as recommended by the Long Range Basing Study.

When the San Antonio housing market collapsed in 1988, USAA changed the relocation package help dispose of departing employees' homes in San Antonio. In California, a second building was completed in December 1988 to house increasing numbers of employees, including 131 migrants from San Antonio. Also in 1988, USAA announced it would abandon its Corporate Oaks Park Florida facility and build a new one especially for USAA in a campus setting in Tampa Palms. In late 1989, the USAA migration to Tampa was complete, reducing Florida's premium tax $200,000 in 1990 alone. In April 1991, the Rocky Mountain Regional Home Office was detached from the North Central Region located in San Antonio. Fully independent, it was now headed by retired Air Force Colonel Michael Quinlan.

In other developments, McDermott announced in April 1989 that USAA would move its Mid-Atlantic Region to Norfolk. USAA leased space temporarily, and held the official opening of the Mid-Atlantic Regional Office under retired Air Force Colonel John "Jack" Wolcott on March 14, 1990. (The new building in Norfolk was dedicated on April 7, 1993.) Finally, USAA opened a major claims office on Federal Way in Seattle, Washington, on November 7, 1989.

In hindsight, the decision to decentralize property and casualty operations was a sound one. Not including the USAA Federal Savings Bank employees who worked in a separate building, USAA grew from 5,248 employees in 1980 to 11,845 employees by the end of 1989. Over 30 percent, or over 3,600 employees, worked in regional offices. The combination of solid leadership, migrating home office employees, sound training, and superb telecommunications and computer technology helped to preserve the service culture in the regions.

Also useful was the methods department established by property and casualty chief Ted Michel. Headed by Terry Shea, the unit worked to keep as much uniformity as possible in the regions.

Jack Wolcott

Geographically separated and headed by independent-minded officers, the regions needed guidance. For example, the opening of the SERHO region in Tampa was heralded there as an Independence Day Celebration. Accompanied at the reception by his wife Sue, dressed as Betsy Ross, SERHO Assistant Vice President Joe "Uncle Sam" House, spoke to his employees. He emphasized that SERHO's independence wasn't from USAA, but rather from the confusion and turmoil created by split responsibilities.[23] In spite of the disclaimer, selection of the independence theme suggested why the home office believed that close communication and coordination with the regional offices were very necessary. Working for Bob Brakey, Shea used the employee newsletter *Highlights* extensively to help build better communication between the home office and the regional offices.[24]

Easier transportation between San Antonio and the regional offices also helped. In March 1984, USAA leased a Gulfstream Aerospace II (G-II) corporate aircraft pending purchase of a Gulfstream Aerospace III (G-III).[25] The G-III entered USAA service on January 8, 1985, and the G-II was returned. Because of the constant and efficient use of the G-III, USAA purchased a second jet, a used G-II, in 1989. Incidentally, the jets bore the tail numbers of "429" and "430," two of McDermott's WWII squadrons. These aircraft improved USAA's ability to move employees back and forth from home office to regional sites for training and operational activities and helped preserve the corporate culture.

Gulfstream Aerospace III (G-III) aircraft

In spite of the migration losses and decentralized functions, the number of home office employees grew from about 4,800 in 1980 to over 8,000 at the end of the decade. The slowed growth rate, however, gave USAA the time to build additional facilities it needed in San Antonio. The first additional office space considered for San Antonio was for a new building for the USAA Life Insurance Company. In 1981, Skidmore, Owings, and Merrill (SOM) completed a building feasibility study which included a recommendation to build the new building on the northern end of the USAA property. Vic Ferrari briefed the Board on the various options for expansion in February 1982. When the Board raised the question of adding more space to the main building, which had been designed for expansion, McDermott said that it would not be feasible at that time. Existing recreational facilities close to the south end of the building were in the way. The Board approved the design of the new facility.[26]

In late 1983, the architects from SOM and James Turner of Project Control briefed the Board. By this time, McDermott had shifted the proposed building's principal tenant from the Life Company to the planned USAA bank. The Board authorized $23 million to build

USAA Federal Savings Bank

the financial service structure. The building opened its doors as the USAA Federal Savings Bank on September 16, 1985.

In February 1986, the Board was briefed on the need for additional parking in San Antonio. Even with 126 vans and car pools, the addition of over 2,000 employees in five years made parking a difficult chore for those last to arrive each morning. The Board authorized management to invest over $10 million in a five-level, 1,000-car parking garage and necessary road improvements.[27] The garage was to be connected to the main building, giving employees access without going outside.

In June of the same year, USAA began construction of an operations building. The new 327,000-square-foot building was designed to house industrial functions such as printing, mail operations, and fleet maintenance. When this main-building addition was completed, it provided more efficient space for these services and also opened up additional office space in the home office building.

In accordance with the Long Range Basing Study, Phase I of the building plan for San Antonio was put into operation in July 1988.

Expanding, Safety, And Succession

Senior Vice President Bob Hayden continued to guide the construction of the home office expansion. The main portion was the construction of buildings E and F that were attached to the end (Building D) of the existing home office building. Before this could begin, however, USAA had to move employee recreational areas off the proposed construction site to the southeastern portion of the USAA campus. The other prerequisite project was to excavate a 750-car parking lot which was also in the way. To make up the parking spaces, the Association built a 1,200-parking-space addition to the North Parking garage. When it was completed, USAA Security programmed identification cards for summer hires, vendors, and temporaries for access to the turnstiles leading from the garage to Building A. The additional spaces were a welcome relief to employees who had previously parked in the open lot near the building and in the distant lots near recreation areas southeast of the main building. Even though shuttles were available during normal work hours, the employees did not always find them to be convenient. Walking through wooded areas, employees were occasionally startled by wild deer and foxes that still resided there.

Bob Hayden

The E and F addition was a massive project. Besides removing the recreation and parking areas, more than a half-million cubic yards of earth had to be removed to make way for the 1.25-million-square-foot addition. HCB Contractors of Dallas built the addition to the same specifications as the original concrete structure. The buildings contained many of the same employee amenities included in the original structure as well as some new features. These included a much larger fitness center, a suite of classrooms and seminar rooms for Training and Development, and an electronic media center with television studios and video editing suites. In the E Building was the American Courtyard, featuring a twenty-two-foot version of the torch-holding hand of the Statue of Liberty. The huge sculpture was lowered by crane through the roof and into the court. Along with this project was the construction of a wide variety of

American ("E") Courtyard

recreational areas including picnic pavilions, basketball courts, and softball fields.

The F Building included a cafeteria and another medical clinic. Its International Court featured a terrazzo floor map of the world and five gazebos representing Asia, Europe, the Middle East, South Pacific, and North America. In January 1990, over 82,000 square feet of office space in E Building was opened to relieve pressure on the main building, and garages were partially opened in both E and F. In July, both buildings were dedicated.

The additional workspace was badly needed, and its completion was very important to USAA. Perhaps more important was McDermott's continued insistence on a comfortable and appealing work environment for the employees. New improvements were made for the employees, including better lighting. The new fitness center design reflected the increasing interest of women in wellness and physical fitness by providing sufficient lockers for women.

USAA employee Doris Suarez works out in the Mountain States Regional Office fitness center

A Tradition Of Service

In addition to the garage and home office building expansions were other construction projects. These included a backup computer center and renovation of the drive-in claims building to allow for drive-through service and to house USAA's employment screening center. Finally, the area in C Building containing the Company Store, USAA Federal Credit Union, and health clinic was renovated. It now became the Commercial Courtyard, with the look of an old town square, and featured bronzes of children admiring aircraft sculptures overhead. In the next decade, this courtyard was also known as the Children's Courtyard.

For the future, the November 1989 Long Range Basing Plan Annual Review projected construction of a G Building addition and a Bank Operations Building. In a 1990 interview, strategic planner

"C" Courtyard

Ed Bradley noted that USAA was using a planning formula that "dictates an expansion project whenever a facility reaches 85 percent capacity or 80 percent in the FSOs (regional offices)."[28] For the time being, USAA's construction plans seemed to be enough to take care of anticipated growth.

* * * *

Meanwhile terrorism, which had been a staple in the Middle East, began having a direct impact on America. In April 1983, bombs hit the American Embassy in Beirut, killing sixty-three. In October of the same year, a terrorist drove a truck filled with explosives into a building that housed sleeping U.S. troops. That night 241 service personnel were killed. The blood of terrorism flowed beyond the Middle Eastern borders. Airplane hijackings and attacks on busi-

General Robert T. Herres, Vice Chairman of the Joint Chiefs of Staff and Acting Chief, briefs President Reagan and Secretary of State Casper Weinberger on the USS *Stark* incident.

nesses often targeted Americans in overseas areas. In 1985 alone, over 800 terrorist incidents claimed 900 lives, twenty-three of them Americans. When terrorist incidents at airports escalated, the U.S. blamed Libya, and bombed that state twice. Besides the terrorism it spawned, the instability in the Middle East continued to affect the United States. In May of 1987, two Iraqi sea-skimming missiles struck the U.S. frigate *Stark*.[29]

The concerns about terrorism forced changes in how USAA conducted business in some overseas areas. Previously, most USAA members drove cars bearing armed forces license plates. To reduce the threat to military personnel, many overseas commanders decided to blend their forces in with the local population wherever possible. In Italy, for example, USAA members began using Italian plates on their cars and insurance stickers provided by insurers licensed in Italy. USAA was not licensed to do business in Italy at first, but within two weeks, it had contracted with a subsidiary of the Zurich Insurance Company of Switzerland to handle USAA members. The officers' vehicles now appeared to be licensed and insured like those of all Italian citizens. They continued to pay for their insurance through USAA, and received service as usual from their Association, however. In addition, the Association removed visible signage bearing "USAA" from Frankfurt and London offices and substituted "Automobile Association" instead.[30] The fear was that "USAA" was too close to "USA," and the Association, like the U.S. Armed Forces, wished to lower its visibility. Incidentally, the name of the USAA London subsidiary had been changed from the "American Officers' Insurance Company LTD" to "USAA LTD" on January 1, 1983.[31] This brought the name of this subsidiary in line with all other USAA companies. The use of the United Services Automobile Association LTD was considered. It was not possible, however, because the name "United Services" had already been registered in England by another company.

In the United States, in response to the general worldwide wave of terrorism, USAA installed new security systems in all of its office buildings. While there had been no problems or visible threats, USAA decided to take no chances. The turnstiles also helped protect against theft and safeguard sensitive data and technical equipment. Vic Ferrari told the employees that the goal was "to be sure that USAA remained a safe place for everyone."[32]

Employees were issued identification cards with individualized magnetized strips. When run through an electronic reader at an entrance, the system verified the card and opened the turnstile gate designed to let in only one person at a time. In addition to the outside entrances, many internal areas, such as some computer facilities and cash handling, were made limited access. Only employees authorized to be in those areas had their identification cards keyed to give them admittance. At first, the turnstiles, inside doors, and later the bank were on three separate security systems. In 1990, however, the entire system was put on one expandable system with software developed commercially by Software House. The threat of terrorism also resulted in hardening the computer backup center to make it less vulnerable to attack.

* * * *

In 1980, McDermott was pessimistic about the American economy. Wide fluctuations in various economic factors made it more difficult for insurers to control underwriting profits and losses. Investments were also problematical. For many years, the surplus-to-earned-premium goal of the Association had been at least 50 percent. McDermott set the new goal at 100 percent. Board Chairman Sam Phillips was concerned about the impact of this policy on member dividends. McDermott assured him the impact would only be for the short run and probably meant only a 2-percent difference in dividends. Board member Ed Travers asked how this would be viewed by the industry. McDermott said that it would be viewed as "super conservative," but USAA had to do what it believed to be right. The Board approved the new goal unanimously.³³

The year 1981 seemed to justify McDermott's worries. It was marked by record-breaking underwriting losses for the property and casualty industry — around $6 billion. USAA's underwriting gain declined for 1980, but still was $14.1 million after dividends. In 1982, USAA did even better, with an underwriting gain of $24 million. By 1984, however, USAA was experiencing underwriting losses and continued to do so until 1987. In that year rate increases, expense control, and unusually low catastrophe losses combined to produce an underwriting gain of 3.9 percent. The gains continued for the rest of the decade. Part of the reason for the gains was a number of imaginative programs designed to cut costs and improve profits at USAA.

Reduction of claims expenses was a major thrust of the initiatives. Another was to improve service to the members. One thoughtful program suggested developing a claims replacement service instead of paying individual claims off in cash. If USAA bought items like diamonds in large lots, the cost per diamond would be less than buying them one at a time. Replacing a lost diamond with an equivalent stone would satisfy the member, and cost USAA much less on each claim. The vehicle to do this was a buying service and it received Board approval on May 5, 1983.

On July 5, USAA hired retired Air Force Major General Bobby W. Presley to head the USAA Special Services Company and to begin the USAA Merchandising Division under this company. Presley, formerly the Commander of the Army and Air Force Exchange Service, was a good choice. He had operated one of the largest retail businesses in the world. Presley began building a team with the right expertise, including super merchant Sheldon Blitslow and other marketing experts to help get started.

The primary role for the new division was to replace — at reduced cost — articles destroyed or stolen in an insured loss, such as fire or theft. For example, one member had his Bundy saxophone stolen. USAA replaced the instrument, which retailed for $759, at a cost of about $510.[34]

The secondary role was to offer members merchandise at attractive prices through direct mail. In spite of its subsidiary role, the merchandising function was developed first. McDermott feared Congressional legislation effective in 1984 that might prohibit USAA from getting into such services. He wanted the USAA Merchandising Division operating before December 31, 1983, to grandfather the function. Presley developed three catalogues, gold jewelry, Citizen watches, and pearls, which were displayed in USAA buildings and mailed to members' homes in Tampa, San Diego, and San Antonio. With markups of only 5 to 7 percent, the merchandise was a tremendous buy. Member response was much greater than expected. At first, with only six telephones, Presley's people could not meet the telephone answering service standards used by USAA. Even when he increased those on the telephones to thirty, the merchandising employees still couldn't keep up. To hire more people and mitigate costs, the USAA Buying Service began charging a $15 fee to join — similar to the way that membership fees were charged by other low-market merchandisers such as Sam's.[35] The Spring 1984 issue of *Aide Magazine* included the first USAA merchandise catalogue, with a limited but varied offering of products. At first, the Army and Air Force Exchange

Bobby Presley

A Tradition Of Service

Service (AAFES) expressed some concern about USAA's newest operation. That quickly dissipated, however, because most of USAA's merchandise was not carried by the AAFES. In addition, the vast majority of USAA's non-officer customers were not even eligible to shop at the AAFES outlets on military installations.[36]

The actual claims replacement service began in March 1984 in the Rocky Mountain Region, with all regions included by August 1. Overall, the program was a successful one. In 1985, USAA eliminated the membership fee for the Buying Service that was making the claims replacement process more difficult.[37] In 1987 alone, the claims replacement service reduced the costs of the Property and Casualty Division by $1 million.[38]

The claims replacement specialists were a special breed of people. The positions required highly technical knowledge, intuition, determination, and empathy towards the members with losses. They worked from the office or out with the Catastrophe teams. Sometimes items could be found in regular catalogs. Sometimes law enforcement helped. One older couple in Houston were beaten and the thief stole a 5-carat marquise stone. This particular stone had a Gemological Institute of America certificate that spelled out the technical details of the stone. The specialist put out an alert and the diamond was recovered in New York City from a dealer in hot merchandise. The couple was delighted to see their own stone back. Sometimes the claims were for items that USAA had no intention of trying to replace — a human eye ring, a hand from 15,000 BC, and a shrunken head. In these cases, the specialists negotiated cash settlements. The bottom line was that the claims replacement service would save USAA tens of millions of dollars in future years and bring members peace of mind.

Another successful cost reduction effort that saved claims costs for USAA and provided a service to the members was "structured settlements." Useful in certain types of large claims settlements, the program established an annuity to finance payment of the settlement. Instead of one large payment, USAA often bought an annuity from the USAA Life Insurance Company to fit the claimants' needs and desires. The industry had used such settlements for a long time, but when a 1979 IRS ruling confirmed that structured settlement payments were tax-exempt to the claimant, their popularity grew. Not only were they tailored to meet individual needs, but also they provided protection for a large settlement. Studies had shown that 50 percent of individuals who received a large "windfall" settlement had nothing left after one year; 90 percent had no money after five years.

The structured settlements saved money for the Association as well. In one case, a twenty-year-old college student received permanent disabling injuries in an accident caused by a USAA member. USAA estimated its liability was about $375,000. With the agreement of the injured student, USAA set up a structured settlement. The student received $50,000 at once and his attorney's fees of $100,000 were covered. A USAA annuity assured that after two years, the claimant would receive monthly payments of $2,000. These payments would continue for forty years, and would include a $250 monthly increase every five years to cover inflation. The bottom line? The student received a guaranteed settlement of $1.5 million at a cost to USAA of about $330,000, or a savings of $45,000. Senior Vice President for Claims Al Kirsling said the settlements were a solution "where everyone is a winner."[39]

Another cost reduction program with an emphasis on helping the member was the creation of the USAA Medical Management Team. Begun in 1982, the program provided rehabilitation services for severely injured policyholders and third parties if the USAA insurance were adequate. Pauline (Nesbitt) Burkholder, USAA's first Medical Management Administrator, told an interviewer that the rehabilitation program worked to restore the patient to a normal lifestyle. Part of the program tried to get the individual in good enough shape to return to work as soon as possible. Studies demonstrated that for the long term, individuals who returned to work received about half the amount of insurance monies paid to those who remained unemployed. Besides this was the great feeling of helping restore a member to as normal a life as possible. One case in point was Amy Harris, daughter of USAA member Captain Edward A. Harris, USAR (Ret.). She was paralyzed in an automobile accident. USAA arranged for the Harris' home to be modified for Amy's home care, and outfitted a van to handle her wheelchair so she could return to school. When she graduated, her father wrote to thank "USAA's wonderful people" who made it all possible. His letter reflected his gratitude at being insured "with the finest insurance company in the country."[40]

One unusual initiative to cut operating costs was USAA's venture into satellite communications. With long distance expenditures spiraling upward, USAA looked into the feasibility of satellite alternatives with San Antonio-based Datapoint Corporation. In May 1981, USAA management proposed building an earth station on the campus and formed a subsidiary — the USAA Satellite Communications Company. This would enable USAA to reduce communications costs and to resell services to other companies. Board Chairman Sam Phillips applauded the move and encouraged McDermott to hire someone soon with the technical expertise to make it successful. USAA Board member Vice Admiral Edward Travers recalled that the Board members were enthusiastic because they believed the proposal would pay "a great deal" of USAA's bills and would make USAA "even more competitive and greater." Allocating $4 million for start-up costs, the Board authorized setting up the new company.[41]

On July 15, 1983, an eighty-ton crane hoisted USAA's thirteen-ton satellite dish into place on a twenty-five-foot pedestal on the

EXPANDING, SAFETY, AND SUCCESSION

east side of the USAA building. Jerry E. Piatt, the Executive Director for the new satellite company, announced to the press that it would begin to look for outside markets for its 154 satellite channels. This would be in addition to USAA's links with New York, Los Angeles, San Francisco, and Chicago. USAA's earth station communicated using Western Union satellite *Westar III*. Started with great optimism, the USAA Satellite Communications Company never fulfilled the Association's hopes. Rapidly changing technology, including fiber optics and intense competition from the breakup

USAA's Earth Station

A Tradition Of Service

of the Bell telephone company, outpaced USAA's pioneering efforts. The company was dissolved in September 1990. At first used as a backup communications link to the field offices, the disk itself was removed from the USAA campus about a year later.

Another cost control program that many thought was an oxymoron at first was a unit to combat insurance fraud at USAA. The USAA membership was believed to be immune to committing fraud. True anecdotes of member honesty surfaced regularly and became part of USAA's oral tradition. Everyone knew (and knows) about U.S. Naval Academy graduate and former Dallas Cowboys star Roger Staubach's claim. In the mid-1970s, Staubach and his wife Marianne went on vacation and she mislaid the Super Bowl pendant she received for the Cowboys' 1972 win. They filed a claim with USAA and were paid nearly $1,000. Years later, Staubach's wife found the pendant in a briefcase and promptly repaid the claims payment to USAA. In a 1988 interview with *Forbes,* Lodwrick Cook, Chairman of Atlantic Richfield, related a similar story. While he was on leave from the Army, his mother took his clothes to a dry cleaner which burned down. USAA promptly reimbursed Cook. Later, when he found out that his clothes were really safe at another dry cleaner, he sent the claims money back. "They trust me and I trust them," he said.[42]

USAA member Roger Staubach

At other times, when members did slip, they often returned to USAA with the truth. In the early 1970s, one young officer being transferred overseas didn't know what to do with a mechanically challenged European sports car. Friends told him that if he left it on a certain street it would be stolen, and then he could collect $1,000 from his insurance company — USAA. He did, and received the claim payment promptly. Some sixteen years later, the officer wrote to McDermott, revealed what he had done, offered restitution, and asked for forgiveness. USAA accepted the apology and the restitution, leaving a contrite, relieved, and loyal USAA member.

The Claims Security Unit (CSU) came about in 1979 through the initiative of two USAA employees in the Northeast and Overseas Region. Steve Brite and another employee sought out regional Vice President Jim Patterson and told him that they'd like to begin a "CSU." Patterson had to ask what a CSU was. Convinced by their enthusiasm, he received clearance from McDermott. The unit looked for fraud in body shops and with third-party claims as well as in USAA's membership.[43] The two-man team detected over $250,000 worth of fraudulent auto claims in the first year.

McDermott directed Ensley to conduct a study into the feasibility of establishing a permanent CSU for all of USAA. The study recommended to do so and USAA brought Donald B. Nettle to the Association to head the CSU. Nettle was an attorney and CPA with seventeen years of investigative experience with the Internal Revenue Service. By 1984, the unit had grown to twenty employees and had provided assistance leading to the recovery of more than $8 million in fraudulent claims. Cases included a $58,000 yacht that was sold, not sunk, and $250,000 worth of belongings hidden, not stolen. As USAA claims employees became more sensitive to fraud possibilities, referrals made the CSU more effective. Also strengthening the unit's efforts was its cooperation with the National Insurance Crime Prevention Institute and the National Automobile Theft Bureau. USAA helped fund these organizations, and cooperated with local law enforcement agencies by doing such things as loaning vehicles for auto-theft sting operations. In just one case

A Tradition Of Service

in New York City, Brite referred a questionable claim to the police. The police credited USAA for helping break up a large ring, saving insurance companies as much as $170,000.

USAA's most active program for the members' health and cost control was automobile safety. Throughout most of the Association's years, automobile safety was a primary concern, although its active participation ebbed and flowed. In 1979, for example, Joan Claybrook, the director of the National Highway Traffic Safety Administration, presented its "Double Eagle" award to USAA for its help in promoting the 55-mph national maximum speed limit. In 1980, George Ensley briefed the Board of Directors on claims. He pointed out that there were fewer accidents due to a combination of high gasoline prices and the 55-mph speed limit that resulted in less

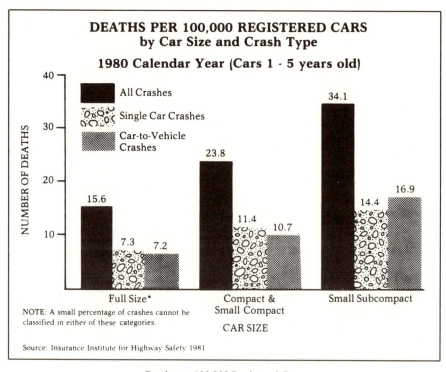

Deaths per 100,000 Registered Cars

driving. The trend towards smaller U.S. and foreign autos, however, was reflected in the more serious injuries and higher number of deaths.[44]

McDermott had continued to work with the National Association of Independent Insurers, and he was a strong supporter of the Insurance Institute for Highway Safety (IIHS) and its research arm, the Highway Loss Data Institute. Dr. William Haddon Jr. headed both organizations and directed a study on the relationship of vehicle size to accident injuries and deaths. The researchers looked at injury claims submitted to ten auto insurance underwriters covering half of the nation's vehicles and federal records on fatal accidents. The results were a dramatic indictment of the small, gasoline-saving automobiles. One of the study's charts illustrates its principal finding in dramatic fashion.

McDermott seized the initiative on the IIHS study findings and held a press conference with Haddon in Washington, D.C., on January 5, 1982. Facing a bank of microphones and a press gathering of over 120 TV, radio, and print reporters, McDermott pointed out that subcompact cars were twice as deadly as full-sized cars. Because Japanese subcompacts held thirteen of the seventeen worst injury-claim records, the *Chicago Sun-Times* reported that McDermott praised the safer American-made vehicles.[45] If all automakers did not improve the safety of automobiles, McDermott agreed with current estimates that annual death rates could climb to 70,000 by 1990. He urged U.S. automakers to incorporate even more safety features into their new designs.

Following the press conference, the national public relations firm of Manning, Selvage and Lee and its San Antonio representative, Jim Dublin, set up fifteen telephone interviews and tapings for two syndicated television shows for McDermott. At the same time, Property and Casualty Senior Vice President Bob Brakey, Actuary Charles Bryan, P&C Claims Senior Vice President Ed Ring, and Charles Weeber, Claims Counsel Vice President, took the same findings to the Dallas, Chicago, Los Angeles, and Atlanta media. After finishing in Washington, McDermott traveled to New York City for a live appearance on the nationally televised "MacNeil/Lehrer Report."

For thirty minutes, two auto experts, a representative of foreign importers and a representative of Ford, fired questions at McDermott. He did well. Ralph Nader, consumer advocate and author of *Unsafe at Any Speed,* watched the program and discussed it in an article that appeared in Rhode Island college newspapers. He wrote, "For an insurance company president, he (McDermott) was most articulate." When the auto representatives tried to pick apart the report, "McDermott coolly and rationally replied point by point."[46] The following day, McDermott's remarks appeared in newspapers from coast to coast.

Next, McDermott placed a full-page advertisement in the *Wall Street Journal* on January 14, 1982, summarizing the high points of the IIHS report. He also had a special issue of *Aide Magazine* entitled "How Safe is Your Car?" published and sent to the members. Except for a handful of defensive members who drove foreign subcompacts, most were very positive about the exposure. One member agreed with the small car danger, calling them "mobile coffins." He brought a smile to a serious issue by telling the story of a young woman in his office whose Volkswagen bug was totaled by a motorcycle.[47] Other letters were sad, like the one from a member in Cocoa Beach, Florida. He said he had read McDermott's information on fatality rates in Japanese cars with interest, but hadn't expected the information would ever touch his family. Four days after the press conference, on January 9, 1982, his son, the father of two, had been killed driving the member's 1972 Datsun. Letters like this put a human dimension into McDermott's drive for safe automobiles.

McDermott also had a special flyer with questions and answers and the table on claims frequency printed and sent to industry leaders. He gave the other insurance companies permission to reprint the flyer using their own company's logo. F. William Hirt, Presi-

EXPANDING, SAFETY, AND SUCCESSION

USAA advertisement "Americans Are Dying" in the *Wall Street Journal*

A TRADITION OF SERVICE

dent of the Erie Insurance Group, thanked McDermott and told him that he would do just that. About fifty other insurance executives also wrote, including Donald P. McHugh, State Farm's General Counsel, who congratulated him "on the very progressive and statesmanlike position" he was taking on the traffic safety issue.[48] Interestingly, General Motors took a table labeled "Best" and "Worst" from the special issue of *Aide Magazine,* "How Safe is Your Car?" and began using it in an advertising campaign which placed the ads in more than 330 newspapers and magazines. It trumpeted that General Motors' cars dominated the "Best" column — and further spread USAA's initiative.

During the rest of the year, USAA continued with a number of safety initiatives. *Aide Magazine* carried extensive material, including letters from McDermott extolling safety. In the Spring 1982 issue, he asked members to try to influence auto manufacturers to

"Buckle-up" advertisement

make safer vehicles. In July, General Motors asked McDermott to set up a meeting with its executives to discuss safety issues. *Highlights* advocated "Buckle-up" campaigns, the 55-mph speed limit and a ten-minute documentary film co-sponsored by San Antonio's Santikos Theaters and USAA. In a June Rotary Club of San Antonio address, McDermott told of a new drug called Acutane which had the potential for curing severe cystic acne, estimated to scar 300,000 American teenagers annually. Another 300,000 Americans could be saved from permanent facial scars, he pointed out, if auto manufacturers would install shatterproof windshields. The antilacerative windshield technology had been used in Europe for years, but not in the U.S. General Motors head Alfred P. Sloan Jr. had refused to install the new automobile safety glass. "It is not my responsibility," he said. "We are not a charitable institution — we are trying to make a profit for our stockholders."[49] Eventually all American cars came equipped with the safety glass.

Over the next few years, McDermott tried a variety of incentives to reduce accidents and improve driver and auto safety for the Association's members. In 1984, USAA allocated $30 million to pay a 5-percent bonus to members who had no accident surcharge. To improve child passenger safety, USAA began offering Century 200 Child Safety Seats for $20, including postage and handling, the same year. In the next four years, USAA sold over 170,000 to members. In 1987, USAA offered a special increase of medical benefits to $10,000 and a death benefit of $10,000. These were payable if the members or anyone in their households, in any vehicle, were wearing a seat belt at the time an accident occurred causing injury or death.[50]

Decisions in the boardroom are often analytical and logical, but lack warmth. Letters from members relating incidents about the decisions give them life and vitality. So it was with the child seat policy. An article from a local Virginia newspaper related the story of a car that plunged down an embankment and overturned. The three-year-old girl was dangling by the straps of her car seat belt. All three occupants were safe in the totaled car although witnesses expected to find them dead. USAA member Lieutenant Colonel Warren Green had purchased the seats and thanked USAA. He said the cost of the car seats was a very small investment for such "an outstanding payback."[51]

All of these incentives assumed that drivers would be taking voluntary actions to mitigate possible injuries because of an accident. Drivers would have to put on their seat belts, for example. In 1981, however, only 8 percent of car occupants aged fifteen to twenty-four were wearing a seat belt when an accident occurred. The historical average of seat-belt use for the entire U.S. population stood only at approximately 11 percent. McDermott believed that passive restraints (seat belts that fastened automatically) or preferably, air bags, were the answer.[52]

As with other safety issues, McDermott continued to work the air bag proposal on the national scene as well as within USAA. In 1977, the U.S. Department of Transportation had revised its 1967 Federal Motor Vehicle Safety Standard 208, which required seat belts in all vehicles by 1984. Since people were not using the seat belts, the revision required passive restraints. In 1981, Secretary of Transportation Andrew Lewis rescinded the passive restraint rule. USAA and other NAII members joined State Farm Mutual Insurance Company in a suit to overturn the Lewis decision. The U.S. Court of Appeals found the Lewis decision to be "arbitrary and capricious," and the U.S. Supreme Court agreed in a unanimous decision.[53] The Court pointed out that the auto manufacturers had waged the equivalent of war against the air bag, but now had lost. In 1984, new Secretary of Transportation Elizabeth Dole issued a "weak and ambiguous" rule on passive restraints. McDermott as Chairman of NAII continued to fight for a strengthened passive restraint standard.[54]

Expanding, Safety, And Succession

McDermott set a positive example at USAA in the air bag debate. In 1983, McDermott announced that USAA would replace its 150-car fleet with cars equipped with air bags. In June 1985, he had IIHS President Brian O'Neill talk to USAA employees about air bags and auto safety. Automobile manufacturers still fought the issue. Lee Iacocca, head of Chrysler, bitterly opposed the air bags and said so in his best-selling autobiography, *Iacocca*. He said that at heaven St. Peter was going "to meet me at the gate to talk to me about air bags."[55] To suggest the depth of McDermott's passion for air bag safety, he later turned down the opportunity to serve with Iacocca's committee to refurbish the Statue of Liberty. He refused the honor because of Iacocca's previous anti-air bag intransigence.[56] In 1988, confronted by the reinstated passive restraint rules, the IIHS, insurers, and the introduction of air bags by Mercedes Benz, Iaccoca surrendered. In his landmark 1988 Chrysler Motors' ad-

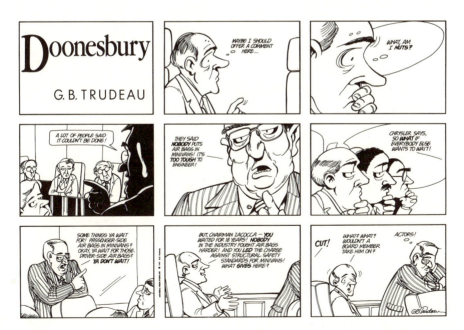

DOONESBURY © 1991 G.B. Trudeau. Reprinted with permission of UNIVERSAL PRESS SYNDICATE. All rights reserved.

vertisements that asked, "Who says you can't teach an old dog new tricks?" Iacocca discussed his conversion and promised air bags in all Chryslers.

When Ford came to much the same conclusion, McDermott announced that USAA was endorsing Ford's plan to make driver's-side air bags standard equipment in the majority of its cars after September 1, 1989. In his Executive Perspective in the November/December 1987 *Aide Magazine*, McDermott announced that 10 percent of 1988 models were equipped with air bags. The air bag would be an optional feature on most, however. He also related that all American auto manufacturers would be equipping most cars with at least driver's side-air bags by 1990.

To coordinate safety issues and to work on new automobile safety initiatives, McDermott had appointed Staser Holcomb to head a 1988 "USAA Safety Committee." The committee's foremost objective was equipping cars with air bags, but improved seat-belt usage and more responsible driving for young people were other goals. The committee developed incentives to encourage members to purchase automobiles with air bags. It also put together a nationwide sales contest with Ford and Oldsmobile dealerships to reward the salesperson who sold the most air bag-equipped cars. The prize was an eight-day cruise for two. The contest drew significant media attention and interest in the air bags rose among new car purchasers.

The committee's efforts culminated in March when McDermott held another press conference in Washington, D.C., to announce air-bag incentives. He also encouraged other insurance companies to do the same. These incentives to members who purchased or leased a new car and took an air bag option included a $300 bonus and a doubling of the discount to 60 percent on premiums for Medical Payments and Personal Injury Protection. Other benefits included an additional $25,000 life insurance benefit to USAA Life Company policyholders who were killed while wearing a seat belt and occupying a seat protected by an air bag, and replacement reimbursement for any air bag accidentally deployed.[57] After McDermott spoke, a note from U.S. Secretary of Transportation Jim Burnley was read. Burnley wrote that the day after he was sworn in as Secretary, he challenged the insurance industry to provide incentives to enhance the appeal of air bags. He went on to say that he was delighted that McDermott "accepted the challenge and in turn is setting the standard for the insurance industry." He offered the hope that other companies would follow.[58] During a later Ford press conference announcing an air bag in its Continental, Ralph Nader also praised USAA's discounts for setting an example for the industry as Burnley had the year before.[59]

McDermott used *Aide Magazine* and other USAA publications extensively to educate the membership about air bags and to announce the incentives he hoped would spur member interest. One effective "advertisement" told of a driver who had a serious accident which caused her air bag to inflate. She walked away with a few minor bruises, but left a perfect lip print on the air bag. *Aide Magazine* also published letters from grateful members who believed they or loved ones survived accidents because of seat belts and/or air bags.

Another USAA publication to stress safety was a new one — the *USAA Car Guide*. It was put together by Bill Hicklin, USAA Consumer Affairs Director, in partnership with property and casualty expert Larry Jockers and financial analyst Myron "Butch" Dye. The guide included safety facts and figures on most cars, accumulated by various safety agencies to assist members in purchasing safer cars. The guide was distributed to all USAA members for the first time in 1988 and became an annual publication because of great member interest. To spread the word further, McDermott authorized NAII member companies to reproduce the guide at no cost.

By the end of the decade, the air bags were still selling slowly,

A Tradition Of Service

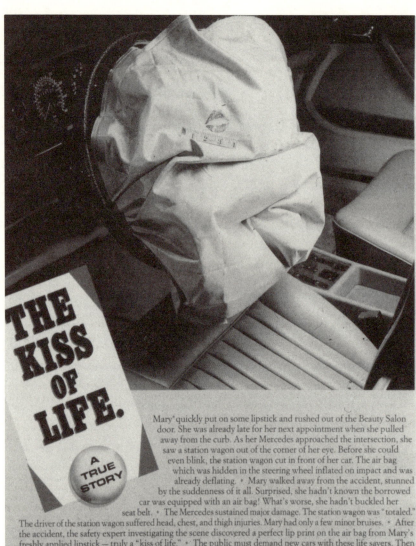

USAA's advertisement, "The Kiss of Life"

according to a General Motors spokesperson. In an October 1989 interview, she related that GM had sold only 6,000 air-bag-equipped cars in the past two years.[60] In the next decade, public attitudes towards automobile safety changed dramatically when automobile manufacturers decided that safety would sell. USAA and McDermott took pride in the roles they had played in bringing about this successful change.

* * * *

USAA members believed in USAA and wanted to buy all their insurance from the Association. In some cases, members had bought things like antique automobiles, large yachts, and private airplanes, which USAA did not cover. In other cases, members were assigned to or lived in areas where USAA did not offer insurance, such as Singapore. When USAA members' driving records dropped below USAA's underwriting standards, the Association was no longer able to insure them and they were lost to USAA. Underwriting Senior Vice President Bob Brakey and Clem Spalding, Vice President-Regulatory Affairs, and others often discussed the problem and conducted studies on expanding the things USAA would or could insure directly. The cost of systems to support the new lines and the lack of expertise made direct writing seem impossible. Then the group came up with the idea to serve the members by acting as an agent for other companies.[61]

In November 1983, Brakey briefed the USAA Board of Directors on the whole issue. He presented the results of a member survey that indicated that USAA was not providing service in terms of coverage that the members wanted. USAA was unable to do so because of the relatively small numbers of members wanting specific coverages, or because of USAA's lack of expertise in specialized areas. The answer was to set up a General Agency that could serve as an agent to other carriers that were willing to provide insurance that USAA was not. The Board agreed, and with the guidance of

General Counsel Bill McCrae, the USAA General Agency was incorporated under the laws of the state of Texas.[62] The first meeting of the USAA General Agency, Inc. was held on January 16, 1984, with Bob Brakey as its first president. Once established, "the hardest thing to do," according to Brakey, was to find someone to run it. He was delighted when Joseph "Joe" R. Calvelli agreed to come to USAA as Executive Director of the new agency. Calvelli knew the business very well and seemed to know everyone who could help USAA build the agency.[63]

Joe Calvelli

Calvelli graduated from East Rockaway High School on Long Island and from Sienna College in New York. For six years, he worked in a variety of underwriting and marketing positions with "Little" Aetna on both coasts. He even accumulated experience in insuring yachts. In 1978, he went with a large general broker in Seattle, where he gained experience in excess lines and became its regional vice president in San Francisco. In 1984, USAA executive recruiter Wayne Brittingham contacted Calvelli and offered him the opportunity to start a brand new company. Calvelli later recalled that at thirty-nine he felt "indestructible," and couldn't turn the offer down. He was willing to give up a "piece of the action" for the chance to do something very special.[64] With his Long Island accent still firmly in place, he plunged enthusiastically into his new job.

The USAA General Agency grew slowly, but steadily. In the beginning, it wrote five lines of business — foreign automobile, Mexican tourist, aviation, non-standard automobile, and antique/classic cars. In 1986, the General Agency added commercial lines representing the Royal Insurance Company. It provided insurance for USAA's corporate insurance program for such things as officers' liability and also for the community. Community insurance coverage included San Antonio's Fiesta celebration and the United Way.

Brakey considered the sale of non-standard automobile business to prospective members who could not qualify for USAA or CIC insurance to be the major service the Agency provided to its members.[65] In April 1988, the General Agency contracted with Progressive Insurance Company as its primary carrier for non-standard auto insurance. From this point on, USAA's underwriters referred all eligible applicants whom they declined to cover in USAA or USAA CIC to the General Agency.[66] The year 1988 was a major benchmark for the Agency. For the first time in its short history, it showed a profit — $281,000. By the end of 1989, it was serving over 22,000 members, had a profit of over $450,000, and its written premium of over $30 million placed the Agency in the top 3 percent of insurance agencies nationwide.[67]

During the 1980s the Life Company continued its rapid growth. Life insurance in force grew from $4.4 billion in 1980 to $34.9 billion in 1989. Assets climbed from $165 million to $2.5 billion. Policies in force quadrupled. The keys to success were the loyalty and trust of the USAA members and the excellent service provided to them. Jack Daye, the Life Company president, built a strong team and encouraged his employees to enhance their professional skills. Daye himself earned his professional designation of Chartered Life Underwriter to both learn new skills and to set an example for his people. Along with this were improvements in information systems. The new systems enabled employees to give quotes to members while still on the phone. This was without the excessive dead time talking about the weather and other unrelated topics that had occurred in the past while calculating the rates.[68] Sales results by individual employees were spectacular. In 1987, Sharon Mitchell was top sales representative — over $113 million in life insurance sold in just one year. A multi-year, industry-wide project, the "I" computer system also promised product flexibility, management reporting and productivity gains. USAA and the other participating companies terminated the project when the costs became excessive. Nevertheless, the need was still there, and the void was eventually filled by the HAL (Health and Life System) project, led by John Douglas.[69] Unlike "Hal," the malevolent computer, in *2001: A Space Odyssey,* USAA's HAL was a positive contributor.

The Life Company continued developing a wide variety of products to serve all sectors of the USAA membership. Conventional whole life and term policies could be tailored to fit individual members through a complete package of options. Flexible premium investment "tax sheltered" annuities gained in popularity. For a few years, USAA sold insurance policies out of both the USAA Life Insurance Company and the USAA Annuity and Life Company, which often confused members. When a new tax law resulted in the annuity company being taxed at the same rate as the Life Company, all the life policies were transferred to the USAA Life Insurance Company.[70]

A successful Universal Life Policy was added in 1981, as was a Group Life Insurance product. When Group Life was offered to the USAF Academy's Association of Graduates in 1985, Life Marketing projected 4,000 sales by 1989. Instead, USAA sold only 527 policies to the graduates. The low-dollar amount of the premiums resulted in a high-risk product that was costly to maintain. Because of this, USAA terminated the program and offered to convert the existing coverage to Universal Life or Annual Renewable Term. A total of 328 policyholders did convert.[71] In addition to these, USAA also began offering a Medical Supplement, CHAMPUS active-duty supplement, and a CHAMPUS retiree supplement.

Expanding, Safety, And Succession

While the Life Company was adding new products, members were asking for new products that USAA did not, and would not, carry. One was temporary medical insurance. When dependents coming of legal age had to be taken off their parents' automobile insurance policies, members asked USAA to help. The result, of course, had been the USAA Casualty Insurance Company which covered the dependents. In a way, the same thing happened to the Life Company. Dependents coming of age were being denied medical coverage on their parents' policies.

The answer was the USAA Life General Agency, which was organized by its first director, Steve Miller. It was incorporated under the laws of Colorado on December 29, 1983. Serving first as an agent for the Golden Rule Company, the first short-term medical policy was issued on September 9, 1984. Written for six months, the policies were designed to provide a transition time for the ex-dependents to find coverage on their own from their places of employment or other sources. In 1985, 96 percent of all applications processed by the Life General Agency were for individual health insurance. USAA signed contracts with more than one insurance company to provide this coverage. When Golden Rule's service levels deteriorated, USAA dropped the company. Fortunately, backup was available. In July 1988, USAA's primary individual health insurance carrier became Time Insurance Company. Other Agency products included long-term care, disability income, overseas medical, and structured settlements. The Life General Agency became a success because it provided services and products members needed and wanted. At the same time, two special benefits assisted the parent company. The General Agency served as the first point of contact for many ex-dependents and opened the way for other areas of business. It also provided a vehicle to test the market for future life insurance and annuity products.

In 1982, long-term Life Company President Jack Daye became

ill with ulcers and was sent to the hospital. Senior Vice President, Life Operations Dale Briscoe had fallen from a horse and also had health problems. About the same time, Air Force Brigadier General Charles Bishop was visiting USAA to give Vic Ferrari a recommendation on a potential USAA employee. Bishop had been a West Point cadet when McDermott was an instructor there and had been on the Air Force Academy faculty when McDermott was Dean.[72] He had served in a number of Air Force flying assignments, including flying F-105 "Thuds" in combat in Vietnam. During the visit, McDermott talked to Bishop briefly. With McDermott's blessing, Ted Michel hired Bishop to be a regional vice president for Northeast Region.

Before Bishop ever arrived at USAA, however, McDermott decided to place Bishop as Vice-President, Operations in the Life Company. He called him at Shaw Air Force Base to tell him the news while Bishop and his wife Pat were packing.[73] McDermott had been concerned about the health of his Life Company leaders and he believed Bishop could eventually replace them. Things worked out well in the Life Company for Bishop. President Jack Daye gave him a goal to increase productivity by 3 percent; Bishop succeeded in increasing it by 39 percent. Daye noted in Bishop's annual rating that year that he had an outstanding "plebe year."[74]

After a rotation tour as a Regional Vice President in Property and Casualty, Bishop returned to the Life Company to take retiring Dale Briscoe's place as Executive Vice President for Insurance Operations on May 1, 1986.[75] In the meantime, Daye had been promoted to President of the Financial Services Division. John Knubel replaced retiring Jack Daye on September 1, 1986. As a practical matter, the responsibility of running the Life Company resided in the Insurance Operations position. In a later shift, on June 1, 1988, David Roe took Knubel's place and former Air Force pilot Edwin L. Rosane replaced Bishop.

Expanding, Safety, And Succession

Rosane was born in New Castle, Wyoming, one of six children. He spent most of his childhood years in Pasco, Washington. A gifted athlete, Rosane went to the University of Washington on a football scholarship. After one year there, he was recruited by the U.S. Air Force Academy as a quarterback. He graduated with the class of 1959 and became a pilot. In 1962, he was flying in Vietnam in C-123s with the classified mission of resupplying strategic hamlets in Project "Mule Train." He was to return to Vietnam twice during the war years, flying as a Forward Air Controller in 0-2s both times. During an intermediate tour at the Air Force Academy as the Executive Officer to the Commandant of Cadets, he got to know Colonel Jack Daye, who was then the Deputy Commandant of Cadets. Daye recruited Rosane for USAA, where he started in Corporate Planning. After six months there, he moved to the Life Company to bring the new universal life insurance policy online.

Ed Rosane

In the area of aviation coverage, USAA Life Insurance Company was forced into an accommodation that benefitted the membership. Virtually all life insurance companies limited coverage for air crews, wrote a surcharge, or refused to write any insurance at all. United Services Life Insurance Company in Arlington, Virginia, removed its surcharge on military aviators effective with 1983 renewals. In early 1983, Briscoe briefed the Life Board of Directors on the problem. With its surcharge, USAA Life was simply not competitive with United Services. In any event, an analysis of USAA death claims revealed few aircraft accidents, and most of them did not involve active-duty military pilots. The Board agreed to eliminate the surcharge and to offer insurance up to a $150,000 limit.[76]

Overall, the USAA Life Insurance Company grew rapidly because of its value to the membership. For example, in 1982, the USAA Life Board of Directors had increased the amount of the family rider on insurance policies at no cost. The members appreciated this benefit. The policies were safe because the company was financially sound, as reflected in its *A.M. Best's* "A+" rating for thirteen consecutive years. Perhaps the best indicator of the members' satisfaction with their USAA life insurance was that they continued to hold the policies. In 1989, of more than 2,000 companies in the industry, USAA Life ranked first or second for three straight years in persistency.[77]

Along with the new insurance products and services, USAA added other new programs. In 1984, USAA began to sell federally-backed flood insurance using the same rates and rules set by the federal government. The main advantage for USAA members was not the price, but that the USAA claims service would take care of them in times of need. Also in 1984, USAA CARDEAL guaranteed members a new-car price well below sticker price without haggling. Under the CARDEAL program, USAA was also able to offer extended service contracts the following year. Cruise services continued and a new auto leasing program began in 1988.

* * * *

On July 31, 1985, McDermott was scheduled to play a round of golf at Sun Valley, Utah. He was there to accept an award as Man of the Year from the Federation of Insurance Counsel for his contributions to the insurance industry. His wife, Alice, had been concerned for his health after seeing a sign at the resort that indicated the elevation was 6,000 feet. McDermott had jokingly told her that it was probably 600 feet and that she had misread the sign. On the first tee, McDermott felt a tingling in his arm and a flutter in his chest. When he described his symptoms to Tom Haggerty, his golf partner and a previous heart attack victim, Haggerty urged him into the golf cart. He drove the cart to a hospital across the street and right up the emergency entrance ramp. McDermott was admitted and upon return to San Antonio had the second of his two heart bypass surgeries.[78]

Fortunately, the USAA Board was prepared for this eventuality. In its November 3, 1984, meeting, the Board had voted to retain McDermott's services "until at least age 70." At the same meeting, the Board had listened to proposals by management and executive search consultant J. Robert Harman, a 1945 West Point graduate who headed his own executive search firm. With McDermott's blessing, Harman proposed that Board member Lieutenant General Robert Pursley be appointed as a "working" vice chairman and consultant to the president and to the Board. Pursley would be paid and would act for and in the absence of the chairman, president, and attorney-in-fact. When McDermott fell ill, the Board reaffirmed that Pursley would run USAA until McDermott returned to work full-time.[79]

Lieutenant General Robert Pursley

Pursley's selection as "working" vice chairman was part of an overall succession plan developed by Harman with McDermott's assistance. In 1984, the Board realized that more than half of USAA's senior executives were over sixty years of age. As such, it was likely that they would retire about the same time. These potential retirees included recent heart attack victim Ted Michel, George Sykes, Jack Daye, and Dale Briscoe, Executive Vice

President of the Life Insurance Division. McDermott later praised these men in a letter to the members in discussing USAA's need to bring in a new management team.[80] The Board was also well aware that McDermott was already sixty-four, and though extended to age seventy, it began to think about his replacement as well.

Harman worked directly with the Board of Directors to get nominations and comments on prospective candidates for top-level USAA positions. The expectation was that "one or more [of these individuals] might qualify in a reasonable time as a candidate for CEO."[81] In 1984, retired Army Major General Donald R. Lasher was the first to be brought to USAA under this plan. Retired Air Force Brigadier General Wilson C. "Bill" Cooney was hired under this plan in 1985, but was not told he was a candidate nor was he ever put in the rotation program.[82] He was followed in 1986 by retired Vice Admiral M. Staser Holcomb.

Holcomb was born in Detroit in 1932. When he was six months old, his family flew in a United Airlines Ford tri-motor airplane to Seattle. The first young family to do so, there were reporters at each of the plane's six stops. His father was a commercial artist who loved the English language and he passed on his interest to Holcomb and his sister. His father and uncle had served in the Navy and the family lived close to the Seattle Naval Air Station. Under the influence of blood, sea, and air, Holcomb went to the Naval Academy and graduated in 1953. As a Navy pilot, he had over 4,300 flying hours and more than 800 carrier landings. In between flying assignments, he completed a Master's degree in Physics. This degree led to a systems analysis assignment to the Pentagon to work with Secretary of Defense Robert McNamara's Whiz Kids. Most of his remaining shore duty was in the Pentagon in the same field. In 1976 and 1977, he was the military assistant to Secretary of Defense Donald Rumsfeld and then Harold Brown. After retiring in 1985, he became an independent consultant for sixteen different clients on national security matters until USAA Board member Vice Admiral Ed Travers recommended him to Harman. Holcomb's first assignment was President of the Property and Casualty Company.

Holcomb was followed by Rhodes Scholar, White House Fellow, and retired Air Force Brigadier General David Roe; retired Army Brigadier General Thomas E. Carpenter; and USNA graduate and Rhodes Scholar John A. Knubel. McDermott's intention was to have these candidates serve at least one rotation in the senior-level positions over the next few years. With the senior staff replacements selected and most already at USAA, the Board discontinued Pursley's working vice chairman arrangement over his objections effective February 21, 1986.[83] In addition to these officers, McDermott also considered hiring an executive from another insurance company to strengthen USAA in the Property and Casualty area. And, finally, the Board discussed creating a Chief Operating Officer position to back up McDermott. McDermott recommended, however, that instead of a COO, the Board approve a Deputy Chief Executive Officer position and move George Ensley into it as an "interim solution" until McDermott retired. In 1987, the Board approved this recommendation.[84]

Staser Holcomb

A new Office of the Chairman was created to support McDermott, headed by Ensley who agreed to postpone his own retirement. The plan was to "take the burden off the CEO and allow more access to the new senior executives." McDermott was positive about this aspect and also appreciated that he would have more time to spend with his family. Retired Air Force Colonel Bill McKinsey was added as an Assistant Vice President, and Carolyn Olivera became McDermott's Executive Assistant.[85] John O'Neill joined the office a short time later and provided additional staff assistance. The practical effect of the new office was just the opposite of the intention. With the additional staff assistance, McDermott added new projects and entries, especially in the community, to his already crammed calendar and was busier than ever.

CHAPTER TEN

A NEW ERA FOR USAA — FINANCIAL SERVICES

When he became president, McDermott's vision for USAA was a full-service insurance and financial services company. He believed in making available to USAA members all the products and services that they needed for their financial security and well-being. It was in this spirit that McDermott had sent George Ensley to Washington, D.C., in 1969 to look into the legal possibility of mutual funds and a bank for USAA. The Glass-Steagall Act prohibited an affiliation between a commercial banking and a financial securities operation. That precluded USAA from both owning a bank and offering mutual funds. McDermott did not give up his dream, but he had decided to start a mutual fund and bide his time on a bank for USAA.[1] The election of Ronald Reagan and the deregulation of business provided the opportunity.

In December 1982, McDermott and Ensley talked about the changing regulatory climate for financial services. Ensley had developed a briefing for McDermott to explore how USAA could be reorganized to facilitate the process. As the Executive Vice President for Finance and Treasurer, Ensley was spread too thinly. He suggested that his job be split, with internal responsibilities such as accounting and the pension funds transferred to someone else. This would free him to work on expanding financial services, including a bank. McDermott agreed and told Ensley to begin working on developing a bank for USAA. General Counsel Bill McCrae went with Ensley to Washington, D.C., where they hired a banking consultant firm, Golembe and Associates. Golembe then assigned John Mingo to work with USAA.[2]

Next McDermott asked Ensley to brief the USAA Board of Directors at its February 1983 meeting. The purpose was to start building a consensus on the Board to support USAA's entry into a broad spectrum of financial services. On the first day of the meeting, February 24, the briefing, entitled "The Restructuring of Financial Services in America," took all morning. It covered changing demographics, consumer interest, investment incentives, and technology. Ensley explained the Depository Institutions Deregulation and Monetary Control Act of 1980 and the Garn-St. Germain Act of 1982, which opened the possibility that USAA might own a bank. Next he discussed six different financial services networks already in existence. One example was Sears with its building blocks of Allstate, Coldwell Banker, and Dean Witter Reynolds. Ensley referred to John Naisbitt's *Megatrends,* that posited a mass society breaking down into fractured groups with different tastes and values. And he quoted a Harvard study that said tomorrow's suppliers of financial services would need to serve customers' broad needs with a "nationwide delivery system" and with "personalized customer service."[3] Ensley concluded by quoting from that week's *Forbes.* The magazine warned that for non-bank companies to get involved in financial services, "the time to move is now. By year-end, or in 1984, some doors may swing shut."[4]

The Board members were receptive and interested in the briefing and the overall plan to move into financial services. They told McDermott to continue to study the issue, but to get back to them before USAA made firm commitments. Board member and retired U.S. Coast Guard Vice Admiral Donald C. Thompson later recalled that McDermott didn't ask for a yes or no on each piece, but that the briefing was laid out like a strategic plan, "a springboard" for the future.[5] Two days later, on the last day of the Board meeting, the Directors authorized the President to apply for a charter and take whatever other actions were necessary to begin a bank.[6]

A NEW ERA FOR USAA — FINANCIAL SERVICES

At the next Board meeting Dave Myers, the Executive Director of Manpower and Organization, briefed the Directors on a new proposed organization for USAA to enable it to move into the new era of financial services. In essence, the new organization mirrored Ensley's briefing to McDermott months earlier. The Board approved the new organization.[7] The newly created Financial Services Division was an umbrella that included all the Financial Services pieces plus the Life Company. Retired Army Colonel Ray Otte took over the internal accounting functions. In this capacity, Otte guided the automation of accounting to provide rapid and accurate information to assist management in making decisions. Ensley regarded this as a major contribution that enabled USAA leadership to make better business decisions.[8]

With the overall go-ahead from the Board, McDermott held a Financial Services Planning Conference on March 15, 1983, at the Tapatio Springs conference facility in San Antonio, Texas. Each financial services product was briefed. In his opening comments, McDermott talked about the importance of financial services for USAA's future, and the tough competition that would face the Association. That day, he noted, was the first of many steps into a new and challenging market. The only way USAA could be a player would be to deliver products and services in a manner consistent with USAA's tradition of excellence. It was a time of great change, and USAA with a financial services wing would be significantly different. He concluded "One thing that won't change, however, is our commitment to serving our members. When that is lost, nothing else matters."[9]

McDermott listened carefully to separate briefings on each possible financial product or service. Then he listened to the discussion that followed, and made a decision. If it were positive, he assigned an action officer. He decided not to proceed with limited partnerships for oil and gas leasing and personal financial planning. He deferred action pending further study on both USAA becoming a transfer agent and Ensley's proposal for a marketing and communications program to broaden USAA's image. He approved and gave directions to proceed on a USAA High Venture Fund, real estate partnerships, a discount brokerage, and most importantly, a bank. He selected Ensley as the action officer to establish the new bank. As insurance, Ensley was to identify an existing bank or savings and loan for purchase, in addition to seeking approvals for a new bank.[10]

Kelly Field Bank soon became the prime candidate for purchase. The owners had physically moved the Kelly Bank off Kelly Air Force Base and into the Leon Valley section of San Antonio and tried to convert it from a military bank into a commercial bank. But the owners were in financial difficulty. They contacted McDermott, who told Ensley to negotiate a purchase with the idea of later converting it into a non-bank bank. (A non-bank bank was one that did not issue any commercial loans.) Golembe and Associates' John Mingo evaluated the Kelly Bank, and Ensley negotiated the purchase price as $17 a share, or about $14 million. At this juncture, the U.S. Comptroller of the Currency in Washington, D.C., announced that he would not approve any more non-bank banks. That put the sale on hold, and eventually USAA terminated the negotiations. It wasn't fair to make the Kelly owners wait because of the uncertainty of USAA being able to own a non-bank bank.[11]

On April 14, 1983, the formal process to start up a new USAA bank began. Working with General Counsel Bill McCrae, USAA Vice President, Associate General Counsel Michael D. "Mike" Wagner proposed and delivered the Association's application to Supervisory Agent J. Thomas Hall of the Federal Home Loan Bank Board regional office in Little Rock, Arkansas. In the application, USAA proposed to offer credit and deposit products primarily to the citizens of San Antonio and Bexar County, Texas. The Association included in the application that it would also serve USAA's members. The actual applicant for the bank was USAA's subsidiary, the USAA Development Company, which had been incorporated in Texas on August 10, 1982. Special considerations in the application that were noted included parent USAA's $2 billion backing and 25,000 USAA members in the San Antonio area.[12]

While this was transpiring, McDermott went back to the USAA Board of Directors in May to provide more details on the financial services programs. The banking portions of the briefing were to prove a little controversial in spite of previous Board action to authorize a bank. Mingo briefed the Board on the process of establishing the bank. Next, Ensley briefed the Board on a concept called USAA Golden Eagle Service. It spelled out in great detail the services that the bank could provide in the future and its relationship with other USAA financial services products. At this point, the U.S. Navy officers on the Board raised serious concerns because of the competition it would bring to Naval financial institutions and associations in Washington, D.C.[13] While the others on the Board considered their misgivings, the final decision was to continue to get a bank for USAA. Also, Vic Ferrari briefed about a Buying Service, Jack Saunders about a Discount Brokerage, and Richard Thomas about Real Estate Partnerships.[14] The new ideas and programs raised many questions by the Board members. Board member and retired Rear Admiral H.C. "Bud" Donley recalled, however, that "once we heard his [McDermott's] reasons and his logic . . . he got the votes."[15] Following this Board meeting, McDermott then briefed all USAA managers on the changes that were to sweep USAA.

Meanwhile the process to get approval for a USAA bank continued. The regional office of the Home Loan Bank Board had approved USAA's application and had sent it on to Washington. McDermott hired Larry J. Lanie, a Tulsa, Oklahoma, Guaranty National Bank executive, to run USAA's proposed bank. As predicted earlier by *Forbes*, legislation that would prohibit USAA's entry into the banking field was proceeding in Congress. Time was critical, but hopes were high. Then Mingo called USAA and told Ensley that the USAA request for a charter, that had been approved in Dallas, was now suspended. A Home Loan Bank Board member had learned from a FSLIC employee that USAA owned a mutual funds management company (a securities broker dealer), so the Board opposed the link. Ensley and Wagner flew to Washington and met with Loan Board executive Laura Patriarca. Ensley pointed out to Patriarca that as of September 30, 1983, the Investment Management Company contributed only one-tenth of 1 percent of USAA's consolidated assets.[16] The Loan Board was embarrassed that the previous approval had been followed by a suspension, and was willing to negotiate. When USAA agreed never to put more than 5 percent of its surplus in its broker dealer, the Home Loan Bank approved the charter.

Wary that the proposed legislation being debated in Congress would prohibit USAA from owning a bank, McDermott wanted to have USAA's bank in operation by December 31, 1983. By doing this, USAA hoped to be grandfathered by having started in 1983 and not in 1984. Sam Pinnell, Vice President for Facilities and Services, procured a trailer and modified it for a bank, installing a safe and a service counter. On Tuesday, December 27, a new roadblock appeared. USAA was notified that the application form for establishing a bank had been changed and that the old one was invalid. USAA had to present to the Home Loan Bank Board the new form with all the organizers' signatures on it before the charter could be approved. By Thursday, USAA's revised form was ready to go to Washington when tremendous snowstorms hit, closing many airports. Ensley sent two copies of the revised charter by Federal Express to two different Washington, D.C., addresses and a third with a USAA courier. The courier was told to take whatever planes were flying in the general direction of Washington.

A New Era For USAA — Financial Services

Friday, December 30 was the last business day of the year and USAA wanted the bank to be open by nightfall. By Friday morning, the USAA courier had made it to Washington. He went to the Golembe office to pick up Mingo to go to the Home Loan Bank Board to file the charter. When they arrived, the Bank Board building was locked up because of the storm and a pipe that had frozen and broken inside. Mingo contacted someone he knew personally who worked for the Board and who lived in the D.C. suburbs. The Board employee agreed to come in to the office to process USAA's charter in spite of the storm. They still had to get FSLIC approval, and ran into the same problem. FSLIC was closed. Once again, Mingo talked someone from FSLIC into coming in to process the papers to insure USAA's bank. This done, Mingo called USAA and told Ensley it was okay to open the bank. McDermott, Ensley, and a few others hurried to the trailer serving as the bank. McDermott opened account #0010001-1, and the USAA Federal Savings Bank was in business, barely under the deadline.[17] It was San Antonio's first federal savings bank. Originally capitalized at $20 million by USAA, at the close of 1984, the USAA Federal Savings Bank had more than $49 million in deposits. And it was one of the fastest-growing financial institutions in the nation. One wag said that it was a tribute to the members' faith in USAA that they would send their life savings by mail to be deposited in a bank located in a trailer pointed towards an international border.

One of the plans for the bank from the start was issuing a credit card. USAA applied to both Visa and MasterCard for permission to issue credit cards. MasterCard replied first, and so USAA decided to go with MasterCard for its initial offering. The timeline for the whole credit card operation was accelerated because of Larry Lanie. Having just come from Tulsa, he was aware of a Tulsa bank merging with an Oklahoma City bank and vacating its credit card operations center in Tulsa. Lanie went to Tulsa and arranged for USAA to take over the lease, purchase its computer equipment, and take over the telephone lines into MasterCard's credit card center in Omaha. He even hired seventeen of its twenty-five employees — so USAA had a fully operational credit card center with existing manager Doug McCoy and staffed by experienced employees.[18]

Now USAA was ready to market credit card accounts. McDermott decided to solicit active duty members only at first and to give them pre-approved credit limits based on their military ranks. Further, he did not want credit checks run on any of these officers.[19] On Monday, November 5, 1984, USAA mailed out 240,000 pre-approved credit card applications. The cards had no fee, low interest rates, and a twenty-five-day free float on purchases. By the end of the week, a few hundred applications had arrived.

After processing these applications, everyone at the Tulsa credit card center was ready for the three-day Veteran's Day weekend. On Tuesday morning, Vice President Doug McCoy called Senior Vice President-Retail Banking John Gosnell at the bank in San Antonio. He needed $40,000 immediately to pay the U.S. Post Office for the postage due on about 40,000 applications that had accumulated over the weekend. The response had been phenomenal and overwhelming. USAA hired forty temporaries to process the cards and almost brought down the MasterCard processing center in Omaha. Then USAA ran out of blank plastic cards. They ended up buying MasterCard blanks from a dozen other sources, so the new USAA credit cards were not identical. Before the mailing, Lanie said that the most optimistic response rate predicted was 10 percent, which was good because similar mailings by other companies harvested only 2 to 3 percent returns. The USAA member response was 52 percent.[20]

All the bank operations grew rapidly, and the bank offered a complete line of products and services except for a trust department. It soon became evident to Lanie that he needed a Chief Financial Officer, and he hired Jack Antonini. Antonini was the youngest of four born in Grand Rapids, Michigan, to Italian immigrant parents. One day his father took him to spend a day at the automotive parts manufacturing plant where he worked. The temperature inside the plant was well over 100°, and the plant was very noisy and dirty. After a long day, they walked to the car. His father said, "That's why you are going to get an education."[21] That was a good enough argument for Antonini.

Jack Antonini

Over the objections of his parents, in his second year of college he married his wife Susie, whom he had known since third grade and dated since he was sixteen. Graduating from Farris State University with a degree in accounting, he worked as a certified public accountant and then as a comptroller for a manufacturing plant. From there he went to work with First National Bank in Midland, Texas, and watched other banks collapse and his taken over by Republic Bank. Next he went to Kansas City Thrift. It was there that an executive recruiter sought him to be Chief Financial Officer for the USAA Federal Savings Bank in San Antonio. Having both bank and thrift experience made him an ideal candidate for USAA. After a visit, the thirty-two-year-old Antonini took the job and stayed with the bank for more than ten years. Beginning March 11, 1985, he would run the operations of the bank under four different presidents before becoming president himself.

On September 16, 1985, the USAA Federal Savings Bank opened its doors for business in the newly completed building. The 180,000-square-foot building was located on the northeast sector of the USAA campus with access to Interstate 10. The seventy-some bank employees moved into the building in September, with the Financial Services employees moving in over the next three months. In anticipation of servicing USAA members mailing important papers to safeguard, a large storage area was built into the bank. It was never used for its intended purpose, however.

Ironically, just when the USAA Federal Savings Bank finally looked solid in its new building, it came dangerously close to closing. The USAA members were not only signing up for the new MasterCards at a record rate, but they began using them like crazy. Every day the bank had to wire the money to pay MasterCard for the charges, but it didn't have enough cash to do that. So the USAA parent was making deposits in the bank to cover the MasterCard payments. Lanie asked Antonini to figure out where to get some money. Accumulating savings deposits was an option, but the USAA bank could not match the interest rates the failing thrifts were paying. The result was that the deposits were too small to cover the credit card charges. In addition, since the USAA bank had grown at more than a 25-percent annualized rate for two consecutive quarters, it had to get permission to continue to grow from the Federal Home Loan Bank.

Each year, thrifts had to pass a thriftness test, to insure their viability. With the huge amount of money owed to the bank by credit card users, and the much smaller amount of deposits in the bank, USAA Federal Savings would fail to meet the test. If this occurred, the rules indicated that USAA would have to sell the bank or dissolve it on December 31. Many thrifts were failing because they held large amounts of fixed-rate mortgages at low interest rates. In 1984, to keep the thrifts from failing, the Federal Home Loan Bank had authorized the thrifts to create finance subsidiaries, and to place these mortgages in the newly created subsidiaries. Antonini came up with the idea to do the same thing with the credit card debts owed to USAA. The thriftness test applied only to the principal company and not the subsidiaries — so the USAA Federal Savings Bank would meet the test, if it moved the credit card debts into a subsidiary. The Bank included this provision in its growth application, and the Federal Home Loan Bank of Dallas approved Antonini's concept.

Now USAA had to find $80 million to fund the credit card receivables or the money owed by customers to the bank — the sum total of all the customers' balances. The dramatic — and ironic — precedent to this was that USAA had never borrowed money in all the years it had existed. It even paid cash for massive construction projects, like the home office building. Antonini's idea was to issue commercial paper by December 15 and then to transfer the debt to a new finance subsidiary created for this purpose. (Commercial paper is a type of short-term promissory note that businesses issue to lenders, usually corporate investors, in return for a loan.) One contact Antonini made to sell commercial paper for USAA was Salomon Brothers. Instead of providing cash, the Salomon representative delivered a subtle threat instead. The representative called Lanie and told him that the scheme was going to fail. Nobody had ever funded credit card receivables with commercial paper, let alone through the unusual way USAA was going to use a financial subsidiary. The Salomon Brothers representative told Lanie that they would be willing to buy all the bank's credit card assets. If USAA did not agree, the representative suggested that perhaps USAA would have to close its bank on December 31. Lanie panicked, but was reassured by Antonini.

Antonini had already worked out a funding source with Merrill Lynch in New York, and it looked like everything was going to work out okay. He was able to do this because USAA had developed a means by which the Bank could get credit ratings based on the financial strength of the parent. This resulted in the highest ratings given by Standard & Poor's. On December 7, however, a lawyer working with USAA in Washington, D.C., went to a party. While there, he heard that a new thrift regulation was being issued shortly. It would limit the amount a thrift could put in a subsidiary to 30 percent of its total assets. USAA Federal Savings Bank's credit card receivables were close to 100 percent of its assets, and for Antonini's scheme to work, almost everything had to be moved to a subsidiary. It looked like all might be lost. The next morning, the Washington lawyer faxed the draft 150-page regulation to Antonini. To make a long story short, Antonini found a waiver provision and exercised it successfully. When Antonini flew to Dallas to get approval on the waiver, the Bank Board people there saw the draft regulation and the waiver provision for the first time. Nevertheless, Antonini convinced the Board to approve the waiver.

To save the Bank, Merrill Lynch still had to sell the $80 million worth of USAA's commercial paper before the end of the year. It was December 31 and Merrill Lynch found erratic interest rates and buyers leery of unknown USAA, but succeeded nonetheless. With the financial markets closing at noon, Merrill Lynch notified relieved USAA bankers that it had sold the paper. But Antonini had a nagging feeling and checked the total dollars actually paid. The total had to include 60 percent of assets in a qualifying investment — and it did not. It was about $3 million short because of the fluctuating interest rates. When a panicked Antonini called Merrill Lynch, he was told it was too late — that the market was almost closed. With just seven seconds to go, before USAA would have had to sell the bank, Merrill Lynch agreed to buy the $3 million worth of the commercial paper itself. Now the Bank had the right numbers to pass the IRS thriftness test. "A very exciting day!" remembered Antonini.[22] The USAA Federal Savings Bank was here to stay.

Homer Holland, who joined the USAA Board of Directors in August 1985, recalled his introduction into the USAA service culture in discussions about the Bank. Holland was the first non-career officer or separated officer to serve on the USAA Board.

A NEW ERA FOR USAA — FINANCIAL SERVICES

Graduating from West Point in the class of 1963, he spent eight years in the Army, including a year in Vietnam. Leaving the Army in 1971, he began a career in banking with the First National Bank of Chicago and later built a reputation on turning troubled banks around. In 1984, Holland was approached by an executive recruiter for a management position at USAA. While he was not interested, he did come to USAA to meet McDermott and to consult on the Bank. Shortly thereafter, McDermott asked Holland to join the USAA Board of Directors. He accepted and that gave McDermott bank expertise on the Board as well as a separated officer.

After Holland's strong focus on the bottom line in the banking business, he was amazed that USAA wanted a credit card business located in Texas. A bank in Texas could only make 12 percent interest at that time, while most other states' laws set an 18 percent ceiling. When he raised this question, McDermott told him that if USAA could make money at 12 percent, that was in the "best interest of the member." Holland's first thought was that naivete in the business world was alive and well in Texas. But he soon realized that USAA was actually far ahead of most companies in business sense. In "the best interest of the member" usually turned out to be in the best interest of the Association too.[23]

The Bank grew rapidly and was very successful. In 1985, assets grew more than $250 million and deposit accounts increased by more than 17,000. At the end of 1986, the Bank reported more than $500 million in assets and over 500,000 credit cards in force. The following year, assets climbed to over $1 billion and more than one million USAA MasterCards resided in members' wallets and purses. The confidence that the Association's members had in USAA and its Bank was well-placed in the face of massive failures of other thrift institutions. At the end of 1987, the USAA Federal Savings Bank received its twelfth consecutive quarterly "Superior" rating for financial soundness from *S&L — Savings Bank Financial Quarterly.*

A TRADITION OF SERVICE

Sheshunoff and Company, a rating service for financial institutions, gave the Bank its highest "A+" rating. The commercial paper of the Bank also received the highest ratings given by Standard & Poor's (A-1+) and Moody's Investor Service (p-1). The Los Angeles-based *Nilson Report* called the USAA MasterCard the "best card buy" of all the nation's standard credit cards.

The next step USAA made in the credit card business was to issue a gold card. In the middle eighties, virtually all banks issuing gold cards were charging an annual fee. This fee paid for enhancements with the card such as common carrier life insurance, and later, free rental car liability and collision insurance. Under Texas law, a bank couldn't charge an annual fee and interest. In 1987, Senator Jake Garn, R-Utah, introduced an amendment to the Bank Holding Company Act to enable troubled Utah industrial loan companies to survive. The amendment permitted the creation of banks whose only purpose was to issue credit cards. Mike Wagner and Jack Antonini flew to Utah to see the state banking commissioner to try to get a Utah charter. Fearing a difficulty in explaining what USAA was and why it wanted a charter, Wagner and Antonini were delighted when the commissioner pulled a USAA MasterCard out of his wallet. The application was approved quickly, but it took until May 31, 1988, to get FDIC approval. Then the USAA Financial Services Association (FSA) opened its doors. It issued its first gold card in June 1988. In 1990, USAA also began offering a Visa card because members found it easier to use than a MasterCard in Europe at that time. The gold card proved to be very successful for the whole banking industry, and the cost of enhancements fell considerably. By 1991, USAA discovered it could offer its gold card at no annual fee and still make a profit. It then closed down the USAA FSA and consolidated the USAA standard and gold credit card operations in San Antonio.[24]

* * * *

A New Era For USAA — Financial Services

Meanwhile, the Investment Management Company (IMCO), under George Sykes, continued to manage USAA's investment portfolio successfully. In 1981, the USAA Property and Casualty companies received 89 percent of their net income from the IMCO investments. By 1989, the USAA equity portfolio exceeded $6 billion. USAA's mutual fund family grew in diversity in response to member requests. The dollar growth in the mutual funds was a positive vote by the members that the Association was offering the right things and combining them with excellent service.

What made the development of new mutual funds relatively easy was a change in structure in 1980. Prior to this time, each new mutual fund required a separate subsidiary. Wagner recommended a new series company arrangement that Boston Company had pioneered in the 1970s. This development permitted organization of new mutual funds by simply a Board of Directors resolution. USAA merged the two existing mutual fund companies into the USAA Mutual Fund Inc. An affiliate of IMCO, this new entity could begin new funds as management and membership desired.

In 1981, USAA added a money market fund and the Sunbelt Era Fund for the more aggressive, risk-oriented members. By 1982, USAA had seven mutual funds, and assets grew from $211 million to $334 million. Tax-exempt funds filled a need expressed by many members. Financial publications such as *Money* magazine routinely noted the solid performance of the USAA mutual funds. In 1989,

Lieutenant General Laurence "Bill" Craigie, USAF (Ret.)

A Tradition Of Service

USAA added two state tax-free funds for California investors. Retired Air Force Lt. General Laurence "Bill" Craigie's appeal to McDermott hastened the establishment of these funds already under consideration. The still-active pilot, at eighty-seven years of age, became the first investor in the USAA California Bond Fund. USAA's offer to allow California members to transfer monies from other USAA mutual funds at no cost was successful. Ken Willman, the Tax Exempt Investments Vice President, reported at a management meeting that USAA's first state tax-free funds were in heavy demand, and they soon met the $100-million break-even point.[25]

The first investor in USAA's Florida Fund also had an interesting background. At the celebration of the fund's opening, he enthralled the USAA participants with his story. Retired Air Force Lieutenant Colonel James Harvey Martin had been assigned to P-40s and his squadron was sent to Australia. Shot down over water by Japanese fighters, he plunged into the ocean and the plane sank immediately. When the aircraft settled in about fifty feet of water, he sat quietly while sea water poured into his cockpit. He put his oxygen mask on and when the cockpit was full, he opened the canopy and swam to the surface. Here was a man who wouldn't panic at a sudden downturn in the market.

On October 19, 1987, the stock market crested after waffling and sending signals for a couple of weeks. The Dow Jones industrial average plunged 508 points, or about 23 percent, wiping out $500 billion in amassed wealth in hours. Actually, since August 25, the Dow had lost about $1 trillion in equity value. Small investors panicked, and *Money* magazine chronicled the futile efforts of many who could not even get their brokers to talk to them. Fidelity's Magellan Fund lost $4 billion in the first three weeks of October. The overall Fidelity staff received about 480,000 phone calls on October 19 and 20.[26] At USAA, the Discount Brokerage was exceedingly busy, but handled the workload. IMCO Executive Vice

A New Era For USAA — Financial Services

President Mickey Roth was especially pleased with the performance of USAA's diversified Cornerstone Fund, which passed the test both in the Bull Market of 1986 and in the Crash. The major impact on USAA itself was on the surplus. McDermott announced to the Board following the Crash that the annual projection for the Association's surplus ratio had been 90 percent. It now was closer to 82 percent, but still the best in the industry. The other impact was on USAA investments. The Association had pegged its equity investments at a percentage of the surplus. When the investments fell below this percentage, Roth advised McDermott that USAA should buy. McDermott agreed.[27]

The rapid growth required tremendous effort to keep the service levels to IMCO customers at a satisfactory level. USAA changed its transfer agent account to State Street Bank and Trust Company as a basic step. With over 100,000 accounts on the books, Sykes told *Highlights* that USAA could run its own transfer agency.[28] On February 6, 1984, USAA opened its agency under Assistant Vice President Bill Flynn. In another program, Senior Vice President Jack Saunders led the development of a discount brokerage that began on September 15, 1983. Over 4,100 members opened accounts by the end of 1983, and over 15,000 one year later. This brokerage met the desires of members who wished to make their own investment decisions. Continuing efforts in cost reduction lowered the expense ratio steadily, making the funds a more attractive purchase. In 1988, the Discount Brokerage improved its services by adding a new software "back office environment" system that enabled customer service representatives to handle customer accounts with more efficiency and accuracy.

In 1988, IMCO took other major steps in improving service to customers. The Investronic plan enabled investors to make regular investments to their mutual fund accounts by electronic debiting of their own bank accounts. InveStart allowed investors to open a Cornerstone Mutual Fund account with $100 and to make monthly investments of as little as $50. The new program was a tremendous benefit for new investors with little disposable income, who wanted to begin building for their futures. USAA Touchline was an automated telephone information system designed to enable members to keep up with the status of their mutual fund investments. All of these service enhancements made investing in USAA's funds easier and more efficient, accelerating the growth of the funds. By the end of the decade, IMCO had 417,000 individual accounts, thirteen mutual funds and over $10 billion in total assets.

In such a period of rapid growth, it would be easy for service to individuals to slip. Not so, wrote twenty-seven-year member, retired Army Major Charles Davis to McDermott in April 1988. He had purchased a new car and paid for it with an old check from a USAA Money Market Account he had previously closed. A USAA employee called Davis and told him that USAA had honored the "bad" check and applied it to another of his USAA accounts. "No pain — no strain — no bad check," he wrote. He asked rhetorically whether any other business in the country would give service like this. He answered his own question by pledging to stay with USAA at least another twenty-seven years.[29]

Mickey Roth

On January 1, 1990, Michael J.C. "Mickey" Roth became President and CEO of the Investment Management Division. Roth was born in El Paso and was raised there. His father gave him the nickname "Mickey" after boxer Mickey Walker. He had two boyhood interests — flying and the stock market. When he was a young boy, his father often took him to the office of E.F. Hutton. Sitting in comfortable easy chairs, investors could watch the Hutton employees change the stock quotations on a huge chalkboard. Flying was his first love, however, and he never believed he would get into business.

Roth graduated in 1963 from the U.S. Air Force Academy where he was the Cadet Wing Commander. He flew A-26s on 146 combat missions in Southeast Asia, principally over Laos, receiving the Silver Star and Distinguished Flying Cross with seven oak leaf clusters. He separated from the Air Force in 1972 and entered the business world as a trust officer at a bank in El Paso. He joined USAA in 1978 as a fixed income securities analyst. He rose rapidly through a succession of promotions in the investments area, culminating in his selection as USAA's investment chief.

* * * *

The Association's real estate program also developed rapidly in the eighties. USAA's formal entry into real estate investments began in early 1982. Ensley briefed the Board of Directors on the advantages of investing in mortgages and equity real estate. These included higher yields, capital gains, and a hedge against inflation. Further, real estate would give the Association one more element to spread the risk. This briefing included an analysis of twenty large life insurance companies and the role real estate played in their investment portfolios. The Board agreed to establishing an office of Vice President-Real Estate Investments and made it effective immediately.[30] Terrie W. Thompson headed this new program.

To serve as a vehicle for making real estate investments, the Board approved the formation of a new subsidiary, the USAA Development Company (DEVCO) which was incorporated under the laws of Texas on August 10, 1982. The next day DEVCO held its organizational meeting and Ensley was elected president. In October,

Ensley briefed the first new DEVCO product — Real Estate Limited Partnership — to the Investment Management Company's (IMCO) Board of Directors. Ensley told the IMCO Board that this tax savings product would add a new element to USAA's full financial services offerings. He proposed that DEVCO be the general partner and IMCO act as underwriter and sales agent with Pacific Mutual serving as the real estate advisor. The IMCO Board approved the concept unanimously.[31]

DEVCO then began making real estate investments for the USAA Group. By February 1983, McDermott reported that DEVCO had contracts signed for $36 million with another $20 million in process. As this arm of USAA's business grew, McDermott decided that he wanted a new name for DEVCO to better reflect its role at USAA. At its May 12, 1983, meeting, the DEVCO Board changed its corporate name to the USAA Financial Services Company (FINCO). All USAA's non-insurance companies that had considerable assets were aligned under this newest subsidiary. It set up a structure to permit access to the capital markets and to facilitate borrowing from these. This eventually was to become CAPCO.

On July 11, 1983, the initial mailing on a Real Estate Partnership was sent to all USAA members in the San Antonio area. The 13.6-percent response was better than expected and the Association extended the offering nationally. This first limited partnership's offering of $25 million sold quickly and Thompson packaged USAA Income Properties II. It went on sale May 1, 1984.[32] That year USAA also became an equity partner in developing the Austin (Texas) Marriott Hotel.

Meanwhile, McDermott had asked Thompson to look into the possibility of developing a high-quality shopping center and a 300-room first-class hotel on the northwest end of the USAA campus. The development was to be a joint (50/50) venture with the Edward DeBartolo Corporation of Youngstown, Ohio.[33] DeBartolo was working plans for two other malls at the same time. Of these two, only

A New Era For USAA — Financial Services

one materialized — the Rivercenter Mall in downtown San Antonio. In February 1986, McDermott told the Board that after a twenty-two-month study, the plans for a mall development on the USAA property were dead. He based the decision on two main factors. First was the traffic congestion that the projected USAA work force growth along with the mall traffic would bring. Without moving employees in the regional offices, USAA employees could be in the 12,000-to-14,000 range by 1995. Second was the entry into the San Antonio market of Saks Fifth Avenue and Marshall Fields, which opened for business in North Star Mall.[34] USAA's mall would not be unique in having "high-end" stores as tenants.

At the same 1986 meeting, McDermott announced that USAA had entered a partnership venture with Redland Development Company and Worth Development Company. The partnership intended to develop approximately 806 acres of land at the intersection of Interstate 10 and Loop 1604, a few miles north of the home office. McDermott's plans were to develop a conference center with a golf course and retirement area on one side of the interstate and a large shopping mall on the other. Called "La Cantera," the development was expected to take fifteen to twenty years to complete.[35] This development was expanded at a later date to include plans for a musical show park in partnership with Opryland USA.

Growth of the real estate function and confusion with other USAA lines resulted in another name change for the real estate corporate entity. Effective on March 1, 1986, the USAA Financial Services Company became the USAA Real Estate Company with H. Drake Leddy as its president. Leddy was previously a junior partner with Arthur Anderson and Company. McDermott brought Leddy in to evaluate USAA's real estate transactions and ended up hiring him to head the company and report to Michael K. Conn, who was promoted to head the Financial Services Division.[36]

In the middle eighties, McDermott watched the development of a growth industry developing and operating residential communities for retired and the elderly. On May 2, 1987, he wrote a memo to George Ensley asking him to make a comprehensive study on the feasibility of doing the same for USAA members. He noted that the World War II membership was already in the right market age and that the Korean War group would soon follow. He looked for the synergism of a real estate investment for USAA, mortgage financing from the bank, and homeowner or condominium insurance.

In March 1985, Thomas R. Brennan of Retirement Resources Associates briefed the Board. Brennan was a 1963 graduate of West Point, a USAA member, and a consultant for retirement centers since 1976. A survey of USAA members suggested that 23 percent would be interested in moving into a retirement community within five years. More than 70 percent of the members responded favorably to the concept of USAA building retirement centers for members. In Brennan's view, USAA's entry into retirement residences would provide an economic return, positive public relations, and a service

USAA Towers

to the membership. He recommended six different sites — San Antonio, Washington, D.C., San Diego, Tampa, Sacramento, and Colorado Springs. After serious discussion about competition in the various areas, the Board voted to support the retirement project beginning at the San Antonio location.

On October 30, 1986, the ground was broken for the USAA Towers. Located near Fort Sam Houston in San Antonio, the USAA Towers was designed as a twenty-three-story structure with 353 upper-scale residences and many amenities for security and a com-

Interior Pedestrian Mall, USAA Towers

fortable quality of life. Increasing the attractiveness of the residence site was the co-location of a 138-bed Healthcare Center, although not part of the USAA Towers. At first, the residences were sold in a cooperative ownership arrangement to USAA members and their parents aged fifty-five or over. Initial marketing was to 38,000 USAA members over age sixty-two. The facility opened for business on October 9, 1988. Initial prices ranged from $86,000 to $590,000, with the average cost of $170,000. The monthly service fee varied by the size of the residence.[37]

Those who bought were delighted by the facility, but in spite of various incentives offered, completed sales were slower than expected. In 1987, after a presentation by Leddy, the Board voted to extend eligibility to purchase residences to other than USAA members when it was in the best interest of the membership.[38] Later, based on experience with sales at the USAA Towers and the intense competition in the retirement community industry, USAA's Board decided not to support any more retirement communities.

In their early years, the youthful subsidiaries of USAA demonstrated that they needed additional transfusions of capital to stay viable. This was not unexpected, but the number of requirements and the large amounts demanded a structural change at USAA. Having the USAA Board of Directors meet each time to allocate surplus or other company funds to the subsidiaries was awkward and inefficient. The incessant need of the USAA Federal Savings Bank for loans to cover its growth in member credit card charges forced a solution.

USAA's answer to the funding problem was the creation of the USAA Capital Corporation (CAPCO). On August 8, 1987, the USAA Board of Directors approved the use of CAPCO to facilitate access to foreign and domestic capital markets. It would also enhance the capability for inter-company funding within the USAA Group.[39] All of USAA's non-insurance subsidiaries signed an inter-

A NEW ERA FOR USAA — FINANCIAL SERVICES

company funding agreement with CAPCO that was effective May 1, 1988. The agreement not only made provisions for loans to the subsidiaries, but also for the subsidiaries to loan excess monies to CAPCO. The first President of CAPCO was David H. Roe. The funds involved were significant. In the year 1990, CAPCO authorized USAA subsidiaries collectively to borrow over $2 billion from it.[40]

One impact of the USAA diversification not anticipated earlier was the need to convert to a new accounting system. In 1985, the USAA Group converted to GAAP (General Accepted Accounting Principles) to provide a better measure of comparability among the various USAA companies. The major change brought about by the system was an approximate 2 percent increase in the property and casualty bottom line and a 2.5 percent increase in the Life Company. The previous system used was the SAP (Statutory Accounting Principles) which lent itself primarily to insurance accounting.[41]

* * * *

The explosion of new products and services led to serious thinking about future directions for USAA. At the 1985 mid-year property and casualty planning conference, the participants discussed the Long-Range System Plan at the end of its five-year point in the cycle. McDermott had also visited with the Long Range Planning Group at IBM to discuss systems support for his financial services expansion. Half of the Group's members, as well as IBM CEO John Akers, were USAA members. The Group discussed Sears, American Express, and other groups that were trying to build financial service empires, but it believed USAA couldn't make it because of its limited niche market. McDermott didn't agree because he felt USAA could make a deep penetration in the market it had available.[42] Decisions on the future of information systems development had to follow USAA's operational plans. McDermott decided that it was time to take an in-depth look at USAA. He wanted to know where USAA should be in the year 2000 and how to get there. To do this, McDermott appointed Jim Patterson, Senior Vice President, Information Systems, to head a task force called "Vision 2000." This was a full-time project for Patterson and he was relieved of other responsibilities.[43] Don Lasher took his place in Information Systems.

Jim Patterson

Patterson selected a team from across the company and held the first meeting of the Vision 2000 Task Force on June 26, 1985. McDermott's charge to the Task Force was to develop an operational scenario that described the types and mix of products and services for the year 2000 and beyond. He wanted a priority on enhancing efficiency and increasing synergy and integration between twelve various lines of business at USAA. The Task Force provided a guide to products, information systems, delivery systems, and supporting functions.[44]

In the following months, Patterson's Task Force interviewed employees at all levels, conducted member focus groups, and obtained information from more than fifty companies. The group found USAA's membership, employees, and financial strength tops and praised the Association's innovative spirit and leadership in technology. Major concerns included developing real synergy and improved communications among USAA's corporate entities. Principal recommendations included consolidation of corporate marketing under the Chief of Staff, encouraging members to establish a banking relationship, and continued leadership in technology. Perhaps most far-reaching was the philosophical shift of member-contact employees from just processing transactions to participating in Event-Oriented Service (EOS).[45]

At the 1986 USAA Strategic Planning Conference, EOS was adopted as a strategic direction for USAA. This concept envisioned providing members with complementary and coordinated products and services related to key life events. These were specific milestones such as marriage, the birth of a child, or retirement. A cross-USAA committee was put together to develop the concept. Under Chief of Staff Staser Holcomb's guidance, it presented its findings to McDermott and the Executive Council in early 1989. The committee identified twenty-nine member life events that could be addressed by maintaining fifteen critical data elements in each member's customer information file. To make the program work required EOS advertising, integrated data systems with communications support, and EOS employee training. Such a program was not cheap, and costs were a key issue. The biggest impact on systems was on the Customer Data Base Systems with its Customer Information File rather than on Applications Systems, designed to support specific business lines. This overall program not only helped improve the "one company image" that McDermott wanted, but also encouraged USAA lines of business to work more closely with each other. [46]

* * * *

Visions and plans, no matter how brilliant in conception, are useless without the capacity to put them into action. McDermott always realized that the key to his plans for the Association lay in the employees' ability and desire to carry them out. Providing a wonderful working environment made the employees feel good about their jobs and themselves. The careful workplace design also helped bring about and maintain high productivity. USAA's attention to employee pay and benefits had always been excellent, and this continued. As the children of the sixties entered the work force, however, different benefit issues surfaced.

Increasing attention was paid to individual needs and health issues. An active counseling program was available for individuals in need. The formal program was operated out of the USAA Counseling Office managed by Barbara Knight, and later Pat Cusik. Most employees brought problems in that were work-related or in the area of career counseling. Some employees became frustrated when they did not get selected for positions posted through the Job Opportunity Program (JOP). In this case, the counselor talked to them about interviewing techniques and improving their personal preparation for new opportunities. The counselors also heard occasional personal problems and discrimination complaints. Supervisors were encouraged to be more sensitive, and received training in ways to be so. Also, USAA ombudsman Bob Gaylor was available for those frustrated by the normal channels. By 1986, USAA added Employee Assistance Programs for employees seeking help with alcohol or drug abuse problems. Towards the end of the decade, the office added an extensive childcare facility referral service.

Education and training had always been important for employees to prepare for future opportunities. The emphasis continued with extensive publicity in *Highlights* on tuition reimbursement and course offerings in both the general education and professional development areas. Education Fairs staffed by representatives of various educational programs were very effective. A business reading club focusing on key books on business and management such as Tom Peters's *In Search of Excellence* encouraged employees to read. USAA General Counsel Bill McCrae sponsored the club, which was for all employees, not just executives. USAA was the only company in the U.S. to offer on-site CLEP (College-Level Examination) testing.

In 1986, USAA established a new bonus program to encourage employees to pursue professional designations. They received cash for each exam passed. Bill Bowen, Assistant Vice President for Train-

A New Era For USAA — Financial Services

ing and Development, praised the program, which combined self-development and knowledge directly related to the employees' jobs. The Toastmaster clubs in San Antonio and the regional offices helped employees build confidence and improve communication skills. In one speech, Kathy Blair, Northeast Sales Representative, pointed out that these clubs were "an investment in the future." And she was right.[47] Annual Employee Achievement Breakfasts recognized the completed college degrees and professional designations of the employees and helped build pride in their accomplishments. By 1989, so many employees were being honored that the breakfasts were held twice each year.

Training also became increasingly sophisticated and more responsive to employees' needs. One innovation was called "House Calls"

Sandy Lengel, keynote speaker for USAA's Sixth Annual Employee Achievement Breakfast. Lengel earned her CPCU designation after 3 ½ years of study.

because training specialists went to the work areas to provide training. Short courses on topics like job stress and handling anger were well-received and effective. One of the projects on the Long Range Systems Plan was Computer-Assisted Instruction, which the training department enthusiastically supported. The Auto Technical Training Center gave hands-on training to claims adjusters and appraisers on such things as repairing unitized frame automobiles. The wide variety and excellence of the training was a major contributor to serving USAA's members by making the employees knowledgeable and confident.

McDermott had become especially interested in health as a result of his own circulatory problems and as health issues became dominant in the eighties. The physical fitness centers were included in the buildings primarily for health and secondarily for fun. Sneakers for health triumphed over the strict dress code. Over the decade, questions and answers on USAA's dress code appeared in *Highlights*. The answer to the quest for more informal dress was always in favor of *Dress for Success* rules. The only exception in the decade was made in 1988, when employees were authorized to wear sneakers while walking for exercise on the service level of the main office building.

Smoking became a major concern and health initiative. USAA had always supported the Great American Smoke Out each year, calling for employees to reconsider their smoking habits, but that voluntary program had minimal impact. In November 1986, USAA announced a limited no-smoking policy that applied to general access areas such as the auditorium, waiting line areas, and the company store. Sensitive or hazardous work areas were also included. USAA's Wellness Committee, made up of employees, recommended more limits. In 1987, many lounges became smoke-free, cigarette vending machines disappeared, and Health Services began offering financially subsidized smoking cessation programs. As of January

1, 1988, smoking was no longer permitted in work areas. Herb Emanuel, Vice President, Human Resources, took most of the heat from frustrated smokers who found areas available for smoking steadily disappearing. Incidentally, Emanuel was a heavy chain smoker who quit smoking cold turkey as an example for the employees. On September 4, 1990, USAA became totally smoke-free. Even smoking in parked cars in the garages was not acceptable. Many of the approximately 10 percent of USAA's employees who still smoked had difficulty with the new policy. For awhile, break and lunch times resulted in more-than-normal traffic around USAA sites as the smokers took to the road to indulge in their habit. While all were not happy, the USAA workplaces were much more healthy than prior to the no-smoking rule.

The Wellness Committee also had a positive impact on the ARA-run cafeterias. ARA Services worked with the Committee and the USAA staff to introduce healthy choices to the daily menus. Low-fat and low-salt popcorn was offered in addition to the buttery, salty variety everyone enjoyed at the movies or the ball game. The "Treat Yourself Right" meal concept ensured at least one meal available on each day's menu for those who wanted to eat more healthy. McDermott agreed with these programs, and his diet was laden with tuna fish, salmon, and fruit because of his circulatory problems. He loved chocolate, however, and spent considerable effort sneaking his favorite in spite of the active policing by his wife, Alice, and his Executive Assistant, Carolyn Olivera. Olivera related that when she had to pack his office for a move, she found caches of chocolate candy hidden behind books and in other unlikely places.

Many other benefits made working at USAA enjoyable and life easier. "Dinner Express" was especially popular. At the end of each workday, USAA employees could buy a variety of prepared foods to go including a family-pack dinner. This dinner provided an entree, two vegetables, and a roll for about $10 for a family of four.

A Tradition Of Service

Even pizza-to-go was added later. Named after Vic Ferrari, it was called "Vittorio's — The Ferrari of Pizza." Also added in later years was a full line of fresh groceries, milk, bread, and delicatessen items. Employees could purchase desserts or breads or even special-order cakes baked on the premises for birthdays and other special occasions.

Special activities also generated enjoyable times for the employees. Teamfest and Fiesta were held on the USAA campus and featured games, food, and fun. The Annual Christmas Party was held in the USAA building at first, and then shifted to San Antonio's Convention Center when the numbers attending grew too large. All the regional offices held similar events.

Discounts on tickets for admission to events ranging from the San Antonio Spurs to the movies were available at the cashier's cage. Merchant discounts negotiated by employee activity special-

Teamfest was held on the USAA campus and gave employees and their families an opportunity to enjoy themselves with their coworkers.

A NEW ERA FOR USAA — FINANCIAL SERVICES

Above: "Land skiing" was a popular activity at Teamfest.
Below: Debbie White with Spurs' mascot, the Coyote.

ist Debbie (Charo) White were also available.

In a 1989 *U.S. News & World Report* feature, "You're in the Office of the Future Now," Beth Brophy highlighted USAA's efforts in creating an outstanding workplace for the employees. Vice President Alice Gannon praised things like the four-day workweek and Dinner Express as "making all the difference in the world" in finding a balance between duties on the job and duties at home. To sum up why he provided such a workplace, McDermott pointed out that "we spend more hours at work than we do at home or anyplace else, so the environment should be pleasant."[48] The employees seemed to agree, because turnover continued to drop and attendance levels were among the highest in the industry. Perhaps that was even a better indication than the rally sponsored by the Employee Activities Committee in 1986 to thank McDermott for his support. San Antonio Mayor Henry Cisneros attended, reading a city proclamation declaring January 15 as "McD Day."

A Tradition Of Service

San Antonio Mayor Henry Cisneros (left) with Robert McDermott on "McD Day"

The employees responded to the positive attitude of the company and provided outstanding service. In 1986, Regional Vice President for the Pacific Region Bill Cooney occasionally listened in on service representatives' telephone calls with members. The representatives knew their calls might be monitored, but never knew exactly when anyone was listening. At the time, the average time for a telephone call was 4.9 minutes, and the guideline was to keep each call as short as possible while still taking care of the member. On his first "eavesdropping" call of the day, Cooney listened to an eighty-year-old woman ramble on about a number of things. The employee was patient, but was obviously trying to bring the conversation to a conclusion. When she asked precisely how she could help the member, the woman confessed that she was a new widow and was confused and frightened. She had a number of USAA matters scattered over the house and didn't know what to do with them.

The USAA employee told her to take her time, collect them, and bring them to the phone. She'd wait. With the fascinated Cooney still on the line, the representative and the widow straightened out all the problems which included various USAA matters — not just property and casualty. One hour and five minutes later they finished. The grateful widow told the employee that their time together in giving her peace of mind was the nicest thing that had happened to her since her husband's death. Cooney later praised the employee for going against the guidelines for shorter calls, because she had made the right decision. The incident deeply affected Cooney, and strengthened his resolve to make sure that USAA members continued to be served well. And to make this happen, he was determined to ensure that the employees were well cared for too.

Cooney was raised in Pennsylvania where his father was in the textile manufacturing business. After three years in a Catholic high school in Philadelphia, the family moved to Emmaus, Pennsylvania, in the Pennsylvania Dutch country. He played football and baseball in high school. After graduating from high school, he worked during the day and went to college at night. Passing required exams, he entered a navigator aviation cadet program, got commissioned in March 1955, and married Fran McAuley one week later. Three years after that he went to flight school. He continued to pick up college courses through evening programs, and he eventually graduated from Park College in Kansas City under the Air Force Bootstrap program.

During his career, he qualified in a number of aircraft including the B-57 and the RF-4 reconnaissance aircraft. During an unaccompanied tour as Chief of Reconnaissance for Korea, he had one of the more interesting opportunities in his service career. He was sent to Kunsan Air Base as a services squadron commander for an outfit beset with race riots. Two previous commanders had already been fired. The first night, Cooney went to the dining hall at 3 a.m. and talked to a cook there. The young African American didn't like cook-

Bill Cooney

ing and said that no one would listen to "us Black guys." He told Cooney that what he really wanted to do was be a driver in the motor pool. Cooney told the incredulous airman to report to the motor pool at eight the same day. He did the same thing the next night to another airman. The Director of Personnel was in consternation, but did the paperwork to back up Cooney's words. The word spread quickly throughout the base. The next day when another racial brawl started in the barracks, the African-American leaders halted the brawl and told the others to give Cooney a chance. Pulling a midnight requisition on a closed American fighter base in Japan, he filled twenty C-123s with items to improve his squadron domain. Cooney succeeded in calming the base and went on to a successful career, retiring as a brigadier general. In 1985, he ended up at USAA because of the recommendation of his former wing commander at Craig Air Force Base, Charles Bishop. After a short stint as a Special Assistant to McDermott, Cooney became the Regional Vice President for the North Central Region.[49]

* * * *

Assisting employees to do a better job at providing service and helping USAA save money were continuous improvements in technology. Projects originally outlined in the Long Range Systems Plan came on line, as did others that were not included. For example, an update in the customer accounting system was able to institute penalties for delinquent accounts. This change alone generated an additional $10 million annually for USAA. Some employees had to work on three different terminals on their desks. They found relief and increased productivity when new software combined functions onto one terminal. Adding an IBM 3090, Model 200 computer in 1985 almost doubled USAA's processing power, according to Rueben Machado, Vice President of the Computer Center.[50] Office automation made contact among USAA employees quick and accurate. Each change came with appropriate training and resulted in improved service and productivity.

One of the more interesting and important technical innovations was the development of the IMAGE processing system. IMAGE enabled a document to be transferred directly to computer optical disk for storage and instant recall. Its genesis was a project developed jointly, but slowly, by 3M and USAA. Jim Patterson and Mike Howard, unhappy with the progress, went to California to visit with Ted Smith, President of File Net System. USAA contracted with File Net to develop an extended prototype at USAA. It would next help develop a request for proposal for a USAA IMAGE system. When the bids came in to develop the system, IBM beat out 3M because it bid less than the cost. In Howard's opinion, IBM saw the potential for the technology and bet on the future.[51]

In 1988, IBM CEO and USAA member John Akers came to USAA for the dedication of USAA's IMAGE system. IBM commended USAA for its role in bringing the system on line at least two years sooner than if IBM had done it alone. At first, USAA had twenty-five IBM IMAGE system display terminals installed in Property and Casualty policy service. This was a significant step on the McDermott 1969 challenge of a "paperless company." One disk stored the equivalent of eighteen file cabinets of information. By July 1990, there were 1,400 terminals online. Each day USAA processed 10,000 new letters into the system. It also stored more than 500,000 pages of outgoing policies and correspondence. Early in 1997, over one billion pages of information were stored on the system.

A TRADITION OF SERVICE

Because the incoming mail for policy service is scanned into the IMAGE system in the mailroom, it is available to all authorized users on the system very quickly. When the system first came on line, a member mailed a policy change request on a Friday and needed action taken by the following Tuesday. On Monday, he called USAA's 800 number and tried to explain his situation to the representative who answered the phone. The representative asked for his member number. As luck would have it, the letter had arrived and had already been scanned into the system. "I have your letter in front of me sir," she politely told the member. She then told him that everything had been done as he wished. The member was amazed that he reached the employee who had his letter. He hung up, but called again because his surprise had made him forget to touch upon another point. He asked for the same representative, whom he could not identify, but a different representative who answered suggested that she could probably help him. When she told him that she also had his letter right in front of her, the member was dumbfounded. How could a letter mailed on Friday be in multiple copies and all over USAA three days later on Monday? In a 1994 interview, then Vice President George A. McCall said that the IMAGE system helped fulfill a slogan that guided systems development, "Customer Convenient, Operator Efficient, and Personal."[52]

In February 1989, *American Programmer* featured an article by Ed Yourdon that called USAA "An Exemplary Data Processing Organization." He praised USAA for melding together technological leadership with a people orientation. Yourdon related advice that Don Lasher, USAA's Chief Information Systems Officer, passed on to his managers. Lasher encouraged them to help subordinates plan career growth as well as to solve present-day problems. Yourdon also praised McDermott because of his positive support for USAA's technological development and his support of the people. Yourdon's final comment on USAA's employees was, "They're proud to work

A New Era For USAA — Financial Services

there [USAA] and I can see why."

Advanced technology was also transforming other parts of USAA. In 1986, the Corporate Business Transaction system included a provision to use the U.S. Post Office's new Zip-plus-four codes. By doing this, USAA received a savings from the Post Office of 4.5 cents on each first-class letter. Since USAA sent out 30 million pieces of first-class mail annually at that time, the savings was significant. Presorting mail by Zip code before taking it to the Post Office saved additional money. And the Association's efforts in upgrading telephone service transformed the community as well as the company. USAA had been the catalyst in the upgrading of Southwestern Bell's telephone system to an integrated network of fiber-optics, electronics, and digital switching and satellite transmission capabilities. By the end of 1988, San Antonio was 100-percent digital, obviating the use of operator assistance for long distance calls.[53] The tremendous communications capabilities built by Southwestern Bell made San Antonio a telemarketing center in the nineties.

* * * *

As USAA grew in size, reputation, and financial strength, so grew the requests for funding for worthy causes. A request by the Air War College for $150,000 to endow a foreign officers' conference prodded McDermott to go to the Board. To help respond to these requests, he asked the Board to state explicitly USAA's philosophy of giving. The Board reconfirmed the policy it had established in 1969. USAA could contribute an amount equal to the employees' United Way contributions, with at least half of that amount going to United Way. The contributions were to be used to maintain and improve the quality of life in the communities in which USAA employees lived.[54] This charitable contributions budget formula remained in effect until 1990, when McDermott decided that USAA's charitable contribution levels were much lower than they should have been given USAA's size. The USAA employees' per-

A TRADITION OF SERVICE

sonal contributions to United Way were without peer, but in his view, USAA's matching was insufficient to cover the Association's responsibility to the community.[55] As a result, the Board agreed to establish the total budget at a specific percentage of pre-tax net income, rather than tying it to the employees' donations to United Way. It also directed that within this budget, USAA contribute to United Ways in San Antonio and regional office locations. The amount contributed was to be one-half of what the employees personally contributed to the United Way.[56]

In addition to the more narrowly defined corporate contributions program, USAA occasionally sponsored other unusual projects for the good of the nation's citizens. One of these was a series of television documentaries produced by Arnold Shapiro in Hollywood. Shapiro had produced the award-winning "Scared Straight" and a military-oriented documentary entitled "Return to Iwo Jima." McDermott had been deeply moved by the latter program. When Shapiro proposed to McDermott and the Board that USAA support a documentary on The Unknown Soldier, he received a warm reception. "The Unknown Soldier," a USAA-sponsored documentary, aired on the PBS national network on Veteran's Day, 1985. It was well-received by members and media critics and led to USAA sponsorship of four other military-oriented films. The next one was "POW: Americans in Enemy Hands — World War II, Korea, Vietnam," which aired in 1986. The Board was a little cautious about the subject matter, but trusted Shapiro to treat the subject with the respect and delicacy that it deserved. Following this sensitive portrayal in 1987 were the documentaries "Future Flight," and "Top Flight," a documentary celebrating the history of the 40th anniversary of the U.S. Air Force. In 1988, Loretta Swit hosted "The Korean War." The Board was pleased with these television documentaries and Shapiro's treatment of these military subjects.

One by product of the Shapiro documentaries was the creation of the USAA Foundation. In 1985, working Vice Chairman Bob Pursley studied financial planning. Because of the multiplying products and services offered by USAA, he recommended that USAA develop an informational and educational program. USAA already had *Aide Magazine* in place, but Pursley suggested more. About the same time, the USAA sponsorship of Arnold Shapiro's documentaries had begun. Management hoped that revenues from these productions could fund Pursley's proposed educational program. This led to the formation of the USAA Foundation, incorporated under the laws of the state of Texas on January 16, 1986. The organizational meeting was held ten days later, and the Board elected McDermott as president.[57]

The purpose of the Foundation was to provide education on safety, security, and good health to USAA members. All of these activities served the general welfare of the membership and advanced the well-being of the public at large. In 1989, the Foundation began the production of booklets to achieve its purpose. These included the *USAA Car Guide* and booklets on subjects such as managing debt and buying a home. The same year, John Cook, Senior Vice President, was elected president of the Foundation and assumed the responsibility for its operation.[58] In the first year, the Foundation filled member requests for 79,000 booklets, and in 1990, 358,000. The program had become an important arm of USAA's educational thrust for members.

In 1988, McDermott was becoming increasingly troubled by the moral and ethical breakdown in American society. He abhorred the deterioration of values, the rise of crime and drug use, the propensity towards violence, and the breakup of families. He wanted to do more to help America's youngest generation have a better life and to give them a better chance to grow into useful and productive citizens. In this light, he asked Shapiro to develop a proposal for an advocacy documentary to promote an improved social climate for the nation's youngsters. Shapiro proposed a two-year, five-part series which eventually was called "Raising Good Kids in Bad Times."

The Board strongly supported the proposal and approved it as presented."[59]

In 1989, McDermott, Senator Bob Dole (R-Kansas), and Senator George Mitchell (D-Maine) co-hosted a premier of the first documentary in the series in Washington, D.C. It was attended by a number of Washington key figures including numerous congressmen, USAA Board members, and FBI Director Bill Sessions. Senator Phil Gramm (R-Texas) and Senator Alfonse D'Amato (R-New York) both spoke at the event and praised USAA's involvement. Hosted by movie star Tom Selleck, "See Dick and Jane Lie, Cheat and Steal — The Teaching of Values to Kids" was greeted at the premier by a standing ovation. This syndicated documentary and the four that followed aired in 98 percent of the national television market and in all 150 top markets. They received great attention from every quarter. Even Barbara Bush, wife of President George Bush, wrote personal notes to McDermott on two different occasions praising USAA's sponsorship of these programs. The other four documentaries on teaching, parenting, and values were hosted by Whoopi Goldberg, Michael Landon, Loni Anderson, and James Garner.

In addition to the television documentaries, an unusual USAA contribution included a small tract of land near the home office that was transferred to the city of San Antonio. The new police substation that was built on the property provided increased police protection for the area around USAA. Another gift was a donation of over $5 million to San Antonio's Cancer Therapy and Research Center for research into anti-cancer drugs. The USAA Life and Health Company decided to release the funds from a reserve it had set aside to pay AIDS claims. When the claims did not materialize as projected, the money was available for a charitable contribution. USAA decided to allocate it for some form of medical research that would most help USAA members. Cancer research was the choice. Ed Rosane, President of the USAA Life and Health Division, told the press that the investment was being made "with enlightened self-interest." Improving the health and longevity of the USAA membership could well result in a decrease in claims experience.[60]

Perhaps more important than USAA charitable dollar contributions to communities were the volunteer hours spent in the communities by USAA employees at all levels. Dozens of USAA employees served on Boards of Directors of non-profit agencies. Their donations of time and expertise were highly valued by the community. Under the banner of the USAA Volunteer Corps, founded in 1983, aqua-tee-shirted employees were seen helping at every conceivable charitable function in San Antonio and regional office communities. Five hundred employees were involved that first year; by the end of the decade over 1,300 employees were participating. In its twenty-fifth year in 1968, Christmas Cheer volunteers assisted over 7,000 San Antonio residents in having a happy holiday.

USAA employees, members of the USAA Volunteer Corps, donate their time in the community. Here employees participate in a telethon.

A Tradition Of Service

McDermott's firm belief in education was a driving force behind his personal support of educational initiatives in the city of San Antonio. Whenever he had the opportunity, he also lent USAA's support. Many officers including Vic Ferrari, Herb Emanuel, Susan Evers, Paul Beyer and Tony Rivera, played strong roles in the community in various educational and literacy programs. McDermott talked to the employees and community groups often about the importance of education. His favorite cartoon strip was one of Charles Schulz's *Peanuts* that talked about doing well in school. He used this panel often as part of his talks. In 1988, McDermott saw an educational opportunity where USAA and its employees could help.

PEANUTS reprinted by permission of United Feature Syndicate, Inc.

In the fall of that year, McDermott was reading in the San Antonio paper yet another article on school dropouts. Some San Antonio schools were experiencing as much as a 40-percent dropout rate. The children who left school early added to the deadly litany of society's problems — teenage pregnancies, unemployment, drug and alcohol abuse, violence, and other criminal behavior. He believed that a mentor program might help, and he asked Vic Ferrari, who had just retired the week before, to look into the possibility. After studying the local schools, Ferrari and a management trainee, Margaret Anderson, prepared a master plan for a USAA Mentor Program. McDermott gave the go-ahead for a pilot program to begin in January 1989.

A New Era For USAA — Financial Services

Seventy USAA employees volunteered to spend one hour each week one-on-one with a student attending either Barkley Elementary School or Cooper Middle School in the San Antonio Independent School District. The faculty at the schools recommended the students based on dropout potential. The pilot was a success, and Ferrari began an ambitious program in the fall of 1989 that grew quickly and enthusiastically. The program was to be more successful than even the optimistic Ferrari envisioned.

The USAA Mentor Program was designed principally for dropouts although a small number of gifted and talented students were included. As the *Peanuts* panel suggests, McDermott believed in encouraging gifted students as well as those who were struggling

Mentors and mentees: Jane Hill, Veronica Salazar, Juan Bernal, and Paul Ringenbach. In 1997, these mentors and mentees had been together for eight school years.

for educational survival. It was for this reason that he began offering USAA college scholarships to the children of Association employees. To ensure that everything was fair and neutral, USAA contracted with the Citizens' Scholarship Foundation of America to administer the program. In 1984, USAA sponsored its first two National Merit Scholarships. Susan Nutt, daughter of USAA employees Larry and Katherine Nutt, exercised her scholarship at the University of Texas at Austin. Tragically, she died in 1992, three years after her graduation and employment at USAA. The other recipient was Simone Farmer, daughter of Jay Farmer, USAA senior claims examiner. Farmer studied pre-med at St. Mary's University in San Antonio and graduated from medical school. Keeping the honor of commissioning in the USAA family, retired Air Force Brigadier General Bill Cooney put on his uniform "one more time" to commission Simone in the Air Force. She was now a member of USAA on her own. These two gifted students helped pave the way for continuing and expanding the program because of their successes in school. This scholarship opportunity was an employee benefit that gave all USAA employees pride in their company — and in the children of their fellow workers.

Simone (Farmer) Morris. She is currently an Air Force Captain and physician.

* * * *

It became increasingly evident over the years that USAA had to become more active politically on its own behalf. This was not an entirely new impulse, but rather an intensification of earlier activities. Consumerism, the cult of the individual growing out of the sixties, general anti-insurance attitudes in society, and the volatility of the financial services deregulation all played a role. It was in USAA's best interest to participate. In 1981, for example, USAA lobbied for a change in Texas premium tax legislation that saved the Association $5 million annually in retaliatory taxes levied by other states. In another effort, Individual Retirement Account (IRA) legislation was needed to enable active duty military members to invest in IRAs. USAA lobbied successfully to have them included.[61]

USAA's growing interest in participating in the political process was matched by an increase in requests for political contributions. To provide a legal and rational process, USAA General Counsel Bill McCrae advised McDermott to begin a Political Action Committee (PAC) to channel future political contributions. McDermott agreed, and an organizational meeting of the USAA Group PAC was held on November 24, 1982, and McCrae was elected Chairman.[62] Membership was voluntary and composed mostly of Association officers and executive directors. The PAC was successful in that payroll deductions made it financially viable, and USAA donated funds to candidates it supported. The less successful part of the PAC was that the PAC members were often unaware of where their contributions were going. They continued to contribute in good faith, however, trusting their PAC Executive Committee representatives to make the right decisions.

In the eighties, the rising tide of radical consumerism was of serious concern to McDermott and the Board. McDermott and McCrae worked actively with trade associations and other insurance companies to stay abreast of developments. With literally thousands of bills touching on insurance in the legislative process in the fifty states and in the federal government at any given time, the trade associations were necessary to help keep track. USAA did not have the resources to do it all alone, but still needed the information. For example, in 1987 a proposed Texas law establishing a 6 percent sales tax on insurance passed the Texas House. The proposal died, but McDermott had threatened to move USAA out of Texas, if it passed.[63] McDermott's fundamental belief was that the only real way to combat misplaced consumerism and adverse legislation was for the insurance industry to improve itself — especially in the area of customer service. As a 1987 Ernst & Whinney survey of insurance company CEOs revealed, service was low on their priority list. Asked to identify the corporate goals and objectives that CEOs would most like to accomplish in the next five years, "improving customer service" came in a dismal eleventh.[64] McDermott used the survey to push for improvement with his fellow CEOs.

McDermott believed that he needed more help in the public relations area of USAA to work with the insurance industry and state regulators, and to help position USAA in the media. At the time, USAA's actual Public Affairs staff numbered only five, and such a limited job would not attract the talent he wanted. Working with Dave Myers and Jim Roberts in Manpower and Organization, McDermott arranged to have all communications activities pulled under a Corporate Communications Department. Employee and member communications, member relations, community services, public affairs, history, corporate marketing, and television production made up the new department. With the management responsibility raised to the senior vice president level, McDermott could recruit the talent he believed that he needed in this new era for the insurance industry. Knowing the experience level, depth, respect of industry officials, and energy levels of John Cook, he recruited him for USAA.

A native of Houston, Cook graduated from the University of Houston and went to work for Allstate Insurance Company. He worked there for twelve years in various corporate relations staff and management responsibilities. Following this, he went to work as Vice President of Public Affairs for the American Insurance Association. Located in Washington, D.C., this association is a trade organization of property and casualty insurance companies. Impressed by Cook's vigor and ability there, McDermott played a role in bringing Cook to the Insurance Institute for Highway Safety (IIHS). As executive vice president, Cook directed the communications and information services for the IIHS and the Highway Loss Data Institute. As Chairman of IIHS, McDermott once again had the opportunity to observe Cook's performance.

McDermott wanted more from Cook than to work only with USAA. He wanted Cook to help him reform the insurance industry itself. USAA already had an outstanding reputation for service, and McDermott believed that more information available in the media about USAA would help spread this ethic in the

John Cook

industry. Public recognition of USAA's service in various ways could influence other companies to improve their service levels to compete with USAA. If the entire industry didn't improve its image, troubles were certainly ahead, as the California experience would demonstrate. In July 1989, when Cook arrived at USAA, the insurance industry's nightmare of an ultimate consumer revolt had already come true in the form of an initiative passed in the state of California.

Many of the democratic reforms in American history had begun in the West and flowed back across the nation. For example, Utah was the first state to grant women the right to vote in its constitution. During the Progressive Period, the democratic principles of initiative, referendum, and recall found fertile ground among western voters. In 1911, the initiative process was included by California in its state constitution. It gave citizens the right to bypass the legislature and to present proposals for legislation directly before the voters in a general election.

The initiative was viewed by consumer advocates and others as the best way to bypass powerful constituencies like business to enact reform legislation. Earlier, Californians had passed Proposition 13, which limited taxes on real estate and threatened significant cuts in government services. Enter Harvey Rosenfield, a lawyer and Congressional lobbyist for Ralph Nader. In 1981, Nader requested that Rosenfield move to California to organize the California Public-Interest Research Group. After unsuccessfully fighting utility companies at rate hearings and insurance industry-backed Proposition 51, Rosenfield decided to seek major insurance reform. The result was initiative Proposition 103. This initiative required a retroactive rollback to November 1987 in property and casualty rates, an additional 20 percent rate cut for good drivers, and approval of future rate increases by an elected insurance commissioner. It was strongly supported by the California trial lawyers.

In the California state elections held in 1988, there were five insurance initiatives on the ballot including Proposition 103. The insurance industry spent tens of millions of dollars in a media campaign against 103 in what turned out to be a futile effort. Proposition 104 was one that called for no-fault insurance and was strongly supported by USAA and the insurance industry. In fact, USAA's Sacramento office played a strong role in getting the initiative on the ballot. USAA employee Deanna Stoddard organized mailings to California members. She included signature petitions for the initiative and USAA members returned thousands of signatures to support Proposition 104. Some members even included financial donations that were not even requested. When USAA needed support, the members were there for the Association. After this Proposition joined the others on the ballot, USAA exhorted members to vote and sent pocket-sized cards spelling out USAA positions on each proposition. When the votes were counted, only Proposition 103 passed, and just by a bare majority.

USAA believed that Proposition 103 was unconstitutional and

joined other insurance companies in an attempt to have the courts declare it so. The California Supreme Court, however, declared that Proposition 103 was constitutional and ordered the rollbacks. To the dismay of the consumer activists, the court also said that insurance companies were entitled to a "fair rate of return" on investment and income before being forced to cut rates. Insurance companies prepared a nineteen-page application to show that the rollback guidelines were, in fact, "confiscatory." USAA's further concern, later borne out in such states as New Jersey and Maryland, was that Proposition 103's passage in California would encourage similar movements in other states.[65]

In the meantime, California legislative hearings on the rollbacks were held. Consumer advocate Ralph Nader testified that the insurance companies could afford to pay the rollback. He stated that companies like USAA were hoarding too much surplus — USAA's ratio of premium to surplus was about 1:1. He praised USAA's efficiency, however. He stated that the industry's operating-expense ratio was 35.3 percent, while USAA's was about 20 percent. He quoted from a National Insurance Consumer Organization (NICO) report that stated "auto liability insurance rates would drop by an average of 19 percent nationally, if the industry on average were as efficient as USAA."[66]

Then at the same hearings, Senator Waddie P. Deddah asked about the "take all comers" provision in Proposition 103. Earlier, Fred Wooscher, Special Counsel to the California Attorney General, had suggested that USAA would be required to sell insurance to any "good driver." The California law defined a good driver as a motorist with one or less moving violation in the past three years. (Under this definition, accidents would not be counted.) USAA's concern was a major one. If the Attorney General's opinion prevailed, USAA would be subject to "take all comers" — to sell automobile insurance to virtually anyone. Senator Deddah mentioned USAA specifically and stated that he planned to introduce legislation to protect the "exclusivity rights" of it and similar companies. Harvey Rosenfield voiced no objection, noting that there was nothing in 103 that said companies couldn't serve an exclusive group. Senator Alan Robbins agreed with Deddah's goal, and suggested legislative action. At the session, no one opposed USAA's eligibility rules, but the tenor of the session suggested that a legislative remedy was necessary.[67]

The path to legislation to guarantee USAA's membership eligibility criteria clearly illustrates the supportive nature of USAA's members. Legislation was introduced that would grant USAA and similar companies an exemption to the "take all comers" provision in Proposition 103. McDermott sent a letter to all California members asking them to contact their legislators to obtain support. Thousands did. Although not asked to do so, hundreds of these wrote personal letters to General McDermott and told him what actions they had taken. All said they had made contact with their legislators. Some said that they wrote, called, or sent telegrams to every single California legislator and asked what else they could do. The amendment passed the Legislature unanimously, and was sent to the Governor's office for signature. Then USAA learned that the Governor might not sign before the legislation expired — the unsigned bill was languishing in his office, and would expire on a Monday. McDermott sent a letter by Federal Express to about 100 influential members who had written him about this issue earlier. He asked their help in getting the Governor's signature. By close of business Friday, most had already contacted the Governor's office and the Governor had signed the bill. In the opinion of those familiar with California politics, the Association would have lost its unique status in California without this positive intervention of USAA's members.

While that took care of this section of Proposition 103, USAA was still waiting to hear about its request for an exemption to the rollback. After reviewing the some 4,800 requests from insurance companies for exemptions, California Insurance Commissioner Roxani Gillespie initially ordered seven insurers to refund $305 million. Her staff had determined that an 11.2 percent return on equity was fair. Since USAA's return was 37.3 percent, she directed USAA to refund $56.7 million, or 17.3 percent of its annual premiums. No one was satisfied. Rosenfield had demanded the 20 percent rollback included in the law. The overall average for all companies was 6 percent, with Progressive Casualty required to pay only 1 percent. Steve Miller of the Insurer Consumer Action Network criticized her formula, which he said penalized the most efficient companies "like USAA."[68] USAA protested Gillespie's decision, and USAA spokesman John Walmsley said that "Their figures just don't jibe with ours." Harvey Rosenfield agreed, and said that USAA had good reason to be confused because what Gillespie had done "made no sense at all."[69] Months of hearings on the rollback and rate increases followed, with little progress. Frustrated by Gillespie's seeming inability to get companies to pay the rollbacks to their policyholders, in November 1990 the California voters turned her out in favor of John Garamendi. He immediately declared war on the insurance industry. USAA waited to see what actions the new Commissioner would take.[70]

The following year, natural disasters followed the manmade version. The first was Hurricane Hugo, the largest single storm in USAA's experience. When the storm hit, USAA's losses totaled over $130 million, affecting almost 23,000 members. The USAA Catastrophe team was on the scene quickly, and members responded approvingly to the quick and fair settlement of their claims. Hurricanes were expected occasionally, but earthquakes were not. At 7 p.m. on October 18, 1989, a major earthquake, 6.9 on the Richter scale, struck with its epicenter near Santa Cruz, sixty miles south of San Francisco. In 1985, the state had required insurance companies to offer earthquake coverage. USAA actively encouraged members to

A Tradition Of Service

buy the coverage, while other companies did not. As a result, USAA had four times as many members with earthquake coverage as its closest competitor. Over 4,300 members suffered losses totaling almost $23 million. USAA's total catastrophe loss for the year was $233 million; the net loss after reinsurance was $143 million.

At the end of 1988, USAA's surplus was 88 percent. McDermott pointed out to the membership that 1989 disasters such as Hurricane Hugo and the earthquake in Northern California validated the need for a high surplus.[71] The natural disasters for members at home were matched by troubles for USAA members in overseas areas. The numbers were smaller there, but no less tragic because of the loss of lives.

On the morning of April 21, 1989, USAA member Colonel James Nicholas Rowe, U.S. Army Special Forces, was on his way to work in Manila, the Philippines. A 1960 graduate of West Point, Nick Rowe had gone to Vietnam in 1963 as a Green Beret. Captured by the Viet Cong, he had been a POW for five years before making a dramatic escape in 1968. He resigned his commission in 1974, then wrote a book on his experiences called *Five Years to Freedom*. In 1981, he had returned to active duty to start a survival school at Fort Bragg, North Carolina. This member's story had been profiled in the USAA-sponsored Arnold Shapiro documentary, "POW-Americans in Enemy Hands," produced in 1987. Soon after, Rowe went to the Philippines as an advisor on combating communist insurgents. On that spring day in 1989, the terrorists lay in wait for Rowe and riddled his armored car with bullets, killing him. *Aide Magazine* honored him with a special salute. The salute made the point that

Nick Rowe

although the United States seemed to be at peace in 1989, many USAA members were "in harm's way" every day, no matter how peaceful the world might appear from the vantage of American living rooms. That knowledge was a very special element of being an employee and serving the members.

Meanwhile, anti-American sentiment was rising in Panama. In 1987, a former Noriega aide disclosed that Panamanian head General Manuel Antonio Noriega was involved with the drug trade to the U.S. The Reagan administration took increasing sanctions against Panama including freezing that nation's assets in the U.S., and held back foreign aid. Noriega and his allies incited anti-American riots in Panama and harassed U.S. military personnel there. On December 15, 1989, the Panamanian National Assembly passed a resolution that a state of war existed with the U.S. Noriega named himself the "Maximum Leader." On the following day, a Panamanian soldier shot three American officers; USAA member and Marine Corps Lieutenant Robert Paz died of his wounds. A junior U.S. Naval officer and his wife who witnessed the incident were arrested and assaulted by the Panamanian Defense Force (PDF) soldiers while in custody. The PDF interrogators kicked and punched the officer. They then forced his terrified wife up against a wall and groped her until she collapsed. President George Bush had heard enough and ordered Operation Just Cause, the invasion of Panama.[72] Just prior to the U.S. surprise attack, an American female dependent was shot and wounded at Albrook Air Force Station.[73] These incidents further served to remind USAA employees that members' families shared the dangers and hardships of a military career — even in times of apparent peace for America.

At 12:45 a.m. on December 20, U.S. special forces operational units received their orders to attack Panamanian power centers. The U.S. forces moved quickly to seize the PDF command center, to capture other important points in Panama City and to protect the

U.S. Embassy. The resistance was much greater than expected, but as the PDF collapsed, looting erupted and refugees and wounded overwhelmed the hospitals. By Christmas, U.S. casualties stood at twenty-three killed and 322 wounded.

At the same time, the Americans discovered that Noriega had been given political refuge by the Catholic Church to end the bloodshed. The Papal delegate had granted sanctuary on the basis of a political dispute. To refute this rationale, the Americans gave the Panamanian Catholic bishops the opportunity to visit Noriega's residences to view evidence of Noriega's acts of torture, devil worship, witchcraft, murder, drugs, and voodoo. The bishops then wrote to the Vatican and urged the Pope to remand Noriega to U.S. custody. The Pope sent Monsignor Giacinto Berloco to negotiate with U.S. Lieutenant General Marc Cisneros and Deputy Assistant Secretary of State Michal Kozak. When the Americans agreed that they would not pursue the death penalty for Noriega, Monsignor Berloco agreed to try to persuade Noriega to surrender. On January 3, when church officials told Noriega that anti-Noriega Panamanians might enter the Vatican Compound in the capitol, he agreed to surrender. That signaled the end of Just Cause.[74]

As soon as the invasion started, evacuations of the wounded began from Panama to the San Antonio military medical hospitals of Fort Sam Houston and the Wilford Hall Medical Center. What made the evacuations especially poignant for the wounded personnel and their families was that it was Christmas season. The hospitals were brightly decorated, as were the homes of military personnel hospitalized in San Antonio. The families were joyful that their loved ones survived, but sad at the separation. At this point, U.S. Naval Academy graduate Ross Perot called General McDermott. Perot told McDermott that if USAA would make the arrangements, he would pay for the airfares of family members who wished to come to San Antonio to be with their wounded loved ones for Christmas. The

A New Era For USAA — Financial Services

only condition he requested was anonymity.

McDermott agreed, and asked Duane Divich to head the project. Divich contacted all the families to see if they wanted to come, and if so, when and how. He worked closely with the USAA Travel Agency to make the necessary reservations and have the tickets delivered to the appropriate airports. Eventually, complimentary accommodations courtesy of local hotels and free transportation were arranged for 119 family members who wanted to come to the bedsides of sixty wounded and dying servicemen. In spite of Perot's request for anonymity, wounded servicemen praised him and USAA to reporters, and this appeared in the San Antonio papers. Reflecting later on the operation, Rear Admiral Jesse J. Hernandez, USAA Board member, complimented the USAA staff on their efforts.[75]

Another form of praise came from a past member of USAA who lived in Santa Ana, California. A former Marine, he had switched to local insurance carriers after getting out of the service. In his letter to McDermott, he said USAA never crossed his mind again until he read about what the Association was doing to reunite servicemen wounded in Panama with their families. He wanted to express his appreciation and respect. So that he could say thank you in his "own small way," he asked McDermott to have someone call him so he could get USAA insurance again. He also wanted some information on investment opportunities from "a company that really cares."[76]

For a company that claimed service to military members as a birthright, the efforts for those wounded in Panama were a perfect cap to the decade. It was unusual only in the size of the undertaking and its genesis. In microcosm, USAA employees served individual members daily, often in personal events every bit as traumatic and tragic as those that followed Operation Just Cause.

USAA's dedication to service was well-known and even expected by its members. In the 1989 Member Satisfaction Survey, 98.6 percent of members rated USAA's overall service as outstanding or

A Tradition Of Service

satisfactory — the highest ratings since these surveys were initiated in 1979. By the end of the decade, a number of public recognitions raised the Association's visibility as a national model of a service provider. In 1980 and again in 1985, *Consumer Reports* reported that Amica Mutual and USAA were rated as the two top-rated insurance companies in the nation by its survey participants. In 1985, *In Search of Excellence* author Tom Peters praised USAA's employees and their skills in his nationally syndicated column. He called them, and representatives of other selected companies, "A New Class of Heroes" because of their service ethic. In the 1989 book, *The Service Edge: 101 Companies that Profit from Customer Care,* USAA was selected to join the nation's elite service providers.[77] In a 1988 *Forbes* interview, McDermott emphasized the importance of service for a successful company: "If you put service number one, everything else will follow." USAA's growth in membership reflected his belief. At the end of 1989, USAA had over 1.9 million members, a 60 percent increase since the past decade.[78] At USAA in the nineties, considerable efforts would be made to ensure USAA's continued outstanding service into the next century and beyond.

CHAPTER ELEVEN

THE NINETIES – A DECADE OF WORLDWIDE CHANGE

At the outset of the 1990s, two historic events occurred which underscored that this would be a decade of worldwide change. This change would have a particular impact on the American military mission and on USAA, the company dedicated to facilitating the financial security of the military community. Most important was the dissolution of the Soviet Union and its captive empire. And in the midst of this dissolution process came the Persian Gulf War, precipitated by the Iraqi invasion of Kuwait and culminating in the successful U.S.-led international rescue effort to free Kuwait and prevent Saddam Hussein's move to get a stranglehold on the crucial Middle East oil supply.

While it is impossible to say exactly when it began or pick the precise day it concluded, the almost half-century long Cold War confrontation between the Soviet Union and its captive empire on the one side, and the United States and its allies on the other, was clearly ending as the Soviet empire began self-destructing on the eve of the 1990s.

It started in Poland, where after a decade of challenge to the Communist regime by Lech Walesa's Solidarity movement, the Polish government agreed on April 5, 1989, to a broad range of reforms including free elections. The communists were swept out of power in parliamentary elections by Solidarity candidates and Lech Walesa became president on June 4, 1990.

With startling rapidity and with a surprising lack of violence except in Romania, the other Warsaw bloc nations pulled away from Soviet dominance. Hungary dissolved the Communist Party in October 1989. In East Germany, after massive anti-government protests and demonstrations, President Erich Honecker was forced to resign October 18, 1990; the border with Czechoslovakia was opened for travel with the west on November 4; and the Berlin Wall, the symbol of separation between the Communist world and the West, came down on November 9. In Czechoslovakia, the first cabinet in forty-one years with a non-communist majority took office on December 10, 1989, and Vaclav Havel, playwright and human rights advocate, was elected president on December 29. In Romania, after brutally suppressing a series of anti-government protests, army units joined the protesters in a battle against security forces in Bucharest on December 21, 1989. On December 22, a group known as the Council of National Salvation announced it had overthrown the government. On December 25, President Nicolae Ceausescu and his wife were executed. Finally, Albania, long considered the last bastion of Stalin-style communist rule in Europe, re-elected its communist government in the March 1991 elections. But the communists were swept out of office the next March following a virtual economic collapse and widespread social unrest.

The independence movement spread to the three Baltic states held captive by the Soviet Union and to the Soviet Union itself, where ethnic provinces began agitating for separation. Lithuania declared its independence from Moscow on March 11, 1990, and Estonia declared itself a free nation that same month. Latvia declared itself independent on August 21, 1991, in the midst of an unsuccessful coup attempt against vacationing President Mikhail Gorbachev launched by Kremlin hardliners. On August 24, Gorbachev resigned as leader of the Communist Party and recommended that the Central Committee be disbanded. On Christmas day 1991, Gorbachev resigned as president and the following day, the Soviet Union was officially disbanded and the Soviet hammer and sickle over the Kremlin was lowered to be replaced by the flag of Russia.

The Nineties — A Decade of Worldwide Change

The end of the Cold War drew a huge, collective sigh of relief from people around the world who for too long lived with the threat of nuclear holocaust hanging over the globe. This sentiment was of course shared by American service personnel and by employees at USAA. But accompanying this feeling of relief was the question of what impact this change would have on their lives. It turned out that the U.S. military appeared to be less surprised by the dissolution of the Soviet Union than the press and public. In early November 1989, before the fall of the Berlin Wall, chairman of the Joint Chiefs of Staff General Colin L. Powell had already considered such a possibility in a briefing entitled "Strategic Overview – 1994." Powell had subtitled the briefing, "When You Lose Your Best Enemy."[1] His proposal was a Base Force Concept which shifted emphasis from a threat-based to a threat-and-capability-based force. The new base force would be smaller — dropping the active-duty military force from 2.2 million to 1.6 million.[2]

But in spite of the overall force reductions, new officers entering active duty annually stabilized at about 20,000. With the earlier addition of dependents and former officers to its pool of eligibles and its expansion into financial services and other areas, the company appeared well-positioned to manage the change. USAA's continued growth was reflected in major new milestones at the beginning of the decade. In 1990, Navy Ensign William Prevo became USAA's two millionth member (counting Regular and Associate members) and Air Force Major Mark Clodfelter signed up for USAA's one millionth homeowners policy in January 1991.

The dissolution of the Soviet Union ended the bi-polar Cold War confrontation, but it also created new global peacekeeping responsibilities for the United States as evidenced by the Gulf War. It started on August 2, 1990, when some 140,000 Iraqi troops, supported by 1,800 tanks, began crossing the Kuwait border in the pre-dawn darkness. Iraq had at least one major motive for the invasion — money.

Robert McDermott with two millionth member, Ensign William Prevo and family

USAA's one millionth homeowner policyholders, Major Mark and Donna Clodfelter.

It owed billions of dollars to Kuwait for monies borrowed to finance its long war with Iran. But a more troubling secondary motive was also suspected, the possibility that Iraqi leader Saddam Hussein's ultimate target was Saudi Arabia and its huge oil reserves. If Saudi Arabia fell to Iraq, Saddam Hussein would control 40 percent of the world's known oil reserves, a frightening prospect to the United States and other world powers that relied heavily on Middle Eastern oil. As the world's sole remaining superpower, only the United States was capable of mounting a credible reaction.

THE NINETIES – A DECADE OF WORLDWIDE CHANGE

Responding to a request from Saudi King Fahd Ibn Abel-Aziz, President Bush acted. Working through the United Nations, the United States put together a powerful international coalition to oppose Iraq's takeover of Kuwait — a coalition that included Arab states traditionally hostile to U.S. interests in the Middle East and support from the Soviets, who in the past could have been counted on to lead the opposition to such a move. On August 7, President Bush ordered U.S. military aircraft and troops to Saudi Arabia. On August 22, with about 200,000 U.S. troops en route to the Gulf, Bush activated 12,000 members of the Army National Guard. The Pentagon announced that some 200,000 other reservists might be called to active duty. The troops joined a multinational peacekeeping force led by the United States to defend Saudi Arabia in an operation called Desert Shield.

USAA reacted swiftly. On August 22, the Association's Human Resources specialists held briefings for its employee-reservists on re-employment rights and various benefit programs. About 200 of its employees were then active in the National Guard or the Reserves. USAA had long supported employees who participated in Reserve and National Guard programs. In fact, USAA received a Texas state award for its support of these programs in 1985. The company had routinely paid the difference between its employees' normal pay and what they received from the Reserves or Guard during their annual two-week, active-duty training. Further, the employees' military leave was not deducted from their vacation or personal leave. McDermott not only supported employees already in such programs, but also encouraged employees to join Reserve and Guard programs.

Also on August 22, a letter from USAA Chairman McDermott reached each employee's desk. He reminded them of "the unlimited liability clause"— the willingness of service personnel to die for their country. It was this that made the military profession dif-

Lieutenant Colonel Hilton Garnes
United States Marine Corps Reserve

Private Toni Charette (Southeast Regional Office)
United States Army Reserve

ferent from other professions. He wrote that this was the special ingredient that forged the service-family tradition, and that USAA was proud to be part of this extended military family. Tension would be high in service families affected by the impending conflict, McDermott said. As part of the military family, he asked the employees to "be especially sensitive" and to "exercise more patience than usual." By doing this, USAA could help relieve stress for the families affected by the war.[3]

USAA's support of its reservists during the Gulf War was extraordinary. McDermott announced that the Association would pay employees who were called to active duty the difference between their military pay and their USAA pay for twelve months. Their jobs would be held for them during this period. The national media picked up the story and USAA received strong praise. On Christmas Eve 1990, Army Lieutenant Colonel Hal Schade, USAA public relations expert and Executive Officer of the 114th Evacuation Hospital, arrived at his unit's assigned location about twenty miles from the Kuwaiti border. During his six months there, he was able to concentrate on his military duties without having to worry about his future at USAA. It was not that way with other reservists in his unit, however. Many doctors and other self-employed medical professionals of the 114th suffered severe financial hardships. Others who were called up had no assurances or support from their employers beyond the two weeks' paid training leave mandated by the Soldiers and Sailors Relief Act. And so it was with many Reserve and Guard units during the war.

Lieutenant Colonel Hal Schade
United States Army Reserve

The Association went all out to serve its members and the entire military family as well. All military members ordered to the Persian Gulf could buy initial life insurance policies or add to existing ones from USAA, although the Association reluctantly put a cap on how much new or additional insurance they could buy — $25,000 for lieutenants and captains and $50,000 for officers in the grade of major or above. At the same time USAA was expanding its coverage of the military in the Gulf, the *Navy Times* reported that 117 companies in Virginia refused to offer any coverage at all to those going to the Middle East.[4] In Operation Desert Greetings, USAA employees prepared thousands of holiday greetings addressed to "any service member" in the Persian Gulf region. The Association forwarded them in batches overseas. Melissa Baldwin headed a project to develop a special Desert Shield packet and guide to provide information on deployments for members and their families. The USAA Federal Savings Bank reduced all interest payments on loans to 6 percent, as required by law, but also deferred principal payments. USAA Bank President Jack Antonini reported to the press that over 4,200 members took advantage of this program at a cost to the Bank of about $100,000 a month during the war.

As tensions heightened, USAA opened a Desert Shield Assistance Center on January 15, 1991. Staffed by experts from the various lines of USAA business, its purpose was to provide extra-sensitive service to surviving relatives of Desert Shield casualties, prisoners of war, and those missing in action. The following day, when Desert Shield became Desert Storm, the Center was ready to help. Finally, the USAA board declared a 25 percent dividend on auto insurance for six months for members who served in the war's area of operations from January 17 to February 29. USAA advertised this offer widely and wrote to over 400,000 members that the Association identified as possibly being involved in Desert Storm. The members and employees greatly appreciated USAA's support. In 1992, the Department of Defense echoed the members' and employees' gratitude by presenting to USAA the Department's highest honor for a civilian agency — the Pro Patria Award.

USAA member General Colin Powell visiting the 726th Tactical Control Squadron in Saudi Arabia during Desert Storm.

Two permanent improvements in service grew out of the Desert Storm experience at USAA. First, the special military rapid deployment guide, developed for this war, was modified into a general one that could be used by USAA members for any conflict. This guide was updated when conflicts arose and made available to members. It was used as recently as 1996 for those assigned to Bosnia. Second, the Desert Storm Assistance Center concept was modified to assist survivors of all member deaths. The new organization was called the Intercompany Survivors Assistance Team (ISAT). Operations analyst Sylvia Hilbig led the development of the new organization. The team developed policies and procedures to make it as easy as possible for survivors of members to work with USAA. When a member died prior to the establishment of ISAT, individual USAA companies wrote letters of condolence and occasionally asked individual members for the same documents, such as death certificates. The team developed correspondence and an information packet to provide a single USAA response to each tragedy. After this, members' survivors received initial information and requests from only the Survivors Assistance Team. This made it much easier for the bereaved and demonstrated the unity of USAA's efforts as one company.

And as the war faded into history and redeployments and remobilization loomed ahead, USAA began an information program to assist those affected by military downsizing. Articles on the transition from military to civilian life appeared in *Aide Magazine*. In 1992, the USAA Educational Foundation published the booklet *Leaving the Military: Your Guide to Separation and Retirement*. Containing information on résumé preparation, salary negotiation, goal setting, and financial planning, the free booklet was a popular one with those caught up by the end of the Cold War.

The 1990s quickly tested USAA's much-praised financial strength and its vaunted service to members by dishing up a variety of major catastrophes in areas of considerable member density.[5] In 1991, USAA Catastrophe (CAT) Teams settled fire claims in the Oakland, California, area totaling over $106 million. Another CAT team sifted through dust and debris outside of Clark Air Base and the

Subic Bay Naval Station in the Philippines looking for members' cars and other belongings in the wake of a massive volcanic eruption. And a series of nasty hail storms struck north Texas and Colorado. All told, 1991 turned out to be the second worst catastrophe year in USAA's history. Fortunately, by 1992, USAA had developed catastrophe management into a well-tuned process and its operations became a model for the insurance industry. Average rates for closing claims in catastrophes was 50 percent in four weeks and 75 percent in eight.

But the greatest test for Steve Marlin, Assistant Vice President-Catastrophe Operations, and his CAT teams was yet to come. It began on August 24, 1992, when Hurricane Andrew, the costliest single catastrophe in U.S. history, smashed into the South Florida coast and cut a twenty-five-mile-wide swath across the state, taking forty-one lives and causing more than $20 billion in property damage. Moving across the Gulf, it caused another $1.5 billion in damage in Louisiana. USAA had over 22,000 claims totaling $615 million in insured losses. However, USAA was ready. Marlin had been monitoring the progress of the storm and called his team together when landfall was predicted. Before Andrew made landfall, USAA media placement specialist Michelle Cook had placed advertisements on radio and in newspapers in South Florida telling members where USAA's claims facilities would be. Dozens of claims employees were already in the general area, and hundreds more were standing by. USAA Travel procured rental vehicles and made airline and hotel reservations. USAA Buying Service was ready to help replace lost possessions and Information Services readied cellular phones and laptop computers to relay claims from the scene.

After Hurricane Andrew hit, USAA's sophisticated telephone switches rerouted incoming calls in coordination with the AT&T network to claims representatives in other regional offices as far away as Seattle. More than once, members living in South Florida were curious about the unfamiliar accents that greeted them on the phone. Because of the tremendous volume of losses, it was impossible to provide enough claims personnel on scene to handle immediate member problems. To help, a new concept was created. Special customer contact teams were formed that walked the now signless streets looking for USAA insureds and their property. They provided them with soft drinks, coffee, and telephones while identifying those members whose needs were critical. Eventually, 400 USAA employees and independent adjusters were on the scene, along with USAA's senior leadership.

Robert McDermott (center) and Charles Bishop (right), President of USAA's Property & Casualty Division, talking to USAA member at Homestead Air Force Base, Florida, following Hurricane Andrew.

In 1992 alone, USAA paid over $800 million in catastrophic claims. USAA's business line diversification, successful investments, and strong reserves enabled the Association to pay all claims fairly and promptly. Catastrophic reinsurance mitigated the severity of the financial losses. The reserves were quickly rebuilt by suspending SSA distributions in 1992 and automobile insurance dividends for six months.

Hurricane Andrew sent a strong signal to the insurance industry on the importance of financial strength. Nine property and casualty companies went out of business and the Florida Insurance Guarantee Association paid the claims for the failed companies. At the Association's request, USAA sent experienced claims experts to help resolve the cases. Concerned about their high exposure rates in coastal Florida, many companies began restricting their agents from writing new policies on residences. In December 1992, the Florida legislature created the Residential Property and Casualty Joint Underwriting Association (JUA) with the support of USAA and other property and casualty insurers. The JUA acted like an insurance company in that it wrote insurance for individuals who were unable to purchase homeowners coverage from other carriers. This destructive hurricane and other major catastrophes served as a catalyst for property and casualty companies to seek ways to transfer risk. The reinsurance industry was no longer able to handle the demands. USAA formulated a set of catastrophe principles that USAA used as guidance for involvement in future initiatives. They stressed use of private sources of funding and suggested the government serve only as an insurer of last resort.

Reducing loss costs in auto insurance coverage was another area of USAA leadership as well and the company earned a good reputation for its long tradition for aggressiveness on safety issues. McDermott was an industry leader in opposing Nissan's advertisement extolling speed that aired during the 1990 Super Bowl coverage. But McDermott's special safety interest was the air bag. On March 12, 1990, USAA member Priscilla Van Steelant was driving her 1989 Chrysler LeBaron along a rural road near Culpeper, Virginia. Suddenly, Van Steelant's car collided head-on with an-

Re-creation of the Culpeper Crash. *(Courtesy of Insurance Institute for Highway Safety)*

other 1989 Chrysler LeBaron. The cars were both totaled, but their drivers were not seriously injured to the amazement of rescue crews at the scene. The air bags that were standard equipment in that Chrysler model inflated, enabling both drivers to emerge from the twisted vehicles with only minor cuts and bruises.

McDermott urged maximum publicity; with the assistance of safety organizations, the story was well publicized. Later, the Insurance Institute for Highway Safety surveyed 227 car dealerships in the Washington, D.C., area about the crash. An amazing 81 percent had heard of the Culpeper accident and, of these, 46 percent said that customers had expressed an interest in air bags because of the crash.[6]

In addition to its efforts in promoting air bags, USAA and Staser Holcomb's cross-company safety committee had developed programs for drivers too. USAA had long worked at educating members

A Tradition Of Service

on auto safety. A National Family Opinion Survey revealed a full ten-percentage-point pro-safety differential between USAA members and policyholders from other companies. Traffic safety education did make a difference, and the committee's DRIVE SMART program held this as a basic assumption. The overall purpose of USAA's DRIVE SMART campaign was to educate audiences about safe driving techniques and practices. It concentrated its efforts on encouraging drivers to avoid drinking and driving, use safety restraints, properly maintain autos, and buy "smart cars" — those with the latest safety technology. The San Antonio pilot program had been considered a success and provided organizers with significant lessons learned for future campaigns including the necessity for communication and cooperation among the various public and private safety organizations.

Building on the experience of the San Antonio campaign, USAA

Assistant Vice President Mike Quinlan with the crash test dummies. Quinlan was eventually to be Regional Senior Vice President for the Mountain States Region.

exported the DRIVE SMART concept to all the regional office communities. The DRIVE SMART programs were similar in all locations, although each developed unique features. For example, in Colorado Springs, in addition to the basic precepts, a new wrinkle, "Drive Cool," urged drivers to keep their emotions in check while driving. Success in Colorado Springs led to a DRIVE SMART COLORADO and John Henry of the USAA Mountain States Regional Office became president of the statewide program. Jack Wolcott and his team from USAA's Virginia regional office developed DRIVE SMART Hampton Roads (Virginia) which also led to the formation of a state counterpart and it attracted the interest of the Armed Services in the area.

DRIVE SMART VIRGINIA logo

Other safety initiatives surfaced. Deaths of unbelted or improperly positioned young children caused by deploying air bags led to USAA educational programs on the proper use of seat belts and child safety seats. Encouraging drivers to secure young children in the rear seats of automobiles was stressed. Further efforts included advice for elderly drivers, imaginative articles on safe driving, and production of an award-winning video called *Shattered Lives* on the perils of drunk driving. Discouraging driving over the speed limit and supporting the use of reduced speed limits were also part of USAA's efforts.

Meanwhile, on the eve of McDermott's retirement, retired Rear Admiral Ben Hacker was named to head the Western Regional Office effective August 1, 1993. Hacker had joined USAA in 1988 after a successful thirty-year Navy career. After an orientation in San Antonio's home office, he had been transferred to Sacramento

Ben Hacker. Hacker later became USAA's Chief Administrative Officer and the first African American to serve on USAA's Executive Council. In 1997 he moved to head USAA's regional office in Norfolk, Virginia.

as an Assistant Vice President under Senior Vice President Joe Meyer. When California Governor Pete Wilson asked Hacker to head the state's Department of Veteran's Affairs office, he did so for two years. Afterwards, he returned to USAA, where he was promoted to Regional Vice President replacing Meyer.

At its August 21, 1993, meeting, the USAA Board of Directors reaffirmed the appointment of Robert T. Herres, USAA Chief Operating Officer, as Chairman and CEO to replace McDermott effective September 1,

Alice and Robert McDermott

1993, as spelled out in the succession plan approved by the Board in November 1991.

In recognition of McDermott's outstanding accomplishments, the Board appointed McDermott Chairman Emeritus and named the USAA Home Office Building in San Antonio the McDermott Building in honor of both McDermott and his deceased wife, Alice. The Board praised McDermott's "superlative leadership" and his development of a truly outstanding work force based on integrity and the Golden Rule. It also cited training, self-development, and the intelligent use of leading-edge technology.[7] Key USAA statistics covering McDermott's era from 1968 to 1993 speak for themselves.

USAA Growth Statistics 1968-1993

USAA	1968	1993
Members	653,000	2,400,000
Employees	2,683	15,240
Assets, owned & managed	$207 million	$29.5 billion
Private Auto Insurer Rank	16	5
Homeowner Insurer Rank	45	4

Whenever McDermott received an award, he was always quick to praise the USAA employees. Typical was his acceptance speech upon his selection to the Junior Achievement National Business Hall of Fame by the editors of *Fortune*. "Although I am accepting this, I am doing so in the name of the employees — they really made it possible," McDermott said. At the USAA Annual Members' Meeting in 1993, McDermott told the members that "passing along the leadership of such a treasured institution to the right person is important to me." He said he was proud to announce that "the right person" was General Bob Herres.[8]

CHAPTER TWELVE

THE TRANSITION TO NEW LEADERSHIP: GENERAL ROBERT T. HERRES

The ascension of retired Air Force General Robert T. Herres to Chairman and Chief Executive Officer of USAA on September 1, 1993, came as no surprise to the employees and top management of the company. Instead, it was the product of a careful search and grooming process personally orchestrated by McDermott. In retrospect, Herres' elevation constituted one of McDermott's most important decisions. He did not make the decision without long deliberation. As he pointed out to members in passing the mantle of leadership, Herres was the man he considered most qualified to lead the Association into the challenging future.[1]

McDermott's association with Herres began in 1983, when he interviewed Herres at a Washington, D.C., luncheon for an upcoming vacant position on the USAA Board of Directors. Both men hit it off from the start. Herres recalled that McDermott fit the mold of what he expected — an impressive in-charge person, very thoughtful, with a firm understanding of his job, and with the intellectual capability to cope with the issues of running a major company.[2] Similarly, McDermott was very impressed with Herres. When he returned to his room after the interview, he told his wife, Alice: "I've met my successor."[3] With McDermott's strongest recommendation, Herres was elected to the USAA Board at the next Annual Members' Meeting.

Six years later, Herres was on the threshold of retirement from his thirty-six-year military career. During the November 1989 USAA Board of Directors Meeting, Director Herres was excused from the room in order for the Board to discuss the role he might play in USAA's future. McDermott told the Board that his successor should be someone who would be "a leader for the future" and Herres was his choice. McDermott also had great admiration for Herres' wife, Shirley, whom he thought a perfect partner to help Herres represent the Association. He proposed that Herres join USAA as president of the Property and Casualty Division. The Board agreed and Herres was called back and congratulated by the Board members.[4]

Herres retired from active duty after a distinguished career on March 1, 1990, and joined USAA's management team one month later. Until that time, the bylaws of the Association allowed only one USAA employee (the President of USAA) to serve on the Board. On March 3, 1990, the bylaws were changed at a Special Members' Meeting in Tampa permitting two USAA employees to serve on the Board. Herres was elected to fill the newly established position, and was thus able to continue to serve as Board Vice Chairman.[5]

Bob Herres was born in Denver in 1932. His paternal grandparents had left New Jersey, settled in Denver and raised a family there. His mother came to Colorado by way of Arizona. Her father was diagnosed with tuberculosis soon after law school graduation and was sent from Washington, D.C., to Arizona for the drier climate. He later moved to practice law in Denver where Herres' parents met and were married. They had three children — Fred Willard "Bill" Jr., Margaret, and Robert, who was the youngest.

Herres was raised in a hard working and close-knit family. After eating dinner together many evenings, the family frequently gathered around the radio to listen to such favorite radio shows of the era as the "Lux Radio Theater." His father worked for sixty years in various areas of residential building and real estate development in Denver, and he taught his children the virtues of hard work. By example, he also taught his son Bob the value of listening to the opinions of others, a habit that would serve him well and which became a cornerstone of his management philosophy. Another influential building block in Herres' character was the Boy Scouts, where he earned the rank of Eagle Scout.

When the Japanese struck Pearl Harbor, Herres was barely nine years old, but he was well aware of the war and followed events closely. His older brother Bill was a cadet at West Point and a contemporary of McDermott when the war broke out. Soon after graduation, Bill joined the Second

Robert T. Herres as a high school senior

Infantry Division in France during the siege of Brest and served throughout the subsequent campaigns to liberate Europe. When the war in Europe ended, Herres' brother was commanding a company of infantry troops in Pilsen, Czechoslovakia. After the war, Bill remained in the Army as a career officer in the Infantry. His experiences and those of his classmates and colleagues exerted considerable influence on Bob, as did the fact that the Herres' family home in Denver was within one-half mile of Lowry Air Force Base. Bob Herres and his young friends watched from across the alfalfa fields as B-24s took off and landed all hours of the day and night. He and his friends sometimes sprawled on the grassy area near the base fence to watch the planes and to dream of flying. An interesting side note was the fact that Herres' father had served in the Signal Corps and ultimately the Air Service in World War I, and in later years would remind his son that he was a "charter member" of the Air Force.[6]

Affected by these various influences, when Herres graduated from

East High School in Denver, he decided in favor of a military education. Although he won a full Naval ROTC scholarship and admission to Princeton, Bob Herres opted instead to accept an appointment to the U.S. Naval Academy in the class of 1954, where he later became captain of the Academy's rifle team and a company commander.

U.S. Naval Academy Midshipman 3/C Robert T. Herres aboard the USS *Albany*, August 1951

When he entered the Naval Academy, Herres did not at first consider flying, but instead followed the rule that New York Yankee Manager Casey Stengel later made famous, "You play the ball game one inning at a time." But, after five orientation flights in the old N-3-N "Yellow Peril," Herres knew that he wanted to fly. At that time, the surest way to do that was to join the 25 percent of the graduating class who were to be commissioned in the Air Force. The opportunity to do this was to be based strictly on the "luck of the draw." On the Sunday night after the Army-Navy football game, a hat full of numbered papers was carried from room to room by Class President Dick Dean to determine the assignment preference

NEW LEADERSHIP

United States Naval Academy. *(Courtesy United States Naval Academy)*

sequence. (Dean would later become a Lieutenant General in the U.S. Marine Corps and a fellow USAA Board member.) The number Herres drew was low enough to give him his preference, an Air Force commission and the opportunity to go directly to flight training.

After winning his wings, Herres qualified in the F-86D Interceptor and was assigned to an Air Defense squadron at Kirtland Air Force Base in New Mexico. As a young single officer, he was a cautious but willing candidate for blind dates. Shirley Jean Sneckner, a young woman who was dating a fellow bachelor officer, fixed Herres up with dates from her Chi Omega Sorority at the University of New Mexico. Before long, Herres' Air Force cohort had separated from active duty and returned to Georgia where he married his high school sweetheart. Herres promptly went back to Shirley one more time for a date — this time with her. They started dating regularly in mid-September 1956, were engaged on December 1, and married at St. Paul's Lutheran Church in Albuquerque during Easter Week in 1957. They had their first child, Julie, in Albuquerque. Son Mike arrived next while they were stationed in Dayton, Ohio, and Jennifer was born later in Montgomery, Alabama.

Herres excelled in a variety of early assignments in the Air Force, receiving successive early promotions. An enthusiastic sportsman, he enjoyed hunting, skiing, golf, and playing intramural softball in Air Force leagues after work. After his Kirtland assignment, Herres went to the Air Force Institute of Technology, where he earned an M.S. in Electrical Engineering. He served three years in the U.S. European Command Intelligence Staff and at Chateauroux Air Station in France supervising flying training operations. Back in the United States as a student at the Air Command and Staff College, he simultaneously completed work on a second Master's Degree. During a follow-on assignment, a call went out from the Air Force for individuals interested in space programs — NASA's and the Department of Defense Manned Orbiting Laboratory (MOL). In 1967, he successfully completed test pilot school at Edwards Air Force Base in California and entered the MOL program. Unfortunately for its participants, this program became a victim of budget strains induced by the war in Southeast Asia and was canceled by President Nixon in 1969.

Subsequently, Herres served as a Strategic Air Command Wing Commander in northern Michigan and Thailand and in a number of important program staff positions. He was commander of the Air Force Communications Command and, later, Commander of the 8th Air Force. Then he served his second Pentagon tour — this time on the staff of the Joint Chiefs of Staff, leading to his final promotion and a fourth star. As a general, he was Commander-in-Chief of the binational North American Aerospace Defense Command, and be-

Lieutenant Colonel Robert T. Herres (far left) as a member of Manned Orbiting Laboratory program. Shown with (left to right), Major Bob Lawrence, Major Don Peterson, and Major Jim Abrahamson.

came the first American military officer ever to testify before an open committee session of the Canadian Parliament. On its formation in 1985, Herres also served as the first Commander-in-Chief of the United States Space Command.

The wide variety of experiences in a dynamic and flexible Air Force prepared Herres well for his next and final assignment — Vice Chairman of the Joint Chiefs of Staff. An education with the Navy, a brother in the Army, and experience in

General Robert T. Herres
Vice Chairman of the Joint Chiefs of Staff (1987)

joint service activities were also a plus. Herres was the first officer to hold the position that Congress had designated as the nation's second highest ranking officer in the military. His first task was to develop a description of the duties and responsibilities for the newly created post. Herres and his Executive Officer, Colonel Randy Blanks, worked out a draft based on the enabling legislation in coordination with the Joint Staff personnel. Chairman Admiral William Crowe and the Secretary of Defense approved the list as did General Colin Powell later when he replaced Crowe as Chairman. Basically, the Vice Chairman was the extra pair of knowledgeable and influential hands that the Chairman badly needed. Important duties included chairing the Joint Requirements Oversight Council (JROC) and serving as Vice Chairman of the Defense Acquisition Board (DAB). He also represented the Chairman on a number of important councils and agencies. As Chairman of the JROC and Vice Chairman of the DAB, Herres "institutionalized the role of the military in setting requirements for major weapons systems." *Defense Weekly* declared that he "put the process back in the hands of the military and the Joint Staff."[7]

Herres also spent considerable time attending and testifying at important Congressional hearings and committee meetings. Periodically, he hosted counterparts and other senior foreign military officials visiting the U.S. from various allied nations. Most importantly, Herres served as acting chairman when Crowe or Powell were out of pocket — about one-third of the time. In 1990, after retiring from a highly successful military career, Herres several times was asked again to serve his country, most prominently on the Vice President's Space Policy Advisory Board, and then, in 1992, as Chairman of the Congressionally mandated Presidential Commission on the Role of Women in the Armed Forces.

McDermott was pleased to land Herres for USAA. Herres had been a USAA Board Member since 1983 and Vice Board Chairman since 1985 and therefore knew the Association's operations well. McDermott told USAA employees of Herres' "superb reputation as an executive and innovator" during his Air Force career. "We are delighted to have a man of his ability and experience join us at USAA."[8] General Powell agreed with this assessment. In his memoirs, *My American Journey,* Powell wrote that when Admiral Crowe retired, he believed Herres was a "superb choice" and a "shoo-in" to succeed Crowe as Chairman of the Joint Chiefs of Staff.[9] Powell said he was surprised to get the position himself. In a later interview with the *San Antonio Express-News,* Powell called Herres "a great leader and a superb manager" and said that USAA and San Antonio were "fortunate to have him."[10]

Herres was described as "brilliant" and possessing "outstanding intellect" by individuals who had the opportunity to observe him and work for and with him. An Academy classmate, Tony Correnti, pointed out that of their class of 800 at Annapolis, Herres was the only one to earn four stars. Colonel Art Forster, who worked for Herres in several assignments, said he was "the most multi-talented man I've ever served for." The Commander of Operation Just Cause in Panama, General Maxwell R. Thurman, called Herres "unflappable in the face of crisis." William Hoover, former Assistant Secretary of the Department of Energy, noted that in spite of his stellar career, Herres remained "unassuming."

It was the unassuming part that the USAA employees in the Property and Casualty Company noticed first. He moved easily among them and engaged in conversation on business as well as his favorite recreational pursuits of skiing, fly-fishing, woodworking, and golf. He ate breakfasts and lunches with small, mixed groups of employees to help him understand how USAA worked from their perspective. On a holiday evening, he often drove to the USAA campus to offer good wishes to those required to work. Soon the employees also learned about the brilliant part, watching Herres quickly absorb information on the insurance business. His thoughtful and probing questions encouraged them to be well-prepared for meetings with him. In later years McDermott recalled that he was "very impressed" at the time by how quickly Herres was learning the business. He was "very, very sharp," McDermott said.[11]

Another trait that Herres demonstrated early was his tenacity to push ahead in the face of "too hard to do" objections. Soon after he arrived at USAA, Herres began receiving complaints from members about the difficulty of changing their addresses at USAA. The number of individuals changing an address was significant — over 600,000 in 1992 alone. If a member had auto and life insurance, a credit card, and a mutual fund, it took four separate calls to different operating companies to make the changes. In spite of its financial product diversification, USAA wanted members to feel that their Association was still a unified whole. And it was clear that members didn't get the "One Company" feeling when they had to call several different numbers to accomplish a simple change of address. When Herres asked why they could not just update a common data base on the computer, done after one call, he was told it was too complex, fraught with regulatory problems, and would require expensive software changes. He continued to press for the software development to implement the change, however, and the systems were modified to accommodate this need. The new service was announced to members in the December 1993 issue of *Aide Magazine.*

Another example was Herres' insistence that employee involvement in member service would continue to be the key to USAA's success in the future. He believed that an initiative in the Property and Casualty area, PRIDE (Professionalism Results in Dedication to Excellence) was just the right mechanism to enhance employees' growth and role in the Association. Herres became PRIDE's chief advocate in its infancy in 1990 and promoted it broadly within the Property and Casualty Division.[12] The seed for this employee involvement program had been contained in an earlier initiative called Leadership '86. Bill Cooney and a team including Mary Pieper, Billy Bowen, Janice Marshall, and others had put it together. Charles Bishop, then Regional Vice President of the Western Region, recalled that Leadership '86 had most of the elements that later surfaced in PRIDE, but at that time the program did not have wide support in the Property and Casualty Division.[13]

Instead of Cooney's proposal with its emphasis on empowerment, people, and service, management's focus in the mid-to-late 80s had moved to the claims area, and USAA brought in McKinsey and Company to help study it. Its claims effectiveness study analyzed 2,000 closed claims files looking for what improvements could be made. The study suggested that USAA wasted as much as $100 million annually through loss cost leakage — excessive and redundant payment for a variety of insured losses. In November 1986, the PACE (Professionalism and Claims Excellence) program was organized under Assistant Vice President Bill Hutton to help correct these problems. Ed Schrenk joined USAA to help improve the USAA claims process. PACE added manpower and automation which materially improved the situation. Finished with its study, McKinsey and Company began working on another study with Terry Shea and Walt Doughton for the improvement of sales, service and underwriting. This, along with the impetus that Leadership '86 provided, resulted in what eventually became PRIDE.

The actual PRIDE program in its refurbished form began in 1990. Besides its forerunners within USAA, it was also influenced by the quality movement that was getting significant attention in corporate circles. USAA was twice a finalist for the national Malcolm Baldrige Award. The experience in the competition led to the internal recognition that USAA's service to members was fine, but that many processes needed improvement. Beverley J. McClure headed a new Quality Office to help guide these efforts. The Association's success was so great that many other companies wanted to benchmark USAA. A monthly Quality Journey was established to handle the large influx of visitors who wished to tour the company and observe its operations. On occasion, USAA's experts were requested to assist other institutions and agencies. When Tanis Jenschke retired as Vice President of USAA's Communications Center, the Clinton White House asked her to serve as a consultant to help the President's staff develop procedures to handle its huge volume of mail. She received a commendation for her efforts.

In 1991, Bill Cooney was reassigned from USAA's Support Services to the Property and Casualty Company as Senior Vice President with the responsibility for planning, marketing, sales, systems integration, and a charter from Herres to assume overall responsibility for PRIDE. Cooney released McKinsey and Company and USAA ran its own program. Under Cooney's overall direction and with Herres' strong support and involvement, Janice Marshall, followed by Doris Dent, and then Del Chisolm led PRIDE as it grew into a key USAA program in the nineties. The vision of the program was "to provide member-driven service delivery that is flexible and ever improving." PRIDE's foundation was a values-based philosophy spelled out in the ten principles of PRIDE developed by employees who synthesized guidance from Dent, Cooney, and Herres. The principles espoused leadership, teamwork, and the pursuit of excellence. It empowered employees at all levels to participate and contribute. The principles guided employees to "live the Golden Rule" and to "have fun." It encouraged employees to exceed member expectations. The

The PRIDE logo, created by Myron "Butch" Dye.

essence of PRIDE was to encourage and capitalize on vertical communications within the company. This helped create an atmosphere in which change was accepted more easily. More importantly, it gave all employees the opportunity to contribute to improving USAA's ability to meet the changes and challenges that the Association was facing.

Another important initiative in Phase I of PRIDE consisted of a Sales, Service and Underwriting (SSU) Closed File Review, a study of member needs and expectations, and a best practices study. Completed in the first quarter of 1991, these process reviews also identified six projects that were called "early wins," projects with great potential for early implementation.[14] For example, one was discovering that members often had gaps in coverage. This led to a "service alert" program where claims representatives notified policy service representatives if they found gaps in coverage. The policy service representatives, in turn, notified the members. Discovering the advantages of claims and policy service representatives working closely together planted a seed that would develop into the Customer Insurance Team that would come later.

Phase II of PRIDE continued projects identified in Phase I, but its primary accomplishment was a process called Engaging the Organization. Simply put, this was the vehicle for providing employees with the skills and training they needed to be players in the PRIDE process. The training was extensive. Each Property and Casualty employee received twenty hours of training. Wherever possible, employees took the training together in classes of about fifteen to twenty students who were in the same service unit. It took about three years to train the close to 11,000 people in the changes involved. Courses taught facilitating, team building, and action planning. The ultimate goal was to challenge employees to take ownership of their company and to work on continuously improving it by substantially increasing the dialogue between the work force and management at all levels. Increased vertical communication made it possible to identify solutions to ongoing problems and to get problems out in the open so that they could be addressed. The process helped the focus shift from a project orientation to a new way for employees to look at USAA and their roles in its improvement.

Herres encouraged USAA's other companies and staff agencies to introduce PRIDE or PRIDE-like programs to their employees as well. And they all did. For example, the Bank's version was called ESP (Extraordinary Service Partnerships) and the Life Company's was LEO (Life Engaging the Organization). Whatever the PRIDE-like programs were called, the efforts paid positive benefits to the employees and the Association.

McDermott and the Board praised Herres' innovative leadership of USAA's core business and his efforts with PRIDE, and they were convinced he was the right man to succeed McDermott. To make the transition a smooth one, an Executive Succession Plan was developed and approved in November 1991 by the Board.[15] In accordance with the first step of the plan and effective January 1, 1992, Herres was selected as Chief Operating Officer for Insurance and Information Services and was designated Deputy Attorney-in-Fact. As specified in the second step of the plan, on September 1, 1992, Herres became President, Chief Operating Officer for USAA, and Attorney-in-Fact. As such, Herres' focus was on internal operations with the responsibility for the P&C Insurance Division, Life and Health Insurance Division, Information Services Division, and Investment Management Division. McDermott remained Chairman and CEO with a focus on external activities and direct oversight responsibility for the Banking and Real Estate Divisions. In another personnel change the following month, USAA Board of Directors' member and retiring Air Force General Hansford (H.T.) Johnson joined USAA's management team,

New Leadership

to later become USAA's Chief of Staff upon George Ensley's retirement. Johnson was a 1959 graduate of the U.S. Air Force Academy and the first graduate of that institution to earn four stars. His last Air Force assignment was Commander in Chief of the U.S. Transportation Command and the Air Mobility Command.

As he moved up the ladder of leadership at USAA, Herres demonstrated a management style that mirrored McDermott's in terms of innovation and boldness, but that differed in terms of emphasis on process, on employee empowerment and on focus. Like McDermott, Herres would prove to be a "big picture" leader, and he also displayed an extraordinary command of and interest in the detailed operations of the complex USAA organization. As McDermott and the Board realized, Herres' management style was well suited to meet the challenge posed by the rapidly changing competitive market, the revolutionary developments in communication and information technology and the need to refocus USAA's now wide-ranging business lines to take advantage of the synergy they presented.

CHAPTER THIRTEEN

MEETING THE CHALLENGES OF CHANGE

Herres assumed the leadership as Chairman and Chief Executive Officer of USAA at a pivotal time in the Association's history. No longer a niche reciprocal company providing auto insurance for military officers as it had begun, USAA was now a highly successful, Fortune 500 company, which owned and managed more than $31 billion in assets. The Association had become a huge, complex organization with more than seventy-five subsidiaries and affiliates with over 15,000 employees and 2.4 million members. It was the nation's fifth largest private automobile insurer, fourth largest homeowners insurer, thirty-seventh largest life insurance company, and its Investment Management Company (IMCO) ranked twenty-ninth of 348 companies with assets under management. In addition to its insurance and investment services, USAA's ownership extended to the USAA Federal Savings Bank; a travel agency; a member's buying service; a twenty-three-story retirement community; a health care facility; and joint ownership with Opryland USA in the Fiesta Texas Musical Theme Park in San Antonio; along with other real estate holdings across the U.S.

But the rapid growth had come at a cost. Externally, the diversification had tended to dilute USAA's powerful and attractive "one company" image. And internally, restructuring and the institution of process management were necessary to better integrate the operations of the many subsidiaries and to improve the vertical and horizontal communications between all the employees across the many companies. While most of the new lines of business were profitable and adding financial strength to the Association, the development aspect of the USAA Real Estate Company, particularly the La Cantera development project and its Fiesta Texas musical show park, was draining resources from the Association.

At the same time, outside in the marketplace, competitive pressures became more intense than ever as the nineties evolved, which together presented a serious challenge to the Association's position as an industry leader. For instance, overcapacity in the property and casualty industry precipitated increased competition for customers. And mergers and consolidations were changing the landscape of the insurance industry. Also, new competition was developing from the mergers in the banking and financial services industries. Finally, rapidly improving technology in the information and communication industries was accelerating the pace of change, driving management, business and work processes to move faster and become more interactive. All of this was happening at a time when it appeared that the Association's growth prospects would be limited in the years ahead with the likely military drawdown due to the end of the Cold War. It was clear to Herres that in order to keep USAA ahead of the competition, he would have to gradually restructure the company, deploy the latest information and communication technology to serve the members, and enlist the Association's top management and all of its employees in the rebuilding process.

Herres had thought long and hard about how USAA had to adjust to these challenges of change even before moving up to the Chairman and CEO slot. While still head of the Property and Casualty Company, Herres in February 1993 formed the Great Lakes Region as an operational test bed to evaluate new processes and technologies in an operational environment. The Great Lakes Region, headed by Assistant Vice President Rick Fowler, served Michigan, Indiana and Ohio, states with moderate regulatory requirements and a membership sample large enough for testing, but small enough to minimize risk and cost. Growing out of this were such innovations as Needs Based Sales and Service, and a knowledge-based expert system to better serve customers during a phone call. Aside from improving operations, Herres believed the closer contact with members in the Great Lakes Region would foster a closer relationship between USAA employees and members and generate ideas for additional products within existing lines of business. The idea of a test region caught the attention of the Harvard Business School, which developed a case study on the region to use with its business students.[1]

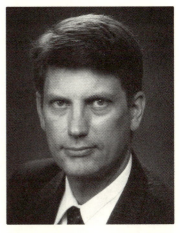

Rick Fowler was later to become Regional Senior Vice President at USAA's Western Regional Office at Sacramento.

Another major structural innovation, this time in the service area, was launched later by Bill Cooney, Herres' hand-picked successor as president of the Property and Casualty Company. Cooney developed the Customer Insurance Team (CIT) concept as a means of providing all property and casualty services to members in a specific geographical location. In the past, USAA policy service and claims employees served the members from separate units. Thus coordinating service to a particular member was more difficult. The CIT was a team of policy service, underwriting, and claims employees who would provide all of these services in a given area. Under the concept, some team members would be trained to handle policy service and simple claims functions. Cooney chose Oklahoma for his test site and put Esther N. Huff in charge. Started August 28, 1995, the team worked to achieve what Cooney referred to as "that small company soul inside our big company body." On the Oklahoma CIT's first anniversary, USAA management praised Huff and employees for their success and began using CIT in the Great

Lakes Region. USAA management believed that the CIT concept was to be the wave of the future in member delivery service.

When he became CEO of USAA, Herres focused internally on introducing processes and a more defined structure into how the Association went about its business. Most important was the revision of the way USAA did its planning. Herres believed that fundamental to USAA's future success was a clear vision for the future — the mission statement itself. While the revised mission statement remained constant in spirit with the earlier versions, he approved one that was simpler and more easily understood by employees and members alike. For planning, he continued to use the Key Result Areas (KRAs) construct that his predecessor had established as USAA's response through the creation of objectives supporting mission fulfillment. He then tightened up and strengthened the procedures used to put together an integrated plan. Senior Vice President Bill Flynn and his planning team provided the guidance to operating companies and staff agencies on the process. Strategic goals were developed at an annual Strategic Planning Conference in the spring and then continually reviewed and revised by senior management and reported to the Board of Directors. At the Operational Planning Conference each fall, specific market performance, financial performance, and program objectives derived from the strategic goals were developed for corporate USAA and for each line of business and the staff agencies that supported them. The Key Result Areas constituted the organizational framework for these goals and objectives.

The market and financial objectives were quantitative in nature and provided a picture of how well USAA's business was currently doing. The program objectives were qualitative and provided an avenue for innovation to spur business in the future. The market performance measurement constituted 40 percent of the corporate performance evaluation. This category, which included objectives in the Key Result Areas of Service, Product Value, and Growth, measured how well the Association was delivering value to the members through products and services and its ability to sustain that close member relationship over time. Financial performance measures accounted for 30 percent of the corporate performance score. This category, which included Financial Strength and Resources KRAs, sought to evaluate efficiency and how financially sound USAA was as a company. The performance in this area ensured that USAA would continue to be there when the Association's members needed it most. Lastly, the program objectives comprised 20 percent of the corporate performance evaluation and overall mission performance comprised the final 10 percent. This category related to any of the Key Result Areas as the Association sought new ways to sustain future performance.

Central to the planning process was the tasking of USAA officers to meet the specific objectives as part of their own responsibilities. By the end of 1996, a bonus component was added to the compensation of all employees that was tied to meeting their objectives. The USAA Board of Directors had agreed to instituting performance pool dollars to reward employees for achieving the objectives outlined in their individual line of business or staff agency plans. Each employee's bonus was subsequently adjusted by the overall corporate performance measure determined by the Board. Accomplishments judged beyond USAA's pre-determined "target" performance could result in an increase in the employee bonus pool. Similarly, shortfalls in pursuit of corporate objectives could reduce the size of the pool. This management system intended that all employees would focus on achieving the objectives for their own organizations while working as a team to achieve corporate objectives for USAA. Finally, in 1996, the Board approved a revision to the mission statement to establish a more inclusive characterization of the market upon which USAA would focus:

The mission of the Association is to facilitate the financial security of its members, *associates,* and their families through provision of a full range of highly competitive financial products and services; *in so doing USAA seeks to be the provider of choice for the military community.*[2]

A key factor in Herres' rebuilding effort was to change the structure and improve the procedures of the USAA Board of Directors itself. He wanted the Board to engage in developing and finally approving the strategic plans. Herres saw as the Board's major role, the independent oversight of USAA. As part of this responsibility, Herres wanted the Board to engage in developing and approving the Association's strategic plans. He also wanted the Board to evaluate the CEO and the Association's functional leadership on their efforts in executing the plans and in operating USAA. Board Member Homer Holland vividly described the process in this way — "nose in, fingers out." In essence, Herres wanted the Board to ask questions, but to let the Association's management handle operations. In Holland's view, Herres struck the proper balance between the Board and the management of the Association.[3]

To institutionalize the process, Herres asked the Board to develop new charters for all Board committees. First were charters for the Finance and Audit Committee and Personnel Policy Committee. In 1995, the new Nomination and Ethics Committees gave way to the Board Governance Committee, which combined these and other functions.[4] The new Governance Committee charter specified duties that included filling Board vacancies, Chairman and CEO succession planning, CEO compensation, Board performance, and ethics. The Board members themselves worked to identify potential Board nominees from a broader base of relevant experience with the assistance of the consulting firm of Heidrick & Struggles Inc. New nominees were sought and elected who had specialized expertise and/or business experience to help in the oversight of the diversified business of the Association. For example, Board member Bill

Hybl had the experience of running a major foundation and had legal and political experience as well. Such Directors were able to make valuable and specific inputs to assist Herres in making business decisions. To provide a link with the membership, the makeup of the Board continued to include at least 20 percent drawn from members on active duty.

However, a problem for active duty Board membership arose when President Clinton on June 5, 1996, nominated USAA Board member Admiral Jay L. Johnson for appointment as Chief of Naval Operations (CNO). Senator Strom Thurmond, Chairman of the Armed Services Committee, raised a question about Johnson's position as a Director of USAA because his financial disclosure statement indicated that he had been paid for Board service. Compensation for services performed by military personnel while on personal annual leave was common and at the time was unconstrained by the Department of Defense as long as such services did not interfere with military duties. Just a few months earlier the Senate had confirmed Johnson's promotion to his fourth star and appointment as Vice Chief of Naval Operations without objection with full knowledge of his role on the USAA Board as Johnson had fully disclosed.

USAA's reply to inquiries in this matter were straightforward. Active duty officers had served on the Board since 1922 and had always been paid. The Board members always took leave and no government resources were used in carrying out Board duties. USAA was never a government contractor and carefully avoided using the military ranks or position of any active-duty member of the Board in company publications, even on such things as ballots for Board elections. Independent consultants confirmed that the amount of compensation paid to USAA Board members was substantially less than that paid members of boards of comparable companies.[5] Nevertheless, to avoid any appearance of conflict, Admiral Johnson resigned from the Board effective August 17, 1996, as had been his previous intention upon confirmation as CNO. With compensated active-duty representation under fire, Herres looked for an alternate way to ensure that the concerns of active-duty members were heard. His solution was the creation of an Advisory Council to the Board made up of representatives of various groups comprising USAA's policyholders.

One of Herres' early structural changes came about when he staffed and assigned functional roles to the USAA Capital Corporation (CAPCO). CAPCO was originally formed in 1985 solely as an administrative legal entity and served as a type of central bank for all of USAA's subsidiaries. The purpose of the change in 1993 was to activate CAPCO as an operating entity and consolidate the non-insurance subsidiaries under one manager. Herres appointed H. T. Johnson as its first president, with the financial services subsidiary chiefs Jack Antonini, Ed Kelley, and Mickey Roth reporting to him along with the president of the Buying Services, Bobby Presley. CAPCO was charged with the responsibility of oversight of the retail investment products and banking services. Also included was the Buying Services' support of property loss replacement and its retail services to members. Most important, however, was the assignment to CAPCO of full responsibility for consolidated investment portfolio management of all surplus and reserves of the Association and its affiliates. To further solidify this critical investment portfolio management role, the Investment Advisory Council was formed to periodically review portfolio performance and develop recommendations for the CEO on investment policy and strategy. The president of CAPCO was appointed chairman of the Investment Advisory Council and line of business CEOs and key staff officers were appointed to membership. The insurance lines of business continued to report to Herres. Herres also strengthened the CAPCO Board by adding outside Directors who had experience to provide proper oversight in the realm of financial services.

CAPCO's previous primary function remained — to secure funding for USAA's subsidiaries, primarily to cover the credit card receivables for the USAA Federal Savings Bank. With its "AAA" ratings, CAPCO, with the backing of USAA, was able to get very favorable interest rates on loans.

USAA's investments and investment services were enormously valuable to the Association by providing a large and steady flow of profits which helped offset losses in heavy natural disaster years such as 1992, the year of Hurricane Andrew. As he reviewed the Association's investments, one trouble area, real estate development, drew Herres' attention. Following Herres' guidelines, USAA Real Estate Company President Edward Kelley worked to improve the profitability of USAA's real estate operations across the board.

A San Antonio native, Kelley graduated from Harlandale High School, but he didn't have money for college and joined the Coast Guard Reserve. After six months of active duty, he accumulated enough funds to start at San Antonio Junior College. While a student there, he first met his wife Nancy at the San Antonio Public Library. Kelley received a BBA in Finance from St. Mary's University in 1964 and an MBA in Finance in 1967. After a stint at college teaching and working in the mortgage investment business, he became president of Barshop Enterprises, a commercial real estate development and management firm. He had joined USAA in 1989 as head of the USAA Real Estate Company with the primary charter to develop Fiesta Texas along with maintaining USAA's real estate portfolio.

Under Herres' direction, Kelley

Ed Kelley

shifted investment emphasis into income-producing rather than the pursuit of developmental projects. The Austin Marriott and Four Seasons Resort at Las Colinas in Dallas did well, and occupancy levels of USAA commercial properties exceeded 90 percent. A number of undeveloped properties were sold as well as some properties with marginal potential, and the real estate portfolio was repositioned for profitability. The end result of all this activity was that the USAA Real Estate Company moved into the black and began to pay dividends to its holding company beginning in 1994.

Also in 1994, the USAA Board decided to limit further expenditures for the La Cantera development project to the golf course and development of infrastructure of other La Cantera properties to the extent necessary to attract and facilitate non-USAA capital investment.[6] The centerpiece of La Cantera was now the golf course, which hosted the Texas Open for the first time in 1995, less than one year after the course opened. The tournament was a prestigious one, the third-longest running on the Professional Golf Association Tour. In 1996, with a new golf clubhouse and the participation of PGA Tour newcomer Tiger Woods, the Texas Open drew over 100,000 fans. The announcement of the signing of a letter of intent was made to form a partnership and to build and operate a destination resort hotel at La Cantera with the Westin Hotel Company, Woodbine Development

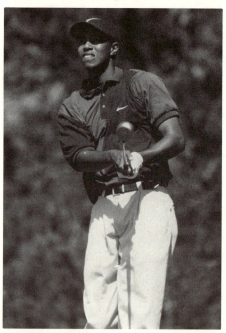

Tiger Woods, son of USAA member, retired Lieutenant Colonel Earl D. Woods. *(Courtesy San Antonio Golf Association)*

Company, and La Cantera development Company participating in the joint venture.

Fiesta Texas, which was to have been the centerpiece of the 1,600-acre La Cantera tract northwest of the USAA campus in San Antonio, fared less well. The musical show park built by USAA had opened in 1992. Operated by Opryland USA (which also held a minor partnership position), the park was beautiful, set in an abandoned quarry surrounded by 80- to 100-foot white limestone cliffs. Unfortunately, through its first four seasons, the park was not profitable and annual infusions of capital were required to develop new recreational areas and rides. Herres had been approached by the

Fiesta Texas

A Tradition Of Service

Six Flags subsidiary of Time-Warner regarding a role in either management or ownership of Fiesta Texas. Subsequently, he decided to look for a suitable buyer for Fiesta Texas and retained Goldman, Sachs to advise USAA in this process, stipulating that a Six Flags role should be considered. After lengthy deliberation and negotiations, USAA decided not to sell the park, but structured a ten-year lease-purchase agreement with the Six Flags organization. After the first year of operation, Six Flags heralded a significant rise in attendance, managed the park's first profitable year in operation, and committed millions of its own funds to additional capital improvements.

A highly successful USAA venture that demanded top management's attention because of its rapid growth was the Association's credit card business. USAA was serving almost two million accounts and was outgrowing its credit card operations in Tulsa. After looking at all of the options, including leasing or building in Tulsa, USAA decided to relocate the 420-person Tulsa operation to San Antonio. All full-time employees were offered an option to move to San Antonio, including reimbursement for moving expenses. Alternatively, they were offered placement service and generous severance packages. Beginning in September 1993, USAA flew more than 300 Tulsa employees to San Antonio to help them decide whether or not to move. Meanwhile, construction was underway on a Bank Services Building on the USAA Campus to house the credit card operations, and on January 27, 1995, the official grand opening was held. The new structure, along with an addition already begun and completed in 1996, had space for 2,500 employees,

David Robinson, USAA member and member of USAA Federal Savings Bank Board of Directors.

including the credit card operations.[7]

USAA's no-annual fee cards, low interest rates, and determination to have no ancillary charges for things like late payments attracted huge numbers of new cardholders. Constant praise from financial columnists and periodicals all over the country gave USAA tremendous free publicity. Virtually every column that recommended cards had USAA's cards high on their lists.

To protect its customers, the Bank installed a Falcon Fraud Detection System, which scored each credit card transaction for potential fraud. It worked. For example, just after New Year's Day in 1997, Bank Fraud Control Specialist Liz Cruz called a member in San Antonio to confirm his move to a small town in Ohio. The Bank had received a U.S. Post Office change of address card informing USAA of the pending change so she ran a routine check. The member said he was not moving. The USAA Bank representative took rapid action and in minutes canceled the member's existing card, notified the credit bureaus of the attempted fraud and issued a new card. This sophisticated system and an alert employee had stopped a fraud before it was successful. Feedback from members indicated that the Bank was routinely providing great service. For example, one member opened a credit card account with another bank because its initial interest rates were cheaper. She left her USAA credit card at home and went to Hawaii. Late one night she tried to check into a hotel and was told her card was over the limit; blocks for potential charges by hotels and rental car companies had eaten up her balance. She called the card issuer, but got no answer. She then called USAA. The USAA representative called the hotel, guaranteed the USAA credit card that the member did not have with her, and overnight expressed a new card to her.

Such overall superior service and products earned the USAA Federal Savings Bank a very special recognition. In June 1995, *Money* magazine selected the Bank as the "Best Bank in America."

The *Money* article declared that the Bank's "combination of safety, generous savings rates, minimal fees, unparalleled convenience, and five-star service beats the dividends off the competition." As a result of the article and subsequent publicity on ABC's *Good Morning America,* the Bank received over 20,000 telephone calls. These calls translated into 6,000 new accounts and over $20 million in new deposits.

Concurrent with changes in structure and business process, Herres began building a leadership team to push new initiatives. At his November 1994 management meeting, he announced some key promotions to help him fill the "need to accommodate changing business processes." He selected Bill Cooney as the president of the Property and Casualty Group effective February 1, 1995. Herres called this appointment perhaps "the most important decision I've made" so far at USAA. He said that Cooney was "well tuned to the problems of the future."[8] In addition, the regional vice presidents were given increased responsibilities, promoted to senior vice presidents (RSVPs, as they became affectionately known), and they would begin reporting directly to the president of the Property and Casualty Company.

In 1996, Staser Holcomb was appointed the new president of CAPCO to replace H. T. Johnson, who left USAA. During Holcomb's tenure at USAA, he had been at various times, President of the Property and Casualty Division, Chief of Staff, Chief Financial Officer, and Chief Information Officer. This diverse background gave Holcomb a unique perspective on CAPCO's role at USAA. Then, on Holcomb's retirement in early 1997, Herres appointed Robert G. "Bob" Davis as his successor. Davis had served nearly seven years in the U.S. Army, including service in Vietnam, and he separated as a captain in February 1973. After leaving the Army, he entered the financial services industry and chalked up more than twenty years experience. Prior to joining USAA, he had been President and Chief Executive Officer of Bank One in Columbus, Ohio.

To face the critical challenge of maintaining USAA's leadership in employing the latest in information technology, Herres established the Information Technology Acquisition Process (ITAP) in 1994. It created a life-cycle approach to the introduction and acquisition of new information systems with a phased review and approval structure for critical project design milestones. This was done to make sure that each information technology capability was clearly aligned with business objectives. It also ensured that funds were committed to development of such capabilities in increments that corresponded to the review and approval milestones. The system placed the business sponsor in the lead role in the acquisition process. In addition, it called for designated individuals to make information technology investment decisions. Responsible for this effort after November 1995 was the then new Chief Information Officer Donald R. Walker who followed Staser Holcomb into that role. Walker was another key addition to Herres' leadership team. An Air Force Academy graduate and retired Air Force Brigadier General, Walker's military career had centered around a number of large, software-intensive space and communications systems and programs. His new job was a challenging one: over 2,000 USAA employees worked for him, providing information technology and telecommunications services to the Association. The Information Services (IS) organization operated around the clock and was truly the nerve center of USAA. Thousands of daily telephone calls and millions of transactions were managed by IS to maintain what many

Bob Davis

Don Walker

regarded as the industry's model service environment.

Walker's statement of his mission sounded simple enough: "Information when and where you need it."[9] But simple it was not, and it required a massive rearchitecting effort. USAA's mainframe legacy system consumed significant maintenance and resources that would be better spent for more modern systems. For the time being, however, it had to be maintained with a new systems environment in development. USAA began migrating into Windows NT-based platforms on both desktops and in servers. The first step in the development of the new architecture was to understand the business processes in place and being developed and then to develop systems to support each product line of business. Always in the back of Walker's mind, however, was Herres' challenge to him to ensure the compatibility of all information systems.

Once plans for new or revised business processes had been determined, Information Systems had to build plans to support these changes. The costs were great, but steering committees monitored the progress to see that the expenditures were reasonable and justifiable in terms of business purposes. Proper use of systems had paid big dividends in productivity throughout USAA's history. For example, while USAA membership more than doubled between 1982 and 1997, the Property and Casualty Company's number of additional policy service representatives ratio to members declined 28 percent. One way costs were minimized was by exploiting the use of existing systems in property and casualty lines by modifying them for other lines of business. For instance, the IMAGE system, which was originally developed for property and casualty use, was subsequently used by the USAA Federal Savings Bank to put customers' signature cards on optical disk, making them instantly available for tellers and other bank employees.

In some cases the systems changes were more tactical in nature — even though the impact would be in the future. One such case was the Change of the Century Project under Jay Holmes. USAA's business application software, and virtually everyone else's, used only two digits to specify the year in order to conserve computer memory storage. With the new century looming, modifications had to be made so that systems could discriminate between the years 1900 and 2000. As often had been the case in the past, USAA began working on the crucial problem before most other companies and will be prepared for business as usual when the year 2000 rolls around.

Other changes were more strategic. At Herres direction, a Strategic Telecom Committee chaired by Bill Cooney reviewed telecommunications technology. The cross-Association committee developed a strategy for the future which included replacing the entire USAA telephone switching system. After spirited competition, and a very deliberate and extensive evaluation, USAA selected AT&T to provide its new telephone switches. Through the interface and use of key computer data, these switches have the potential to identify callers and route their calls to the most appropriate service representative. Information system interfaces also provide members' information on the employees' computer terminals so they can handle members' problems more efficiently. Among other things, the new switching system promised increased productivity and improved answer rates, not to mention better service to the members.

Another strategic information systems effort was the Blue Eagle Alliance. Herres and IBM Chief Executive Officer Lou Gerstner agreed to reengineer USAA's Property and Casualty Insurance business processes. The focus was to accomplish claims handling more efficiently and to achieve a higher level of member and employee satisfaction. Both companies stood to gain substantially from the alliance. IBM would benefit from an understanding of updated business requirements which would give direction to its continuous technology development. It would also give IBM exposure to the implementation of the newest technology and methodologies. USAA would receive the support of IBM's technical expertise in its quest for improved systems development. This included the intellectual assets of IBM's worldwide laboratories and research facilities.

As he was making these changes, Herres set about to get the best advice and guidance he could from top management across USAA's subsidiary companies. Herres' leadership style was to get as much input as possible before making key decisions. Important to this end was hearing the ideas of his Executive Council members and increasing communications among various lines of business. He began holding Executive Council meetings on a frequent regular basis. Proposals for new programs and services were briefed before the Council to enable all council members, staff, and business heads alike to comment on any issues or problems they felt needed more considerations. Weekly staff meetings gave Herres further opportunities for cross-discussion of issues facing the company. And weekly activity reports by each member updated Herres on new and pending issues and kept other Executive Council members in the loop at the same time.

Besides gathering input from the Council, Herres sought the views of others. An important channel was through member correspondence addressed to him as USAA's Chairman and CEO. Herres insisted on personally signing replies to as much of this correspondence as possible. At first, his staff was incredulous. They believed that the large volume of correspondence would surely discourage him after awhile, but it did not. A prodigious worker, Herres read the correspondence and monitored actions taken by the involved business activity to deal with key issues in order to gain valuable insights into the issues troubling the members. And he continued to sign the letters of response personally. Member comments kept him in touch with day-to-day problems at all levels and helped him to develop his own ideas on needed future directions of USAA.

Another source of input came from members' telephone calls. Members' letters had normally been seen by USAA officers, but verbal comments to member-contact employees were most often not. In August 1992, the ECHO (Every Contact Has Opportunity) program enabled these member-contact employees to pass on the members' comments. Snapshot comments were combined, analyzed, and passed along to the senior staff. These comments revealed patterns of positive and negative reactions to every facet of USAA's operations. Corporate Research continued to administer a wide variety of surveys and to conduct focus groups of members. Herres valued real-time data and in 1994, all these information-collecting functions were automated and gathered into a Member Relations and Feedback unit under Tim Timmerman. At this point, over 6,000 member-contact employees input more than 1,600 items weekly, using an automated electronic network. This new system became a model and attracted national interest. It was an important program for the Association and gave the employees more frequent direct input to USAA's senior managers, and broadened feedback far beyond the conventional methods of the past. Rules for input were simple; they had to be voluntary, beyond the representatives' ability to fix, and had to pertain to USAA operations. These were then collected and integrated into a tremendous body of information about the membership that was distributed for the benefit of senior leadership and other users. While all the input was important and answering the mail was a must, Herres continually reminded his staff that these things were not enough. USAA needed to react to the

A Tradition Of Service

comments to fix the problems. PRIDE was an important contributor to this problem-solving process.

Employees reacted to problems and fixed them routinely when they were able to do so. PRIDE teams undertook group efforts to identify difficulties that members experienced in doing business with USAA; they also sought to make things easier for employees to serve each other. For example, in the southeast Region, a team reduced courier service costs and an After Hours Operations team developed a system to save member-contact employees significant time while serving members. The Mid-Atlantic Region took on the problem of simplifying property loss settlements after automobile accidents. Central Region employees came up with the idea of improving the procedures for quoting homeowners coverage prices.

At the individual level the PRIDE philosophy sparkled. For example, Becky Nicholson, a field adjuster from the Southeast Region, visited the home of a member to handle an accident investigation process. What she found was the wife of the member in a state of shock. Her husband had been in intensive care for several days as a result of the accident, and she hadn't been able to visit him because she had no transportation. She had little food in the house, her morale was very low, and her personal effects were still in their car, which was in the salvage yard. Nicholson took the wife to the junkyard to recover her personal items, to the hospital to visit her husband, and to the store to stock up on groceries.

In another case, Sandi Stanford, a service manager, took up the case of a deaf member who did not understand her homeowners policy. Instead of trying to communicate through notes, Stanford hired an American sign interpreter. The result was a happy member who knew that her insurance company cared for her. These special services evolving naturally out of the PRIDE philosophy strengthened the members' belief in the Association's special status in their lives.

MEETING THE CHALLENGES OF CHANGE

The mutual trust and respect between the Association and its members clearly evident in these actions underlined the unwritten core beliefs under which the Association operated. Herres decided to introduce a more formal process into the ethics of the Association. That employees should be governed by strong ethical principles was not new to the Association. But a written code of ethics and a structured program, including training, was. In 1996, Herres briefed the Board and showed the new USAA Code of Ethics to them. Liz Gusich was selected as the Ethics Coordinator and reported to the USAA Ethics Council chaired by Staser Holcomb.

Central to USAA's success has been the Association's strong commitment to both its members and its employees. As McDermott put it in an interview with the Harvard Business Review in 1991, "Customers and employees are both precious resources." By treating both members and employees as "precious resources" during his twenty-three-year tenure as CEO, McDermott reduced the employee defection rate from 43 percent to 5 percent and pushed the customer retention rate to an incredible 99 percent.[10] Herres strongly shared those views and believed that crucial to success of process management was the necessity of recruiting, training, empowering, and retaining employees who fit into the company culture and accepted its core value of customer service. "We want to keep our employees when we shift to new processes," Herres said. "They come with assets like loyalty, commitment to customers, and understanding of our culture and our mission."[11]

The goal of training and empowering employees, Herres has told top managers, is to continue to improve and adapt to change. "We must keep getting better because everyone else is," Herres said. "Change will be a way of life. But we must also stay focused on corporate goals and our core values will not change."[12] These core values were later published in the *USAA Code of Business Ethics & Conduct* and are service, loyalty, honesty, and integrity.[13] A key to employee development and retention were company-wide education and training programs, begun under McDermott. Even though USAA's employee training programs were extraordinarily intensive and costly when Herres took over, he greatly expanded them. Herres believed they were essential in order to continually upgrade employee skills and help employees cope with sweeping change and the introduction of new technology and processes.

"We're training everybody right now," Herres told the *Journal of Business Strategy* in a panel discussion on the "Role of the Corporation." "We have a big role in training people. But that doesn't take the individual responsibility away from them to train themselves too."[14] Herres cited as an example the success story of Janice E. Marshall, President of USAA Buying Services, Inc. " as a woman who took advantage of the self-development we offer our employees."[15]

Training and career development are not only important requirements in creating an empowered work force with high productivity and the ability to cope with change. They are also key components for supporting employee retention, along with a modern, well-equipped workplace and attractive employee benefits, all of which have long been provided by USAA. Herres' introduction of child development to USAA was a major new initiative. In 1995, the USAA Child Development Center opened in a new building across Fredericksburg Road from the McDermott Building in San Antonio. This Center, operated by Corporate Family Solutions, and a medical facility, operated by MacGregor Medical Health Center, serve USAA employees and their families. Child Development Centers at all USAA's major regional offices were planned and construction began in 1996 and 1997. The second USAA Child Development Center opened on August 5, 1996, in the Colorado Springs office.

USAA Child Development Center, San Antonio, Texas

USAA has been a leader in other employee areas as well. After the passage in 1990 of the Americans with Disabilities Act, the Association hired a full-time Accommodation Specialist to consider the special needs of employees and prospective employees with disabilities. Newly developed accommodations included audible floor indicators in elevators for visually impaired employees and sign language interpreters to assist hearing-impaired prospective employees. By mid-1997, over 200 physically-challenged employees were in the USAA work force.[16] The Association was also quick to respond to repetitive motion injuries such as carpal tunnel syndrome brought on by the extensive time on computer keyboards. USAA started an ergonomic program in 1989 and in 1993, it opened an ergonomics laboratory and assigned three people to work on ergonomic-related problems. These specialists evaluated work sites and conducted safety and ergonomics training sessions for employees. Hank Austin, USAA's safety manager, pointed out that an important part of the program was to improve the individual workstation to prevent or minimize injuries. Sometimes this meant new equipment and sometimes it required making adjustments to existing workstations.[17]

Two other programs also received positive reception from employees. Employee Benny Knudsen, retired leader of the U.S. Air Force's Band of the West, began a USAA Concert Band. This band and its breakout jazz band brought enjoyment to the employee-musicians and to everyone else.

USAA Concert Band

The second was the advent of the Black History Month Celebration. Conceived of and started on her own by IMCO employee Brenda Butler, the program became a popular one. Employees enthusiastically joined in and developed outstanding programs year after year. A number of outstanding African-American speakers, such as Colonel Herbert Carter, one of the original Tuskeegee Airmen, made a major contribution to the programs. Exhibits and contests had great educational value. And the USAA Gospel Choir made up of employees who loved to sing was remarkable — a hit whenever it performed.

USAA Gospel Choir

Perhaps the most popular Herres' initiative among the employees was his introduction of a relaxed dress code on Fridays, Saturdays, Sundays, and after 6:30 p.m. on weekdays.[18] The program worked so well and was so enthusiastically received that in February 1997, Herres announced a sweeping revision of the USAA Dress Code that expanded to include "business casual" dress on Monday through Thursday.

The internal changes in management style at USAA were quite naturally closely watched by all employees, including the managers. While taken seriously, the changes also were the source of some amusement. A cartoon strip lampooning management fads that became popular during the nineties, Scott Adams' *Dilbert,* became

A Tradition Of Service

DILBERT® reprinted by permission of United Feature Syndicate, Inc.

popular among USAA employees as well. Adams' strips, portraying the "cubicle's eye view of bosses, meetings, management fads, and other workplace afflictions,"[19] appeared here and there in work areas around the McDermott Building. Management took it in stride, however, and Dilbert appeared in company briefings and even made appearances in Herres' talks to his management meetings.

While what was occurring inside USAA was important, during the nineties it became increasingly important for the Association to stay abreast of external developments. Especially critical were regulatory actions affecting USAA, varying from federal insurance legislation and possible banking law revisions, to state programs for assigned risks and special disaster fund authorities in Florida and California. USAA General Counsel Bill McCrae brought in Fred

DILBERT® reprinted by permission of United Feature Syndicate, Inc.

508

Bosse as Vice President, State Legislative Affairs, to monitor activities in state governments. Christopher Seeger became Assistant Vice President to the General Counsel, serving in USAA's Legislative Liaison office in Washington, D.C.; Jim Jinks and Robert Henderson filled similar positions in California and Florida respectively.[20] After McCrae's retirement, the leadership of these activities passed to Bradford W. Rich, who was appointed USAA's General Counsel and Corporate Secretary.

Brad Rich

Holding a law degree from George Washington University, Rich had served as a Staff Judge Advocate in the Air Force and held executive positions with several reinsurance and insurance companies including ACE Limited and Crum and Forster Corporation. He joined USAA in January 1996. Rich's office worked closely with John Cook and George Tye of Corporate Communications and the Property and Casualty staff on issues confronting USAA in various states.

One such state was New Jersey. In May 1994, Herres briefed the Board about the Association's significant losses in New Jersey's assigned risk claims.[21] One avenue explored was to form a new company, USAA of New Jersey, and to renew all USAA new Jersey policyholders in the new company beginning in January 1995. Fortunately, positive changes in New Jersey's political climate, economy, and accident rates enabled USAA to continue serving its policyholders there without resorting to this unpopular solution.

In California, a serious external regulatory problem for USAA persisted in the wake of passage of Proposition 103 in November 1988. On October 16, 1991, California Insurance Commissioner

A Tradition Of Service

John Garamendi had ordered fourteen of the state's largest insurers to refund $1.5 billion to policyholders in accordance with computations based on a formula developed by the Department of Insurance. The Department's interpretation of this formula and the formula itself failed to credit USAA with significant unique features that caused lower rates. Insurance companies were appalled at the size of the refunds required and none agreed to pay, and instead returned to the courts, contending that Garamendi's methodology for calculating the refunds was flawed and illegal. In August 1994, the California Supreme Court upheld the Commissioner's authority to order immediate rollbacks.

In light of the Court's decision, Herres decided it was time to get the whole rollback issue settled. He flew to California, met with Garamendi and indicated a desire for a fair settlement which would not require members in other states to subsidize a rollback in California. Then Herres dispatched the Association's Chief Actuary Steve Goldberg to attempt once more to negotiate a settlement with Garamendi. The effort succeeded and on December 21, 1994, Garamendi issued a press release announcing the settlement. The rollback obligation was settled at $75 million, $44 million of which had already been credited to various policyholder accounts in 1989 and again in the years 1990 through 1992 through cash distributions to policyholders from Subscribers Savings Accounts and other means. In essence, Garamendi had agreed with much of USAA's position that the rollback amount he had ordered did not take these distributions into account. USAA emerged with its integrity intact in a state with the Association's largest number of members. Several USAA members in California returned their rollback dividend checks to the Association because they believed that USAA was correct in its position and that no rollback was warranted. These checks found their way into the USAA Charitable Trust.

On the national scene, USAA strongly supported the Insurance

Institute for Property Loss Reduction (IIPLR). The IIPLR was founded in 1993 by combining the purposes and activities of two long-standing committees — the National Committee on Property Insurance and the Natural Disaster Loss Reduction Committee. Charles E. Bishop, USAA's Property and Casualty President, was elected founding Vice Chairman of the new organization. The new Institute was modeled after the Insurance Institute for Highway Safety (IIHS) in which USAA had been active and which had experienced great success over its thirty-five-year history.[22] USAA played a significant and active role in facilitating the merger and promoting broad, high-level industry support for the industry's significant potential in the loss mitigation arena. Founders intended that their new organization would have the same positive impact in reduction of property damage as the IIHS had accomplished in automobile safety.

In 1995, USAA's Property and Casualty chief Bill Cooney was elected chairman of the Institute and other USAA employees were assigned to various committees. A strategy was developed to energize IIPLR in its mission to reduce injuries, human suffering, deaths, property damage and economic loss caused by natural disasters. Herres and Cooney hosted a meeting of CEOs that unveiled the new strategic direction for IIPLR and generated industry-wide commitment to ensure the success of this important organization.

The new IIPLR strategic plan specifically addressed the five most threatening natural hazards: earthquake, flood, wildfire, hail, and windstorm. It also implemented three major initiatives: retrofit of more than 92,000 not-for-profit childcare centers across the nation; a new seal of approval was proposed to identify structures that adhered to upgraded property loss mitigation construction standards; and it also established a program where communities will serve as models for mitigation efforts. Finally, under Cooney's and IIPLR CEO Harvey Ryland's leadership, a critical partnership was estab-

A Tradition Of Service

lished with the Department of Energy, Department of Agriculture, the United States Geological Survey, the Federal Emergency Management Agency, and others in a cooperative effort to reduce losses from natural disasters. Overall, these initiatives could result in billions of dollars in savings to consumers and to the insurance industry.

Two other important external activities of USAA and its employees were charitable giving and community volunteer efforts for worthwhile causes. Corporate giving and community volunteer efforts over the years played a major role in shaping USAA's positive public image, but they were never the primary motivation for these efforts. The corporate goal was to improve the quality of life for all the citizens of communities where its employees lived and worked. To better manage USAA's philanthropy, in 1996 all community activities functions were organized under Assistant Vice President, Community Relations, Barbara Gentry. Gentry, who was promoted to Vice President in 1997, reported directly to Herres and served as the primary interface between USAA and the community. This included volunteer efforts as well as philanthropic support. Gentry also served as executive agent for the Corporate Contributions Committee composed of USAA senior officers. Each year the USAA Board of Directors was briefed on USAA philanthropy and plans for the future year. The USAA Foundation, a Charitable Trust, was established and funded to serve as the principal vehicle for disbursing funds.[23]

Since its early years of operation, the USAA Federal Savings Bank had maintained a separate charitable contributions budget administered by Judy McCormick, the Bank's Assistant Vice President of Compliance and Community Investments. The Bank's special role was to help provide funds to organizations developing affordable housing for low-income families. Neighborhood Housing Services of San Antonio was a major recipient of these funds. The Bank and USAA also provided funds for Habitat for Humanity, and volun-

Habitat for Humanity Volunteers (left to right) Barbara Gentry, Jill Weinheimer, and Mary Schoff

teers to help eligible families build their own homes under this program. These employees, part of USAA's Volunteer Corps, played a role in activities throughout USAA employee communities.

In 1996 alone, USAA employees contributed over 190,000 hours to their communities. The USAA Volunteer Corps aqua tee shirts with the USAA logo were a familiar sight at community activities, especially those supporting children. Employees at every level contributed, including Herres and his wife Shirley, who included the Santa Rosa Children's Hospital Advisory Board among their

Shirley and Bob Herres with two new friends at Santa Rosa Hospital. *(Courtesy of Santa Rosa Hospital)*

A Tradition Of Service

many community service activities. They also helped build houses for Habitat for Humanity.

Christmas Cheer remained popular, and Santa and elf-dressed volunteers delivered fun and presents to local institutions and families. The USAA Chorus also participated in Christmas activities throughout San Antonio, including singing at retirement communities. While the employees helped bring the Christmas cheer and spirit into the community, they took care of their own too. During Christmas of 1986, USAA employee Felix Barba suffered two heart attacks which left him comatose. Every year for the past ten years, Christmas finds his former fellow employees at the Barba family door with cash and gifts to help brighten the family's holiday. Barba's wife Gloria appreciates the gifts, but more important to her

USAA Chorus

is that even though her husband has been retired for years, the USAA employees remember. "That is a gift of love," she says.[24]

The USAA volunteers in San Antonio and the regional offices gave more than their time. They contributed dollars to the United Way and blood to the community blood banks as well. They also

Christmas Cheer volunteers Damian Vazquez (Santa), Yolanda Lewis (sitting), and (left to right) Diana Villarreal, Margie Arriaga, Eileen Ortegon, and Diana Hill. *(Courtesy of the Victoria Courts Childcare Center)*

WESTRO Volunteers Gwen Smith, Robin Tumble, Vince Costello, and Bonnie Jackson on Fire Safety Day (1994).

served on a wide variety of Boards in leadership positions in non-profit agencies and institutions.

USAA's major thrust in corporate contributions was towards education, which was a prominent thrust for the Association's volunteers as well. Although there were many successful programs, the most significant were the USAA Mentor and Junior Achievement programs.

The USAA Mentor program, underway since 1988, became a national model. It won a number of national, state, and local awards, including the prestigious President's Volunteer Action Award in 1994. The Mentor program had a positive impact on all the mentored students. Two dramatic examples were eighth-grade girls who entered the program because the school counselor judged them to be at high risk to become dropouts. Their mentors, Valerie Heflin and Rachel Gutierrez, did an outstanding job and the girls not only completed high school, but graduated as valedictorian and salutatorian in the class of 1994. Both went on to college with scholarships, one to Dartmouth College and the other to St. Mary's University in San Antonio. In 1997, the Mentor program included 830 mentors in 125 schools in San Antonio.

To provide opportunity for employees who could not commit to mentoring every week, other programs such as team mentoring and pen pals were available. USAA also continued the effort begun by President Bush's Point of Light selectee Vic Ferrari, now retired, to encourage other organizations, businesses, and institutions to join in mentoring school children. Over sixty-eight groups of volunteers from military bases, the Office of the Mayor and many businesses provided an additional 2,700 mentors to the city's students. The USAA Tampa office continued to run its Saturday Scholars program, which it started in 1988. The program featured two six-week sessions each fall and spring. Twenty USAA employees worked with twenty-five students from Edison Elementary School to provide information on careers and one-on-one tutoring in mathematics and reading.

Junior Achievement, a team program to teach business principles and encourage students to stay in school, attracted 215 USAA volunteers. The 1996 Junior Achievement National Business Hall of

Employees Hank Johnson (left) and Janet Wells (center) participating in the Southeast Regional Office's Saturday Scholars Program.

Fame Dinner was cosponsored by USAA and held in San Antonio. Lanier High School (San Antonio) student Yesenia Cardenas, president of her graduating class, was a speaker. Cardenas said that when she began in Junior Achievement in the eighth grade she never would have believed that she would see such people as the volunteers, except in magazines. "These consultants became not only tutors, but our friends and role models," she said. She thanked the guests for "all the lives you have changed." Herres, who was in the audience and joined in the standing ovation, served as Vice Chairman of National Junior Achievement in 1996, a position that leads to chairmanship in 1997.

The most significant USAA corporate good citizenship effort directed nationally was the Arnold Shapiro documentaries sponsored by the Association. The series of programs that had begun in 1988 with *Raising Good Kids in Bad Times* continued to focus on improving the quality of life for children and their families. In 1994, Walter Cronkite hosted *Victory Over Violence,* which suggested ways for communities to reduce violence in their neighborhoods. One columnist reported that Vice President Al Gore praised the documentary lavishly around the White House.[25] *Scared Silent*, hosted by Oprah Winfrey, covered physical, emotional, and sexual abuse of children. This pioneering special appeared on all four major networks (NBC, ABC, CBS, PBS) and was the most-watched documentary in television history, attracting an estimated 56 million viewers. The production elicited over 110,000 telephone calls to the National Child Abuse hotline during the show alone. Calls to the hotline tripled the normal amount for more than nine months and today are still running double the former average rate. Winfrey called it the most important show she had ever done on television. Since its initial airing, *Scared Silent* has appeared in over forty nations worldwide.

The 'Eyes' logo from "Scared Silent"

When child abuse agencies asked for something on abuse that could be shown to children, USAA sponsored *Break the Silence*. Hosted by Jane Seymour and aired on CBS, the documentary combined with animation won the George Foster Peabody Award for Broadcasting in 1995. Other USAA-sponsored documentaries included *Bad Dads,* hosted by heavyweight boxing champion George Foreman on the FOX network, and *Everybody's Business,* carried by NBC and hosted by Katie Couric, of the *Today Show.* Designed to encourage businesses to increase their efforts to help children in their own communities, *Everybody's Business* was also distributed to Chambers of Commerce across the nation. The latest USAA-sponsored Shapiro special, *What's Right With America,* is scheduled to be shown on CBS on July 4, 1997, in conjunction with USAA's seventy-fifth anniversary. The USAA-sponsored documentaries have won dozens of awards and television rating services estimate that they were watched in aggregate by more than 185 million Americans.

The planning, restructuring, employee education and empowerment, and cost containment measures focused on by Herres showed up strongly on the bottom line in 1995. Despite the fact that it was the third worst year ever for catastrophe losses due largely to an unusually active hurricane season, USAA recorded its highest net income on record up to that time — $730 million, a 29 percent increase over 1994. The Association's net worth increased 28 percent and revenues increased 7 percent. At year's end, USAA's owned and managed assets grew to $38.8 billion, up from $33.6 billion in 1994 enabling the largest dividend distribution in the history of the Association. Still, as he looked to the future, Herres felt it was time to deal with the growth issue, which would inevitably be impacted by the reductions in U.S. military force levels.

In what was possibly his most far-reaching decision, Herres recommended to the Board of Directors extending eligibility for access to USAA's property and casualty products to enlisted members of the armed services. He pointed out that this was a logical next step to find better, more comprehensive ways to serve the nation's entire military community. After months of dialogue and detailed study, on October 14, 1995, the Board approved a resolution that permitted management to begin phased extension of associate membership to active duty enlisted service personnel and Reserve and National Guard enlisted men and women on active duty.

The move expanded USAA's military niche significantly. It benefited the nation's enlisted men and women by providing them access to very competitive rates for insurance coupled with the Association's outstanding service. Finally, USAA would be able to serve the entire military family. In earlier days, the enlisted market was quite large and USAA was too small to adequately fund such an ambitious undertaking. But by 1996 when the program would begin to be phased in, the situation was different. The enlisted force was much smaller because of military downsizing and USAA could serve it without sacrificing the Association's quality service and competitiveness. Additionally, the enlisted corps was part of an all-volunteer force that was better educated and trained than ever before. The Association was large enough to accommodate the new group and USAA's financial position was strong enough to capitalize the added growth.

Herres told the Board that even though the number of enlisted personnel was smaller than in the past, the market was still very significant. The active duty enlisted men and women exceeded one million and the other enlisted segments were triple that number.[26] Herres reported that phasing of eligibility meant that the active enlisted force would be brought in carefully planned geographic segments a few states or overseas areas at a time. If assimilated gradually, USAA could continue to sustain its competitiveness and high-quality service to all members, new and old. A reasonable growth rate would assure that capitalization requirements would be manageable and not dilute the Association's strong financial position.

In early 1996, active-duty enlisted personnel being reassigned to Germany were the first of the new group to be served. Next on the agenda for eligibility extension were six states, one from each of the six operating regions in November 1996. Two more states followed in early 1997 and completion of the extension of eligibility to active-duty personnel was planned for the end of 1998. The first policy under the new eligibility rules was issued to Army Master Sergeant Carol McGibbon-Haskins by New Member Sales Representative Michael Ramirez. McGibbon-Haskins had fourteen years

MEETING THE CHALLENGES OF CHANGE

Advertisement which appeared in the 1996 issue of *Off Duty* magazine's "Welcome to Germany" guide.

of service and was under orders for assignment to Germany.

Another long-term effort for future growth was USAA's youth marketing program aimed at developing closer relationships with dependents of USAA members. Developed by Corporate Communications were two new magazines. The first magazine, *Under 25,* was mailed to dependents between the ages of sixteen and twenty-three. That magazine featured articles about cars, money management, college life, and other subjects of interest to that age group. The second, *"U" Magazine,* was geared to members' children aged ten to thirteen. Both won wide acceptance from both member-parents and their children. And in its February 1995 issue, *Aide Magazine* received a new name, *USAA Magazine.*

Herres saw as an important dimension of corporate growth and service to its market the creation of new products and service delivery methods within the Association's existing business lines. One such new product was Life Company's variable annuity. In November 1996, *Money* magazine picked the USAA variable annuity as a "best choice" for growth. IMCO continually looked into new product offerings that might capture member interest, to include state unique funds. The fund with the widest interest was the USAA S&P 500 Index Fund. While there were other index funds on the market, USAA capped expenses at 0.18 percent, which financial columnists pointed out was lower than Vanguard's Equity Index Fund, the previous lowest.

Future products and services under consideration included a new credit card offering with fringe benefits. The Association was unable to offer such a card out of the USAA Federal Savings Bank because Texas usury laws prohibited charging both interest and an annual fee. But the fee was necessary to help pay for the ancillary services that came with the card. In the fall of 1996, the Association opened a new subsidiary in Nevada, the USAA Credit Card Bank. Mark Wright, President and CEO of the USAA Federal Savings Bank, selected Nevada because its law permitted the use of annual fees to subsidize services. Wright had joined the Bank in December 1993 as Senior Vice President; he was a graduate of Mississippi College and had over twenty-five- years experience in the banking industry. Wright was selected as President of the Federal Savings Bank in January 1996, replacing Jack Antonini who had departed the previous year.

Mark Wright

When opportunities to exploit synergism arose, USAA offered new products and services delivered by alliance relationships. In 1991, the Buying Service began offering a USAA Road and Travel Plan featuring amenities such as a toll-free 800 emergency number and locksmith reimbursement. The Buying Service also provided discounted long distance service through Sprint. Special incentives resulted in nearly 300,000 members joining in the first year.[27] Other alliance relationships included a floral service and home mortgages offered by PHH. Mover's Advantage, operated by PHH Home Equity Corporation, helped members buy and sell homes and receive a cash bonus back. USAA also contracted with Federal Express to give members discounted prices on overnight delivery service. Another service, tested in the Great Lakes Region, was a Home Help Line program to match USAA's homeowner's insurance policyholders with skilled tradesmen in their areas for homeowner emergency services and repair work.

The widening use of alliance relationships enabled USAA to meet members' needs that the Association itself could not. But no matter what alliance was providing the service, the member considered it to be a USAA product. So it was important that the Association

Joe Robles

monitor and review the alliances' operations for such things as corporate culture, quality, complaint data, and data integrity. Herres entrusted this review to USAA's Chief Financial Officer and Treasurer, retired Army Major General Josue (Joe) Robles Jr. Robles was born in Puerto Rico and received his commission through the Army's Artillery Officer Candidate School. He held a wide variety of staff and command positions, serving in both Vietnam and Desert Storm. Robles served on the USAA Board of Directors from 1990 to 1994. When he joined the Executive Council as Chief Financial Officer on his retirement, Robles became the first Hispanic on the Council.

Because of the manner in which it handled the tremendous growth in business over the years, USAA has long been recognized as an innovator and pioneer in the use of information and communications technology. In 1996, USAA's Automated Call Distribution System, the world's largest with more than 23,000 telephone lines and 8,000 AT&T trunk lines, handled 120 million voice calls, over 400,000 daily from the 3,200 domestic offices and twenty-nine international locations on the network. With its advanced computer system, USAA completed over 16 million computer transactions each day. The Association's Property and Casualty customer accounting system produced 23 million billing statements each year, over 90,000 each day. USAA also has the world's largest Image System, with 5,921 terminals, and its unique mail system processes over 300,000 pieces of out-going mail daily, while handling an incoming mail volume of more than 96,000 pieces per day.

While continuing to service members through telephone, mail

and fax, Herres also moved to provide service for those members wishing to handle business transactions from their home computers. A survey showed that in 1996, some 62 percent of the membership had home computers and the percentage was especially high among families with children, a key target for future membership.

Melinda and Brandon Chen, children of USAA employee and member, Shiang Chen, have their own home page on the Internet.

Some efforts to take advantage of these and other newer developments in technology are already underway. For instance, the Bank developed its own brand of customer access technology called USAA DIRECTBanking. This gave Bank customers many access channels to use their accounts at the Bank, including ATMs, Voice Response Systems, and PC Home Banking. The goal was to provide a twenty-four-hour-per-day interface between the members and the Bank. Also, IMCO began using DIRECTInvesting software,

A TRADITION OF SERVICE

which allowed customers PC access to brokerage and mutual fund accounts. In the 1995 Operational Planning Conference, Herres expanded USAA's strategic direction for customer access by including developing mechanisms that would provide customer access at the time and place convenient to them. And in his Statement From the Chairman in the *USAA 1995 Annual Progress Report,* Herres declared that in the future, "heavy investments will be needed in information systems technology and the development of a growing work force which has ever-changing needs of its own."[28]

High praise for USAA's business practices, its focus on service, its financial strength and its commitment to its members, employees, and the communities in which it operates was voiced by management experts, financial publications, and other industry leaders in the years preceding the Association's seventy-fifth anniversary. In the book, *The One Hundred Best Places to Work in America,* published in 1993, USAA was not only included, but no other company was rated higher. In 1995, Arthur D. Little, Inc. Recognized USAA as one of Little's "Best of the Best" process management practitioners. A blue ribbon panel of experts selected USAA and nineteen other companies that were "most effective at consistently improving cross-functional business processes and achieving bottom-line benefits through effective process management."[29] In the same year, DALBAR, a Boston-based firm that conducts customer satisfaction surveys, named USAA the nation's "best-liked" provider of investment and savings products along with life and homeowners insurance. In 1996, USAA made *Working Mothers* magazine's list of "100 Best companies for Working Mothers." *Consumers Digest* picked USAA Life Insurance company as one of "America's 25 Safest Insurance Companies." Standard ratings agencies for insurance and banking consistently accord USAA their highest marks. In 1997, *Fortune* ranked USAA 212 out of the 500 largest industrial and service companies in the United States. Finally, in its

March 3, 1997, issue, *Fortune* selected USAA as one of "America's most admired companies." More than 13,000 senior executives, outside directors, and financial security analysts rated USAA first among all property and casualty companies and twenty-sixth among all 431 companies measured.

The Loyalty Effect, a book written by management expert Frederick F. Reichheld and published by Harvard Business School Press in 1996, singled out USAA as a "company that has earned its way into the front ranks of loyalty leaders by adhering to the principle of putting customer value first — followed closely by employee value." Reichheld gave great credit to McDermott for USAA's financial success, stating that he "enriched jobs with education, career opportunity, empowerment, greater job content, decentralization, and a battery of extra morale-boosters." And he praised Herres for building on McDermott's legacy, stating that "Robert Herres, another ex-general, is equally committed to USAA's concept of true north."[30]

In *Grow To Be Great,* a management book based on the study of 1,000 large companies, the authors praise USAA's exceptional service to its members while maintaining a high level of profitability. A most important reason for its success, the authors state, is that "USAA's operating systems and technology make it possible to provide all of these services in a manner that is simple, convenient for the customer and profitable for the company."[31] The book points out that through "a highly coordinated set of improvements to its information systems, this insurer has increased its productivity from one employee for every 152 policies to one employee to more than 1,000 policies today."[32]

Clearly, the Association was growing, satisfying members, and staying financially sound. The years 1995 and 1996 were exceptionally profitable. To some it might appear that USAA could relax and enjoy its celebrity and success. But on the contrary, the very

A Tradition Of Service

success energized Herres and his management team to avoid complacency and prepare for another seventy-five years of progress and prosperity for USAA and its members.

EPILOGUE

As it reached its seventy-fifth anniversary, USAA found itself well positioned to meet the challenges of change and to continue on its path of steady growth and profitability for the foreseeable future. By 1997, the Association's financial strength was most impressive. It was regarded as an industry leader across the breadth of its business lines and its subsidiaries were well managed and profitable in 1996.

The Association's annual report to members for the year ending December 31, 1996, noted these solid financial achievements:

Total Assets Owned: $23.6 billion, up from $22.2 billion in 1995.

Consolidated Net Income: $855 million, up from $730 million in 1995.

Policyholders' Net Worth (Surplus): $5.9 billion, up from $5.2 billion in 1995.

Perhaps even more impressive was the comparison of key financial indicators from 1990 to 1997; the Association's assets, owned and managed, grew from $19.7 billion to $42.7 billion. USAA's surplus ratio, a measure of the Association's ability to withstand above-average losses in any given year, climbed from 89.6 percent, against an industry average of 63.5 percent in 1990, to 113.5 percent, against an industry average of 69.7 percent in 1996. And during the same seven-year period, the annual Policyholder Dividends paid out by the Association climbed from $159 million to $485 million.[1]

These and many other impressive accomplishments drew rave reviews from industry analysts and financial publications and, more importantly, earned the highest possible financial strength ratings for the Association's Property and Casualty, Life, and Bank companies.

The foundation for USAA's success has been the close relationship between the Association and its members, a relationship driven by gifted management and an extremely loyal, well-trained, and dedicated work force, a work force encouraged and empowered to provide exceptional service to members and to anticipate their needs.

The Association's family of companies now provides a full range of insurance and financial products and services: property and casualty insurance, life and health insurance, annuities, no-load mutual funds, a discount brokerage service, retail banking, credit card products, and a fledgling financial planning network. And it currently serves 3 million customers worldwide, in a niche market composed principally of members of the military and their families.

A major challenge to the Association's future growth as the decade of the nineties began was the end of the Cold War and the downsizing of the U.S. standing military force. This challenge was met in large part by the Board's approval of Herres' initiative to enlarge the Association's base by making active enlisted personnel and their dependents eligible for the Association's property and casualty coverages, thus making all USAA products available to all military personnel and their families. This expanded the eligibility pool by approximately 100,000 men and women per year up to and beyond the year 2000.

Looking further into the future, Herres is considering the possibility of serving the future generations of USAA families when they reach adulthood and come off their parents' policies and who might not be eligible for direct property and casualty coverage from USAA. Under the current policies, the USAA Casualty Insurance Company will continue to cover the first generation of offspring for all USAA policyholders who have served in the military, but the eligibility of future generations who have not grown up in a military household, but are direct descendants of military people is an open question. One means of serving this segment of the niche that is being studied by the Association is the formation of a new subsidiary to serve as a separate property and casualty enterprise.

This "Fourth Company" would be a "take all" mutual, but would limit marketing efforts to persons who have had an affiliation with USAA and are not eligible for Association coverage. The policy of restraint from marketing beyond those who have relationships with its niche would remain operative. While broadening its base, USAA is determined to stay within its traditional mission of serving the military community. "We made the decision that we are not going to allow ourselves to become a company that slowly drifts away from its niche market," Herres said.[2]

Herres is comfortable with an annual market penetration growth rate of between 4 percent and 8 percent in the decade from 1997 through 2006 and he is optimistic that goal is reachable without going beyond the company's military community service mission. "But it will take highly focused marketing with a group that can't be economically reached through traditional marketing," Herres said. "But we know how to reach and serve that market; we've been doing it for years."[3] The USAA membership census and various data bases used by the company support this estimate.

The Association's Strategic Plan, updated annually and most recently in the spring of 1997, contained the following estimates of children of members and children of ex-dependent associates under the age of thirty who were transitioning to independence:

Transitioning To Independence

Year	Children of Members	Children of Ex-Dependent Associates	Combined
1998	69,099	25,381	94,480
2002	59,040	37,199	96,239
2006	50,996	48,473	99,469

Based on these data and projections coupled with projections gathered by the Association regarding annual new entrants to the officer and enlisted corps, Herres' annual membership growth target of roughly 6 percent appears reasonable and prudent. Growth rates much above the 8 percent boundary run the risk of threatening the competitiveness of product delivery to existing members, since growth capitalization must come from retained earnings. There is also concern about the sustenance of high quality service delivery levels above that boundary. The Association has already begun an ambitious outreach effort to the children of members and ex-dependent associates through its youth marketing program. The centerpiece of this program is the combination of two new magazines, *Under 25,* featuring articles about cars, money management, college life, and other subjects of interest to that age group, and *"U" Magazine,* geared to members' children aged ten to thirteen.

One area where marketing focus is crucial is the newly enlisted men and women and the enlisted senior grades who have already established a relationship with other companies. "But we know how to reach them and we intend to concentrate on them," Herres has said.[4] Another key marketing area, Herres said, is Selected Reserve and National Guard. "We haven't penetrated [this market] as deeply as the active duty force," Herres said. "We are at about 60 percent, which is not bad, but we can do much better."

USAA's internal projected membership growth exceeds Herres' more cautious estimate of future growth. Starting with actual figures of USAA members and ex-dependents for the year 1994 through 1995, the Association grew from a combined membership of 2.72 million to a combined membership of 2.97 million at the end of 1996. Looking to the future and including the influx of enlisted associates, the estimated combined figures total 3.41 million in 1998; 3.90 million in 2000; 4.42 million in 2002; 4.83 million in 2004; and 5.23 million in 2006. This would be an estimated growth of 76.1 percent over the period 1996 through 2006, with most of the growth coming from newly recruited active duty and ex-dependent associates.

The Association's diversification into life and health insurance, banking and credit cards, investment management, financial services, and real estate investments has contributed greatly to past revenue growth, but Herres is opposed to developing new non-financial lines of business. "We are not interested in getting into any more lines of business that do not support our mission," Herres said. "Our strategy is to continue to develop innovative products and services in the lines of business we are in and to expand our relationships with the households we serve. We serve a market that is highly mobile and is connected to military families. We know how to serve this market. We have an understanding of that market. But, because the world changes so fast, we have to be agile and alert in order to provide the products the members need to facilitate their financial security on a continuing basis."

The goal will be an emphasis on developing those new products to fit the changing needs and lifestyles of members and associates of all age groups. Recent examples include the Financial Planning Network, the establishment of a self-clearing brokerage by IMCO and the offering of a wide variety of mutual funds, annuities, and city and state tax-exempt funds. A major new focus will be a more aggressive new product creation process by the Bank and Life companies.[5]

USAA's emphasis on well-managed growth goes beyond just improving its value to members, which is of course an important consideration. But another factor is the very strong commitment to retain its able and dedicated work force during a period when communication, information and electronic transaction technologies are enabling fewer employees to serve greater numbers of customers. "From the standpoint of our work force, we need to grow our business at a comfortable minimum rate of at least 5 to 10 percent a year so that as we become more efficient, we don't have to lay people off," Herres said. "We can absorb our needs for improved efficiency with market growth and be assured that we provide our employees with a stable view of the future. Our projected market and multiple product relationship growth provides us with a safe margin against this goal."

A Tradition Of Service

Many of the labor-saving benefits of the revolution in information and communication technology have already been realized at USAA, which has always striven to be on the cutting edge of deploying new technology. The Bank and IMCO customers already have the ability to make transactions by computer and Property and Casualty is establishing a Web Page on the Internet for providing communication and information access to its customers. The Property and Casualty Group is also working on a prototype initiative in Utah for full electronic transactions — for billing, to file a claim, to pay premiums, and even for customers to obtain copies of their policies.

Under Herres' direction, the company is moving towards full electronic transaction access cautiously, but with a strong sense of urgency. He is skeptical at the rush of some companies to do this through the Internet without clearly understood objectives. Herres is concerned about the complexity, frequent delays, and security problems posed by the Internet. "Security is a big problem," Herres pointed out. "We need to make Internet access available to all who wish to use that medium, but for others, we want them to be able to bypass the Internet by connecting directly, so the customer's computer can be hooked to conduct transactions with telephone access. The emphasis for all means of access will be on consumer choice, convenience, and dependable security protection."[6]

With seventy-five years of successful experience behind it, USAA is moving toward the new millennium with optimism and assurance. The Association is financially sound, growing at a strong, but measured pace, and positioning itself to meet the challenges of the future. Herres has sought to strengthen the foundation by building and improving USAA's infrastructure, assembling a talented leadership team, and investing the necessary resources to prepare the company and its employees for change. These preparations, along with the continued partnership of USAA employees and its members, will help to assure that the Association's Eagle will still be serving its members for the seventy-five years that lie ahead.

APPENDIX

APPENDIX 1

BOARD OF DIRECTORS
ON
USAA's 75TH ANNIVERSARY*

ROBERT T. HERRES, GENERAL, USAF (RET.)	CHAIRMAN
DANIEL L. COOPER, VADM, USN (RET.)	VICE CHAIRMAN
JOHN D. BUCKELEW, COL., USMC (RET.)	
DANIEL W. CHRISTMAN, LT. GEN., USA	
STEPHEN B. CROKER, LT. GEN., USAF (RET.)	
LESLIE G. DENEND, COL., USAF (RET.)	
FRED A. GORDEN, MAJ. GEN., USA (RET.)	
MARCELITE J. HARRIS, MAJ. GEN., USAF (RET.)	
WILLIAM J. HYBL	
RICHARD D. MILLIGAN, RADM, USN (RET.)	
JOHN H. MOELLERING, LT. GEN., USA (RET.)	
MYRNA H. WILLIAMSON, BRIG. GEN., USA (RET.)	

* as of May 15, 1997

APPENDIX

APPENDIX 2

EXECUTIVE COUNCIL
ON
USAA's 75TH ANNIVERSARY*

ROBERT T. HERRES
WILSON C. COONEY
ROBERT G. DAVIS
WILLIAM T. FLYNN III
JANICE E. MARSHALL
BRADFORD W. RICH
JOSUE ROBLES, JR.
EDWIN L. ROSANE
MICHAEL J.C. ROTH
WILLIAM B. TRACY
DONALD R. WALKER
MARK H. WRIGHT

* as of May 15, 1997

APPENDIX

APPENDIX 3

ORAL HISTORY INTERVIEWS

In writing histories in the modern era, the amount of written material is overwhelming. At the same time, telephone calls and meetings where no notes are taken create gaps in the information available. Oral history interviews of players in the historical process help fill in these gaps, and at the same time, often add warmth and vitality to the cold written word. A large number of individuals spent from fifteen minutes to twelve hours telling me their views of USAA and its people. For all their time, help, and patience, I am exceedingly grateful.

INTERVIEWEES

JACK M. ANTONINI	LEROY V. HONSINGER
LILLIAN BATES	MICHAEL R. HOWARD JR.
CHARLES E. BISHOP	TANIS J. JENSCHKE
ROBERT G. BRAKEY	ANN JOHNSON
HATTIE BROCK	EDWARD KELLEY
LEO A. BROOKS	J. EARL KING
JOSEPH S. CALVELLI	ALBERT J. KIRSLING
MARY E. CLARK	JANICE E. MARSHALL
CHARLES E. CHEEVER JR.	JOHN H. MCCORMICK
WILSON C. COONEY	WILLIAM MCCRAE
ED COX	ROBERT F. MCDERMOTT
DENNIS W. CROSS	MARION MCDOUGALL
JOHN F. DAYE JR.	JOAN MICHEL
H.C. DONLEY	RICHARD A. MILLER
HERBERT L. EMANUEL	FRANCES MOORE
GEORGE H. ENSLEY	JOHN MULLEN
VICTOR J. FERRARI	JAMES A. PATTERSON
MARTIN D. FISHEL JR.	JOHN PERKINS
WILLIAM T. FLYNN III	SAMUEL C. PHILLIPS
ROBERT D. GAYLOR	JANE CHEEVER POWELL
MARGARET P. GRAHAM	BOBBY W. PRESLEY
WINSTON H. HANKINS	WILLIAM J. REGAN JR.
TOMMIE L. HANKS	R. JOE ROGERS
ROBERT T. HERRES	EDWIN L. ROSANE
SHIRLEY HERRES	MICHAEL J.C. ROTH
M. STASER HOLCOMB	TERRY W. SHEA
HOMER J. HOLLAND	CLEM H. SPALDING

APPENDIX

INTERVIEWEES (cont.)

WILLIAM L. STARNES
LENORA TARGAC
DONALD C. THOMPSON
EDWARD TRAVERS
CHARLES WEEBER
MAX H. WEIR JR.
JEAN M. WILLIAMS
ANGELA WONG
DOROTHY WILDENSTEIN

Endnotes

NOTES TO PAGES 1-36

Chapter One

The Road Less Travelled

1. Clay McShane, *Down The Asphalt Path: The Automobile and The American City* (NY: Columbia University Press, 1994), XIII.
2. From 1909 to 1915, the Elkhart Carriage and Motor Car Company's cars were known as Sterlings, but the name changed to Elcar in 1916. The sales peaked at 4,000 in 1919.
3. Edward C. Dunn, *USAA: Life Story of A Business Cooperative* (NY: McGraw-Hill, 1970), 10-11. Dunn was a retired Army Major General and USAA Board member for three years. After leaving the Board, he wrote his book under contract to USAA on the occasion of Charles Cheever's ending tenure as USAA's head. While the name "United States Army Automobile Association" was used in the June 20, 1922, organizational minutes, the bylaws that were passed two days later officially adopted the name "United States Army Automobile Insurance Association." This was the official name until the present name was adopted in 1924. To reduce confusion, the initials "USAA" to represent the Association have been used throughout the text.
4. Ibid., 20.
5. Major William Garrison, USAA, letter to President Warren G. Harding, 7 July 1922.
6. G.B. Christian Jr., Secretary to the President of the United States, letter to Major William Garrison, 19 July 1922.
7. Dunn, 48.
8. Jack Hayes, United States War Department, letter to USAAIA, 6 June 1924.
9. USAA Annual Members' Meeting Minutes (AMM), 18 June 1924.
10. B. Werkenthin, Texas Department of Insurance, letter to USAA, 5 August 1924.
11. The first known interinsurance exchange began in 1881 in New York City where six dry goods merchants banded together to contribute $2,000 each to a pool to protect against losses by fire. These merchants appointed a manager with a power of attorney to take care of the insurance business for them. Many other exchanges sprang up, but most fell by the wayside. As of 1996, there were forty reciprocal companies making up 3.7 percent of the casualty market.
12. Dunn, 51-52.
13. USAA Executive Committee Meeting Minutes, 13 August 1924.
14. Dunn, 83.
15. AMM, 15 June 1927.
16. USAA Board of Directors Minutes, 7 November 1927.

Endnotes

NOTES TO PAGES 37-59

Chapter Two
Depression and Revolution

[1] Gary B. Nash, *The American People* (NY: Harper & Row, 1986), 783.
[2] Edward C. Dunn, *USAA: Life Story of a Business Cooperative* (NY: McGraw-Hill, 1970), 120
[3] Seventy-Second Annual Report, *Association of Graduates of the USMA (AOG)*, June 10, 1941, 167.
[4] Ibid., 168.
[5] Ibid., 170.
[6] Ibid. General Snow extract from military records quoted in the report.
[7] Ibid.
[8] USAA Board of Directors Minutes (BOD), 7 November 1927.
[9] William K. Klingaman, *GEICO: The First 40 Years* (D.C.: GEICO Corp., 1994), 5.
[10] Colonel Margaret P. Graham, USA(Ret.), interview by author, 10 May 1996.
[11] Memo to employees, 13 September 1929.
[12] General Hinds to BOD, 20 June 1934.
[13] USAA Annual Members' Meeting (AMM) minutes, 20 June 1934.
[14] USAA BOD, 3 February 1937.
[15] Ibid.
[16] USAA BOD, 5 November 1938.
[17] AMM, 21 June 1933, 25.
[18] William A. Ganoe, *The History of The United States Army*, (New York, Appleton, 1924), 505.
[19] USAA BOD, 21 June 1933.
[20] USAA BOD, 15 March 1933.
[21] Ibid.
[22] AMM, 15 June 1932.
[23] E.g., see AMM, 16 June 1938. Brigadier General Barton K. Yount was named to the "Air Corps slot" effective upon his arrival in San Antonio and the "Corps Area Engineer's slot" was left vacant pending the military reassignment of the incumbent. To ensure that individuals did not remain too long, however, the bylaws specified that no more than 40 percent of Board members at any one election could be reelected. If more than 40 percent were eligible, the Board member with the longest continuous service was forced to step down. In 1940, this happened to Colonel F.R. de Funick Jr., USA (Ret.) as one example.
[24] USAA BOD, 13 February 1929.

ENDNOTES

NOTES TO PAGES 59-88

25 USAA BOD, 27 January 1932.
26 Commander Bain, letter to USAA President, 17 January 1933.
27 USAA BOD, 1 February 1933.
28 AMM, 19 June 1935.
29 USAA BOD, 5 December 1934.
30 AMM, 17 June 1931.
31 Ibid.
32 USAA BOD, 1 February 1933.
33 USAA *Annual Report,* 1937.
34 *Army and Navy Register,* 4 February 1936, 307.

Chapter Three

THE WAR YEARS

1 Morison, Commager, and Leuchtenberg, *The Growth of the American Republic* (NY: Oxford, 1980), vol II, 534.
2 Edward C. Dunn, *USAA: Life Story of A Business Cooperative* (NY: McGraw-Hill, 1970), 203.
3 *Assembly* (USMA), January 1955, 45.
4 USAA *Annual Report,* 1941, 3.
5 Ibid., 6.
6 USAA Board of Directors Minutes, (BOD), 18 March 1942. Annual Members' Meeting Minutes, 17 June 1942.
7 USAA BOD, 13 May 1942. To protect themselves against catastrophic losses, insurance companies often take out insurance on their own risks with a second company. If catastrophic losses do occur, the original insurer pays total claims up to an agreed-upon limit. The second insurance company or reinsurer pays the rest.
8 USAA BOD, 17 November 1943.
9 USAA BOD, 13 December 1944.
10 USAA BOD, 16 September 1942.
11 USAA BOD, 18 February 1942.
12 *Annual Report,* 1942, 4.
13 USAA BOD Executive Committee Meeting Minutes, 2 June 1943.
14 USAA BOD, 7 May 1944.
15 USAA BOD, 19 March 1941.
16 Colonel Herbert Arthur White, letter to Lieutenant Colonel Charles H. Dowman, 19 March 1941.

Endnotes

17 *Annual Report,* 1941, 5.
18 *Annual Report,* 1944, 2.
19 *Annual Report,* 1945, 4.
20 "Death on the Highways," *New York Times,* 10 May 1946, 18.
21 *Annual Report,* 1945, 4.
22 Dunn, 235, 236.
23 Ibid., 238.
24 USAA BOD, 16 October 1946.
25 *Annual Report,* 1946, p.5.
26 USAA BOD, 19 December 1945.
27 Dunn, 243.
28 *Annual Report,* 1946, 5.
29 *Annual Report,* 1947, inside front cover.
30 Ibid.
31 Ibid., 5.

Chapter Four
THE COLD WAR BEGINS — SERVICING AN EXPLODING MEMBERSHIP

1 Thomas G. Paterson and J. Garry Clifford, *America Ascendant* (Lexington: D.C. Heath and Company, 1995), 48-49.
2 USAA Board of Directors Minutes (BOD), 17 December 1947.
3 James Parton, *Air Force Spoken Here: General Ira Eaker and the Command of the Air* (Bethesda: Adler & Adler, 1986), 445.
4 Frances Moore, interview by author, 12 July 1996.
5 USAA BOD, 19 January 1949.
6 USAA BOD, 15 March 1950.
7 USAA BOD, 20 December 1950.
8 "Proposed Change — Membership Eligibility Rules" (USAA Committee Report, 17 January 1951), 3.
9 Ibid., 6.
10 USAA BOD, 21 January 1951.
11 USAA Annual Members' Meeting Minutes, (vote taken at meeting on membership eligibility), 20 June 1951.
12 Paterson and Clifford, 102.
13 USAA BOD, 16 May 1951.
14 USAA BOD, 18 April 1951.
15 USAA BOD, 21 February 1951.

Endnotes

NOTES TO PAGES 117-135

16 USAA BOD, 18 April 1951.
17 USAA BOD, 20 June 1951.
18 Colonel William Fitzhugh Jones, letter to Commanding General, HQ EUCOM, 21 September 1951.
19 Ibid.
20 Colonel C.R. Hutchinson, EUCOM, letter to USAA, 9 October 1951.
21 USAA BOD, 21 November 1951.
22 EUCOM Cable to USAA, 5 January 1952.
23 Ad Hoc Committee Report to the BOD, 19 March 1952.
24 Charles Cheever, cable to USAA, 22 April 1952.
25 HQ EUCOM, Provost Marshal Division, "Comparative Offense and Performance Levels of Various Categories of EUCOM Civilian Vehicle Registrants," 25 April 1952.
26 Cheever, cable to USAA, 22 April 1952.
27 Ibid.
28 USAA BOD, 23 April 1952.
29 USAA BOD, 20 April 1949.
30 USAA BOD, 16 August 1950.
31 "Savings from Modern Office Lower Cost to Policyholders," *American Business*, February 1951.
32 USAA BOD, 19 September 1951.
33 USAA BOD, 19 March 1948.
34 USAA BOD, 14 December 1949.
35 USAA BOD, 18 February 1948. Lest the reader suspect a spelling error, Mitchel Field was not named after Billy Mitchell, but after New York City Mayor John Purroy Mitchel who plunged to his death from a two-seater aircraft. The Mayor was a passenger and had neglected to fasten his seat belt. And when the airplane flew upside down, he simply fell out.
36 USAA BOD, 14 May 1948.
37 USAA BOD, 19 January 1951.

Chapter Five
MODERNIZING THE ASSOCIATION – A BEGINNING

1 USAA BOD Executive Committee Meeting Minutes, 4 February 1953.
2 The Zimmerman Telegram was a cable sent by German Foreign Secretary, Arthur Zimmerman, to the German minister in Mexico. If war broke out, it directed the minister to offer to Mexico the states of Texas, New Mexico, and Arizona in return for Mexico's joining with Germany against the United States. Intercepted

ENDNOTES

and released to the public by the U.S., it caused a furor among the American citizens.

[3] Charles E. Cheever Jr., interview by author, 31 July 1996.

[4] Edward C. Dunn, *USAA: Life Story of A Business Cooperative* (NY: McGraw-Hill, 1970), 303.

[5] In 1970, because of his intimate knowledge of Patton, Cheever guested on NBC's "Today" show to discuss Patton in conjunction with the release of the movie *Patton, A Salute to a Rebel.*

[6] Cheever Jr., interview, 31 July 1996.

[7] Colonel C.E. Cheever, letter to Jones, 28 April 1952.

[8] Carniero, Chumney and Company, letter to Cheever, 14 April 1953.

[9] "Report of the Executive Committee and Management on the Acquisition of a Suitable Site Upon which to Erect a New Home Office Building," 13 May 1953.

[10] USAA Board of Directors Meeting Minutes (BOD), 23 July 1953.

[11] Atlee B. Ayers and Raymond Phelps, letter to Cheever, 16 July 1953.

[12] Cheever, memo to BOD, 14 December 1953.

[13] *San Antonio Express-News,* 23 May 1956, 1B.

[14] Ibid.

[15] Frances Moore, interview by author, 12 July 1996.

[16] T. Laverne Hanks, interview by author, 20 September 1989.

[17] USAA BOD, 15 April 1953.

[18] Jean Moye Williams, interview by author, 14 October 1988.

[19] Williams, interview, 15 August 1996.

[20] USAA BOD, 15 March 1955.

[21] Charles Weeber, interview by author, 12 July 1996.

[22] Michael S. Sherry, *In the Shadow of War; The United States Since the 1930s* (New Haven: Yale University Press, 1995), 219.

[23] USAA BOD, 27 March 1957.

[24] USAA BOD, 19 June 1957.

[25] USAA BOD, 7 May 1954.

[26] USAA BOD, 27 November 1957.

[27] USAA BOD, 25 September 1957.

[28] USAA BOD, 27 March 1957.

[29] *Andrews Ambassador,* 20 March 1953.

[30] USAA Annual Members' Meeting Minutes, 18 June 1958.

[31] Tanis Jenschke, interview by author, 29 June 1993.

[32] Consuelo Kerford, Helen Wallace, Max Wier, "Recommendations on USAA Insurance in Japan," 14 May 1956.

Endnotes

33 USAA BOD, 21 November 1956.
34 James T. Patterson, *Grand Expectations: The United States, 1945-1974* (NY: Oxford University Press, 1996), 312.
35 USAA BOD, 20 October 1954.
36 USAA *Annual Report,* 1959, 15.

Chapter Six
The Sixties – Maturity And Progress

1 John Kenneth Galbraith, *The Affluent Society,* quoted in Todd Gitlin, *The Sixties: Years of Hope, Days of Rage* (NY: Bantam Books, 1987), 2.
2 David Halberstam, *The Fifties* (NY: Villard Books, 1993), 712.
3 USAA Annual Members' Meeting Minutes, 28 June 1961.
4 USAA Board of Directors Minutes, (BOD), 20 January 1961.
5 Frances Moore, interview by author, 12 July 1996.
6 *Navy Times,* 31 August 1960, 32.
7 USAA BOD, 28 June 1961.
8 Eric T. Goldman, *The Crucial Decade - And After* (NY: Knopf, 1971), 324. Van Doren's rise and fall was later the subject of the movie *Quiz Show.*
9 USAA BOD, 27 December 1961.
10 USAA BOD, 22 March 1961.
11 USAA BOD, 23 February 1965.
12 USAA BOD, 27 March 1963. One of these shares was held jointly by Cheever and USAA because British law required a minimum of two shareholders.
13 Gitlin, 17. (See footnote #1).
14 USAA BOD, 27 March 1963.
15 Ibid.
16 President's Report, Annual Members' Meeting, 26 June 1968.
17 Jean Moye Williams, interview by author, 15 August 1996.
18 Alan F. Gropman, *The Air Force Integrates 1945-1964* (Washington, D.C.: Office of Air Force History, 1985), 145-174.
19 Interview, *San Antonio Evening News* clipping.
20 USAA BOD, 27 April 1960.
21 USAA BOD, 28 June 1961.
22 USAA BOD, 25 May 1966.
23 USAA BOD, 27 March 1968.
24 USAA BOD, 27 July 1963.
25 USAA pamphlet, "A Day in the History of USAA," 18 March 1967.
26 USAA BOD, 28 August 1963.

ENDNOTES

NOTES TO PAGES 213-228

[27] From a slave song quoted in James Baldwin, *The Fire Next Time* (NY: DID Press, Inc., 1962), 141 in the Dell paperback, March 1968.
[28] John Hope Franklin and Alfred A. Moss Jr., *From Slavery to Freedom,* 7th ed., (NY: McGraw-Hill, 1994), 514.
[29] *Barron's,* 23 August 1965, 1.
[30] *Army Navy Air Force Register,* 11 November 1960, 15.
[31] "Crisis in Auto Insurance — What Can Be Done About It," *U.S. News and World Report,* 14 June 1965, 112-114.
[32] President's Report, Annual Members' Meeting, 28 June 1967.

Chapter Seven
HIGH ENERGY

[1] Admiral Elmo R. Zumwalt Jr., CNO, letter to Major General John McCormick, Chairman of USAA, 24 October 1970.
[2] USAA, Executive Committee Meeting Minutes, 28 February 1968.
[3] USAA Life Insurance Company BOD Minutes, 23 February 1966.
[4] Life Company BOD, 28 September 1966.
[5] President's Report, Annual Members' Meeting, 28 June 1967.
[6] USAA BOD, 28 February 1968.
[7] "What Was Said," summary of opinions expressed by USAA employees to the survey administered by the Psychological Corporation of New York in 1968, January 1969.
[8] Clem Spalding, 15 August 1990; Laverne Hanks, 20 September 1989; Martin D. Fishel Jr., 6 June 1989, interviews by author.
[9] Jean (Moye) Williams, interview by author, tape recording, 15 August 1996. Moye Memo to Cheever *et al*, "Special 'Overtime' Project," 19 June 1968.
[10] USAA BOD, 24 July 1968.
[11] Charles Cheever Jr., 31 July 1996, Jane Cheever Powell, 13 August 1996, and Lil Bates, 16 August 1996, interviews by author.
[12] Brig. General Robert F. McDermott, letter to Colonel Charles Cheever, 22 December 1967.
[13] USAA BOD, 24 January 1968.
[14] Major General John H. McCormick, USAF (Ret.), interview by author, 4 April 1988.
[15] Ed Cox, interview by author, 18 March 1991.
[16] Ibid.
[17] United States Military Academy, *Howitzer,* January 1943.
[18] Cox, interview, 1991.

Endnotes

NOTES TO PAGES 232-249

[19] *Denver Post,* 8 May 1968, 5.
[20] Speech made by Anne Foreman, then Undersecretary of the Air Force, in San Antonio, 30 November 1989.
[21] Samuel Huntington, Harvard University Professor, letter to Robert F. McDermott, 1968.
[22] USAA BOD, 28 August 1968.
[23] Edward Clare Dunn, *USAA: Life Story of A Business Cooperative* (NY: McGraw-Hill, 1970), 412.
[24] USAA BOD, 28 August 1968.
[25] USAA BOD, 25 May 1966.
[26] USAA BOD, 22 May 1968.
[27] Spalding, interview, 15 August 1990.
[28] First Executive INSCO Meeting, 12 November 1968.
[29] Lt. Colonel George Ensley, USA (Ret.), interview by author, 12 May 1988.
[30] Lillian Bates, interview, 16 August 1996.
[31] Charles Cheever, President of USAA, letter to Major General William W. Berg, Director of Manpower and Organization, HQ USAF, 18 December 1968.
[32] Commander Jeremiah E. Lenihan, letter to Cheever, 10 April 1969.
[33] San Antonio *Express*-News, 12 January 1969, 5H.
[34] Bates, interview, 16 August 1996.
[35] George Ensley, Memo "Trip to Washington, D.C., 25-27 August 1969," 4 September 1969.
[36] USAA BOD, 24 September 1969.
[37] Jack Daye, memo to General Robert F. McDermott, 5 November 1969.
[38] USAA BOD, 22 January 1970.
[39] USAA BOD, 25 February 1970.
[40] Life Company BOD, 25 February 1970. Ensley, memo, 4 September 1969.
[41] USAA BOD, 22 April 1970. McDermott, interview with author, 28 October 1996.
[42] Clark Aylsworth, President MSIA, letter to McDermott, 12 July 1969. McDermott, letter to Aylsworth, 28 July 1969.
[43] USAA BOD, 26 March 1969.
[44] USAA BOD, 25 June 1969.
[45] Ibid.
[46] USAA BOD, 25 August 1969.
[47] Families purchased from and the approximate acreage of land purchased from each: Straus (135), Taylor (56), Tips/Adams (20), Rogers (15), Spangler (5), Morris (.7), and Kirkpatrick (55).
[48] USAA BOD, 28 October 1970. Authorized McDermott to purchase.

Endnotes

49 USAA BOD, 16 December 1969.
50 Colonel Martin Fishel, interview by author, 6 June 1989.
51 USAA BOD, 18 December 1969.
52 USAA BOD, 30 October 1968.
53 USAA BOD, 25 August 1969.
54 USAA BOD, 23 February 1972.
55 June Rogers, memo to John F. Daye Jr., Vice President, Plans and Programs, 8 August 1969.
56 USAA called them Subscribers' Credit Accounts until 1971.
57 USAA BOD, 27 May 1972.
58 Ibid.
59 Colonel Jack Daye, interview by author, 8 January 1991.
60 Max Wier Jr., interview by author, 6 November 1989.
61 USAA Long Range Plan, 1970.
62 General Robert F. McDermott, interview, *Coverage,* June 1970.
63 President's Report, BOD, 24 March 1971.
64 USAA BOD, 18 November 1972.
65 Daye, interview, January 1991.
66 USAA BOD, 18 July 1971. The actual start was delayed briefly until November 15 because of President Richard Nixon's wage-price freeze.
67 Sean McNulty, "USAA Sets Pace with 4-day Work Week," *San Antonio Light,* 26 August 1971.
68 McDermott, memo to BOD, 15 February 1972.
69 *San Antonio Express-News,* 5 March 1972, 9E.
70 Colonel Victor J. Ferrari, interview by author, 2 September 1988.
71 USAA Press Release, 19 November 1971.
72 USAA Management Directive No. 20-71, "Organization Development Program," 18 June 1971.
73 Paul Thompson, *San Antonio Evening News,* 3 and 6 October 1970.
74 USAA member Major Clarence Wentz, correspondence to USAA, 19 April 1971.
75 Daye, interview, 8 January 1981.
76 USAA BOD, 25 March 1970.
77 Gabriel M. Gelb, "Marketing Comes of Age," *Texas Business Review,* March 1971.
78 USAA Executive Committee Minutes, 26 May 1971.
79 USAA BOD, 29 October 1971.
80 United States Casualty Insurance Company BOD, 22 July 1970.
81 USAA BOD, 29 April 1972.
82 "The Problem of Assigned Risks," *Aide,* Winter 1971.
83 General McDermott, memo to Jefferis, Cook, Spalding, et al., 6 January 1972.

Endnotes

NOTES TO PAGES 271-288

[84] USAA BOD, 24 February 1971.
[85] Southwestern Bell Telephone Company, "USAA Mail Order Insurance by Phone," *Signal,* Spring 1971, 16-19.
[86] Life Company BOD, 16 December 1972.
[87] USAA *Annual Report,* 1969, 16.
[88] USAA BOD, 24 February 1971.
[89] CDR H.C. Holt IV, letter to General McDermott, 18 August 1972.
[90] General Omar N. Bradley, letter to Kenneth D. Childs Jr., President, Southern California Savings & Loan Association, 22 July 1970.
[91] *Consumer Reports,* June 1970.

Chapter Eight
TURBULENT TIMES

[1] Captain Howard J. Hill, letter to USAA, 24 March 1973.
[2] *The Report of the President's Commission on an All-Volunteer Armed Force,* 20 February 1970, 5.
[3] Eliot A. Cohen, *Citizens and Soldiers: The Dilemmas of Military Service* (New York: Cornell University Press, 1975), 178.
[4] Hattie Brock, interview by author, 12 January 1997. About twenty-five years later, a similar situation was the subject of a Delta Airlines television commercial.
[5] M.C. Kerford, Vice President-Secretary of USAA, letter to Colonel Robert S. Giles, USAR, 4 January 1972.
[6] Captain J.D. Riner, USN (Ret.), letter to Robert F. McDermott, 16 August 1973.
[7] McDermott, letter to Clem Spalding and Clifford Jefferis, 29 May 1973.
[8] Rear Admiral Walter J. Whipple, letter to McDermott, 13 July 1969.
[9] Cliff Jefferis, note to McDermott, 12 February 1973.
[10] USAA General Indemnity Company (GIC) Board of Directors Minutes (BOD), 28 April 1973.
[11] Bill McCrae, General Counsel, Memo to McDermott, 11 July 1973.
[12] USAA GIC BOD, 28 July 1973.
[13] USAA Casualty Insurance Company (CIC) BOD Minutes, 28 July 1973.
[14] McDermott Memo to CIC BOD, 19 October 1973. CIC BOD Minutes, 27 October 1973.
[15] Lt. Col. Davis S. Kahne, letter to McDermott, 9 November 1987.
[16] Dankwart A. Rustow, *Oil and Turmoil: America Faces OPEC and the Middle East* (NY: W.W. Norton & Co., 1982), 167. James T. Patterson, *Grand Expectations: The United States, 1945-1974* (NY: Oxford University Press, 1996), 784-785.
[17] USAA BOD, 17 November 1973.

Endnotes

18 USAA BOD, 12 May 1977.
19 *Aide Magazine*, Summer 1979.
20 Patterson, 786.
21 USAA BOD, 29 October 1976.
22 Bob Brakey, interview by author, 13 July 1993.
23 *Washington Post,* 1 February 1976.
24 USAA BOD, 11 May 1976.
25 President's Report to the CIC BOD, 19 February 1977.
26 Brakey, interview, 21 July 1996.
27 William K. Klingaman, *GEICO: The First Forty Years* (D.C.: GEICO Corp., 1994), 91-122. "Seeking Money for GEICO," *Business Week,* 29 March 1976.
28 George Ensley, memo to McDermott, "Evaluation of GEICO Bailout," 14 June 1976.
29 USAA BOD, 18 June 1976.
30 USAA BOD, 28 January 1978.
31 USAA BOD, 16 December 1972.
32 USAA BOD, 15 February 1975.
33 USAA Annual Members' Meeting Minutes, 16 June 1973.
34 USAA bylaws, 28 June 1972.
35 USAA BOD, 28 July 1973.
36 USAA Fund Management Company Board of Directors Minutes, 12 July 1976.
37 Jack Daye, interview by author, 8 January 1991.
38 Dennis Cross, interview by author, 31 May 1991.
39 Ibid.
40 USAA BOD, 20 January 1979.
41 USAA BOD, 12 May 1979.
42 USAA BOD, 28 July 1973.
43 Marty D. Fishel Jr., "The Computer and You," *Aide Magazine,* Summer 1976.
44 "Prospects for '77 Are Exciting," *Aide Magazine,* Summer 1976.
45 Marty Fishel, memo to McDermott, "Computer Services' Talent Drain," 28 October 1976.
46 "Cutting Mail Room Costs," *Best's Review,* vol. 74, no. 7, 101.
47 Major General William L. Starnes, memo to McDermott, 20 June 1974.
48 USAA BOD, 16 February 1974.
49 *Assembly,* September 1990, 171.
50 Al Kirsling, interview by author, 16 May 1989. USAA *Annual Report,* 1977, 4.
51 Rabbi Asher BarZev, letter to McDermott, 28 August 1976.
52 USAA BOD, 27 October 1979.

Endnotes

NOTES TO PAGES 304-323

[53] *Washington Post,* 10 September 1972.
[54] *Coverage,* October 1972, 2.
[55] Member #85-85-66, letter to USAA. *Coverage,* May 1973, 3; Kay Prosk in *Coverage,* December 1976; Joe Massett, telephone interview, 15 January 1996; Mrs. Clayton Bissell, letter to USAA Group, 6 November 1976; 2/Lt. Ethel M. Knapp, USAR (Ret.), letter to McDermott, 20 July 1976; C.W. Thomas, letter to McDermott, 17 March 1973.
[56] "Have Team Will Travel," *Aide Magazine,* Fall 1976.
[57] General Omar Bradley, letter to McDermott published in *Aide Magazine,* Summer 1978.
[58] Claims briefing to USAA Staff, 27 March 1979.
[59] Telecom, Chris Head with David Dosker, 19 February 1979.
[60] Lt. Colonel Raymond J. Hengel, letter to McDermott, 2 March 1979.
[61] *Air Force Times,* 10 September 1979.
[62] Lt. Kevin A. Garvey, letters to USAA, 16 July 1976 and 18 October 1976; Bernice Gideon, USAA, letter to Lt. Garvey, 7 August 1976; Max Wier Jr., USAA, SVP Claims Staff, letter to Lt. Garvey, 4 November 1976; Colonel Kevin A. Garvey, letter to author, 8 May 1996.
[63] *San Antonio Express-News,* 6 November 1973.
[64] USAA BOD, 17 March 1973.
[65] Major General William L. Starnes, interview by author, 25 May 1989.
[66] Ibid.
[67] In 1974, USAA sold the Broadway Building to Southwestern Bell for about $4.5 million. Bell did not take over the building until 1975, however.
[68] USAA purchased the house from Straus in 1969, but the Straus family remained in it until 1971. The stables that came with the residence were destroyed in an accidental fire during the construction of the home office building. After McDermott moved from the residence, it was converted to the USAA Conference Center and dedicated to Alice McDermott.
[69] USAA BOD, 20 January 1979.
[70] *Coverage,* July 1975, 3.
[71] Ronald J. Bowers, Manager, Management Development and Training, "Trip Results: AOR Recommendations," to Leonard J. Otlen, Organizational Development and Training, 6 January 1975; USAA BOD, 27 October 1977.
[72] USAA BOD, 27 October 1977.
[73] McDermott, memo to Starnes, "Organizational Development," 27 June 1974.
[74] USAA BOD, 26 July 1975.
[75] USAA BOD, 24 July 1976.

Endnotes

NOTES TO PAGES 323-335

[76] *Highlights,* 30 November 1977.
[77] Victor Ferrari, interview by author, 2 September 1988; USAA BOD, 22 April 1978.
[78] Earl King, interview by author, 29 October 1996.
[79] Ferrari, interview 25 September 1988; McDermott, interview by author, 29 October 1996.
[80] George Ensley, memo to Brinker, Cook, Goring, Westbrook, "Minority Races in Management Positions," 23 March 1972.
[81] Starnes, memo to McDermott, 10 July 1974.
[82] Lt. General Samuel Phillips, interview by author, 23 June 1988.
[83] Phillips, memo to USAA Board, "Improvements in Board Operations," 17 June 1978.
[84] Ibid.
[85] USAA BOD, 17 June 1978.
[86] USAA BOD, 17 February 1979; Phillips interview, 23 June 1988.
[87] USAA BOD, 28 April 1973.
[88] USAA BOD, 20 January 1979.
[89] Phillips interview, 23 June 1988.
[90] USAA BOD, 24 January 1980.
[91] USAA BOD, 15 September 1973.
[92] General McDermott, interview by Sterlin Homesly, 5 December 1994, Institute of Texan Cultures, University of Texas, San Antonio; USAA BOD, 24 July 1974; USAA Life Company BOD, 27 July 1974.
[93] For a background of COPS and the EDF, see Joseph D. Sekul, "Communities Organized for Public Service," *The Politics of San Antonio* (Lincoln: University of Nebraska Press, 1983),175-190.
[94] McDermott, interview by Homesly 5 December 1994; "Economic Push Needs Grassroots Support," *San Antonio Express-News,* 2 January 1980, 3a.
[95] USAA BOD, 16 February 1980.

Chapter Nine

Expanding, Safety, and Succession

[1] Thomas G. Paterson and J. Garry Clifford, *America Ascendant: U.S. Foreign Relations Since 1939* (Lexington, MA: D.C. Heath & Co., 1995), 292.
[2] Michael S. Sherry, *In the Shadow of War* (New Haven: Yale University Press, 1995), 374.
[3] Paterson and Clifford, 257.
[4] Reagan quoted in Paterson and Clifford, 258.

Endnotes

NOTES TO PAGES 335-362

[5] Ibid., 258. Robert Dallek, *Ronald Reagan: The Politics of Symbolism* (Cambridge: Harvard University Press, 1984), 141.
[6] USAA Board of Directors Minutes (BOD), 24 October 1981. Robert F. McDermott, interview by author, 4 December 1996.
[7] USAA BOD, 6 August 1983; USAA BOD 4 May 1984. The official name of the Naval Investigative Service became the Naval Criminal Investigative Service in 1992.
[8] USAA BOD, 1 March 1985.
[9] USAA BOD, 15 November 1986.
[10] Dallek, 66.
[11] Edwin Meese III, *With Reagan: The Inside Story* (Washington, D.C.: Regnery Gateway, 1992), 17, 75. Richard Levine, "Unfinished Business," *Management Review,* March 1989, 18.
[12] Garrick Utley, "The Reagan Legacy," Discovery Network, 3 November 1996.
[13] Naisbitt quoted in "Working Smarter," *Aide Magazine,* Fall 1980.
[14] *Highlights,* 7 January 1981.
[15] George Ensley, memo, 25 June 1981.
[16] Bob Gaylor, interview by author, 10 May 1995.
[17] "Quality Circles," *Aide Magazine,* Fall 1983.
[18] *Highlights,* 1 May 1985.
[19] USAA BOD, 30 October 1982.
[20] *Highlights,* 3 June 1987.
[21] "Long Range Basing Plan Study," 12 October 1987.
[22] *Highlights,* 11 May 1988.
[23] *Highlights,* 15 July 1987.
[24] Terry Shea, interview by author, 29 May 1991.
[25] USAA BOD, 18 February 1984.
[26] USAA BOD, 6 February 1982.
[27] USAA BOD, 21 February 1986.
[28] Ed Bradley quoted in *Highlights*, 11 July 1990.
[29] Paterson and Clifford, 274-276.
[30] USAA Board Newsletter, July 1986.
[31] American Officers' Insurance Company LTD Board of Directors' Minutes, 10 July 1982.
[32] Vic Ferrari quoted in *Highlights,* 13 February 1985.
[33] USAA BOD, 26 April 1980.
[34] *Highlights,* 13 January 1988.
[35] Major General Bobby W. Presley, USAF (Ret.), interview by author, 30 November

ENDNOTES

1995.
36 Ibid.
37 USAA Board Newsletter, 20 October 1985.
38 *USAA Annual Report,* 1987, 17.
39 "Nothing Left," *Aide Magazine,* Fall 1983.
40 Captain Edward A. Harris quoted in *Aide Magazine,* Spring 1987.
41 USAA Board member Vice Admiral Edward Travers, interview by author, 12 August 1988. USAA BOD, 19 May 1981.
42 "Premium Treatment," *Business Week/Quality,* 1991, 124. Staubach related this story to *Business Week* in a 1991 interview. Cook quoted in Toni Mack, "They Have Faith in Us," *Forbes,* 25 July 1982, 182.
43 Senior Vice President Jim Patterson, interview by author, 13 April 1995.
44 USAA BOD, 26 April 1980.
45 William Hines, "U.S. Cars Rated Safer Than Japan's," *Chicago Sun Times,* January 82, 3.
46 Clipping dated January 20-27, 1982, forwarded to General McDermott by USAA member Lt. Tony Esposito, USAR.
47 Major A.L. Thompson, letter to McDermott, 23 January 1982.
48 F.W. Hirt, President, Erie Insurance Group, letter to McDermott, 21 January 1982; Donald P. McHugh, VP and General Counsel, State Farm Mutual Automobile Insurance Company, letter to McDermott, 18 January 1982.
49 Quoted in Maryann N. Keller, "Safety Sells — At Last," *World Monitor,* April 1990, 71.
50 *Aide Magazine,* May/June 1987, 3.
51 *The Gazette-Virginian,* 3 October 1988, 3. LTC C.W. Green, letter to R.F. McDermott, 20 October 1988.
52 Remarks by Robert McDermott, 5 October 1983, quoted in *Congressional Record — Senate,* S 15712, 8 November 1983.
53 Motor Vehicle Manufacturers Association of the U.S. et al. *v.* State Farm Mutual Insurance Company et al, Case # 82-354, U.S. Supreme Court, 1983.
54 NAII, *Fifty Years of Independents: The Story of an American Insurance Revolution,* 1995, 73.
55 Lee Iacocca, *Iacocca: An Autobiography* (NY: Bantam Books, 1984), 299.
56 McDermott, interview, 5 December 1996.
57 USAA Life Insurance Company BOD, "Written Consent to Action," 30 March 1988; "Executive Perspective," *Aide Magazine,* April 1988.
58 U.S. Secretary of Transportation J. Burnley, quoted in *Highlights,* 6 April 1988.
59 USAA Board Newsletter, July 1988.
60 Tony Boylan, "Driving Improves Through Technology," *Florida Today,* 13 October

ENDNOTES

1989.
61. Bob Brakey, interview by author, 13 July 1993.
62. USAA BOD, 19 November 1983.
63. Brakey, interview, 13 July 1993.
64. Joe Calvelli, interview by author, 3 December 1996.
65. USAA General Agency (GA) BOD, 8 April 1987.
66. USAA GA BOD, 29 March 1988.
67. USAA GA BOD, 19 April 1990.
68. Dennis Cross, interview by author, 31 May 1991.
69. USAA Life Company BOD, 27 July 1982.
70. USAA Life Company BOD, 4 November 1982.
71. USAA Board Newsletter, October 1989.
72. Bishop's brother was in McDermott's class at West Point, but they did not know each other.
73. Brigadier General Charles Bishop, USAF (Ret.), interview by author, 18 January 1995. Life Company BOD, 30 October 1982.
74. The "plebe" reference is to the term used for first-year cadets at West Point.
75. Life Company BOD, 9 April 1986.
76. Life Company BOD, 25 January 1983. United Services Life Insurance Company had a $100,000 limit, so USAA's policy provided more coverage than the United Services policy.
77. *A.M. Best*; persistency refers to the percent of policies that remain active over a period of time.
78. Robert F. McDermott, interview by author, 28 October 1996.
79. USAA Board of Directors Executive Committee, 13 August 1985.
80. *Aide Magazine,* Fall 1986.
81. USAA BOD, 3 November 1984.
82. Brig. General Wilson "Bill" Cooney, USAF (Ret.), interview by author, 20 December 1996.
83. USAA BOD, 11 May 1985. USAA BOD, 21 February 1986.
84. USAA BOD, 12 August 1987.
85. USAA BOD, 23 May 1987.

Chapter Ten
A New Era For USAA – Financial Services

1. Lt. Colonel George Ensley, USA (Ret.), letter to Colonel Rolfe Salin, USAFR, 19 May 1992.
2. Ensley, interview by author, 19 March 1993.

Endnotes

NOTES TO PAGES 392-410

[3] George Ensley, "The Restructuring of Financial Services in America," 24 February 1983.

[4] Ibid.

[5] Vice Admiral Donald C. Thompson, USCG, interview by author, 9 August 1988.

[6] USAA Board of Directors Minutes (BOD), 26 February 1983.

[7] USAA BOD, 7 May 1983.

[8] Ensley, interview, 19 March 1993.

[9] Robert F. McDermott, "Opening Comments: Financial Products and Services Planning Conference," 15 March 1983.

[10] McDermott, memo to Executive Council, "Financial Services Planning Conference," 24 March 1983. This was a summary of decisions and directions made at the Tapatio Conference. McDermott, interview by author, 4 December 1996. Ensley, interview, 19 March 1993.

[11] *San Antonio Express-News*, 16 December 1983. Ensley, interview, 19 March 1993.

[12] Application for "Permission to Organize a Federal Stock Savings Bank" in San Antonio, Texas, USAA, 14 April 1983.

[13] McDermott, interview, 4 December 1996. Ensley, interview, 19 March 1993.

[14] "USAA Financial Services Plan Briefing" delivered to the USAA Board of Directors, 5 May 1983.

[15] Rear Admiral H.C. Donley, USN (Ret.), interview by author, 9 August 1988.

[16] Ensley, letter to Laura Patriarca, Deputy Division Director, Corporate and Regulatory Structure, Federal Home Loan Bank Board, 21 November 1983.

[17] Ensley, interview, 19 March 1993.

[18] Ibid.

[19] Ensley, interview with Joseph "Ed" Braswell and author, 6 December 1992.

[20] Jack Antonini, interview by author, 30 August 1995.

[21] Ibid.

[22] Ibid. USAA Counsel Mike Wagner related to the author on December 17, 1996, that USAA had a backup plan in the wings in the event Antonini's ploy failed.

[23] Homer Holland, interview by author, 14 December 1995.

[24] Ibid.

[25] Ken Willman, briefing, USAA Management Meeting, 15 August 1989. Michael J.C. Roth, interview by author, 31 December 1996.

[26] *Business Week,* 2 November 1987; *Money,* January 1988, 13.

[27] USAA BOD, 14 November 1987. Roth, interview, 31 December 1996.

[28] *Highlights,* 1 February 1984.

[29] Major Charles E. Davis, letter to McDermott, 7 April 1988.

[30] USAA BOD, February 1982.

ENDNOTES

NOTES TO PAGES 410-437

[31] USAA IMCO BOD, 19 October 1982.
[32] USAA BOD, 4 May 1984.
[33] USAA BOD, 19 November 1983.
[34] USAA BOD, 21 February 1986.
[35] Ibid.
[36] USAA FINCO, "Written Consent to Action," 1 March 1986. Leddy had replaced Michael K. Conn as real estate head on December 1, 1985.
[37] *Aide Magazine*, Fall 1986.
[38] USAA BOD, 6 March 1987.
[39] The USAA Capital Corporation (CAPCO) had been incorporated under the laws of the state of Delaware on December 27, 1985. Its first organizational meeting was held on January 20, 1986.
[40] USAA CAPCO BOD, "Written Consent to Action," 28 December 1989.
[41] USAA BOD, 1 March 1985.
[42] McDermott, interview, 14 December 1996.
[43] USAA BOD, 11 May 1985.
[44] "USAA Looks into the Future with Vision 2000," *Highlights*, 29 May 1989; Jim Patterson, interview by author, 13 April 1996.
[45] USAA Board Newsletter, January 1986; "Vision 2000 Recap" briefing.
[46] Staser Holcomb, memo, "Event-Oriented Service Concept Paper," to Executive Council, 9 Jan 1989; "EOS," *Highlights*, 25 January 1989.
[47] *Highlights*, 5 March 1986.
[48] Beth Brophy, "You're in the Office of the Future Now," *U.S. News & World Report*, 17 April 1989, 51.
[49] Wilson C. "Bill" Cooney, interview by author, 2 December 1996.
[50] *Highlights*, 20 November 1985.
[51] Mike Howard, interview with author, 18 October 1994.
[52] Quoted in Gregory H. Watson, *Business Systems Engineering* (NY: John Wiley & Sons, Inc., 1994), 195.
[53] Chuck McCollough, "Business Line Wire," *San Antonio Express-News*, 6 March 1988.
[54] USAA BOD, 30 October 1982.
[55] McDermott, interview, 14 December 1996.
[56] USAA BOD, 20 March 1990.
[57] USAA Foundation BOD, 14 September 1994; 26 January 1986.
[58] USAA Foundation BOD, "Written Consent," 23 August 1989.
[59] USAA BOD, 14 May 1988.
[60] Press Conference held by CRTC, 1988.

ENDNOTES

61 USAA BOD, 19 May 1981.
62 Bill McCrae, interview by author, 17 January 1996.
63 *San Antonio Express-News,* 10 July 1987, 2F.
64 Ernst & Whinney, "Insurance Company CEOs," 1988.
65 California Department of Insurance Press Release, 19 June 1990. *San Antonio Light,* 16 May 1989, E8. USAA Property and Casualty History, 1989.
66 Ralph Nader quoted from testimony before California legislators, 9 March 1989.
67 Interoffice Memo, Deanna Stoddard to Joe Meyer, "Robbin's Finance and Insurance Committee," 10 March 1989.
68 *San Francisco Chronicle,* 2 August 1989; Kenneth Reich, "7 Insurance Firms Told to Return $305 million," *Los Angeles Times,* 2 August 1989.
69 Erik Ingram, "Auto Insurer Questions Figures," *San Francisco Chronicle,* 3 August 1989.
70 Jerry Goldberg, "New Insurance Czar Set for War in California," *New York Journal of Commerce,* 9 November 1990.
71 "Executive Perspective," *Aide Magazine,* December 1989.
72 Ronald H. Cole, *Operation Just Cause: The Planning and Execution of Joint Operations in Panama, February 1988-January 1990* (Washington, D.C.: Joint History Office, Office of the Chairman of the JCS, 1995), 2, 27.
73 Ibid.
74 Ibid., 62-63.
75 USAA BOD, 2 March 1990.
76 John Murphy, letter to McDermott, 8 January 1990.
77 Ron Zemke with Dick Schaaf, *The Service Edge: 101 Companies that Profit from Customer Care* (NY: New American Library, 1989), 232-235.
78 Toni Mack, "They Have Faith in Us," *Forbes,* 25 July 1988, 182.

Chapter Eleven
The Nineties – A Decade of Worldwide Change

1 Colin L. Powell, *My American Journey* (NY: Random House, 1995), 438.
2 Ibid., 458.
3 USAA Chairman Robert F. McDermott, letter to "Dear USAA Employee," 22 August 1990.
4 *Navy Times,* 21 January 1991.
5 A "catastrophe" is defined currently as a natural or other disaster which generates insured losses that exceed $25 million in a single event. In 1992, the amount was $5 million.
6 IIHS news release, 1 May 1990.

Endnotes

NOTES TO PAGES 465-496

7. USAA Board of Directors Minutes (BOD), 21 August 1993.
8. USAA Annual Members' Meeting minutes, 21 August 1993.

Chapter Twelve
THE TRANSITION TO NEW LEADERSHIP: GENERAL ROBERT T. HERRES

1. USAA Annual Members' Meeting minutes, 21 August 1993.
2. General Robert T. Herres, USAF (Ret.), interview by author, 9 August 1988.
3. Brig. General Robert F. McDermott, USAF (Ret.), President's Remarks, Annual Members' Meeting, 20 June 1992.
4. USAA Board of Directors Minutes (BOD), 10 November, 1989.
5. USAA BOD, 2 March 1990; Special Members' Meeting, 3 March 1990.
6. Herres, interview by author, 4 January 1995.
7. Quoted in Ron Cole, *The History of the Chairman of the Joint Chiefs of Staff* (U.S. Government: Washington, D.C., 1996), 7.
8. *Highlights,* 16 November 1989.
9. Colin L. Powell, *My American Journey* (NY: Random House, 1995), 406-407.
10. Leslie Hicks, "Smooth Transition," *San Antonio Express-News,* 7 August 1994, 1H.
11. McDermott, interview by author, 4 December 1996.
12. Admiral Staser Holcomb, USN (Ret.), interview by author, 2 January 1997.
13. Ibid.; Also Brig. General Wilson C. "Bill" Cooney, USAF (Ret.), interview by author, 2 December 1996.
14. Property and Casualty Annual History, 1991, 6.
15. Major General Herb Emanuel, USAF (Ret.), interview by author, 22 February 1996.

Chapter Thirteen
MEETING THE CHALLENGES OF CHANGE

1. Harvard Business School, "USAA: Business Process Review for Great Lakes Region," Case #N9-694-024, 5 August 1993.
2. USAA Board of Directors Minutes (BOD), 17 August 1996.
3. Homer Holland, interview by author, 14 December 1995.
4. Herb Emanuel, interview by author, 22 February 1996. USAA BOD, 4 March 1995.
5. USAA BOD, conference call, 22 June 1996.
6. USAA BOD, 4 March 1994.
7. USAA BOD, 4 March 1995.
8. General Robert T. Herres USAF (Ret.), USAA Management Meeting, 16 November 1994.

Endnotes

NOTES TO PAGES 498-534

9. "The Race is On," *Inside USAA,* 29 January 1997.
10. Frederick F. Reichheld, *The Loyalty Effect* (Boston: Harvard Business School Press, 1996), 30.
11. "Leveraging Processes for Strategic Advantage," David A. Garvin, *Harvard Business Review,* September-October, 1995, 86, 87.
12. Herres, Management Meeting, 18 January 1996.
13. *USAA Code of Business Ethics & Conduct,* December 1996, 3.
14. *Journal of Business Strategy,* July/August, 1996.
15. Ibid. Also see Janice Marshall's biography on pages 319 and 320.
16. See William B. Tracy, "United Services Automobile Association," in *Reasonable Accommodation,* Jay W. Spechler, ed., (Delray Beach, FL: St. Lucie Press, 1996), 229-236.
17. Thelma Garza, "The Growing Menace of RSI," *San Antonio Express-News,* 9 September 1996.
18. USAA BOD, 27 May 1995.
19. Scott Adams, *The Dilbert Principle* (NY: Harper Business, 1996), title page.
20. USAA BOD, 17 August 1996.
21. USAA BOD, 6 May 1994.
22. IIPLR, *UPDATE,* December 1993.
23. USAA Foundation BOD, 14 September, 1994.
24. Gloria Barba, letter to USAA, February 1995.
25. Morton Kondracke, "Pennsylvania Avenue," *Roll Call,* 19 September 1994.
26. USAA BOD, 2 December 1995.
27. *Aide Magazine,* December 1991.
28. *USAA Annual Progress Report,* 1995, 7.
29. Arthur D. Little, Inc. Press Release, 14 February 1995.
30. Reichheld, *The Loyalty Effect,* 284, 285.
31. Dwight L. Gertz and Joao P. Baptista, *Grow To Be Great* (New York, NY: The Free Press, 1995), 53.
32. Ibid., 145.

Epilogue

1. *USAA Annual Progress Report,* 1997.
2. Herres, interview by Jim Wieghart, 25 April 1997.
3. Ibid.
4. Ibid.
5. Ibid.
6. Ibid.

INDEX

Illustrations are indicated in bold type

AAFES (Army and Air Force Exchange Service), 362
ARA, 421, 422
Abdel-Aziz, King (of Saudi Arabia) Fahd Ibn, 453
accidents
　carelessness and speeding, 91
　condition of cars, 91
　early instructions for, 21
　of enlisted personnel in Europe, 120
　of officers in Europe, 120
　rates, climbing in 1930s, 64
Accommodation Specialist, 505
accounting (GAAP), 415
ACE II, 340
Adjusted Building Cost (ABC), 289
advertising and marketing, 14, 17, 19-21, 30, 61, 114, 155, 268, 269
　active duty advertisement, **268**
　"An Unusual Sight," **17**
　"Bragging Rights," **16**
　Cheever as 1954 spokesman, **156**
　confusion with United Services, **62**
　"Do You Believe in Signs," **18**
　enlisted, **521**
　Event-Oriented Service, 417
　40th anniversary advertisement, **211**
　Good Luck Symbols, **17**
　Group Research and Marketing, 294
　Life Marketing, 296
　Member Relations Team, 269
　missed eligibles, **336**
　on military installations, 212
　pre-commissioning efforts, 153, 210, **210,** 212
　promoting careful driving, 65
　typical 1930s advertisement, **61**
　typical 1950s advertisement, **114**
　USAA car emblem, **29**
　USAA Diamond, **19**
　USAA Life, **194**
　World War II, rate reductions, **81**
Afghanistan, 333
After Hours Operations, 502
African-American employees
　BOD changes policy, 196, 197
　early policy, 196
　Moye and, 197, 198
　Ollie Smith, **196**
Akers, John, 427

Aide Magazine, 251, 267, 289, 297, 320, 336, 339, 377, 444, 457, 476
　becomes *USAA Magazine,* 522
air bags
　and Culpeper crash, 460, 461
　increased interest, 461
　safety, 463
Air Force
　establishment of, 104-105.
airplane, corporate, 350, **351**
Aldrin, Col. Edwin E. "Buzz", **272**
　first active member on the moon, 272
Allen, George, 344
alliance relationships, 523-524
　Federal Express, 523
　PHH Home Equity Corporation, 523
　Sprint, 523
Allstate, 162
　supports tax on reciprocals, 162
All-Volunteer Armed Force, 281
Altgelt, Ernest J. and Mary (Heard), 315
Alvarez, Lt (jg) Everett, Jr., 218, **218**
American International Underwriters Corporation, 67, 95, 116, 170
American Management Association (AMA), 152, 153, 328
　Cheever, 152
　Company Program, 255
American Officers Insurance Company Limited (AOIC), 190-191, **192,** 545n 12
　employees, **191**
　renamed, 358
American Reciprocal Association, 162
American Red Cross, 188
American United, 219
Americans with Disabilities Act, 505
Anderson, Margaret, 434
Anderson Bill, 128
Annapolis, 346
Annual Members' Meeting (first), 18
Annual Organizational Review Program (AOR), 320
"Annual Peer Ratings", 320
anti-insurance attitudes in society, 436
Antonini, Jack, 398-399, **399,** 490, 523
Army Cooperative Fire Association (AFCA), 10, 12, 63, 88
　"friendly competitor", 89
Army Exchange Service, 116, 120

Army Mutual Aid Association, 10
assigned risk plans, 129, 130, 270, 271
  associate members, 129
  move to CIC, 286
  policyholders become voting members, 130
  study to use USAA CIC, 270
Atkins, Brig. Gen. Joseph A., 71
  as Second Assistant Secretary-Treasurer and Attorney-in-Fact, 71
Attorney-in-Fact, 12, 13
  multiples terminated, 158
Auburn automobile, a 1926 Auburn 4-door sedan with a USAA emblem, **29**
Austin (Texas) Marriot, 492
Auto Issue and Maintenance System (AIMS), 297
Auto Technical Training Center, 420
Automation
  ACE (Automated Claims Environment), 340
  AIMS (Auto Issue and Maintenance System), 297
  EDP as separate unit, 234
  equipment upgrade postwar, 96
  first Long Range Systems Plan, 340
  Fishel and, 249
  HAL (Health and Life System), 382
  IBM 650 installed, 154
  IBM 7074, 1401, and 360, 234
  IBM 3090, 427
  IMAGE, 427, 428, 498
  INSCO, 235, 254
  ITAP, 497
  mail and telephone advances, 429
  multi-car, 234, 253, 255
  "paperless company," 273
  problems in 1970s, 298
  USAA's first "computer" (1936), 96
Automated Claims Environment (ACE), 340
automobile
  air bags, 375, 376
  Auburn, 1926 4-door Sedan with USAA emblem, **29**
  Elcar Landau Touring Sedan, **13**
  history and impact of, 5-7
  increasing number of, 124
  insurance premium rate tables, 25
  insurance in New York City, 116
  Model "T" Ford, 5, **5**
  new, acquisition of after the war, 90

popularity, 178
repair costs, 164
shatterproof windshields, 373
smaller sizes, 369
Automobile Underwriters of America (AUA), 12
Ayres, Atlee B. and Robert M., 144
aviation coverage, 385
Aylsworth, Clark, 244, 245

B-17 Flying Fortress, **105**
Bailey, Col. Neill E., 158
  Chairman of the Board, 160
  death of, 160
Bailey Committee on Mandatory Retirements, 158
Baldwin, Melissa, 455
Bank of America (B.O.A.), 175
Bank Services Building, 351, 493
Barba, Felix, 514
Barnard, Lt. Col. J.H., 1
Base Force Concept, 451
Bates, Lillian, 193, 239
Bates, Former POW Lt. Richard L., **278**
Baumhefner, C.H., 175
Baxter and Korge, USAA logo, 265-266
Beck, Henry, 182, 312
Benham-Blair and Affiliates, 310
Berg, Maj. Gen. William W., 237
Berlin Wall, 195, 450
Best's ratings, 163, 176, 299
  gives USAA consistent A+ ratings, 232, 297, 368, 386
  cut dividend to protect rating, 250
  gives USAA Life "Policy holder's Recommendation", 270
  1940s rating of USAA, 97
Biegler, Lt. Col. George W., 1-2, **22**
  as USAA president, 18-19
Bishop, Brig. Gen. Charles, 296, 384, 426, **459**, 477, 511
Black History Month Celebration, 506
  USAA Gospel Choir, 507, **507**
Blair, Kathy, 419
Blanks, Col. Randy, 474
Blitslow, Sheldon, 360
Blue Eagle, 499, 500
Board of Directors (USAA), **10**
  Advisory Council to, 490
  and active duty membership, 489

INDEX

Audit Committee created, 325
BOD members from outside San Antonio, 246
 directors' fees, 327, 328
 Executive Committee removed from operations, 246
 Executive Council, 12
 first, 11
 instability during World War II, 85
 membership requirement, 58, 540n 23
 Personnel Policy Committee created, 326
 Phillips recommends McDermott as Chairman, 325
 reorganized with new committees, 488
 tenure becomes five two-year terms, 327
 withdrawal from operational decisions, 186, 187
boatowner's insurance, 189
bonus referral, 257
Bosnia, 457
Bosse, Fred, 509
Bowen, Bill, 418, 477
Bowles and Tillinghast, 204, 270
Bowles, Andres, and Towne, 199
Bradley, Ed, 357
Bradley, Gen. Omar, 275-276, **275**, 306
Braeuler, Peter, 345
Brakey, Robert G., 289, 292, **303**, 337, 379
 as president of USAA General Agency, 380
Brett, Lt. Cmdr. James E., first U.S. Navy officer on USAA BOD, 86
Brinker, Brig. Gen. Walter, 236
Briscoe, Dale, 384, 385
Brite, Steve, 367
Brock, Hattie, 282,
Brooke, Col. Roger, USAA President, 58, **58,** 59
Brooks, Nancy, 115, 200
Broussard, Debbie, Miss Fair Share Contest, with Tracie Martin and McDermott, **259**
Buis, Dale, 217
Burkholder, Pauline (Nesbitt), 363
Burnley, Jim, 377
Burstein, Dr. Alvin, 256
Bush, U.S. President George, and Iraq, 453
business reading club, 418
Butler, Brenda, 506
bylaws – key changes (other than eligibility)
 to create subsidiaries, 190-191
 to enable two employees to serve on the Board, 468
 to offer non-insurance products, 294
 to sell insurance other than P&C, 191

Caldwell, Lt. Col. R.G., 2, **15**
 background, 15
 contract renewed, 34
 reduced to Assistant Secretary-Treasurer, 41
 Secretary-Treasurer, 15
Calvelli, Joseph "Joe" R., 380, **380**
Calvert, Dale, 303
Camp, William, 244
CAPCO, *see* USAA Capital Corporation
Caperton, Cape, 340
Cardenas, Yesenia, 517
"Career Fashions", **263, 264,** 263-265
Carneiro, Chumney and Cagney, 50, 142
Carpenter, Brig. Gen. Thomas E., 389
Carpenter, Jeanette, 304
Carrington, Bob, 267
Carter, Col. Herbert, 506
Cashen, Shack, 318
Cassiday, Lt. Gen. Patrick F., 324
catastrophes (CAT), 443-444, 457-459
 CAT Teams, 274, 305, 306, 331, 459-459
 catastrophe principles, 460
 claims replacement, 362
 first CAT to Virginia, 209
 first overseas to Guam, 209
 reinsurance
 team concept, 209
Celler, Congressman Emanuel, 215
CHAMPUS, 382
Chandler, Brig. Gen. Rex E., 158
 chairman, 160
 expense reduction initiatives, 164, 165
Change of address, 476
Change of the Century, 499
Charbonneau, C.K., 300
Charette, Private Toni, **454**
charitable contributions
 computation changed, 429, 430
 first formal program, 187, 188
 justifiable business expense, 188
 McDermott's attitude, 328
 reorganized (1996), 512
 The USAA Foundation, a Charitable Trust, 512
Chartered Financial Analyst (CFA), 318
Chartered Property Casualty Underwriter

563

(CPCU), 234
classes, 259
Cheever, Col. Charles E.
  and enlisted, 237
  as a young man, **134**
  as an instructor at the US Military Academy, **137**
  as General Counsel, 128
  as Managing Director, 190
  as Secretary-Treasurer, General Manager, and Attorney-in-Fact, 132
  at Hitler's Eagles Nest, **138**
  background, 133-140
  Betty and Charles at his retirement coffee, **238**
  guides USAA as a modern company, 141
  in 1954 USAA advertisement **156**
  negotiating licenses, 126
  on NAII Board of Governors, 152, 233
  president of NAII, 152
  retires, 236-237
  role in Germany, 120, **120**
  USAA President, 160
Chen, Melinda and Brandon, **525**
Chen, Shiang, 525
childcare facility referral service, 418
Chisolm, Del, 478
Children's Courtyard, 356
Christmas Cheer, 188, 514
  volunteers, **515**
Christmas shopping, half-day off cartoon, **151**
CIA, 451
Cisneros, Henry, 330, **424**
CIT, *see* Customer Insurance Team
civil disorders, 213-214
civil rights struggle, 196-197
Civil Service Commission, 123
Civilian Conservation Corps Camps, 54, 69
claims
  "actual value" (1939), 67
  adjusters convert to USAA employees, 303
  replacement service, 360
  structured settlements, 362, 383
  study, 477
  worst year (1992), 459
Claims Security Unit (CSU), 367, 368
Clark Air Base, 458
CLEP (College Level Examination) testing, on-site, 418
Clodfelter, Maj. Mark, 451, **452**

CLU (Chartered Life Underwriter), 257
Cockrell, Mayor Lila, 316
Cold War, 100, 530
  accelerated by Korean War, 113
  Afghanistan and new Cold War, 333
  Cuban Missile crisis intensifies, 194, 195
  ends, 451, 484
  intensifies, 177, 178
Combination Automobile Insurance Manual, 25
Combs, Brig. Gen. Cecil E., 158
Communities Organized for Public Service (COPS), 329
compulsory auto insurance, 167, 181
Comprehensive Personal Liability Policy, 173
computer-assisted instruction, 420
computers, 525
concentration camp survivors, **139**
Conference Board, 328
Conn, Michael K., 411
consumer cooperatives, 8
Consumer Reports, 276, 331, 448
consumerism, 436
Continental Insurance Company of New York, 235
Contingency Plan (Presidential), 326
Cook, Charles, 318
  as Chief Actuary, 247, 253, 285, 318
Cook, John, 431, 438-439, **439**, 509
Cook, Michele, 458
Cooney, Brig. Gen. Wilson C. "Bill", 388, 424-426, **426**, 477, 478, 485, 499, 511
  as president of Property and Casualty, 496
  background, 425-426
cooperative movements and mutuals, 8, 9
corporate good citizen
  computation changed, 429-430
  education, **434,** 434-436, **435**
  first formal program, 187-188
  justifiable business expense, 188
  McDermott's attitude, 328
  Shapiro documentaries, 430-432, 517-519
Corporate Communications Department
  organized, 438
Corporate Family Solutions, 504
Corporate Research, 488
Correnti, Tony, 475
Costello, Richard, 254
Couric, Katie, 518
Coverage, 265

INDEX

Covington, Guy, 297
Covo, Bertie, 45
Craigie, Lt. Gen. Laurence "Bill", **405**, 406
Craven, Gloria (Patterson), 341
Crawford and Company, 168
credit cards (USAA)
  booming business, 494
  Falcon Fraud Detection System, 495
  funding payments, 414
  gold card, 404
  insurance, 189
  MasterCard, 397
  overwhelming response, 398
  Tulsa Center closing, 494
  USAA MasterCard rated "best card buy", 404
  use of, 400-404
  Visa, 397, 404
Crime Prevention Institute, 252
Crocker, James W.T., 190, **191**
Cronkite, Walter, 517
Cross, Dennis, 296
Crowe, Adm. William, 474, 475
Cruse, Maj. Fred, 23
  USAA board member, 40
Cruz, Liz, 495
Culpeper Crash, 460-461, **461**
Cushman and Wakefield, 312
Cusik, Pat, 418
Customer Data Base Systems, 417
Customer Information File (CIF), 417
Customer Insurance Team (CIT), 485

DALBAR (research company), 526
Dau, Beate, 121
Davidson, Waid J., 269
Davis, Col. Michael F., first Air Force officer on Board of Directors, 106
Davis, Robert G., 496, **497**
Daye, Col. John F. "Jack", 236
  as a pilot in World War II, **242**
  as Vice President and President in the Life Company, 269, 381, 383, 384
  as Vice President, Plans and Programs, 243, 257
  background, 242
  expansion site plans, 248
Dean, Dick, 470, 471
death rate climbs in 1960s, 213

"deaths per 100,000 registered cars", **368**
Deddah, Senator Waddie, 441
Defense Acquisition Board (DAB), 474
Defense spending, 334-335
DeLorean, John, 251
Denenberg, Herbert S., 304
Dent, Doris, 203, 478
Department of Defense (DOD), 180
  letter from Cheever, 237
  licensing directive, 224
Depository Institutions Deregulation, 392
Depression
  Bonus Marchers, 54
  employees during, **47,** 55, 56
  Hinds takes voluntary pay cut, 54, 55
  payless furlough, 54
  reduction in federal salaries, 54
  USAA investments during, 48-51
deregulation of business, 391
Desert Shield, 453
Desert Shield (Storm) Assistance Center, 456
Desert Storm, 456
  and USAA Federal Savings Bank, 455, 456
  and USAA Life Insurance, 455
  and Operation Desert Greetings, 455
  and service immprovements resulting from, 456-457
  auto dividend, 456
Dilbert (cartoon), 507, **508**
DIRECTInvesting, 525
"Dinner Express", 421
Discount Brokerage, 394, 406, 407
Divich, Duane, 447
documentaries
  Bad Dads, 518
  Break the Silence, 518
  Everybody's Business, 518
  Future Flight, 430
  The Korean War, 430
  POW: Americans in Enemy Hands, 430
  Raising Good Kids in Bad Times, 517
  Return to Iwo Jima, 430
  Scared Silent, 518, **518**
  Top Flight, 430
  The Unknown Soldier, 430
  Victory Over Violence, 517
  What's Right With America, 519
Donley, Rear ADM H.C., 395

Donohue, Antoinette, 163
DOONESBURY (cartoon), **375**
Double Eagle award, 368
Dougherty, Maj. Russell, in Korea, **113**
Doughton, Walter, 477
"Drive-In Claims Facility", 267
dress code relaxed, 507
DRIVE SMART, 462, 463
DRIVE SMART, "Drive Cool", 463
DRIVE SMART COLORADO, 463
DRIVE SMART Hampton Roads (Virginia), 463, **463**
Draude, Capt. Thomas, **220**
Drucker, Peter, 339
Drumm, Bob, 318
Dunn, Edward C., 539n 3
Dunton, Harold, 9, **10**
   as first general manager, 11, 16, 17
   leaves USAA, 22
Duryea, Charles E., 5
Dye, Myron "Butch", 377, 478

ECHO (Every Contact Has Opportunity), 501
Economic Development Foundation (EDF), 329
education and training
   employee achievement breakfast, **419**
   Ferrari, Col. Victor J. and, 260-262
   house calls, 419, 420
   management development program, 260
   Managerial Insurance Seminar (1971), 262
   professional development, 259, 260, 318, 418, 419
   Project Campus, 262, 318, 324
   tuition reimbursement, 319, 418
   women in programs, 324
Education Fairs, 418
Eisenhower, Dwight
   addressing USAA employees, **154**
   and Bonus Marchers, 54
   appoints McDermott, 231
   military and cold war, 153
   supports Air Force, 104
   Vietnam, 217
Elcar, 1925 Elcar Landau Touring Sedan, **13**
eligibility, *see* membership eligibility
Emanuel, Maj. Gen. Herbert L., 343, **343**, 344
   and smoking, 421
Employee Activities Committee, 423
Employee Assistance Programs, 418
Employee Benefit Association, 321

Employees
   African-American, 196, 197
   and service in the Reserves, 453, **454**
   bonus refund program (1971), 257
   correction clerk, 223
   equal pay for equal work ordered (1978), 323, 324
   exempt and non-exempt, 199
   handicapped, 199
   high school dropouts, 198-199, **198**
   Mexican-American, 150
   "Operation: How Are We Doing," 256
   President's Employee Merit Award, 199
   survey (1966), 204
employees at work
   Depression era, **47**
   in the mid-1960s, **221**
   modeling career fashions, **264**
   modeling mini-skirts, **263**
   Policy and Ratings Departments, **55**
Employee benefits
   discount tickets, **423**
   Employee Assistance programs, 418
   Employee Benefit Association, 321
   Employees' day at Hemisphere, 205
   employee dependent scholarships, 435, 436, **436**
   four-day work week, 257
   group retirement plan, 200, **200**, 201
   New Year's Day Reception, 258
   physical fitness centers and health, **355**, 420
   Retirement Savings Supplement Plan, 201
   retirement, social security offset, 201
   special events, **422, 423**
   summer camp for employees' children, 202-203, **202**
   tuition loans, 201
   USAA Savings and Investment Plan (SIP), 321
Employers Reinsurance Company, 79, 92
energy shortage, 287-288
England, *see* American Officers Insurance Company
Enlisted eligibility, *see* membership eligibility
Ensley, George H., 236, 246, 318
   as Deputy CEO, 389
   as president of DEVCO, 409
   background, 240-242, **241, 242**
   designed Employee Benefit Association
   Financial Services briefing, 392
   management control system, 246, 247
   twenty-year forcast, 248
Engaging the Organization, 467

INDEX

ergonomics, 505, 506
Erie Insurance Group, 372
Ernst & Whinney Survey, 438
ESP (Extraordinary Service Partnerships), 480
ethics, 184, 503
　first USAA formal ethics policy, 185
　USAA Code of Ethics, 503
Europe, selling insurance in, 169
European Command (EUCOM), 117
　assisting with insurance in Germany, 117-119
Event-Oriented Service (EOS), 417
Evers, Susan, 318
Eversole, Inez, 273
Executive Management Group (EMG), 339
Executive Succession Plan, 464, 480

Falcon Fraud Detection System, 495
Farm-related insurance, 255
Federal Express, 299, 523
Federal Highway Act, 6
Federal Home Loan Bank Board, 394-396, 400, 402
Federal Income Tax Law (1942) USAA exempt, 162
Federal Minimum Wage Law, 199
Federal Motor Vehicle Safety Standard 208, 374
Federal Services Finance Corporation, 31
Federal Trade Commission, 215
Ferrari, Col. Victor J., 260-262, **261**, 517
Fidelity & Guaranty Fire Corporation of Baltimore, 64
Fiesta, 422
Fiesta Texas, 483, 493-494, **493**
File Net, 427
Financial Planning Network, 523
Financial Responsibility Laws, 91-93, 125-129
　certificates, 127
　strengthening, 180, 181
financial services deregulation, 426
Financial Services Division, 393
Financial Services Planning Conference, 393
Fire Insurance
　for non-AFCA members, 63, 64
　available for all officers, 88, 89
Fishel, Col. Martin D. "Marty" Jr., 236, 240, **240**, 246
Florida Insurance Guaranty Association, 460
Florida, Irene, 260, 265
Flynn, Bill, 347, **347**, 407, 486
Ford, advertisement in *San Antonio Light,* 1922, **6**

Forster, Col. Art, 475
Fort Sam Houston, 1, 25, 35, 37, 39-41
Fort Sam Houston Clock Tower, **26**
four-day workweek, 257, 258, 548n 66
Four Seasons Resort, 492
"Fourth Company", 531
Fowler, Rick, 484, **485**
Fox, Charles, artist, 182
fraud, insurance, 27, 366-368, **366**
Frees, Beulah, 151, 175, **175**
French, Maj. Marion O., 2
Frieden Flexowriters, 254
Frost National Bank of San Antonio, 115
FS-1, (New York), 167

GAAP (General Accepted Accounting Principles), 415
Gannon, Alice, 249
Garamendi, John, 510
Garletts, Larry, 342
Garnes, Lt. Col. Hilton, **454**
Garn-St. Germain Act of 1982, 392
Garrison, Maj. William Henry
　and Charles Cheever, **146**
　background, 2-3, **3, 4**
　daughter and USAA CIC, 285
　financing autos, 31
　first president 11, 12, 15
　founding USAA, 9-11
　sell USAA insurance, 25
Gasoline Alley (cartoon), 6
Gates, Thomas S., Jr., 281
Gates Commission, 281
Gaylor, Robert D., 340-341, **341**, 418
GEICO (Government Employees Insurance Company), 57
　advertisement for, 80
　compared with USAA, 163
　poor performance, 292
　USAA helps save, 292, 293
Gelb Marketing Research, survey of members, 243
　modernizing image, 265, 267
General Motors, 251
Gentry, Barbara, 512, **513**
George Foster Peabody Award, 518
Germany
　Cheever role, 120-121
　decision to insure members in 116-121

567

EUCOM HG supportive, 117-119
first overseas office, **121**
International Motor Insurance (Green) Card, 169
LAW 22, 118
Status of Forces Agreement, 169, 206
Gerstner, Lou, 499
Glass-Steagall Act, 391
Goldberg, Steve, 249, 510
"Golden Eagles" club, 321, **322**
Golden Rule Company, 383
Goldman, Sachs, 494
Golembe and Associates, 391
Goodwin, Leo, Sr., 22, 42, **42**
  as Chief Accountant, 42
  deceased, 292
  founded GEICO, 57
  lobbies against Federal regulation, 93
  resigned from USAA, 57
  working for Perry L. King, 42
Governance Committee, 488
Governor's Island, 116
Government Service Policy, 64
Graham, Margaret P., 46
Great Lakes Region, operation test bed, 484, 485, 523
Green, Warren V., 121
Griffith, Col. Jack, 234
Griffith, Lt. Jack H., first life insurance policy, 194
Gring, Wade, 250
Group airline charters, 293
Group Life Insurance, 382
Grow To Be Great, 527
Gulfstream Aerospace III (G-III) aircraft, **351**
Gunter Hotel, **xx**, 1, 7, 18
Gusich, Liz, 503
Gutierrez, Rachel, 516
Gwyn, Stuart, 94, **94**, 129, 154
  as Chief Assistant in underwriting, 44
  as principal assistant to the Office Manager, 44
  as a Vice President, Underwriting, 185
  welcome home telegrams, 94

Habitat for Humanity, 512, 513, **513**, 514
Hacker, Benjamin T., 463, 464, **464**
Haddon, Dr. William, Jr., 369
Hains, Maj. Gen. Peter C., III, 165
HAL (Health and Life System), 382
Harding, President Warren G., 14

Harman, J. Robert, 387, 388
Harris, Amy, 364
Harris, Col. William, 109
Hawaii, John Mullen Agency, 208
Hawker, Mike, **191**
Hayden, Bob, 353, **353**
Head, Chris, 308
health, 420
Health Services, 420
Heflin, Valerie, 516
Heidrick & Struggles Inc., 488
Heidt, Col. James V., 31
  as president and Chairman of Executive Committee, 32-35
HemisFair, 205
  USAA tour guides, **205**
Henderson, Capt. Harry McCorry, 1, 26
Henderson, Robert, 509
Henry Beck Construction Company, 146
Henry, John, 463
Hernandez, RADM Jesse J., 447
Herres, Bill, 469
Herres, Robert T., 464, 465
  and Junior Achievement, 517
  appointed Chairman and CEO, 464
  as a high school senior, **469**
  as a member of MOL Program, 472, **473**
  as a Midshipman 3/C on the USS *Albany*, **470**
  as COO for Insurance and Information Services and Deputy Attorney-in-Fact, 480
  as President, COO for USAA and Attorney-in-Fact, 480
  as Vice Chairman of the Board, 468
  at USNA, 470, **470**
  background, 467-474, **469**
  briefs Reagan and Weinberger, **357**
  children, 472
  elected to USAA Board, 467
  Executive Succession Plan, 480
  president of the Property and Casualty Division, 468
  Vice Chairman of the Joint Chiefs of Staff, 473, 474, **473**
  with Shirley, volunteering, **513**
Herres, Shirley, 471, 472, 513, **513**
Hertz, discount program, 273
High school dropout program, **198**
"High Tech, High Touch," 339

INDEX

Highway Loss Data Institute, 369
Hilbig, Sylvia, 457
Hildebrandt, Charlotte, 121, 157
   staffing New York office, 168
Hill, Capt. Howard J., 280
Hinds, Maj. Gen. Ernest, **41**, 182
   and financial houses, 51
   and USAA employees, 55-56
   as a West Point Cadet, **37**
   background, 37-40
   entertaining visitors at Fort Sam Houston Quadrangle, **40**
   death, 71
   managing USAA, 45-46
   new ten-year contract, 58
   reduces salary by 15%, 55
   report to the Finance Committee in 1938, 70
   salary restored, 56
Hirt, F. William, 370
Hittle, James D., 274
Hobbs, Congressman Sam, 93
Holcomb, Vice Adm. M. Staser, 376, 388, **389**, 503
   as president of CAPCO, 496
   as President of Property and Casualty Company, 389
Holland, Homer, 402-403, 488
Holmes, Jay, 499
Home Help Line, 523
Home Loan Bank, 395
Home Office Building, USAA
   first, Kelly Field #1, Texas, 11, **11**
   second, Calcasieu Building, San Antonio, Texas, 16
   third, Fort Sam Houston, Texas, (Wilson and Shirley Streets), 25, 30
   fourth, (1400) Grayson Street, San Antonio, Texas, 35, **122**, 141, 142, 144
      additions, 122, 123
      American Business, picked as one of Best 100 (1951), 122
   fifth, (4119) Broadway Building, San Antonio, Texas, 143-148, **147**
      addition, 182, 183, **183**
      cafeteria, **148**
      dedication, 146, **146**
      leased supplemental space, 248, 249, 296
      Ovenshine Committee picks site, 142, 143
      planning, design, engineering, 144
      proposed addition, (1968), 233
      Summer Day Camp, **202**
      terminated, 235, 551n 67
   sixth, McDermott Building, San Antonio, Texas, 316
      American ("E") Courtyard, **354**
      Commercial (Children's) Courtyard, **356**
      Conference Center, 551n 68
      dedication, 316
      expansion, 353-355
      groundbreaking, **311**
      inspiration for, 310, 311
      interior, 316-317
      landscape, 310, 313
      named for McDermott, 464
      parking garage, 352, 353
      role of Starnes, 312, **313**
      San Antonio ("B") Courtyard, **317**
      site planning, 233, 247, 248, 310, 547n 47
      turnstiles for security, 359
      under construction, **314**
home ownership, 173
homeowners insurance, 174
   first policy issued, **174**
   resistance from banks, 275
Hoover, William, 475
Hopkins, Rita, 106
House, Joe, 344, **344**, 350
"House Calls", 419
Huff, Capt. Leslie B., first homeowners' policy, **174**
Huff, Esther N., 485
Huntington, Samuel, 232
Hurricane Andrew, 458-460, 491
Hutton, Bill, 477
Hybl, Bill, 488, 489

Iacocca, Lee, 375
IIHS, *see* Insurance Institute for Highway Safety
Illig, Al, 295
IMAGE, 427, 428, 498
IMCO, *see* USAA Investment Management Company
inflation impact, 289, 292, 293
Information Services (IS), 498-499
   see also automation
Information Technology Acquisition Process

569

(ITAP), 497
INSCO Systems, 235
insurance, fraud, 366
  of automobiles during military transfer, 27
Insurance Crime Prevention Institute, 253
Insurance Department of State of Texas Report of Examination in 1944, 97
Insurance Information Institute, 250
Insurance Institute for Highway Safety (IIHS), 214, 215, 369, 438, 439, 461
Insurance Institute for Property Loss Reduction (IIPLR), 511, 512
Insurance Institute of America, 259, 318
insurance, no-fault, 252
Insurer Consumer Action Network, 443
Intercompany Survivors Assistance Team (ISAT), 457
Internal Revenue Act of 1962, 212, 253
International Motor Insurance Card (Green Card), 169
Internet, 534
INVESTART, 407
Investment Securities Company of Dallas, 48
Investronic plan, 407
In-WATS testing, 302, 303
  see also WATS
Iran, 307-309
  revolution, 307
  denial of claims, 308
Iraq, 449, 451
ISAT, *see* Intercompany Survivors Assistance Team
ITAP, *see* Information Technology Acquistion Process

Japan, institutes compulsory insurance law, 171-173
  insurance in, 207, 208
Japan surrendering ceremonies, **99**
Jefferis, Clifford, 246, 285, **290**, **339**
Jenschke, Tanis, 171, 478
Jinks, Jim, 509
Job Opportunity Program (JOP), 418
Jockers, Larry, 377
Joe's Car (cartoon), 7, **7**
John Mullen Agency, 208
Johnson, ADM Jay L., 489
Johnson, H.T., 480, 481, 490
Joint Underwriting Association (Florida), 460

  see also Residential Property Casualty Joint Underwriting Association
Jones, Col. William F., 51, 71, 182
  announces retirement, 131
  as Attorney-in-Fact and Assistant Secretary-Treasurer, 71
  as Commanding Officer of the 12th Field Artillery, 1935-1937, **101**
  as General Manager of USAA, 1948 to 1952, **104**
  as Secretary-Treasurer and Attorney-in-Fact, 100
  background, 101-104
  in the Philippines, ca. 1910, **103**
  recommends Proctor as his replacement, 131
  resigns, 132
Joseph, Robert E., 163, 168
Junior Achievement program, 516-517
  see also USAA Mentor and Junior Acheivement Program.

Keeter, James E., 313
Kelleher, Marie, 320, 322
Kelley, Edward, 490, 491, **491**, 492
Kelly Field #1 (Duncan Field), 3
Kennedy, President John F., 183, 184, 195, **203**, 204, 217
Kerford, Consuelo, as secretary to Hinds, 44, **95**
  as Secretary to USAA Board of Directors, 44
  as USAA's first woman officer, 160
  as a Vice-President-Secretary, 185
  in Japan, 172
Key Result Areas (KRAs), 256, 486
Keyes, Col. Edward A., 160
Kilday, Congressman Paul J., 93
King, Earl, 323
King, Perry L., Auditing Company, 22, 29
Kirn, RADM, 188
Kirsling, Albert J., 283, **285,** 303
Knight, Barbara
  manages Counseling Office, 418
  heads office to assist minorities, 324
Knubel, John A., 384, 389
Knudsen, Benny, 506
Korean War,
  action, 112, 113
  and Cold War, 113
  impact on USAA, 113, 114, 153
  and Ensley, 240, 241
Korge, Fred, 267

INDEX

Korn/Ferry, 328

Labor Union activity, 204, 322, 323
La Cantera Golf Course, 492
Lackland, Maj. Frank D., 2
  as Acting Secretary-Treasurer, 15
Lackland Air Force Base, 2
Laird, David, 318
Lange, Morton, 117
Lanie, Larry J., 395, 397-402
Lasher, Don, 428
Lasher, Maj. Gen. Donald R., 388
Leadership 477
  see also PRIDE
League of Families of American POW and MIA, 279
Leaving the Military, Your Guide to Separation and Retirement, 457
Leddy, H. Drake, 411, 557n 36
Lengel, Sandy, **419**
LEO (Life Engaging the Organization), 480
Leonard, Col. A.T. "Benny", 234
  retires, 235
  Vice President and Attorney-in-Fact, 186
Lewis, Andrew, 374
Lewis, Major H.B., 1
licensing
  by Germany, 171
  by states, 224
  dynamics of, 130
  en mass, 181
  for life insurance, 193
  in Canadian provinces, 91
  in Hawaii, 126
  in Maryland, 157, 158
  in Massachusetts, 92-93
  in New York, 92, 126-128
  in Texas, 28
  securing licenses in all states, 126
  state, 130, 131, 180-182
  states changing the rules and requirements, 130
  USAA GIC, 286
  USAA moves for in all states, 181, 209, 224
Lichens, Lucille, 240
life insurance, see USAA Life Insurance Company
Life Insurance Company of North America, 219
Life Insurance Marketing and Research

Association (LIMRA), 296
Lifsey, Capt. Robert J., 297
Lincoln, Col. Lawrence J., 158
Lloyd's of London, 76, 167
Logan, Welby, 120, 171, **171**, 206
  as AOIC Board member, 190
  European manager, 121
  resident Vice President, Europe, 186
Long, Eva, 43, **43**, 44
Long Range Systems Plan, 340
Long-Range Basing Plan Study, 347
Look magazine, 251
Loughborough, Maj. William B., **24**
  appointed General Manager, 24
  background, 24
  removed from office, 34
Loyalty Effect, 527
Lumberman's Mutual Casualty Company "Not Over 50" Club, 65

MacArthur, Gen. Douglas, 54
  a USAA member, **136**
MacGregor Medical Health Center, 504
Machado, Reuben, 254, **254**, 427
Mahon, Bill, **300**
Malcolm Baldrige Award, 477
management intern program, 260
Managerial Insurance Seminar (MIS), 262
Managing in Turbulent Times, 339
Manning, Selvage and Lee, 369
Markette, Shirley, 259
Marlin, Steve, 458
Marshall, Janice, 319, **319**, 477, 478, 504
  as first woman on Executive Council, 320
  as President of USAA Buying Services, 320
MARSO (Mid-Atlantic Regional Services Office), 299
Martin, Lt. Col. James Harvey, 406
"Marty's War Room", 250
Massett, Joe, 305
McCarran Act (1945), 93
McClure, Beverley J., 477
McComsey, John, 170, 173
McCormick, Maj. Gen. John, 161, 173, 224
  as Chairman of the Board, 190
McCormick, Judy, 512
McCoy, Doug, 398
McCrae, William, **247**, 508

as General Counsel, 247, 286, 323, 328, 380, 437
sponsors reading club, 418
McDaniel, Col. W. A., 53
McDermott, Alice, 225, 551n 68
McDermott, Robert F.
  and Alice, 228, **464**
  and community economic development, 328-330
  and two-millionth member, **452**
  as automobile safety advocate, 251, 252, 370
  as Executive Vice President, 225, 233
  as USAFA Dean of Faculty, **230**
  as West Point Cadet, **228**
  as World War II fighter pilot, **229**
  background, 225
  Chairman Emeritus, 465
  Cheever's interest in, 224-225
  elected Chairman, 325-326
  joins USAA, 225
  National Business Hall of Fame (JA), 465
  President and Attorney-in-Fact, 237
  Principles of Insurance, 115
  promotes airbags, 330, 460-461
  successful leadership praised, 527
  succession, 387-389
  suffers heart attack, 386-387
  views destruction of Hurricane Andrew, **459**
  vision for financial services, 391
  with Miss Fair Share contestants, **259**
McDougall, Marion, London office, 191, **191**
McGibbon-Haskins, MSgt. Carol, 520
McHugh, Donald P., 370
McKinsey, Col. Bill, 390
McKinsey and Company, 477, 478
McWilliams, Patti, 341
Melnick, Herb, 322, 323
member relations and feedback, 501
Member Relations Team, 269
membership eligibility
  all officers of Reserve forces, 283
  Air Corps Cadets, 59
  Air Force officers, 106
  British officers on U.S. Assignment, 86
  divorced spouses - 20/20/20, 337
  Emergency officers (WWI), 59
  enlisted personnel, 59-60, 120, 179, 237, 239, 284, 488, 519-522, 530, 532
  FBI Special Agents, 337
  field clerks, 30
  Foreign Service officers, 60
  former dependents, 284, 285, 337
  former officers, 335, 336
  former warrant officers (WWI), 59
  former World War I Emergency officers, 59
  Naval Investigative Service, 337, 553n 7
  Navy and Marines (active), 19
  "once a member, always a member," 178, 179
  permanent employees, 107
  Public Health Service officers, 30
  Ready Reserve, 282, 283
  Reserve and Guard, not members on active duty, 271, **283**
  Reserve and National Guard (separated), 108-112
  retired officers, 27, 108
  Specialist Corps officers, 86
  U.S. Coast and Geodetic Survey officers, 30
  U.S. Secret Service Agents, 337
  widows of USAA members, 60
Mercherle, George and State Farm, 9
Merrill Lynch, 401, 402
Metcalfe, Lt. Col. Raymond F., 1, 32
Metzen, Rolf E., 346, **346**
Meyer, Capt. Joe, 345, **345**, 464
Michel, Theodore James "Ted", 300-301, 305, 326, **327**, 349
Mid-Atlantic Regional Services Office (MARSO), 299
migration and corporate culture, 348
migration, 347
military rapid deployment guide, 456-457
Military Services Investment Advisors, Inc. (MSIA), 245
military strength, reduction in, 451
  increase during 1960s, 220
Miller, Steve, 383
Minus, Maj. Josiah C. "Josh", 33, **52**
  background, 51, 52
  joining Service Finance Corporation, 52
  Minus "revolution," 52-54
  resigned, 53
Mir, Tammy, 348
Mira Flores, 202

INDEX

Miss Fair Share, **259**
Mission Statement (USAA), 486
Mitchell, Senator MacNeel, 167-168
Mitchell, Sharon, 381
Mobile Homeowner's policy, 294
Model "T" Ford, 5, **5**
Monetary Control Act of 1980, 392
Money, 495, 522
Moore, Frances, 106, 181
Moore, Maj. Walter, 14
moral and ethical breakdown in U.S. society, 431
Morgan, Roy, 297
Morris, Lt. Col. W.W., 1
Morris, Simone (Farmer), 436, **436**
Motor Insurers' Bureau, 169
Moye, Jean, 149-151, **150**
  as Vice President, Personnel, 234, 255
  institutes wide range of programs, 150-151
Multi-car discounts, 255
Multiple Lines Bill, 128
Muscle cars, 250, 251, **251**
mutuals and cooperatives movements, 8, 9, 539n 11
Myers, Dave, 393, 438

Nader, Ralph, 370, 441
Naisbitt, John, 339, 392
National Association of Independent Insurers, 152, 167, 180, 369
  cost of autos, 250
  displeased with insurers, 215
  energy crisis, 288
  fraud, 252
  no-fault, 252
National Association of Insurance Commissioners, 152, 161, 180, 184
National Automobile Theft Bureau, 367
National Automobile Underwriters Association, 116, 165
National Bureau of Casualty Underwriters, 116, 165
National Convention of State Insurance Commissioners, 30
National Guard, 109, 453
National Highway Traffic Safety Administration, 368
National Insurance Consumer Organization (NICO), 441
National Insurance Crime Prevention Institute, 367
National Safety Council, 165, 251

alcohol as a traffic death factor, 330
National Security Act, 105
National Security Council Paper Number 68 (NSC-68), 113
National Surety Company of New York, 48
National Title and Trust Company of San Antonio, 48
Needs Based Sales and Service, 485
Neighborhood Housing Services of San Antonio, 512
Neilson, Marynel, 106
Nettle, Donald B., 367
Neuhaus and Taylor, 310
new cars, acquisition of after war, 90
New York, NY, 168, 267
Nicholson, Becky, 502
Nomination and Ethics Committee, 488
Norgaard, Richard, 232
Norrgran, Val, 345
Noriega, Manuel, 445-446
North Atlantic Treaty Organization, 208
Nutt, Susan, 436

Ocean Marine Insurance, 189
Office and Professional Employees International Union (OPEIU), 322
office movement, 349
Office of Civilian Defense, 195
Office of Price Administration, 84
officers, USAA, same level as other companies, 185, **186**
Olivera, Carolyn, 390, 421
Ombudsman, 418
One Hundred Best Places to Work in America, 526
O'Neill, Brian, 375
O'Neill, John, 390
OPEC (Organization of Petroleum Exporting Countries), 288
Operation Desert Greetings, 455
"Operation, How Are We Doing?", 256
Operation Just Cause, see Panama
Operational Planning Conference, 486
Organizational Development Program, 262, 320
Otte, Col. Ray, 393
Ovenshine, Brig. Gen. Alexander T., 85, **85**, 142
  as President, 85
Ovenshine committee, 142-143
  chooses Dr. Urrutia property for next building, 143

PACE (Professionalism and Claims Excellence), 477
Pagelow, Maj. J.A., 2
"Paint the Bridge," 320
Panama, 445-447
Panek, Kathie, 341
Patriarca, Laura, 396
Patterson, James A., 320, 367, 416, **416**
Patterson, Sharon, 297
Patton, George, 54
Payne, Oleta, 96
Peace Corps, 184
Peanuts (cartoon), **434**
Peat, Marwick, Mitchell and Company, 209
Pension (first employee) plan, 97
Perkins, John, 228
Perot, Ross, 446
Persian Gulf War, 451-453
  and USAA employees, 453-455
  see also Desert Storm
Personal Catastrophe Liability (umbrella) policy, 294
Peters, Tom, 448
Peyton, Col. Ephraim G., 33
Phea, Cleaves, 57
Phelps and Dewees and Simmons, 144
Philadelphia Contributorship for the Insurance of Houses from Loss by Fire, 9
PHH Home Equity Corporation, 523
Phillips, Gen. Samuel C., 324, **325**
  recommends new committees, 325-326
Piatt, Jerry E., 365
Pieper, Mary, 254, 477
Pierce, Maj. Francis Edwin Jr., 336
Pinnell, Col. Samuel W., 267, 396
Planning, Long Range
  1997 Stategic Plan, 531
  AMA Company Program, 255
  and Jack Daye, 255
  establishment of Key Result Areas, 256
  Hamilton, NY, meeting, 256
  revisions under Herres, 486, 488
  USAA Board of Directors role, 488
Political Action Committee (PAC), 437
Poore, Brig. Gen. Benjamin A., 22
Powell, Colin, 451, 474, 475
  in Desert Storm, **456**
Presidential Commission on the Role of Women in the Armed Forces, 474

President's Employer Merit Award, 199
President's house on USAA campus, 315, **315**
President's Volunteer Action Award, 516
Presley, Maj. Gen. Bobby W., 360, **361**, 490
Prevo, Ensign William, 451, **452**

PRIDE (Professionalism Results in Dedication to Excellence), 476-480, 502
  logo, **478**
  Phase I, 479
  Phase II, 479
Principles of Insurance, 115
Pro Patria Award, 456
Proctor, Col. Mert, 129, **131**
  First Assistant Secretary-Treasurer, 101
  as Vice President and Treasurer, 160
Progressive Insurance Company, 381
Project 1969, 249-250
Project 1970, 255
Project 1971, 255
  outcome, 297
Project Administration Services, 312
Project Campus, 262, 318
Project Control, 351
Proposition 103 (California), 440-443, 509-510
  "take all comers" provision, 441-442
Proposition 13 (California), 440
Prosk, Kay, 305
Provident "War Exclusion" clause, 76
Pursley, Lt. Gen. Robert, 387, **387**, 431
Psychological Corporation of New York, 204, 234, 263

Quality Circles, 339, 341
Quality Circle at work, **342**
Quality Journey, 478
Quality Office, 478
Quigley, Capt. Robin, 316
Quinlan, Michael, 349, **462**

Race riots impact on USAA, 213, 214
Ramirez, Michael, 520
Ready Reserve, 282
Real estate
  and Leddy, 411
  and Thompson, 409
  DEVCO, 409
  La Cantera, 411, 483, 484, 492

INDEX

real estate limited partnerships, 394, 410
retirement communities, 412, 413
USAA Towers, **412, 413,** 413, 414
Reagan, Ronald, 333
Reaganomics, 338
Real, Gladys, 341
reciprocal, problems of, 189
Reciprocal Inter Insurers Federal Tax Committee, 163
Red Dog Automobile Insurance of Chicago, 2
Reedy, June (Rogers), 235, **249**, 250
first maternity leave, 150
Regional Offices
California
Cupertino, 301, 344
Sacramento, 344-345, **345,** 349
Colorado
Bill Mahon, 300, **300**
fitness center, **355**
new building, 346, **346**
Quinlan, Michael, 349
Rocky Mountain Regional Service Office (RMRSO), 300
Florida
Pensacola, (SERO satellite), 300
Tampa, Southeast Regional Service Office (SERO), 300, 344, 349
New York
West Point, 267, **334**
Virginia
Falls Church, 267
Mid-Atlantic Regional Services Office, 299, **299**
Norfolk, 349, **464**
Reston, 346
Washington
Seattle, 459
Regional (overseas) Offices
Frankfurt, Germany
1 Siesmayerstrasse, **207**
European Claims Staff (1957), 170
purchase building, 346
USAA's first overseas office, **121**
Welby Logan, 171, **171,** 206
London, England, **192,** 358
American Officers Insurance Company (AOIC), 190-192
Regional Senior Vice Presidents (RSVP), 496
regionalization, 299-302, 343, 350, 356, 357

and corporate airplane, 350, 351
and migration, 347, 348
from terminal digits to regions, 302
Long Range Basing Study, 347, 348
use of In-WATS, 302
reinsurance, 166, 541n 7
rental car reimbursement, 255
Republic Bank of Dallas and USAA investments, 252
Residential Property and Casualty Joint Underwriting Association (Florida), 460
"Revolution" – USAA takeover attempts, 33, 52-54
Ribicoff, Senator Abraham, 215
Rich, Bradford W., 509, **509**
Riner, Capt. John, 283
Road Traffic Certificates, 191
Roberts, Jim, 438
Roberts, Richard C., 193
Robinson, David, **494**
Robles, Joe, 524, **524**
Rocky Mountain Regional Service Office (RMRSO), 300
Roe, Brig. Gen. David, 389
Roe, David H., 384
as first president of CAPCO, 415
Rosane, Edwin L., 384-385, **385,** 432
Rosenfield, Harvey, 440, 442
ROTC, 155, 510
Roth, Michael "Mickey" J.C., 408, **408,** 409
Rowe, Col. James Nicholas, 444, **444**
Royal Insurance Company, 380
Ryland, Harvey, 511

Safety
1980's efforts, 369-379
airbag, 330, 374-379, **375, 378,** 460-461, **461,** 463
"Buckle-Up," **372**
child safety seats offer, 373
"Deaths per 100,000," 368
IIHS, 215
military's efforts in 1950s, 163, 164
NHTSA, 368
"Odds on Death," **125**
opposition to drinking and driving, 66, 215, 463
promoting automobile safety in 1930s, 64-66
promoting automobile safety in 1960s, 214, 215

575

safety campaign (1950), 124
Safe Driver Award Plan (1938), 66
State Safe Driver Rating Plans, 164
USAA Car Guide, 431
USAA joins National Safety Council, 251
Wall Street Journal advertisement, **371**
Salomon Brothers, 401
Salvation Army, 188, 249
San Martin, Dr. Jose, 329
Sarratt, Col. E.O., 53
satellite communications, 364-366
Saturday Scholars Program, 516, **517**
Saucedo, Ric, 341
Saudi Arabia, 452, 453
Saunders, Jack, 318, 407
Schade, Lt. Col. Hal, 454-455, **455**
Schenken, Carlton G., 165, 178, 190, **193**
   Vice President-Treasurer, 186
   retires, 235
   studies of reinsurance, 166
   study of life insurance, 192
Schmidt, Jim, 318
Schoff, Mary, **513**
Schrenk, Ed, 477
search teams, 222, 223
seat belt law, 374 *see also* Federal Motor
   Vehicle Safety Standard 208
Seattle, Washington Office, 349
Security, 353
Seeger, Christopher, 509
Selective Service Act, 74, 281
SERHO, 344
Service Finance Corporation (SFC), 22
   referrals, 23, 61
   Minus and, 52
service-famly tradition, 454
Seymour, Jane, 518
Shapiro, *see also* documentaries
"Shattered Lives", 463
Shea, Terry, 343, 349, 477
Sheldon, George B., 5
Sijan, Capt. Lance P., 279, **279**
"Simplification", 341
Simplification and Quality Circles, 339
Sinclair, Patsy, 345
Six Flags, 493, 494
Skidmore, Owings, and Merrill (SOM), 351
Sloan, Alfred P., Jr., 373

Smith, Ollie, **196**
smoking, 420-421
Sneckner, Shirley Jean, 471
Snyder, Maj. Gen. James L., 193, **194**
SOFA, 169, 171, 206
Soldiers and Sailors Relief Act, 127, 453
Southeast Regional Service Office (SERSO), 300
Southwestern Life Insurance Company, 97
Soviet Union, dissolution of, 449-450
Space Policy Advisory Board, 474
Spalding, Clem H., **235**, 379
   Underwriting Director, 234
   Vice President, Insurance Operations, 285
Sprint, 523
Stanford, Sandi, 502
Starnes, Maj. Gen. William L., 299, 312, 313,
   313, 324
State Board of Insurance Commissioners, 28
State Farm Mutual Automobile Insurance
   Company, 9, 276
State Financial Responsibility Laws, 124-125
   first enacted, 125
State Insurance Departments, 161
State licensing, 92
   by Germany, 171
   by states, 224
   en mass, 181
   dynamics of, 130
   for life insurance, 193
   in Canadian provinces, 91
   in Hawaii, 126
   in Maryland, 157, 158
   in Massachusetts, 92-93
   in New York, 92
   in Texas, 28
   securing licenses in all states, 126
   state, 130, 131, 180-182
   states changing the rules and requirements, 130
   USAA GIC, 286
   USAA moves for in all states, 181, 209, 224
Status of Forces Agreement (SOFA), 169, 171, 206
Staubach, Roger, 366, **366**
Stillman, Maj. Gen. Robert M., 185, 187
Stoddard, Deanna, 440
Strategic Planning Conference, 486
Straus, Joseph R. and Emile, Sr., 315
Straus house, 551n 68
   as President's house, 315, **315**

INDEX

Structured settlements, 362, 363
Suarez, Doris, **355**
Subscribers Credit Accounts, 212, 548n 56
Subscribers' Savings Account (SSA), 253, 510
subsidiary companies authorized, 190, 191
Sunbelt Era Fund, 405
Survivors Benefit Plan (SBP), 273
Sykes, Brig. Gen. George K., 295, **295**

TABLES
   Auto parts cost comparison, 1954 and 1965, **215**
   Positive Trends in the Depression Years, 1929-1933, **57**
   Inflation rates, 1970-1980, **289**
   Japanese personal liability insurance policy payouts, **171**
   Military strength and USAA members, 1970-1979, **331**
   Percentage of USAA Investments in U.S. Government Bonds, 1941-1945, **84**
   Transitioning to Independence, **513**
   USAA Automobile Claims Record, 1941-1947, **91**
   USAA Growth, 1941-1947, **90**
   USAA statistics from 1968-1993, **465**
   Votes in 1952 for attorneys-in-fact, **132**
Tabriz riots, 307
"take all comers," 441, 442
Tallerico, Bernie, 318
Tax Exempt Investments, 405
Taylor, Paul, 128
Teamfest, 422, **422**
Teamfest, "Land skiing", 423
technology, 525-526
Telzrow, Dennis, 318
terrorism, 357
   new security systems, 359
Texas Board of Insurance Commissioners, 176
Texas Highway Commission, 7
Texas Insurance Code, 28
Texas Open, 492
Texas State Insurance Department, 27, 67-68, 97
Thompson, Terrie W., 409-411
Thompson, Terry, 344
Thompson, Vice Adm. Donald C., 392
Thurman, Gen. Maxwell R., 475
Thurmond, Sen. Strom, 489
Timmerman, Tim, 501
Toastmasters, 419

Total Force Concept, 282-283
Townsend, Imogene, 201
Travers, Vice Adm. Ed, 389
Tulsa Credit Card Center, 397-398, 494
Turner, Jim, 312, 351
20/20/20 rule, 337
Tye, George, 509
Typhoon Karen, 209

"U" Magazine, 522, 532
umbrella policy, 294
union, see labor union
"unlimited liability clause", 453
U.S. Department of Labor, 199
U.S. Department of Labor Job Corps, 221
Under 25, 522, 532
Unexpected Losses, raising reserve for, 167
   reserve account, 161
United Fund, 188
United Nations Economic Commission, 169
United San Antonio, 330
United Services Life Insurance Company
   competition, 62, 269
United Services Automobile Association
   (name), 27, 539n 3
United Services Casualty Insurance Company
   (USCIC), 224, 268
   changes to USAA CIC, 268
United Services Fund, Inc., 244
United States Air Force Academy, **231**, 282
   campus setting, 310
   McDermott as Dean of Faculty, **230**
United States Army, increase in size as of 1935, 70
   size of in 1930s, 69
United States Army Automobile Insurance Association, 11
   name changed to United Services Automobile Association, 27
United States Coast Guard Academy, 155, **157**
United States Military, and World War II, 74
   growth in number, 74
   increases strength, 196
   reduction in strength in 1953, 154
United States Military Academy, 555n 74
   and Cheever, 115, 137
   and Daye, 242
   and Garrison, 2, 3
   and Hinds, 37

A Tradition Of Service

and McDermott, 115, 227-229, **228**, 310
and White, 72, 73
Color Guard, **189**
USAA marketing, 155
United States Military Officers, tasks in 1930s, 69
United States Naval Academy, 155-157, 346, 470-471, **471**
United States Trust Company, 200
United Trust Company, 252
Universal Life Policy, 382
USAA
  "Application, Agreement, and Power of Attorney Form", 13, 48
  management control system, 247
  proposed name change (1962), 210, 211
  renaming subsidiaries, 268
USAA Board of Directors, *see* Board of Directors
USAA Buying Service, 361, 363
  fees, 361, 362
  and natural disasters, 458
  and AAFES, 362
USAA California Bond Fund, 406
"USAA Capacity Gap, 1 January 1973-31 December '82" memo, 282
USAA Capital Corporation (CAPCO), 410, 414, 415, 490, 557n 39
  new leadership, 496
  new role (1993), 490
USAA Capital Growth Fund, 244, 294
USAA Car Guide, 377, 431
USAA CARDEAL, 386
USAA Casualty Insurance Company, 268
  Associate members, 327, 328
  early losses, 290, 291
  former dependents, 286, 287
  original purpose, 285, 286
USAA Child Development Center, 504, **505**
USAA Chorus, 188, **514**
USAA Concert Band, 506, **506**
USAA Cornerstone fund, 407, 408
USAA Coverage, 205
USAA Credit Card Bank, 423
USAA Development Company (DEVCO), 395, 409, 410
USAA DIRECTBanking, 525
USAA's Earth Station, **365**
USAA Educational Foundation, 457
USAA Federal Credit Union, 151

USAA Federal Savings Bank, 392-404 *see also* credit cards
  1969 exploration, 391
  and Desert Storm, 455-456
  application, 394
  Bank Services Building, 494-495
  "Best Bank in America", 495-496
  building, 352, **352**
  charitable contributions, 512
  credit card receivables, 400-402, 414
  Financial Services Association, 404
  Kelly Field Bank, 394
  move into new building, 399
  opens, 397
USAA Financial Services Association (FSA), 404
USAA Financial Services Company (FINCO), 410
USAA Florida Fund, 406
USAA Foundation, 431
USAA Foundation, a Charitable Trust, 512
USAA Fund Management Company, 244
USAA General Agency, 379-381
USAA General Indemnity Company, 285
  original purpose, 285
USAA Golden Eagle Service, 395
USAA Gospel Choir, 507, **507**
USAA High Venture Fund, 394
USAA Income Fund, 295
USAA Income Properties II, 410
USAA Investment Management Company (IMCO), 295
  and Roth, 408, **408**, 409
  and Sykes, **295**, 405
  DIRECTInvesting, 525
  discount brokerage, 394, 406, 407, 530
  first tax-exempt funds, **405**, 406
  Index Fund, 522
  InveStart, 407, 408
  money market fund, 405
  origin, 295
  self-clearing brokerage, 533
  transfer agency, 407
USAA Life General Agency, 383
USAA Life Insurance Company, 219
  1980s, 381-386, 555n 76
  and Charles Bishop, 384
  and Dennis Cross, 296, 297
  and Edwin Rosane, 385
  and Jack Daye, 269, 295-297

INDEX

first study, 192
General Agency, 383
HAL, 382
James Snyder, 193, **194**
Richard C. Roberts, 193
sells USAA Fund Management Company, 297
USAA Life, 193
Variable Annuity, 522
weak growth, 269
USAA Magazine, 522
USAA Medical Management Team, 363
USAA Mentor and Junior Achievement Program, 434-435, **435**, 516-517, **517**
USAA Merchandising Division, *see* USAA Buying Service
USAA Newsletter, 204
USAA Pocket Scoreboard, 247
USAA Real Estate Company, 411, 491-492
USAA Retirement Plan and Trust, 200
USAA Road and Travel Plan, 523
"USAA Safety Committee", 376
USAA Satellite Communications Company, 364-366
"USAA Savings and Investment Plan" (SIP), 321
USAA Special Services Company, 293, 360
USAA Touchline, 408
USAA Towers, **412**
  Interior Pedestrian Mall, **413**
USAA Volunteer Corps, 433, **433**, 513
USAA Wellness Committee, 420, 421

Van Pool program, 288
Van Steelant, Priscilla, 460
Vaughan, Mary Ethel, 106
Ventures Investment Club, 244
Vietnam War, 217, **220**
  end, 277
  impact of end on USAA, 281-284
  impact on USAA 218-223, **221**, **223**
  life insurance coverage, 219
  POWs, 218, **218**, **278**, **279**, **280**
  surge in membership, 220
  Zumwalt on POWs, 218, **218**
Virginia National Guard 192nd Fighter Wing, **283**
"Vision 2000," 416

Wagner, Michael D. "Mike", 394
Waldron, Eugene M., 101, **127**

negotiating licenses, 126
2nd Assistant Secretary-Treasurer, 132
as Vice President USAA, 160
Walker, Donald R., 497, **498**
Wallace, Helen, 155, 168
  in Japan, 172
Wallach, Max, 292
Ward, Bill, 321
Washington D.C. Area Office (WDCAO), 342
WATS, 273, 279, 291, 302
Weeber, Charles, 152
Weinberger, Cliff, 491
Weinheimer, Jill, **513**
Welden, Lt. Cmdr. Frank, 75
West Point (Highland Falls), 267, **334**
Westin Hotel Company, 492
WESTRO volunteers, **515**
Wheelus, Bob, 341
Whipple, Rear Adm. Walter J., 284
White, Col. Herbert A., 44, 55, 71, **182**
  as Assistant-Secretary Treasurer, 44
  as West Point Cadet, **71**
  background, 71-74
  on USAA Board of Directors, 44
  new ten-year contract, 58
  defending Gen. Billy Mitchell, 73
  death, 100
  as a Director, President, and Assistant Secretary-Treasurer, 71
  as Secretary-Treasurer and Attorney-in-Fact, 71, **80**
  as Staff Judge Advocate, **73**
White, Debbie (Charo), 423, **423**
Wier, Max H. Jr., **172**
  hired at USAA, 172
  in Japan, 172
  storm damage claims, 209
  as a Vice President-Claims, 186, 309
Wier, Max H., Sr.
  background, 42, 43, **43**
  claims, 43
  Vice President Emeritus and General Counsel, 186
Wier and Wier, 172
Williams, Jean (*see* Moye)
Willis, Meta (Nemkey), 45, **45**, 96, 164, 185
Willman, Ken, 406
Wilson, Gary, 243
Wilson, Lillian, **57**

579

Wilson, Pete (California Governor), 464
Winfrey, Oprah, 518
Wolcott, Jack, 349, **350**
Woodbine Development Company, 492-493
Woodcock Building, 296
Woods, Tiger, 492, **492**
World War I
    demobilization, 4
    Zimmerman Telegram, 543n 2
World War II
  background, 69, 70
  carpools, 79
  Concentration Camp survivors, **139**
  impact on USAA, 74
  investments during, 83, 94
  post-war insurance overseas, 95, 96
  reduced rates, 80, 81
  special services, 81-83
  war exclusions, 75-79
  War Labor Board, 84, 96
Wright, Mark H., 523, **523**

yacht insurance policy, 294

Zumwalt, Admiral Elmo R., 218, **218**
Zurich Insurance Company, 170